perception

edited by Kathleen Akins

New York   Oxford
OXFORD UNIVERSITY PRESS
1996

Oxford University Press

Oxford   New York
Athens   Auckland   Bangkok   Bombay
Calcutta   Cape Town   Dar es Salaam   Delhi
Florence   Hong Kong   Istanbul   Karachi
Kuala Lumpur   Madras   Madrid   Melbourne
Mexico City   Nairobi   Paris   Singapore
Taipei   Tokyo   Toronto

and associated companies in
Berlin   Ibadan

Copyright (c) 1996 by Oxford University Press, Inc.

Published by Oxford University Press, Inc.,
198 Madison Avenue, New York, New York 10016

Oxford is a registered trademark of Oxford University Press

Library of Congress Cataloging-in-Publication Data
Perception / edited by Kathleen Akins.
p.   cm. — (Vancouver studies in cognitive science : ISSN v. 5)
Chiefly papers presented at a Vancouver studies in cognitive science conference,
Vancouver, Canada, February 1992.
Includes bibliographical references (p.   ).
ISBN 0-19-508461-6; ISBN 0-19-508462-4 (pbk.)
1. Visual perception—Congresses.   2. Perception—Congresses.   I. Akins, Kathleen.
II. Series.
BF241.P397   1996
152.14—dc20   95-11810

9 8 7 6 5 4 3 2 1

Printed in the United States of America
on acid-free paper

Acknowledgments

The majority of the papers in this collection were presented at a Vancouver Studies in Cognitive Science conference in February 1992 in Vancouver, Canada. This conference was funded by a grant from The Social Sciences and Humanities Research Council of Canada. I would like to thank the participants of that conference and the many members of the Simon Fraser University community who helped with its organization and financing: in particular, the VSCS committee members; Deans Robert Brown and Evan Alderson, the past and current Deans of Arts respectively; John Perry, director of the Cognitive Studies Programme; and Tanya Beaulieu, for organizational assistance. My gratitude as well to Eleanor O'Donnell, who copy-edited the volume, to Lindsey Thomas Martin, who prepared a camera-ready copy of the manuscript and to the Simon Fraser University Publications committee for their financial support. And finally a special thanks to Steven Davis, the general editor of this series, without whom neither the conference nor this volume would have been possible.

PERCEPTION

Edited by Kathleen Akins

Vancouver Studies in Cognitive Science is a series of volumes in cognitive science. The volumes will appear annually and cover topics relevant to the nature of the higher cognitive faculties as they appear in cognitive systems, either human or machine. These will include such topics as natural language processing, modularity, the language faculty, perception, logical reasoning, scientific reasoning, and social interaction. The topics and authors are to be drawn from philosophy, linguistics, artificial intelligence, and psychology. Each volume will contain original articles by scholars from two or more of these disciplines. The core of the volumes will be articles and comments on these articles to be delivered at a conference held in Vancouver. The volumes will be supplemented by articles especially solicited for each volume which will undergo peer review. The volumes should be of interest to those in philosophy working in philosophy of mind and philosophy of language; to those in linguistics in psycholinguistics, syntax, language acquisition and semantics; to those in psychology in psycholinguistics, cognition, perception, and learning; and to those in computer science in artificial intelligence, computer vision, robotics, natural language processing, and scientific reasoning.

VANCOUVER STUDIES IN COGNITIVE SCIENCE
forthcoming volumes

VOLUME 6   *The Biological Basis of Language*
              Editor, Myrna Gopnik, Linguistics   2004
              McGill University

VOLUME 7   *Modeling Rationality, Morality and Evolution*
              Editor, Peter Danielson, Philosophy
              University of British Columbia

Contents

Contributors

Kathleen A. Akins, Department of Philosophy, Simon Fraser University

Dana Ballard, Department of Computer Science, University of Rochester.

Patricia S. Churchland,Department of Philosophy, University of California, San Diego.

Paul M. Chrchland, Department of Philosophy, University of California, San Diego.

Daniel C. Dennett, Center for Cognitive Studies, Tufts University.

Frances Egan, Department of Philosophy, State University of New Jersey, Rutgers.

C. Randy Gallistel, Department of Psychology, University of California, Los Angeles.

John Grimes, Beckman Institute for Advanced Science and Technology, University of Illinois, Champaign-Urbana.

John Haugeland, Department of Philosophy, University of Pittsburgh.

John M. Henderson, Department of Psychology, Michigan State University.

Kirk Ludwig, Department of Philosophy, University of Florida.

Brian P. McLaughlin, Department of Philosophy, State University of New Jersey, Rutgers.

Sarah Patterson, Department of Philosophy, Tufts University.

V.S. Ramachandran, Department of Psychology, University of California, San Diego.

Steven Winger, Department of Philosophy, University of Illinois, Champaign-Urbana.

perception

1

Introduction

Kathleen A. Akins

This volume of the Vancouver Studies in Cognitive Science series arose out of the 1992 annual conference which was entitled "Problems in Perception." The point of such a broad topic, simply put, was to see what was new and interesting in the theory of perception across a broad range of disciplines – philosophy, psychology, computer science and the neurosciences. Despite the wide scope of the intended topic, however, there has been a fortuitous convergence in the subject matter of both the papers presented at the conference and those solicited for this volume: all focus on fundamental questions about the nature of visual perception. Taken together they ask "what is the nature of vision – what does vision *do?*" and more specifically "what are the form and content of visual representations – both of those representations involved in unconscious (or preconscious) visual processing and those that support visual phenomenology, our conscious visual perceptions of the world?"

I sit here at my dining-room table and look out at the panoramic view before me – the city skyline on the left, the snow-capped mountains in the background, the small float plane landing on the glinting water of the harbour. Despite the fact that the information received through human eyes is transient (e.g., it is interrupted by blinks and saccadic-eye movements), serial (I look, first, at one very small point in visual space then at another point) and varies in its informational "texture" (e.g., from the fovea to the periphery, the eye receives information with diminishing spatial resolution and frequency discrimination), the world we *perceive*, say, the panoramic view of which I am conscious, does not bear the mark of its representational origins. Even given the fragmented and serial nature of the incoming visual information, somehow we come to experience objects and properties as stable across time, as unified, as existing independently of our perceptions and actions, and so on. Focusing first on one small portion of the skyline and then on another, I nonetheless perceive the skyline as a whole, existing through time in front of me; the individual buildings do not seem to come into existence, one by one, as my eyes traverse the skyline (first Harbour Centre, then Canada Place, then the Coliseum) nor are the individual buildings seen as fragmented or disunified. Moreover, in thinking about the visual experience itself, my perception of the skyline seems to be truly panoramic: at any moment, it *seems* to me that the visual field encompasses a single large "arc" of the world in front of me, one that is equally rich in detail across its entire broad field. In other words, we both perceive *the world* as independent, permanent and stable and we experience *visual phenomenology* as everywhere rich in information and "non-gappy." How, then, is this possible? How does the rich, unified panorama of human vision come about?

Inference Theories and the Literalist View

Since David Marr, computationalists have assumed that vision is essentially the problem of determining "what is where." Given a series of retinal images (plus some fully general assumptions about the physical nature of the world) the task of vision is to produce, on the basis of a series of (unconscious) inferences, a veridical representation of both what is out there in the world (the properties of various objects and events) and where they are. For example, imagine the images that would be created on your retinas as, say, a golden retriever bounds towards you across the lawn. As the dog gets closer, the golden blobs in left and right images grow larger; across both images, the golden blobs begin to diverge – in the left image, the blob veers downwards and towards the left, while in the right image the blob moves down and to the right. From these two-dimensional images, the visual system must (among other tasks): discern figure from ground (pick out what, in the images, is the dog); "fuse" the two golden blobs of the left and right images (i.e., determine that there is but one golden dog in view); disambiguate relative motion· from either expansion or rotation (i.e., determine that the dog is getting closer to you as opposed to remaining in place but expanding); decide that it is the dog that is moving and not yourself; determine the stable three-dimensional shape of the dog despite the changes in the dog's configuration caused by his bounding motion (i.e., his legs and back straighten and bend as he bounds, his ears flap up and down and, with some luck, his tail wags back and forth); and finally identify the dog as a dog (and indeed as your dog, Bowser). Thus, according to the standard computational account, you come to see the shaggy golden retriever, Bowser, bound across the lawn towards you: our veridical perceptions of events in the visual world are the result of a series of unconscious inferences, inferences based upon the information contained in the retinal image plus general background assumptions about the world. This is what Kirk Ludwig terms an instance of an "inference theory" of perception.

Both Kirk Ludwig and Paul Churchland take issue, based upon the inferential nature of the processes posited, with this widely accepted view of the nature of vision. According to *Churchland*, inference theories – and hence standard current computational theories of vision such as Marr's – start off on the wrong foot by making two unwarranted initial assumptions. They assume, first, that our representations of the world (those that bring about our veridical perceptions) are basically *sentential* or propositional and, second, that the relationships between these pre-conscious states are of the sort "that standardly connect sentences together – relations such as entailment, coherence, probability, truth and so on" (p. 61). In his paper, Churchland argues for a different form of neural representation – high-dimensional activation vectors, or less formally, patterns of activation across neural populations – by presenting a vector activation model of stereo vision. Stereo vision is the ability to perceive the relative and absolute positions of objects based upon the relatively displaced images of the left and right eyes. While it is an intuitively simple task (when *we* look at two photographs taken from the vantage points of the left and right eyes, it is certainly easy for us to see that that is Bowser, just slightly displaced), providing a computational model of this ability has proved extraordinarily difficult – or rather the standard computational methods have failed to provide a model that will solve the problem in anything like real time. So Churchland's argument against the inference theory is a purely empirical one: he provides a vector activation model of a task, stereopsis, that standard computational models have (notoriously) failed to explain.

Ludwig's paper, on the other hand, offers an *a priori* argument against inference theories. The inferences postulated by standard computational accounts of vision, Ludwig points out, are neither conscious nor are they necessarily accessible to consciousness in principle – indeed it is precisely because such states are neither conscious nor necessarily accessible to consciousness that they are thought to explain the success of perception. But if this is so, Ludwig claims, then such inferences violate a "a central conceptual requirement" on the very attribution of mental states or processes to a person, namely they violate the "connection principle" (following Searle 1990). This is the principle that "nothing is a mental state unless it is a conscious mental state or it is a disposition to produce a conscious mental state." Ludwig argues that if such inferences cannot be attributed, qua mental states, to persons at all, obviously they cannot be used to explain or justify our veridical visual perceptions.

Daniel Dennett, Dana Ballard and *John Grimes* are also critical of the standard computational view but for rather more unintuitive reasons. In Ballard's terms, standard computational views – and this includes Churchland's own non-inferential but nonetheless computational theory of stereo vision – are committed to what Ballard calls the "Literalist View" or, to coin a phrase, the "You See What You Think You See" view. This is the commonsense position, the position we adopt, according to Ballard and Dennett, when we simply take our visual phenomenology at face value, when we try to model our theory of vision on how our visual experience *seems* to us, on the unreflective first-person perspective. To put this point in a slightly different way, (Dennett and Ballard) our models of vision start off on the wrong foot by endorsing a seemingly innocuous view: the belief that the *purpose* of vision is to produce visual perceptions – that the end product of visual processing is simply visual perception. Thus, most vision researchers (mistakenly) see their task as explaining *what we seem to see* – our conscious visual experiences – instead of investigating *what visual information is used to do*.

What exactly is the Literalist View, then, and how might it be wrong? After all, if one is having a veridical perception (e.g., the tree that seems to be before you *is* before you) what possible alternative could there be to "seeing what you think you see"? As Dennett and Ballard characterize the Literalist View, it appears to have at least four inter-related strands. First, as Ballard says, computationalists have assumed that visual phenomenology is (largely) the result of having "retinotopic representations in the brain that directly correspond to your conscious precepts." In its most naïve form, this is the view that the imagistic nature of visual perception results from "pictures in the head" – or, more generally (as Kathleen Akins and Steven Winger describe it), the commonsense view tries to explain the veridicality of perception by positing that properties of the world are represented by like properties in the brain, and that these representations, in turn, give rise to phenomenological experiences with similar characteristics. So, for example, a naïve person might imagine that viewing a red apple gives rise to an apple-shaped red representation in the brain, a representation which results in a visual image *of* a red apple, an image which is itself "red" and "apple-shaped" in some metaphorical sense. In its most sophisticated guise (i.e., in the form held implicitly by vision researchers), the Literalist View emerges as the assumption that the "imagistic" nature of visual phenomena is explained by spatial or "pictorial" or retinotopic neural representations (as opposed to, say, sentential ones).

Second, the Literalist View assumes that veridical perception involves (for lack of a better term) "complete" representation. For example, when I look out over the Vancouver skyline and see it in all its glorious detail, this is surely because the detail I seem to see is represented, in its entirety, in a retinotopic or imagistic representation – or so the Literalist assumes. Both Artificial Intelligence (AI) and neurophysiological researchers, by adopting the Literalist view, often assume that the purpose of saccadic eye-movements (which serially fixate the retina on small portions of the visual scene) is to build up, bit by bit from these informational fragments, a complex representation of the scene – a representation that is as detailed as the visual experience *seems to be* to the viewer. By contrast, a non-Literalist approach ("You-Don't-See-What-You-Think-You-See") entertains the unintuitive possibility that visual representations, unlike visual *experiences*, may well be "partial" or "gappy" or "sketchy."

Third, and related, the Literalist assumes that such complete representations are built up as a matter of course, on-line, regardless of the current task(s) of the visual system (e.g., regardless of whether one is staring idly out the window, focusing a camera, or trying to identify a distant building). Again, a non-Literalist admits the possibility of what Ballard calls "just-in-time" representation or what Akins and Winger call "need-to-know access." If there is no pressing, imminent need for a detailed representation (say, no question "what building is that?" awaiting a reply), then no such representation need be constructed.

Fourth and finally, the Literalist posits that visual representations have a certain kind of content, a kind of content that goes hand in glove with the initial assumption of pictorial representation. A (distinct) picture of a brown speckled hen contains the information about every speckle on the hen (or at least, about every speckle on the visible portion of the hen!). This is part of the picture's content. The sentence 'there is a brown speckled hen', on the other hand, merely represents the hen *as* speckled; it does not contain any information, either explicitly or implicitly, about the individual speckles, or their spatial relations, one to another. It is this former kind of pictorial content, call it "explicit" or "concrete" content that the Literalist assumes must underlie our visual experiences. Again, if we see (in good light and at close range) a brown speckled hen, then what we see is what we think we see – we have imagistic representations the content of which is necessarily about every individual speckle.

A more general way of understanding the Literalist View is to see it as a compilation of two sets of common (inter-twined) intuitions. First, there are our assumptions about the relationship of the phenomenology of vision to the material events/neural representations that underlie them – about what kind of representations could possibly give rise to the phenomenology which we in fact experience. These intuitions, I suspect, are what motivate the Literalist assumptions that visual representations must use retinotopic maps or images and that, as images, they have explict or concrete content. Second, the Literalist View embodies the commonsense picture of *veridical* visual perception. We all assume that when we look out at the world, we perceive the world *as it really is* – veridically. All things being equal – assuming the viewer is not wearing distorting lenses or is swimming underwater or has just drunk a pint of scotch – what we see is what is actually there. But what kind of representations are required in order to see the world "as it really is"? What properties must the representations themselves have, what conditions must the perceptions satisfy? Here, veridicality, "seeing the world as it really is" seems to require (intuitively) that spatial properties of the world receive spatial representations (hence be pictorial), that they be complete and that have concrete content about the details of the visual scene. In other words, we can read the Literalist View as providing an intuitive set of necessary conditions for veridical vision.

As an antidote to the Literalist View, *Grimes* presents some fascinating experimental evidence that, during the normal inspection of a presented picture, we retain very little information – either because we fail to integrate the information across retinal fixations or because we simply do not process or retain very much of the available information at all. Grimes also suggests that integration, such as it is, may be more akin to abstraction than actual integration: when we retain the information about features of a scene, we first select the information on the basis of salience and then represent that information only abstractly – "a large hen, with many small speckles."

Ballard, on the other hand, argues for what he calls the "functionalist view" ("You Don't See What You Think You See"), the principal tenet of which is that "the machinery of the brain has to be accountable to the observed external behaviour" (p. 118). He therefore suggests that models of vision posit a "hierarchy of abstraction," one level of which is the "Embodiment Level" – one that emerges between the neural and the cognitive levels – and that specifies how the facts of human embodiment constrain aspects of visual processing. More specifically, he presents a number of models for visual tasks that go against the Literalist paradigm by using "just-in-time" informational access to simplify the visual task and reduce memory requirements, object-centred (as opposed to viewer-centred or retinotopic) representations, "coarse-grained" or "abstract" information derived from non-retinotopic representations ("all the dots moving to the left"), the implicit representation of time and a "deictic" strategy for action.

In the papers contributed by *Daniel Dennett, Patricia Churchland* and *V. S. Ramachandran,* and *Kathleen Akins* and *Steven Winger,* the specific issue at hand is the retinal blind spot. Because the axons of the ganglion cells merge together at one spot as they exit the retina, there is a spot on the retina that lacks photoreceptors; hence the retina has a spot, larger than the fovea, that simply fails to "see" a good portion the world. Under normal viewing conditions – with both eyes open – the retinal blind spots are not noticed, for, in each eye, they "look at" slightly different parts of the world (thus the left eye sees the part of the world that the blind spot of the right eye misses, and vice versa). If only one eye is open, objects that fall entirely within the blind spot are not noticed. But if an object *spans* the blind spot, it appears to be "filled in." *The gap or absence is simply not noticed.* Why, and how, does this occur?

Churchland and *Ramachandran* argue for a view of filling in that seems to fall more or less within the bounds of the Literalist camp. For example, Churchland and Ramachandran pose the nature of the debate in the following way:

> What is going on when one's blind spot is seen as filled in...? Is it analogous to acquiring a nonvisual representation (belief) that Bowser, the family dog, is under the bed, on the basis of one's visual perception of his tail sticking out? Or is it more akin to regular visual perception of the whole Bowser in one's peripheral but non-blind field? That is, is the representation itself a visual representation, involving visual experiences? (P. 133)

Here, as later passages make clear, Churchland and Ramachandran assume that there is a distinction between inferential conclusions/sentential representations and "visual" ones, that visual representations can be equated with the known retinotopic maps/representations of various visual areas (such as the retinotopic map of V1) and that there is a corresponding distinction to be drawn between the contents of visual representations and inferential conclusions (one simply *sees* the tail directly, whereas one *infers* that the dog is under bed). They argue on the basis of empirical evidence that, *contra* Dennett, filling in (at least in some cases) is the result of interpolation mechanisms that serve to complete complex representations at the level of visual or retinotopic representations.

Dennett's response to Churchland and Ramachandran takes issue with the distinction (in his terms) between the perceptual and the conceptual – a distinction that he sees as part and parcel of the "Myth of the Cartesian Theatre," the view that there is a place in the brain where "it all comes together," where consciousness occurs. By Dennett's lights, to posit that visual processing eventuates in a conscious perception (seeing the tail of Bowser poking out from under the bed) and that, on the basis of such conscious events, we then draw conclusions about the further nature of the world, unseen but inferred (that Bowser is under the bed), is to accept a fictitious divide – a juncture before which visual representations are unconscious and after which, in the form of perceptions and conceptual conclusions, consciousness occurs. In other words, Dennett ties the Literalist View to the Myth of the Cartesian Theatre and then argues against Churchland and Ramachandran (and thereby against the Literalist view of filling in) largely on general considerations about the nature of consciousness.

In the article by *Akins* and *Winger*, an attempt is made to sort through what, precisely, divides the two camps. As the title suggests ("Ships in the Night"), Akins and Winger see the two parties as, to a large extent, talking at cross-purposes. Although often couched as an empirical dispute, at bottom, what divides Dennett from Churchland and Ramachandran are fundamental philosophical questions about the relationship of mental representation to conscious experience.

Finally, in the paper by *Brian McLaughlin*, the very general question of the veridicality of visual perception is addressed, here in the guise of the traditional philosophical question about the difference between veridical perception and hallucination. McLaughlin addresses David Lewis's counterfactual theory of vision, a view that, when stated in its most intuitive form, is very much in the Literalist tradition. As Lewis tells us, "it is not far wrong to say simply that someone sees if and only if the scene before his eyes causes matching visual experience" (p. 1986). (Here, a visual experience can be said to "match" an environmental scene to just the extent that the scene satisfies the content of the experience, while "the content of the experience" is defined by McLaughlin as "roughly, the way things look to the subject of the experience in virtue of her having the experience.") The problem, however, is that there are many counterexamples to the intuitive claim, in particular cases of "veridical hallucination". In such cases, the subject hallucinates a particular scene and, as a matter of pure coincidence (trickery, magic or what have you), the hallucinatory experience matches the scene before the subject's eyes. (E.g., With my eyes closed, I hallucinate that a large black bug is crawling across my desk just as, as a matter of fact, a large black bug does crawl across my desk.) In order to preclude such counterexamples, Lewis adds a counterfactual condition to the original conception. He says:

This is my proposal: if the scene before the eyes causes matching visual experience as part of a suitable pattern of counterfactual dependence, then the subject sees; if the scene before the eyes causes matching visual experience without a suitable pattern of counterfactual dependence, then the subject does not see. (1986, 281)

Lewis further spells out this condition in more detail, settling upon a formulation which he calls the "multiple tracking condition," a definition that excludes any explicit reference to causal relations between the scene and the experience. McLaughlin's response to Lewis is that the multi-tracking condition is at best a criterion for when the capacity to see is being exercised, not an explanation of the capacity itself. That is, McLaughlin suspects that Lewis has simply reversed the order of explanation: he has mistaken the conditions that hold *as a result of* the capacity to see for a sustantive explanation of the nature of that capacity, of the nature of veridical vision. But if this is so, why then does the multi-track condition "work"? Why does it, by and large, exclude cases of visual hallucination? As McLaughlin says, a wide pattern of counterfactual dependence provides us with good (although defeasible) evidence that a particular kind of mechanism is at work, a mechanism that serves to discriminate between visual scenes of various kinds. McLaughlin ends his article, then, with a rough proposal that equates the capacity to see with the capacity to make certain kinds of visual discriminations. (Note here that McLaughlin's counterproposal is also a Literalist View, for it takes the content of visual experiences at face value and makes us of the undischarged notion of "matching" content.)

The Intentional Content, Objectivity and Unity of Visual Perception

In the articles by *Frances Egan, Sarah Patterson* and *John Haugeland*, it is the intentional content of visual representations and perceptions that is at issue. Both the Egan and Patterson papers are explicitly engaged in the contemporary philosophical debate over "externalism" – roughly put, the view that mental/neural events are individuated by means of their content or meaning, and that the content of psychological events is itself individuated by events, entities or properties external to the subject. To put the debate in context, Jerry Fodor (1980) has claimed that the very possibility of computational theories of mind – and of cognitive science in general – depends upon the individuation of mental/computational states solely on the basis of properties *internal* to the subject, or as he would say, on the "formal" or "syntactic" properties of computational states. In response, Tyler Burge (1986) has argued that, in fact, typical computational theories of perception, such as Marr's theory of vision, actually presuppose an externalist account of content individuation and, hence, of mental state individuation as well. Under normal conditions, Burge claims, given the evolutionary adaptation of our sensory systems to our present environment, it is assumed that our sensory systems are "successful," that we perceive what is actually there – in other words, that our perceptions are veridical. (Referring to

Marr's theory of vision, Burge calls this the "success-orientation" of Marr's theory.) Moreover, it is the normal distal causes of sensory representations that define their intentional contents: "the information carried by representations – their intentional content – is individuated in terms of the specific distal causal antecedents in the physical world that the information is about and that the representations normally apply to" (1986, 32). Thus, for example, the dotted-lines in Marr's 2½-D sketch represent discontinuities in object surfaces – are "edge detectors" – precisely because the algorithms that produce dotted lines from information contained in the Primal Sketch are designed to produce these primitives when and only when an "edge" is present. (In the case of our own visual systems, of course, the notion of conscious design is replaced by that of evolutionary adaptation within a specific environment; if there are representations of edges in our visual system, it is just because there have come to be regular, law-like relations between certain syntactic elements and edges of objects in the world.)

In this volume, both Egan and Patterson take issue with Burge's understanding of cognitive psychology in general, and in particular, his externalist interpretation of Marr's theory of vision. Egan's main argument hinges upon the formal nature of Marr's theory. Computational theories, Egan argues, are formal, mathematical constructs and as such they carry with them no essential interpretations. This is not to deny that interpretations based on external causal factors are commonly and legitimately made. Given, say, a raw primal sketch derived from an actual photographic array, the primitives of the sketch are reliably correlated with intensity changes across the retinal array. Hence they can be legitimately interpreted as representing intensity changes. Moreover (as Burge would agree) representational primitives "have no content considered independently of the particular environment in which the subject is normally situated." Had the photographic array been produced in a world with quite different light properties, the representational content of those primitives would likewise be different. On the other hand, the facts of evolution – of the adaptation of the organism to a specific environment – do not serve to fix any interpretation as essential to the individuation to the primitives. Such facts could only give us good reason to see the interpretation as privileged, for given the formal nature of the computation, no interpretation can be considered essential. Rather, ascribing intentional content plays three pragmatic roles for the researcher: first, the intentional account makes perspicuous the formal account by stating, informally, the nature of the function performed (e.g., the module is computing depth); second, the intentional interpretation of representational primitives and processes allows us to see how, overall, the

problem of vision is solved – it allows us to see how the formal structures of the model solve the problem at hand; and third, an intentional
interpretation allows us to see how the separate modules of vision are
tied together, the role that each module plays in the overall functioning of the system.

What, then, of some other non-external means of individuating the
intentional content of computational states? That is, what of the proposal that the primitives of Marr's theory of vision are indeed intentional, but that their content does not depend upon external causal
factors? Egan ends her article with an argument against such "narrow
content" views. She argues that even if one could square such an
account with Marr's intentions, and even if one could actually construct the right sorts of contents based upon only "internal" considerations alone, such narrow contents would not yield any additional
explanatory power over and above that provided by a formal charaterization of the computational process.

In *Patterson's* response to Burge, she questions Burge's interpretation of Marr's assumption of success, arguing that this assumption
cannot be equated with the presupposition of veridical perception.
Rather, the assumption of success is best explained as a *methodological
dictate* for artificial intelligence. If we wish to understand the ways in
which the human mind works, our best chance of doing so lies in making an intelligent choice about the kinds of human cognitive abilities
to be modelled. We should choose tasks that people perform both well
and regularly, such that we can formulate a concrete characterization
of the tasks performed. Thus in setting the computational task, we
must look to the human case – to see what we do, what we do well
and, in the unusual circumstance, how we fail when things go awry.
Marr's assumption of success, according to Patterson, is merely the
dictate that we model what people do well – and such an assumption
is a long way from the assumption of veridical perception. Hence,
Burge cannot assume that the individuation of visual representations
will necessarily depend upon factors external to the individual, that in
counterfactual situations, both content and individuation will turn
upon "normal causes."

In contrast to Egan and Patterson, *Haugeland's* view of intentional
content is what one might call "radically externalist" – or at least this
might be said of his account of one class of perceptions, "objective"
perceptions. Objective perceptions, on Haugeland's view, involve the
perception of *objects qua objects*. Thus I see the distant bridge over the
harbour *as* a bridge – as an object of a certain type, as a cohesive spatio-
temporal unit that instantiates a set of mutually compatible and interdependent properties. The question of objective perception, however,

is not merely the question of how it is that, say, my visual perception comes to be about *that thing*, the bridge in the distance, for this way of phrasing the problem already grants objects qua objects a pre-theoretic (metaphysical) legitimacy. Rather, Haugeland claims, "the 'object-hood' of perceptual objects and the 'of-ness' of perceptions go hand in hand, and are intelligible only in terms of one another.... So the deeper question is: *How and why* is such a structure – what one might call the structure of objectivity – imposed on the physics and physiology of sensation?" (p. 273). Haugeland's answer turns on the constitutive standards that govern the "unity" or the "integrity" of objects qua objects. For example, any object, at a given time, if it is an object at all, must exist in one and only one place, have a particular shape, size and so on. Further, its properties must be mutually compatible: given a certain property p (say, the property of being spherical), there may be other properties, q, r and s that the object must have as well (say, having a certain size, certain surface texture) and other properties, x, y and z, that it lacks or could not have (it cannot also be a cube or a pyramid or shaped like a donut). Moreover, these constitutive standards, like those of chess and other games, are ineliminably *social*. In order to perceive objects as objects – to have objective perceptions – we must be able to understand the social standards to which such perceptions are (necessarily) held.

Finally, in the last two papers, contributed by *Randy Gallistel* and *John Hendersen*, the issue is also the unity of our visual perceptions, although here under the guise of what is commonly known as the "Binding Problem." The Binding Problem (or, as there are a number of different binding problems, the problem as portrayed by Hendersen and Gallistel) is roughly as follows. Given a single object in the world, the visual system represents its various properties at a variety of spatially distinct locations in the brain – in a number of different modules each of which has, presumably, its own distinctive system of representation. So the representations of the object are, in some sense, a spatially disjoint and representationally disunified set. On the other hand, our perceptions of that object are not perceptions of a set of disunified or disorderly properties at all. As Haugeland says, objects have integrity – they are, qua objects, unified wholes.

Hendersen's view of unification follows from his more specific hypothesis about the nature of visual attention, the hypothesis that there exists a "rubber band" relationship between visual attention and eye-movement. After the currently fixated location is processed, Hendersen contends, attention shifts to a new location. This location is determined, in the usual case, by pre-attentive, low-level feature analysis combined with a weighted choice structure for the various features so determined. (At other times, higher-level processes can co-opt the attention mechanism, such as when, in reading, semantic considerations require a backwards eye-movement.) At the same time as attention is shifted, a signal encoding the new location is sent to the oculomotor system, while the allocation of attention to a new stimulus instigates higher level analsis of that stimulus. Then, after a lag caused by oculomotor programming, the eyes "snap" to the new position, to what is now the focus of visual attention.

How, then, does this model of visual attention solve the binding problem? Following Triesman's "Feature Integration Theory" (1986), Hendersen believes that individual properties of a visual scene are represented on modular feature maps. These maps are each linked to a "master map" of stimulus locations. When attention fixes on a particular place on the master map – in other words, when attention is fixed on a stimulus in a particular location – the various properties of that stimulus are serially accessed from the individual feature maps through their particular spatial locations on those maps. (In other words, the master map gives an explicit representation of space while modular feature maps only encode features *as* occupying a particular place, implicitly.) The features thus selected are then integrated to form a unitary representation that specifies their structural relations. Here, Hendersen postulates that visual attention, in addition to binding the visual properties of an object, may also combine visual and motor representations. There are two ways this might work. First, when visual attention has made explicit a spatial location of the new stimulus, its co-ordinates might become available to a variety of motor systems that are involved in programming movements directed towards that stimulus (e.g., those readying the brain to, say, grasp the object, look at it or lean towards it). Second, perhaps the explicit representation of the spatial location is used to decide among various competing contradictory motor signals within a single motor system (for example, there is some evidence that a variety of contradictory motor signals for saccadic eye-movements exist at one and the same time and hence that some selective process must be at work). Thus selecting a stimulus for further visual processing also serves to select one action among a host of conflicting ones. In either case, Hendersen's point is that part of what we know of an object as an object is its relationship to our own actions, in addition to our understanding of it as having a unified set of visual properties.

Gallistel's answer to the Binding Problem is what he calls a "recollective" theory of unified perception. Recall that on the Triesman theory of feature integration, attention unifies perception by accessing the features of a stimulus based upon a location on the master map.

Triesman also suggests that primitive object markers or "object files" are created. Each such file contains only a record of the spatial position (given in the coordinate system of the master map) of the object across time – a space-time path of the particular object. It is to these files that the various perceptual systems add information about the other properties of the object – about its shape, colour and so on. In contrast, Gallistel claims that "the records of experience in memory are as fragmented as the sensory perceptual process itself" (p. 333) In each sensory module, there are records with two distinct "fields" (or forms of information): the first field constitutes a space-time "worm," a description of place as a function of time, while the second field species certain stimulus properties (given in the dimensions of that particular sensory space) as a function of time. Thus each sensory module keeps its own records of the position in space and time of various sensory properties. Unification begins with the retrieval of a sensory record based upon a particular salient property – say, the colour or taste of an object which is currently of interest to the organism. Based upon the salient property, the correct sensory files are found; the spatial records of that file are then used to probe various other sensory records – that is, to determine the other properties of the object. Thus, unification occurs through "recollection" – only when information about an object or property is required at some time after intial perceptual processing.

Note here that Gallistel's general theory of mental representation exemplifies aspects of both the Literalist and non-Literalist views. Following the non-Literalist, Gallistel advocates a view of perception that does not take unified perceptual experience as the end state of perceptual processees. Rather unification occurs as a result of a particular behavioural need – the retrieval of unified sensory information occurs in order to carry out some behaviour task. On the other hand, Gallistel believes that each sensory representation in every sensory module is tagged with place and time markers regardless of the system's present task or particular needs; moreover representations themselves are defined by Gallistel (1990) as being structures that are "isomorphic" with certain features of the environment. So these latter aspects of the theory better conform to the standard Literalist View.

References

Burge, T. (1986). Individualism and psychology. *Philosophical Review*, 95: 3-45

Fodor, J. (1980). Methodological solipsism considered as a research strategy. *Behavioral and Brain Sciences* 3: 63-110

Gallistel, C.R. (1990). *The Organization of Learning.* Cambridge, MA: MIT Press

Lewis, D. (1986). Veridical hallucination and prosethetic vision. In Lewis (1986) *Philosophical Papers: Vol. 2.* Oxford: Oxford University Press, 273-86

Searle, J.R. (1990). Consciousness, explanatory inversion, and cognitive science. *Behavioral and Brain Sciences* 13: 585-96

Triesman, A. (1986). Features and objects in visual processing. *Scientific American* 255 (5): 114-126

2

Explaining Why Things Look the Way They Do

Kirk A. Ludwig

1. Introduction

How are we able to perceive the world veridically? If we ask this question as a part of the scientific investigation of perception, then we are not asking for a transcendental guarantee that our perceptions are by and large veridical: we presuppose that they are. Unless we assumed that we perceived the world for the most part veridically, we would not be in a position to investigate our perceptual abilities empirically. We are interested, then, not in how it is possible in general for us to perceive the world veridically, but instead in what the relation is between our environment and its properties, of which we have knowledge, on the one hand, and our perceptual mechanisms, on the other, that results in very many, even most of our perceptions being veridical in everyday life.

In this paper, I am concerned with a certain kind of answer to our question which has been popular in psychological studies of our perceptual abilities at least since Helmholtz (1867).[1] The answer is that we do it by taking account unconsciously of various perceptual cues about objects and events in our environment and then reasoning to what the environment must be like on the basis of these cues, our general knowledge of the environment, and how it impinges on our perceptual organs. It is doubtful that anyone has ever held a pure inference theory. For present purposes, I will call any theory an inference theory that appeals at least in part to unconscious inferences from cues provided by stimulus to the nature of the perceiver's environment in explaining how things look. While the power of these accounts is undeniable, they are, I think, deeply mistaken. When I say this, I do not mean merely that they are as a matter of fact false, or that the evidence in fact is overwhelmingly against them. I mean that the explanans employed *could not* explain the explanandum; the appearance of explanatory force is an illusion. It is not that all the particular

18

explanations of this type have failed, but that no explanation of this type could be correct.

In what follows, I will first give some examples of the sort of explanation that is the target of this investigation. I will concentrate on two examples drawn from explanations of visual perception, the visual perception of size and motion,[2] but many of the points I will make will generalize to other sensory modalities, and to explanations of nonperceptual cognitive capacities as well.[3] My initial aim will be to present these explanations in as strong a light as possible. I will then develop an *a priori* argument to show that they cannot be correct, develop some detailed criticisms of them, and provide a diagnosis of their appeal. I will, however, also argue that despite these explanations being necessarily false, they can be reinterpreted so that they have a legitimate use in psychological investigations of perception. The empirical evidence that psychologists have accumulated is not unimportant, but it is not evidence for the existence of unconscious thoughts and inferences. I will conclude by replying to some possible objections to my argument.

2. Perceptual Achievement as the Result of Unconscious Inference: The Visual Perception of Size and Motion

We take our environment to be a three-dimensional space filled with objects, sound and light which evolves continuously through time. We conceive of ourselves as located within that space, as capable of moving around in it, and as subject to stimulus from surrounding objects. Our problem is to explain how we recover from the stimulus an accurate representation of our environment at a time and through time.

The objects around us are located at different distances and directions from us, are in motion or at rest, and their state of motion and distance from us affect the kind of stimuli we receive from them, if any. To achieve an accurate perceptual representation of their properties, we need to take account both of the similarities among them and their differences. Since their locations make a difference to the stimulus which we receive from them, one of the perceptual tasks we must solve is how to represent as the same those properties of objects (or parts of objects) from which we receive differing stimuli solely because of their different locations. This is the problem of perceptually representing constancies across differences in location. The general solution to this problem for visual perception is to provide a function that maps the physical stimulus on the retina to a representation of the environment which meets the constraint that representations so generated are by and large veridical. This function may take into account more than just the local stimulus on the retina.

Perceptual experience in general is autonomous from cognitive states such as beliefs, judgements, assumptions, suppositions, hypotheses, etc. This is what allows our perceptual experiences to serve as evidence for our judgements about the world around us. The autonomy of experiences from cognitive states means that how a scene perceptually appears to us, how a scene looks, is, by and large, independent of what we believe about it, suppose about it, judge about it, etc. This is most clear in the case of perceptual illusions or hallucinations which we know or believe to be such. It may visually appear to me that there is a pile of leaves on my bed while at the same time I do not believe this because I believe that I am undergoing a drug-induced hallucination. Similarly, as in the Müller-Lyer illusion (Figure 2.1a), one line on a page may appear to me to be longer than another, although I know after measuring them that they are of equal length. The autonomy of perception is even more dramatically illustrated in cases of impossible figures, such as the Penrose triangle in Figure 2.1b. Thus, it is clear that my belief that my experience is nonveridical need not change the character of my visual experience, for if it did, there could not be such a thing as undergoing a hallucination, or experiencing an illusion, while simultaneously believing it to be one. The representational constancies we are interested in, then, are not to be found in what we believe about our environment, but in our perceptual representations of them.

As a general term to cover representational features of our perceptual experiences, as opposed to our beliefs about and other attitudes toward those experiences, or what we believe about the world on their basis, we can use the expressions 'how things look' and 'how things

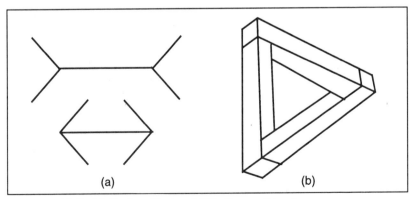

Figure 2.1: (a) The Müller-Lyer Illusion. (b) The Penrose Triangle.

appear', and their variants. Thus, we might speak, for example, of how long a line looks, or how light a thing appears to be, to designate a representational feature of a perceptual experience. Ultimately, we want to talk about the representational character of a visual experience independently of any claim about the objects, if any, of the experience, so that we can talk of the representational character even of total hallucinations; we can use the expressions we introduced above in this sense, that is, to talk about the representational character of an experience from the point of view of the person whose experience it is, without committing ourselves to there being any thing or things the person's experience is of.

Veridical Perception of Size

The correct perceptual representation of size constancy requires that an object's size appear the same when it changes its location with respect to us, and that objects at different locations appear to be the same size if they are. The inference theory offers a compelling account of how the perceptual system accomplishes this task. The perceptual system must recover from the stimuli impinging on the individual, in this case, from the light falling on the retina, a representation of the (relative) sizes of objects in the environment. The actual stimuli from an object relevant to its size is the area occluded by its image on the retina, or, as we will say, its visual angle. (To keep the issues in clear focus, we will set aside changes of visual angle due to changes in an object's orientation, which would have to be treated in a fully general account.) An object's size is proportional to the distance it is from the perceiver and the visual angle of its image on the retina. Thus, the perceptual system can generate an accurate representation of the size of an object provided that it first determines and keeps track of the distance of the object from the observer. Therefore, if we assume that the perceptual system has determined from other cues the distance of an object from the observer, we can explain how the perceptual system keeps track of the size of an object in a visual representation of it by postulating that it infers from the distance of the object and its visual angle how large it is. For example, if the visual angle increases while the distance decreases proportionally, the visual system infers that the object's size has not changed. This explains why an object that approaches us does not look as if it is getting larger. This process is represented in Emmert's law: perceived distance × visual angle = perceived size.[4]

We can contrast the inference theory's explanation of size constancy with that of the stimulus theory (see, e.g., Gibson 1950). The stimulus theory aims to explain size constancy in experience without appeal to unconscious inference. Thus, the dispute between the inference theory and the stimulus theory has the character of an empirical dispute between two contingent theories of the same phenomenon. According to the stimulus theory, size constancy is explained not by unconscious inferences but instead in terms of a constant property of the sensory input which is directly correlated with the representation of an object's size, e.g., constant ratios of the visual angle of an object to the visual angle of some appropriate frame. Thus, in Figure 2.2, *A* is perceived to be the same size as *B* because the number of units of the grid occluded by *A* is the same as the number occluded by *B*. Experiments have demonstrated that ratios of this sort have an important role to play in how things look to us (Rock and Ebenholtz 1959).

However, although constancies in the ratios of the visual angles of objects to a frame seem to be a factor in the perception of size constancy, the stimulus theory does not accurately predict the extent of the appearance of size constancy, and is not applicable to all situations in which size constancy is achieved. For example, the *apparent* size of a line in a rectangular frame, which has the same ratio to the frame as a nearer line and frame, is smaller than that predicted by the stimulus theory. In addition, size constancy can be attained by subjects in a dark room when viewing a single luminous object as long as distance information is available. This appears to be a strong argument, then, in favour of the inference theory providing at least an important part of the account of how size constancy is achieved in visual perception.

Further support for the inference theory is provided by its ability to explain systematic failures to achieve veridical perception. Consider the familiar Ponzo illusion, e.g., illustrated in Figure 2.3. In this illu-

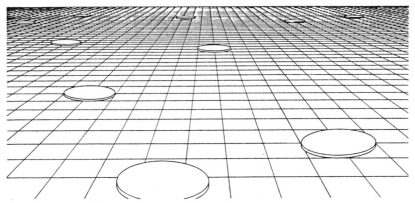

Figure 2.2: The Ratio Theory of Size Constancy. From Irvin Rock, *Perception* (New York: W. H. Freeman, 1984), p. 338. Used with permission.

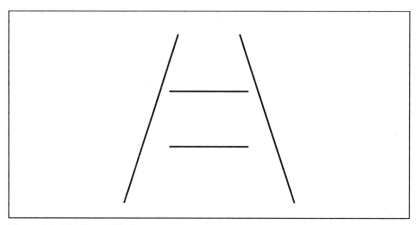

Figure 2.3: The Ponzo Illusion

sion, the upper line appears to be larger than the lower line, although they have the same length. The inference theory explains this as the result of a mistaken inference. The two lines which converge toward the top of the figure are interpreted by the visual system as indicating increasing depth, because the image projected on the retina is similar to the image which would be projected on the retina by two parallel lines receding in a horizontal plane under the observer and orthogonal to him. Thus, the upper line is inferred to be at a greater distance than the lower line, but it produces a visual angle that is equal to that produced by the lower line. In accordance with Emmert's law, the visual system infers that the upper line is larger.

This gives us three sources of support from the inference theory of size constancy. The theory accounts for the veridical perception of relative sizes. It provides an account which at least in some cases is better than its main rival in this area, the stimulus theory. And it explains not just veridical perception of size constancy, but also systematic breakdowns in veridical perception of relative size.

Veridical Perception of Motion

A natural first suggestion for how the perceptual system keeps track of motion is that an object is perceived to move provided that the image it projects onto the retina changes its position on the retina, and that its rate of motion is proportional to the rate of motion of its image on the retina. This would be a pure stimulus theory of the visual perception of motion. A moment's reflection shows that this theory cannot be the correct account of how we achieve veridical perception of motion, because the movement of an image on the retina is a function not just of the movement of the object but also of the movement of the head, eyes and the body of the observer. Thus not every movement of the image on the retina is an indication that the object that projects it is moving. To perceive motion veridically the perceptual system must take into account the reason for the motion of the image on the retina in order to distinguish the motion which is due to the movement of the object from that due to the movement of the retina itself. Since we must appeal to a process that takes into account a variety of different sorts of information, we must appeal to an inference explanation of the veridical perception of motion, and not a simple stimulus theory. Thus, the perceptual system takes into account unconsciously the movement of the image on the retina, and then subtracts from it the movement due to the movement of the eyes and the head, and of the body through the environment, to arrive at a representation of the movement of the object projecting the image. If the eyes are stationary relative to the head, which is rotating to the left, the perceptual system will infer from an image moving at an equal rate in the same direction relative to the retina that the object projecting the image is motionless relative to the observer.[5]

Not every perception of motion depends just on information about the motion of the image relative to the motion of the retina. This is illustrated in the illusion that the moon is moving when it is seen through slowly moving clouds. The inference theory can explain this phenomenon in terms of the system's assumption that the clouds represent the background, and that the background in a visual scene is stationary relative to the observer. The only possible interpretation of the relative motion of the image, then, is that the moon is itself moving. The value of using relative motion of images on the retina as a source of information is that it is sensitive to small changes of position which are otherwise difficult to detect.

As in the case of the visual perception of size constancy, some striking evidence for the inference theory is provided by its ability to explain why we perceive what we do in cases of non-veridical perception of motion, as in cases of stroboscopic or phi phenomena. This is also a case in which the inference theory is apparently able to provide a better explanation than the stimulus theory. Consider two shapes flashed alternatively on a screen, as in Figure 2.4a. It has long been known that at the right speed of alternation the dot will appear to move from position A to position B. How is this to be explained? This presents a difficulty for a simple stimulus theory according to which movement is perceived provided that an image moves across the retina, for in this case there is no movement of an image across the retina at all. In contrast, the inference theory can explain this phenomenon

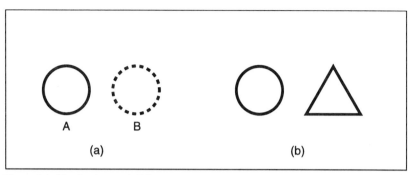

Figure 2.4: The Stroboscopic Effect

in the following way. In ordinary perception of objects which are moving rapidly back and forth, the movement of the object between the points at which it comes to rest can be rapid enough not to register on the visual system. In this instance, there is no image registered as moving across the retina. Instead, what is registered is the image at the end points of its movement. To perceive this as motion, the visual system has to take account of more than simply the information that is provided by the movement of an image across the retina. It must take account of the rapidity and sequence of the appearance and disappearance of the images. Thus, the explanation of the illusion of movement in the case of images flashed alternately on a screen at different positions in rapid succession is that the visual system infers from the alternation and speed of succession that an object is being moved back and forth rapidly from one location to another.[6]

The inference theory also explains the conditions under which the illusion vanishes: (i) when the alternation is slow enough that if an object were moving back and forth at a speed compatible with the alternating images, its image should be visible in between, and (ii) when the rate of alternation combined with the duration of the images is incompatible with an object accelerating and decelerating back and forth between two points.

An interesting example of this process is provided by alternating images of objects of different shapes, as shown, e.g., in Figure 2.4b. At the right speed of alternation, the circle is perceived both to move and to change its shape into a triangle, and then vice versa. Thus, the perceptual system appears to be inferring that the circle has moved because the rate of alternation is appropriate for rapid motion back and forth. But this presents a problem, since it implies that one object is moving, and the image at one end of the trajectory is of a different shape than at the other. The perceptual system solves the problem by inferring that the shape of the object is changing as well, and so representing it.

Further evidence is provided by an experiment in which rectangles are moved over stationary spots on a screen, as illustrated in Figure 2.5 (Sigman and Rock 1974). The experiment is performed under two conditions. In the first, the rectangles are not visible to the subject. In this case, the spot appears to be moving back and forth. If the inference theory is correct, this is because the perceptual system has solved the problem of what the stimulus represents by hypothesizing that an object is moving back and forth rapidly. If so, then with additional information which provides an alternative explanation, the illusion of movement should disappear. This is precisely what happens when the two rectangles which move back and forth over the dots are visible to the subject. The spots are seen as stationary objects, each of which is alternately revealed and occluded. In this case, the perceptual system takes account of the additional information and rejects the hypothesis that the dots are moving back and forth rapidly. That the visible rectangles are occluding and revealing each dot successively provides a better explanation for the alternating images.

To show that the inference theory is genuinely empirical, that is, that it is falsifiable, we can consider one perceptual phenomenon involving apparent motion for which (it seems) it is clearly not the best explanation, the waterfall illusion. The waterfall illusion is generated by having a subject look steadily at moving contours over a uniform background, and then look at a set of stationary contours against a uniform background. The stationary contours appear to the subject

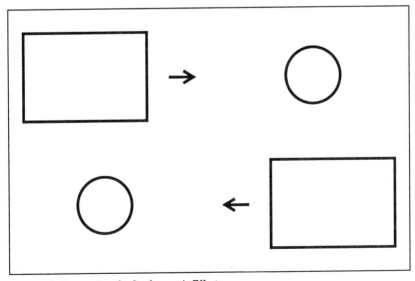

Figure 2.5: Destroying the Stroboscopic Effect

to be moving in the direction opposite to th,
she had previously been looking at. It does no,
theory can explain why this effect occurs, for t,
either the image of the stationary contours or th,
image of the moving contours and then the stationar,
would provide any reason to infer that the contours we.
direction opposite to that of the moving contours. In addi,
a straightforward mechanistic explanation for this effect i,
sensory adaptation to contours moving over the retina (Ans   .d
Gregory 1964). This occurs because some cells in the visual system are
more sensitive to motion in one direct than another. When these
become fatigued, cells sensitive to motion in the other direction are
more active. In the absence of continued stimulus provided by image
motion in one direction, the cells for detecting motion in the opposite
direction now produce a relatively stronger signal, which produces
for a short time an illusion of motion in the direction opposite to that
of the motion most recently detected.[7]

There are two differences between this case and the cases in which
the inference theory seems to provide a better explanation. The first is
that in this case there is a simple mechanical explanation of the phenomenon which does not require taking into account various different
sources of information to arrive at a best guess about the properties of
the perceptual scene. The second is that in this case the perceptual
effect is not in any plausible way thought of as the result of a misap-
plication of a process which in conjunction with the usual nature of
the environment is likely to lead to veridical perception. In the Ponzo
illusion, by contrast, the appearance is explained as a result of an
inference which in the usual case produces a veridical perception. In
the waterfall illusion, representing motion as the direction opposite to
that most recently detected is not likely to lead to veridical perception
in our normal environment. It seems to have no justification in terms
of the goal of achieving veridical perception of one's environment.

Summary

In both of the applications of the inference theory we have considered
so far the perceptual problem is at one level of description the same: it
is to keep track of properties of objects located at different positions
from us through changes in their positions and ours. In the first case,
the property we want to keep track of is an object's relative size. In the
second, it is an object's relative motion. In both cases, the inference
theory seems to provide the best explanation because successful representation requires us or our perceptual system to take account of a

...er of different sources of information simultaneously or sequentially in achieving veridical perception.

These are representative examples of how the inference theory explains veridical perception. The theory gains force as it is seen to be applicable to a wider range of perceptual phenomena. But that it can be applied naturally to a wide range of phenomena should not be surprising, for we can already see that the inference theory is most compelling when generating a veridical perception requires taking into account a number of different interrelated factors, and most of the properties in our environment which we want to keep track of generate peripheral stimuli as a function of their distance from us, ambient light, their orientation, intervening objects, their movement, our orientation, position, movement and so on. Thus, virtually any property we could wish to represent can be expected to admit of an explanation of this form.

In concluding this section, we can note a number of features of the inferences postulated by the inference theory which will play a crucial role in the criticism to come. First, the inferences postulated by the inference theory are clearly not conscious inferences or even readily accessible to consciousness. For example, in the Ponzo illusion, one is not aware of seeing the two lines as having the same visual angle, noting that the two converging lines can be interpreted as representing increased depth, and then consciously thinking that that means the upper line must be further away, and, hence, since it has the same visual angle as the lower line, larger. Instead, we simply see the upper line as larger. Nor does learning the theory help us to identify in ourselves these inferential processes. This is typical of the phenomena explained by the inference theory. We are neither aware unreflectively that any inference is taking place, nor are we able to bring it to our awareness by any act of attention or concentration.

Second, given the way evidence is marshalled for the inference theory, it is clear that the inferences postulated are not thought of as requiring accessibility to consciousness. The evidence for the existence of these inferences is exclusively third-person evidence. The warrant for postulating them derives from their providing the "best explanation" of our achieving veridical perception of the world around us. The absence of any first-person awareness of these inferences, that is, awareness by the subject of the inferences, or the perceiver, is not thought to be relevant to the confirmation of the theory. The absence of such accessibility, even in principle, is not thought to be a refutation of the theory. There is thus no logical requirement that these inferences be connected in any way with our conscious mental lives other than by their output being our visual experiences.

Third, there are positive reasons to require that these inferences be in principle inaccessible to our conscious mental lives. For what we want to explain are perceptual experiences whose contents are by and large autonomous with respect to our conscious mental lives or any of our mental states which dispositionally manifest themselves as conscious mental states. Appeal to such states could not help explain a perceptual phenomenon which we know is insensitive to what we can know, or believe, or want consciously. It is precisely because these states are both unconscious and inaccessible to consciousness that they can be used to explain perceptual experience. They must be as autonomous from our conscious mental lives as the experiences they are supposed to explain; otherwise they could not play the role they are designed to play in the explanation of perceptual experiences. To borrow Helmholtz's expression, unconscious inferences not only are but must be "irresistible."

3. The Connection Principle and the First-Person Perspective

Despite the powerful appeal of the inference theory, I will argue that it cannot be correct. It cannot be correct because it violates a central conceptual requirement on attributing to a person a mental state or process, namely, that that state or process be specially connected to that person's perspective on his own mental states, which is essentially connected to their manifestability in his conscious mental life. It is precisely the autonomy from our conscious mental lives of the inferences which the inference theory postulates which undermines the possibility of regarding them as genuinely mental states of the perceiver.

Searle's Argument

Following John Searle's recent discussion (1990a),[8] I will call this claim the *connection principle*, though my formulation of it and my argument for it are different from Searle's. Searle's version of the connection principle does not deny that there are unconscious mental states, but it requires that every unconscious mental state be potentially a conscious mental state. Searle gives several different formulations of the connection principle. At one place he puts it by saying that every mental state is potentially a conscious mental state, at another by saying that "the notion of an unconscious intentional state is the notion of a state that is a possible conscious thought or experience" (Searle 1990a, 588), and at another by saying that "that ontology of the unconscious consists in objective features of the brain capable of causing subjective conscious thought" (Searle 1990a, 588). I don't think that any of these formulations are equivalent.[9]

I have argued elsewhere (1993) that Searle's argument for his version of the connection principle is unsuccessful. To put the problem briefly, Searle argues for the connection principle by arguing that no non-mental facts are constitutive of mental facts, and in particular no non-mental facts are constitutive of what Searle calls aspectual shape, the fact that we can think of things under more than one aspect, as we can think of the liquid in a glass as H_2O or as water. Searle then raises the question: what fact about one's unconscious mental states make them have aspectual shape? It cannot be, Searle argues, any non-mental facts about them, facts about their neurophysiology, e.g., because no such facts are constitutive of aspectual shape, which is a necessary condition for intentionality. Therefore, it must be their relation to some other states or properties. The only relation that could do the job is some relation to a conscious mental state, namely, that of being a possible conscious mental state.

The difficulty with the argument is that it equivocates on 'make it the case'. Searle's starting assumption, that no non-mental facts are constitutive of aspectual shape, is a conceptual claim. Thus, in the case of unconscious mental states, if we accept this assumption, we can conclude that no non-mental facts about such states are conceptually sufficient for their having aspectual shape. But this does not mean that they cannot have aspectual shape. For some non-mental facts about such states, e.g., facts about their neurophysiology, so far as anything we have said goes, could be nomically sufficient for their aspectual shape. Or, as far as that goes, they may just have aspectual shape as a brute, unexplained fact. The argument could be repaired by holding that some fact must make it the case that unconscious mental states have aspectual shape other than the fact that they do, and that no non-mental fact is conceptually or nomologically sufficient for this. But the second of these claims is clearly question-begging. For it is not advanced as an empirical claim, and if it is a conceptual claim, it is hard to see what could support it other than an implicit appeal to something like the connection principle, which is supposed to be the conclusion of the argument, not one of its premises.

Additionally, even if the argument were successful, it would apply only to states that have aspectual shape. Yet if the connection principle is true at all, one would expect it to apply to all types of mental states. As far as Searle's argument goes, however, although it would be impossible for an individual to have an inaccessible unconscious belief, nothing would bar him from having inaccessible unconscious pains, itches, thirsts, etc. Yet it seems much more difficult to understand how this could be possible than to understand how one could have an inaccessible unconscious belief.

An Alternative Argument

Despite my dissatisfaction both with Searle's formulations of the connection principle and his argument for it, I think the principle is correct in a form stronger than that which Searle gives it, namely:

> (CP) Nothing is a mental state unless it is a conscious mental state or it is a disposition to produce a conscious mental state.

The key to seeing why the connection principle in this form is correct is to appreciate the centrality of the first-person point of view in our conception of mental phenomena.

My approach to this will be indirect. We can begin by noting that for a state to be a mental state it must be the mental state of at least one person, and at most one person. The question I want to push is this: what makes a token mental state the mental state of a particular person?[10] We can further divide this question into two parts, one about unconscious mental states and one about conscious mental states.

What makes it the case that a certain conscious mental state is a particular person's mental state? To answer this question we need to specify a relation between a particular conscious mental state and a particular person such that no one else could bear that relation to that mental state. In the case of conscious mental states, the obvious relation is an epistemic one. One has a kind of knowledge of one's own conscious mental states at the time at which they are conscious which no else could have of those mental states. This difference in the kind of knowledge we have of our own and other people's conscious mental states is well illustrated in the methodology of investigations of perception. Contrast the way we find out how a thing looks to ourselves and how it looks to someone else. In our own case, we do not have to ask ourselves for a report of how a thing looks to know how it looks, or to see this by some observation of our behaviour. In the case of other subjects, however, we have no access to how things look to them other than by their reports about it or what differences it makes to their behaviour or performance on various tasks we set them. I will call this kind of knowledge we have of our own mental states which no one else does or could first-person knowledge.[11] One's having first-person knowledge of a particular mental state is sufficient for it to be one's own mental state and sufficient for it to be no one else's mental state. Thus, in the case of conscious mental states, we can say that a token conscious mental state is X's rather than Y's because X has first-person knowledge of it.

We cannot give this answer in the case of unconscious mental states, because at the time at which they are unconscious, we do not have this kind of knowledge of them. What then makes a token unconscious mental state a particular person's? We can entertain three answers to this question: (1) It is a *sui generis* relation; that a particular token unconscious mental state is a particular person's mental state is a brute fact that admits of no explanation. (2) A token unconscious mental state is a particular person's mental state because it is causally located in his body. (3) A token unconscious mental state is a particular person's mental state because it bears a special relation to that person's conscious mental states. The argument for the third answer will consist in showing that the first two answers are inadequate.

The *sui generis* response can be rejected fairly quickly. If this response were correct, then it would be possible for a token unconscious mental state to bear any combination of causal and epistemic relations to anyone's conscious mental states independently of whose conscious mental state it was. For example, an unconscious mental state which apparently plays a role in your behaviour and produces changes in your mental life, and which is causally located in your body, could still be my unconscious mental state, although it bears no relation to my body, or my conscious mental life at all. This, I think, we will reject out of hand, but since it is a possibility left open by the *sui generis* answer, we must reject that answer as well.

A more plausible answer is that what makes a particular unconscious mental state X's is that it is causally located in X's body. A state is causally located in X's body provided that the intersection of the causal chains in which it is involved is located in X's body. The difficulty with this response is twofold.

First, it requires that it not be possible to make sense of X sharing his body with anyone else, for if both X and Y had the same body, then a mental state's being causally located in X's body could not ground it as being his, since his body is also Y's body. If being causally located in X's body were sufficient for it being X's mental state, then if X's body were Y's body as well, it would be Y's mental state also. But this violates our starting assumption that every mental state is only one person's mental state.

But it is easy to imagine one body being shared by two or more persons. The relations that hold between a person and his body that makes it his are that changes in it affect his mental states, and in particular his conscious mental states, and that his beliefs and desires explain its behaviour, and more generally, his mental states affect more or less immediately his body. But it seems clear that two different people could bear these relations to one body, either at the same or different times, as is shown by the possibility of conceptualizing cases of multiple personalities as cases of multiple persons occupying a single body. Thus, being causally located in a person's body cannot be sufficient for an unconscious mental state to be his.

The second difficulty is that in attempting to explain what makes a particular unconscious mental state one person's rather than another's by appeal to its being causally located in his body, we have to make sense of what makes a particular body one person's body. The only way to do that is to appeal to its relations to his mental states. But then mental states being causally located in his body could not ground those mental states as his, because what makes it his body is that *his* mental states are causally located in it. This difficulty will afflict any attempt to ground what makes an unconscious mental state a particular person's mental state by its relations to any object the person is contingently related to, for then we will have to specify its relation to the person in terms of its relations to his mental states.[12]

Since the only states a person has essentially are his mental states, no appeal to anything other than his mental states could explain what makes some unconscious mental state his. Since it is obviously circular to appeal to a person's unconscious mental states, and we have rejected the *sui generis* approach, this leaves only the third option, that an unconscious mental state is a particular person's in virtue of its relation to his conscious mental states.

We have so far left unspecified what special relation an unconscious mental state must bear to one's conscious mental states in order for it to be one's own. That it causes a conscious mental state is too weak, since it is possible for one of my unconscious mental states to cause a belief in my psychoanalyst, although that would not make it her unconscious mental state, even if the belief it caused had the same content. The relations between a person's unconscious mental states and conscious mental states must be the sort that it is impossible for anyone else's unconscious mental states to bear to his conscious mental states. No contingent relation could secure this. It must be then that our conception of an unconscious mental state is that it is a disposition of a person to (among other things) have certain conscious mental states.[13] Such dispositions are then individuated in terms of the conscious mental states they manifest themselves as.[14]

Application

Let us now apply this result to the inference theory of perceptual achievement. One of the features of this theory that we noted was that it appealed to unconscious inferences and so to unconscious mental states. The crucial question is whether these unconscious mental states violate the connection principle. There are at least three reasons to think that they do. First, note that the condition which the connection principle lays down is very strong. It is not just that the putatively unconscious mental states have a causal effect on my conscious mental states; for this would not distinguish those unconscious mental states that are mine from unconscious mental states that were someone else's. The conception of these unconscious mental states must be of states which are dispositions to produce specific conscious mental sates in the person whose mental states they are. The contents of these states will then be individuated in terms of the contents of the conscious mental states they are dispositions to produce.

The first reason to think that the inferences postulated by the inference theory violate this condition is that our warrant for postulating them is conceived of as independent of the need to verify their occurrence from the first-person point of view. The evidence for their existence is third-person evidence exclusively. This is in contrast to, e.g., the Freudian conception of the unconscious, in which unconscious mental states, though repressed, were in principle manifestable to the consciousness of the intentional agent. This was the ultimate aim of therapy, and was supposed to provide an essential part of the evidence for the theory.[15] The inference theory, however, places no such constraint on the mental states that it postulates. They are thought of as the sort of thing which is independent of the possibility of being manifested in the conscious life of the agent to whom they are attributed. To the extent that they are conceived of in this way, they cannot be mental states at all.

The second reason to think these postulated mental states and processes violate the connection principle is that although they are supposed to play a causal role in the production of conscious mental states, and specifically visual experiences, they are not themselves thought of as dispositions to produce conscious mental states. They are thought of on analogy with a conscious inference of the sort that the theorist might go through in reasoning about how the stimuli impinging on the retina could be used to construct reliable hypotheses about the perceiver's environment. (If my diagnosis below of what has gone wrong is correct, this is not an accident.) But a conscious thought process of this sort is not a disposition of any kind, and would not become so if it were to become, *per impossibile*, unconscious. To borrow Searle's apt metaphor, the inference theory pictures mental states as like fish which can be either at the surface of the ocean or below the surface, so that bringing an unconscious mental state to consciousness is bringing an item of the very same kind as a conscious mental state into, so to speak, a brighter light. The really deep unconscious mental states, such as those involved in perceptual processing, are, as it were, fish trapped in a underwater cave with no route to the surface. The connection principle in the form I have argued for requires us to reject this picture of the nature of unconscious mental states. All unconscious mental states are dispositions manifestable in part as conscious mental states.

The third reason to think that the inference theory violates the connection principle is that it is intended specifically as a theory of autonomous preconscious mental processing which underlies and explains our conscious perceptions. Its autonomy is required by the fact that its putative product is insensitive to those beliefs about the world and our experience to which we have first-person access, either as presently conscious or occurrent mental states, or as dispositions to have conscious mental states. Thus, that these inferences explain conscious states which are autonomous from occurrent and dispositional attitudes requires that they be autonomous from occurrent and dispositional belief as well, and so violate the connection principle.

If the connection principle as I have formulated it is correct, the inference theory is not just false, but necessarily false, for it violates a necessary condition on anything counting as a mental state for a person, namely, that it is something to which the person has first-person access, either as a conscious mental state or as a disposition to produce a conscious mental state through its manifestations.[16] (We will consider below the strategy of denying that these are to be inferences of the perceiver.)

The first of these points against the inference theory could be met only by admitting that so far we have not the slightest reason to suppose that the inferences exist that are postulated by the inference theory, since we have not the slightest first-person evidence that they do, and would require a radical rethinking of the methodology for verifying such a theory. The second and third points, however, cannot be met without substantially giving up the inference theory.

4. Additional Objections

The argument I have just given aimed to provide an *a priori* refutation of unconscious inference theories of perceptual achievement. But even if one is inclined to doubt that the connection principle is true, there are many other reasons to suspect that the inference theory is on the wrong track. These reasons help to support my claim that the inference theory is deeply mistaken, and also help to support the claim that the inference theory is in conflict with the connection principle. In this section, I want to have a close look at the kind of explanation the inference theorist proposes to see whether we can make detailed sense of it. I will argue that we cannot.

(1) Do the Inferences Postulated by the Inference Theory have the Right Form to Be Inferences?

The first problem which I want to raise has to do with exactly how we are to conceive of these inferential processes. Whether or not one agrees with the connection principle, I think it will be accepted that any inference that is unconscious, even if it is not itself capable of becoming conscious for a given person, is at least the sort of thing which could be conscious. If it is not, then we have no conception of what an unconscious inference is supposed to be. A conscious inference is propositional in form. It involves an agent's beliefs, and is psychologically the acquisition of a new belief on the causal and epistemic basis of another belief or set of beliefs. From the point of view of the agent, this appears as one proposition following from or being supported by another proposition or set of propositions. This description of the form of a conscious inference, together with our requirement that any inference, even if unconscious, be the sort of thing we could imagine being conscious (if not for a given agent, then for some agent), amount to requiring that every inference be representable as propositional in form.[17] When we turn to the sorts of inferences postulated by the inference theorist, however, it appears that they violate this constraint. There are at least two ways this occurs, one at the output end of the inference, and one at the input end.

Let us consider the output end first. The output of such an unconscious inference is literally a visual experience, a way things appear to us. But a way things appear to us is not a propositional representation, and its content is not representable as a proposition. My visual experience of my environment is essentially richer than any beliefs I could have about it. I believe that there is a computer on my desk, that it is rectangular, that is face is grey and smooth, its top white and granular, and so on. But none of this comes close to exhausting the representational content of my visual experience, and this is not due simply to the poverty of my beliefs about the visual scene in front of me. The form of representation itself is different. Since it is a minimal condition on a valid inference that the content of the conclusion be contained in the premises, this means that a visual experience could not be the conclusion of an inference all of whose premises are propositional in form. Since an inference must have a conclusion, and a conclusion must be propositional in form, a visual experience cannot be the upshot of an inference. It is as if you were to offer me as an argument a series of sentences which you call premises, and then hand me a picture as the conclusion. This is just to misunderstand what an argument is. While a picture might suggest a conclusion, it cannot literally be one. The input end of the inference is if anything even more puzzling, for it is not always clear what we are to suppose the input is like. Sometimes inference theorists talk as if the input were an image on the retina, or a temporal pattern of stimulations of the retina, as, e.g., in the case of the stroboscopic effect. The difficulty with this is that an image on the retina in the intended sense is not a mental image at all, but instead a sequence of irradiations, which is not the sort of thing that could appear as a premise in an argument, any more than a rock or a shadow could. It is no help to shift from the pattern of irradiation to the pattern of firings of rods and cones on the retina. This as well is simply a pattern of physical events, which could exist in the absence of any minds at all. What goes on at the retina may be informational input to the perceptual system in the sense that it is connected in a law-like way with events in our environments, but in this sense of information the warmth of the outside of my coffee cup carries information about the temperature of its contents, and no one would mistake that for a mental state.

To make sense of the idea that an unconscious inference is taking place whenever we perceive our environment veridically, we must make sense of unconscious representations both of general laws connecting what goes on at our sensory surfaces with the nature of our environment, and of particular events. For when we imagine an inference taking place, we are imagining an inference which is valid, and which produces veridical perceptions of our environment, that is, about particular events and objects and processes around us. The physical events at our sensory surfaces, although particular, cannot play the right role because they are not mental. So to make sense of these inferences we must postulate mental representations of these events. There are two ways we can think of these representations. First, we can think of them as perceptual in character. Second, we can think of them as belief-like in character.

If the former, then of course we have the same difficulty as with the conclusion of the putative inference: its content is inappropriate for it to play the role of a premise in an argument. At best we could think of ourselves as forming beliefs on its basis. We have, in addition, if the experience is thought of itself as unconscious, the difficulty of making sense of an unconscious visual experience. The concept of a visual experience seems to be the concept exclusively of a phenomenal experience, that sort of mental state that, in Nagel's evocative expression, there is something it is like to be in (1979b). Thus, if we take this route with the input, we should treat it as conscious. In any case, if the content of such an experience cannot play the role of a premise in an argument, but at best be a source of information for beliefs whose contents can, we cannot strictly think of it as itself a part of the inference. We must then think of the input to the inference proper as consisting of various beliefs which we have about either what goes on at our sensory surfaces or the content of some perceptual experience.

In the former case, our difficulty is that we lose information in the transition from the perceptual experience to the beliefs which we cannot regain at the putative conclusion of the inference, namely, the final perceptual experience of a scene. This is our first difficulty again. In the latter case, we have this difficulty of course, but also the difficulty of explaining how we come by these beliefs about what is going on at the sensory surfaces. It is evident that at some point explanations in terms of further beliefs must come to an end in a brute fact about the relation between stimulus at the sensory surfaces and our acquiring certain unconscious beliefs. But there seems to be no principle for determining when they should come to an end. In this case, it is at least as reasonable to say that they do not begin at all, and that it is simply a brute fact in the same sense that the stimulation of our sensory surfaces and background conditions produce our conscious perceptual experiences.

If these considerations are correct, then (a) there is no coherent account of the inferences we are supposed to be making unconsciously to arrive at veridical perceptions of the world around us, and (b) there is no reason to postulate them.

(2) Do Perceivers Have the Concepts Necessary to Perform the Inferences Required by the Inference Theory?

The second problem has to do with what concepts we would have to attribute to a perceiver in order to think of him as making unconscious inferences of the sort the inference theory postulates. The conceptual resources required by the inferences postulated by the inference theory are those of the inference theorists. But there can be no general guarantee that the conceptual resources of the perceiver match the theorist's. This is obscured by the fact that typically we have in mind the visual experiences of people who have the conceptual resources to understand the inferences that are postulated. But these theories are not supposed to apply just to perceivers sufficiently like the theorists to have such concepts, but also to, e.g., non-linguistic animals which display a behavioural repertoire sufficient to convince us that they are subject to many of the same illusions and have many of the same perceptual capacities that we do. The evidence is the same in these cases as in the case of human beings. However, it is not plausible to suggest that dogs or fish or pigeons have concepts necessary to entertain the thought that, e.g., the size of an object is proportional to its visual angle multiplied by its distance. Perhaps we have to attribute to dogs and pigeons rudimentary concepts of size and distance to attribute to them visual experiences which represent these, but we have no reason to attribute to them even rudimentary concepts of mathematical operations. Moreover, some of the concepts it would be necessary to attribute to the perceiver to attribute knowledge of principles which must be supposed to be known by him by some inference explanations are not plausibly possessed even by all human beings, for example, the concepts of parallax and luminance, which are invoked in inference explanations of the perception of motion and lightness. For many such concepts the only grounds for attributing them to someone would consist of his speaking competently a language in which some general term expressed the appropriate concept.

This difficulty is a reflection of the fact that the inferences which are postulated to explain conscious visual experiences are treated as autonomous with respect to the perceiver's conscious mental life. This means that no constraints are placed on what concepts can enter into the inferences. But the result of this is that we do not respect the conditions for attributing such concepts to the perceivers. And this shows us that our methodology is mistaken, if we want these inferences to be inferences made *by* the perceiver. For the perceiver could make such inferences only if he was in possession of the concepts which are employed in them.[18]

The Homunculus Response

At this point, it might be replied that it is not the perceiver who makes these inferences, but instead, as is often said, and as I have often said above, it is the perceiver's perceptual system which makes them. It is no accident that explanations of the inference theory so often attribute the inferences to the perceptual system rather than to the perceiver. But this cannot, I think, be a very attractive option once its consequences are appreciated. It commits us to thinking of the perceiver's perceptual system as in effect a different person. For if the perceiver is not making the inference, but the inference is being made, then someone else is making it. If the perceptual system is making the inference, it is a different person from the perceiver. Thus, we would have to

understand the claim of the inference theorist to be that he has not
only discovered that unconscious inferences are made in ordinary
perception of the environment, but that he has discovered that this
inferring is done by a person who inhabits our bodies with us and
passes on to us, somehow, his conclusions, as if, in order to know what
the world were like, we had to call up someone more closely connected with it to ask him to look outside for us.

This is a version of the homunculus fallacy, the attempt to explain
some cognitive function for a agent by postulating a little person inside
him who does part of it for him. The first difficulty with this, apart from
its *prima facie* implausibility, is that in explaining cognitive capacities it
is at best a delaying tactic. This is especially evident if the homunculus
is credited with its own perceptual experiences of the world; and it is
difficult to see how to avoid this once we have in fact postulated a
homunculus, for reasons given below. At some point we must discharge the homunculus if we are to achieve any genuine explanation
of perceptual capacities. If we can do so at some point, then it seems
there can be no need to postulate a homunculus at any point.[19]

Apart from this, appealing explicitly to a homunculus, while it re-
lieves the pressure on the inference theory from the argument from the
unavailability of conceptual resources for the postulated inferences,
also removes a good deal of the explanatory point of the theory. Originally, we were to conceive of the theory as giving us an explanation of
the perceiver's cognitive abilities. But if the form of our explanation is
that the perceiver's perceptions are to be explained by appeal to another person's cognitive abilities, then we have not in fact explained
that person's cognitive abilities at all. We have not explained how the
perceiver achieves veridical perception by appealing to inferences or
knowledge the perceiver has, but to someone else's abilities and
knowledge. What we explain now is not how we achieve veridical perception, but how someone else does it for us. This is not to explain our
cognitive capacities but to deny that we *have* them.

The homunculus response also undermines the claim that what is
going on is that an inference is taking place whose conclusion is in
some sense a perceptual experience. For even if we waive the earlier
objection that a visual experience cannot be the psychological analog
of the conclusion of an inference, we cannot very well allow that an
inference could take place in which all of the premises are in one person's mind while the conclusion is in another person's mind. Thus,
postulating a homunculus is actually incompatible with the claim that
we achieve veridical perception of our environment by an inference
from perceptual stimulus to a visual experience, for this requires that
we think of the premises of the argument and the conclusion as being

in the same mind, and the homunculus theory denies this. Instead, at best what we have is a half-completed inference in one person's mind and a causal transition from this to a mental state in another's, which is as brute as if it had occurred from the blow of a hammer to the head.

Finally, note that if we treat the perceptual system as a separate person, there is no reason to say that the mental inferences which it is making are unconscious. This is true for homunculus explanations generally. For their not being consciously accessible to us is now no more reason to say that they are unconscious than your mental states not being consciously accessible to me are a reason to call all of your mental states unconscious. While this undermines the criticism of the inference theory based on the connection principle, it also, as we have seen, undermines its explanatory power. That inference theorists want to treat these mental inferences as unconscious shows that they think of them as inferences that the perceiver is making; this is what gives them their explanatory relevance. That they attribute them to the perceptual system reflects their awareness that their autonomy requires that we think of them as not properly mental states of the perceiver at all.

(3) How Does the Perceptual System Acquire Its Knowledge?

A third problem is how the system is supposed to know various things about the world which it needs to know in order to make inferences of the sort that result in veridical perceptions. For the inference theory is explaining why we are able to perceive the world veridically in terms of the cognitive powers of our perceptual systems. This is represented explicitly as an intelligent cognitive process which takes information in and produces a perceptual experience as output. The perceptual system does not just make blind inferences, but is in fact attributed knowledge both of what goes on at the sensory surfaces of the individual and in his environment, since it is attributed knowledge of general laws connecting the perceptual stimuli with events, states and objects in the environment. Presumably this is intended in part to explain our knowledge. If the perceptual system did not know what it was about, we could hardly be attributed knowledge on the basis of its products. However, we conceive of our epistemic access to the world around us to be at least partly epistemically mediated by our visual experiences, and we have no conception of how else we could gain knowledge of the world around us. Thus, if we attribute knowledge of the world to our perceptual system, then it must either be derived from knowledge that we have independently, or the perceptual system itself must possess the kind of epistemic access to the environment that we do – that is, it must independently have perceptual experiences, etc.

Neither option is acceptable. If we take the first option, there are two problems. First, if the knowledge we have is to depend on knowledge the perceptual system has independently, then this appeal deprives both us and our perceptual system of any knowledge of the world, since we would presumably have such knowledge only if our perceptual system did. Second, most of us do not have the sort of knowledge that is attributed to the perceptual system at all. The rules which our perceptual systems are supposedly employing in inferring what our environment must be like are supposed to be uncovered not by first-person reflection on what we already know, but by third-person investigation of how our perceptual system achieves veridical perception of the world around us. If we had first-person access to such rules, then there would be no need for psychologists to undertake to discover what they were. If we take the second option, then it is clear that we are attributing to the perceptual system its own perceptual system, and the regress we noticed above is in full swing.

(4) Can There Be Any Evidence for the Inference Theory?

The last objection I want to raise in this section is a methodological one. Philosophers are often interested in claims about what is possible or not even when there is no empirical method for discovering whether or not the hypothesis in question is true. One of the things that sets the sciences apart from philosophy is that scientists are not interested in hypotheses which are not empirically confirmable or which are not needed to account for our observations. Methodologically, scientists are verificationists (thus, the relative lack of interest among physicists about the question of hidden variables in quantum mechanics except as that can be shown to make an experimental difference). In our discussion of the inference theory above, it appeared that it met this criterion for being a scientific theory because we were able to show that in some cases it was superior to the stimulus theory. This appearance, though, is illusory because we know that in principle there is no need to introduce the notion of unconscious inferences to explain our perceptual capacities. All that is necessary is that the actual process that produces our perceptual experiences connect in a law-like way features of our environment with the representational content of our experiences. The process which does this can be entirely physical up to the point at which we know that some mental state occurs. We know that from our first-person access to those mental states. Not only would a physical story be adequate, we are committed to there being such a story, for even if we were to accept that there were unconscious inferences occurring in the production of conscious visual experiences, we suppose that this would not be an irreducible fact about the process, but would itself be instantiated or realized in an underlying process that had a purely physical description. So we are committed to saying that there is an adequate account of how we get from sensory stimuli physically described to our perceptual experiences which does not postulate any unconscious inferences. Thus, the postulation of such unconscious inferences is gratuitous. This shows that, given our commitment to a physical basis for all thought, we could not in principle have a reason to postulate inaccessible unconscious inferences on the basis of the evidence that we achieve veridical perception of the world around us, for we know (or are committed to holding) that this admits of an explanation that does not require inaccessible unconscious inferences. The reason the same argument does not apply to conscious states, or dispositions to produce conscious states, is that these are not theoretical entities for us, but epistemically primary. We have independent reason to believe that they exist. But the only reason there could be to believe that inaccessible unconscious mental processes existed would be that they were explanatorily indispensable. We are committed to their being explanatorily dispensable, so it follows that we can have no reason to think that they exist; hence, they can be of no interest in an empirical theory. Such unconscious inferences, even if we could make sense of them, would have no place in a scientific psychology.

6. Diagnosis

If the arguments I have given are correct, then the inference theory is deeply misconceived. How then does it come to seem so compelling?

It is instructive to begin by considering again the comparison of the stimulus theory and the inference theory. In some of the cases we considered, there seemed to be a clear choice between the inference theory and the stimulus theory. If the mechanism were as the stimulus theory described it, then it would be inappropriate to describe the process as involving unconscious inferences. But this should be puzzling. For *prima facie* we ought to be able to treat the mechanism postulated by the stimulus theory as a matter of unconscious inference as well. For example, consider the stimulus theory of size constancy which holds that size constancy is a matter of the ratios of the sizes of images on the retina. Why should we not represent this way of achieving size constancy as a matter of a very simple inference from the fact that the ratio of the size of one image to that of another at one time is the same as it is at a later time, and a general rule that holds that objects do not change in size as long as the ratios of their visual angles remain constant? Again, consider the case of the waterfall illusion. Why should we not say that the perceptual system infers from the contrast in the pattern of cell discharges that the motion of the scene has not reversed its direction? I think our reactions to these cases contain important clues to the appeal of the inference theory. In the first case, part of what is important is that the putative inference involved takes into account only one factor, and, hence, seems more mechanical than in the case of the process postulated by the inference theory, in which distance and visual angle are independently determined and then brought under a law to determine size. In the second case, this factor is at work, but there is an additional important factor as well. That is that the inference which might be postulated to explain the waterfall illusion is not plausibly thought to be the result of the application of an assumption which would ordinarily be correct and result in veridical perception. Thus, we postulate an inference to explain a perceptual effect only when it is conceived to rest on a true *ceteris paribus* law connecting some feature of the perceptual stimuli with some feature of the environment.

This is a direct consequence of the question that defines our inquiry. We want an account of the process that produces *veridical* perceptions. A necessary condition for this is that the process we describe connect up representations with what they represent in a law-like way. Thus, our goal is to identify a set of laws L_1 that correlates properties of the environment with properties of the stimulus patterns at the retina, and a set of laws L_2 that correlates properties at the retina with representational properties of our visual experiences, so that L_1 and L_2 jointly entail a set of laws L_3 that correlates features of our environment with representations of them. Thus, an inference theory which represents the laws in L_2 as being instantiated by a process of reasoning must attribute to the perceiver or perceptual system assumptions about true laws of the sort that would go in L_1. That these laws are, of course, *ceteris paribus* laws allows for the possibility of perceptual errors and illusions. Thus, the difficulty with the postulated inference in the case of the waterfall illusion is that the assumption that would be attributed to the perceptual system is not a true *ceteris paribus* law connecting features of the perceptual stimuli with features of the environment, while the kind of mechanism we are interested in instantiates a true law of that kind. The trouble with the stimulus theory of size constancy is of a different kind. Here it is simply that there does not seem to be much of a mechanism required and so not much need to think of the mechanism as instantiated in inferences that the perceptual system makes, for lack of any other hypothesis.

But in neither of these cases do we have a reason to deny that the process that the perceptual system is undergoing involves an unconscious inference. The reason to deny this would be, in the case of the waterfall illusions, that the perceptual system makes only correct assumptions about the laws that connect the environment with stimuli at the sensory surfaces; in the case of the ratio theory, it would be that the perceptual system only makes relatively complicated inferences. The evidence we have, however, provides no reason to make these assumptions. As far as the evidence we have goes, we could attribute to the perceptual system a series of false assumptions which fortuitously result in correct conclusions, or very simple inferences from simple features of the perceptual stimuli.

What then explains the pattern of inferences actually attributed to perceivers? What has happened, I think, is the following. We have started out with the assumption that we perceive our environment by and large veridically, and so we want an account of the perceptual system that connects sensory stimuli with veridical representation. We give a set of laws L_1 that connect features of our environment with sensory stimulation. We hypothesize that the laws L_2 that the perceptual system instantiates take account of the sensory stimulations cited in the previous laws. Where it seems that we need to give an account of the *mechanism* which instantiates these laws, given that we want to match representations with what they are of, and think of this as the goal of the perceptual system, *we adopt the expedient of assigning knowledge of the laws in L_1 to the perceptual system, and treat the mechanism as a matter of a rational agent inferring from the laws in L_1 and the stimuli to the nature of the environment.* The mechanism that instantiates the laws in L_2 then becomes a psychological mechanism.

It is clear that this is invalid. Why is it so attractive? There are a number of reasons. First, it is a mechanism that we understand and whose postulation does not require us to do any detailed investigation of the neural mechanisms underlying the process. Second, since we think of the perceptual system as having as its function the production of veridical experiences, it is easy for us to overlook the distinction between the theorist's point of view and the point of view of the perceptual system. That is, thinking of the perceptual system as having a function suggests that it has its own goal, hence, its own point of view; once we have got that far, it is easy to identify its point of view with our own. We can infer, given the laws that connect the environment with surface stimuli, what experiences are needed to have veridical perceptions of the environment. The perceptual system then, we think, having this as its goal, must do the same. This bit of transference is clearly a mistake. What lends to the confusion is that while in the case of many biological functions the output is not a conscious experience – think of the digestive system – in the case of the visual system it is. When we then think of the perceptual system as having veridical perception as its biological function, since the goal itself is an intentional state, it is easy to treat this as an intrinsic goal of the system, and natural to think of the goal driven process by which it is produced as mental as well.

That this is a mistake is brought out in the following two thought-experiments. In the first, suppose that we have added onto the perceptual system a mechanical device that takes into account a number of different factors in pre-processing the image that is projected onto the retina. For example, suppose that it filters out images on the basis both of size and the wavelength of light they reflect. The process that now results in veridical perception includes some additional stages of processing: would we ascribe additional unconscious inferences to the self or the perceptual system? In this case the answer seems clearly to be "No." But our position with respect to the perceptual system is no different from our position with respect to an apparatus designed to pre-process information before it arrives at the retina. In the second, we can suppose that we have designed a machine that can keep track of the movement of objects through keeping track (entirely mechanically) of its own movement, and the movement they generate by changes on a two-dimensional array of light detectors. The machine keeps track of this in the following sense: it has a mechanical model within it of the space around it in which various elements in it correspond to elements in the environment, and their movements to movements of the objects in the environment. We do not, I think, feel any inclination to say that it is making inferences. Suppose we now add a Cartesian soul which has visual experiences of such objects moving as a causal result of this mechanical process. It is obvious that this changes nothing about the process itself.

Similarly, in the case of some physical processes causing in one an experience which is not representational in character, we feel no inclination to say that the process that produced it was a cognitive process, even though the process may be functionally quite complex, as in the case of the digestive system. It could even be at some level of description functionally identical to the perceptual system. But when an upset stomach causes stomach ache we do not suppose that the process that produces the unwanted experience is itself mental. It is only when we start out with a system that has mental states and a process that produces representational states that we feel inclined to suppose that not only the product of the process but the process itself is mental in character.

There are five further possible sources of the seductiveness of the inference theory. The first is the tendency to think of perceptual illusions as cognitive failures. If illusions are cognitive failures, then we are forced to think of perceptual illusion as a matter of some failure in taking proper account of the world. But then this must be represented as our having made some false assumption, and the illusion is treated as an instance of mistaken reasoning. The mistake here is to treat all errors as if they were errors of reasoning.

This is connected with a second possible source of confusion, which is to take the verb 'to perceive' to be analogous to an action verb, and so to be a cognitive achievement verb. If perceiving is something we *do*, in the same sense in which we reason or act, then it must be the result of a cognitive process just as reasoning and acting are. Thus, a proper explanation of perception must bring in a cognitive component. The mistake here is to treat perceiving as if it were something we did in the sense in which we write a paper or solve a puzzle. The sense in which to perceive something is to do something is the same sense in which to breath, or to perspire, or to dream is to do something. None of these implies that what is done is a result of a cognitive process. Perceiving is more like feeling pain that it is like drawing a conclusion.

The move to treating the process by which veridical perception is achieved as an inference is probably also aided by a failure to distinguish between two senses in which we talk of information-processing. There is first of all causal information-processing. In this sense, a system processes information, provided that its states are connected in a law-like way so that a potential observer who had knowledge of the laws governing the transformations of the states could recover information about what happened earlier from later portions of the process. In the second sense, information-processing is just what we consciously do when we reason from our beliefs; in this case 'information' means 'representation'. In the first sense of information-processing, the visual system processes information, but so equally does the digestive system, the immune system and the solar system. In the second sense of information-processing, no one would suppose that the digestive system processes information, but when we turn to perception, since the end of the process is a perceptual state which carries information in the *second* sense, we can be led to suppose that the causal information process must itself carry information in the same sense.

A fourth possible source of confusion is failure to observe the distinction between two senses of rule-following, descriptive and normative. A system follows a rule descriptively, provided that its temporal development is correctly described by the rule. A system follows a rule normatively, provided that its temporal development is explained by its knowing a rule and acting in accordance with the rule out of the intention to follow it. The perceptual system follows descriptively the rule: perceive one thing to be larger than another if its distance is greater but it has the same visual angle. When we think of the output as a perceptual state, and the system as having veridical perception as its biological function, it is easy to read the rule as normative rather than simply descriptive.

A final possible source of confusion is the tendency to conflate two different notions of intelligent behaviour. In the first sense, we speak of a system acting intelligently in the sense that it acts *as if* it were intelligent. This can be a context sensitive classification. Thus, we contrast, e.g., a thermostat which turns on the heater when the temperature drops below 68 degrees, with an "intelligent" thermostat which takes into account, say, the humidity in addition to the temperature. In the second sense, we mean a system is genuinely intelligent in the sense that it has intentional states and engages in explicit reasoning and deliberation to produce behaviour appropriate to its goals. The perceptual system is certainly intelligent in the first sense; that is why the ratio theory of size constancy is inadequate. Since the output of the perceptual process is a perceptual experience, it can be easy to move from thinking of the perceptual system as behaviourally intelligent to thinking of it as genuinely intelligent.

7. Reconstruction

What can be salvaged of the inference theory? Here I think two things can be said. (1) First, if I am right in my diagnosis of the inference theory, there is a stage in the investigation in which we make genuine empirical hypotheses about how the perceptual system achieves veridical perception of the environment. This is in part a matter of discovering exactly which of the features of the perceptual stimuli are both correlated reliably with features of the environment, on the one hand, and with representations of those features, on the other. It is this which the empirical evidence has a bearing on. This is essentially a question from the design standpoint about which features of the sensory stimuli are the ones the perceptual system is causally attuned to in the production of visual experiences. This is an important and interesting empirical question, and conclusions about this can be extracted from the debate between the inference theory and its rivals.

Second, the inference theory is not just about what features at the sensory surfaces are relevant to the production of a veridical perceptual experience but also about the process by which those features produce that experience. Although I have argued that those processes cannot be mental processes, this does not mean that there is nothing of value in the hypotheses of the inference theory, for they can be treated as hypotheses about the functional specification of the process that produces the visual experience. For example, the inference theory holds that we achieve size constancy in visual experience by the unconscious assumption that Emmert's law is true and by the belief that a certain object is a certain distance and that it subtends a certain angle on the retina. We can convert this into the hypothesis that size constancy in visual perception is a function, given by Emmert's law, of two things: (1) the visual angle an object subtends and (2) the features of the stimuli that are responsible for those states in the perceptual system that indicate the distance of the object. Thus, we give a partial functional characterization of the physical process whose upshot is that a certain object looks to be a certain size. What we aim for, on this view, is a functional characterization of the perceptual system which treats events at the sensory surfaces as input and veridical representations as output. The fact that the output is veridical representation requires that the selection of the input and the functional organization of the perceptual system be such that in our actual environment our perceptual representations are by and large correct. Such a functional specification selects from among a number of possible systems, and provides a guide to an investigation of its neurophysiological realization. What it does not do is provide us with a distinctively psychological explanation of how veridical perception is possible. It provides a psychological explanation only insofar as the output is psychological, or the causal processing itself is influenced by conscious psychological processes. The same kind of story can be told about the immune system; this does not make the account of the functional organization of the immune system a psychological account.

Thus, I advocate a retreat from the explicitly intentional language of the inference theory to the functional structure any such inferences must assume.

8. Objections to My Argument

Objection 1. Psychologists are just extending in a principled way the meanings of the terms 'mental' and 'inference', so any objection based on the concept ordinarily expressed by these words does not apply to the inference theory.

Reply. It is not clear that this is the intent of any actual inference theorist, but in any case reformulating the inference theory explicitly as offering an extension to the ordinary conception of the mental would achieve at best a Pyrrhic victory. I can extend the meaning of any word by adding a disjunct to its definition, but then when I argue on the basis of the extension that some item falls under the concept now expressed by that word I do not thereby show that we have discovered that something falls under the concept previously expressed. If I say that henceforth I will call anything that is a human being or a chair "a human being," and then assert, "I am sitting on a human being," I have not discovered a new and startling fact but relabelled an old and mundane one. This discovery would not call, for example, for new legislation to protect the rights of a previously unrecognized segment of humanity. Similarly, to suggest that the inference theorist is or ought to be just extending the meaning of 'inference' is to suggest that the theory is of very much less interest than it seemed to be at first. It might still be urged that the extension is a principled one, and that therefore the theory is making a substantive claim. But if the argument I have given is correct, the extension would consist of including in the extension of 'inference' information-processing in the sense in which a sunflower or a prism processes information; in this sense virtually every causal process is a mental inference, which just trivializes the claim that the perceptual system is making unconscious inferences. There is, furthermore, a point to not changing usage as this strategy urges: in doing so we obscure distinctions important to a clear understanding of what's special about having a mind.

Objection 2. Sometimes conscious knowledge or belief influences the character of perceptual experience. For example, in the perception of ambiguous figures such as the Necker cube, a suggestion to a subject about what the figure is before he views it will often determine how he sees it. Since the input here is clearly mental, the process which selects which one of the two figures the figure is naturally seen as must be mental as well. A similar phenomenon is the autokinetic effect. When a subject views a stationary point of light in a dark room, often it will be seen as moving; and whether it is seen as moving and in what direction is susceptible to suggestion. Thus, it appears that a conscious belief plays a role in how a scene is perceived; this requires that the process which produces the perception be a mental process.

Reply. That what we consciously think we are seeing or likely to see should have a causal effect on the process that generates our visual experience does not require that the process itself be a mental process. If what I think causes my ulcer to act up, which causes me discomfort, it does not follow that the causal process that led to that is a mental process. Similarly, when I type a sentence at my keyboard, I do this because of my intention to write a particular sentence; but it does not follow that each movement of my fingers is itself intended by me to

Figure 2.6: The Duck-Rabbit

move as it does or that each movement is the result of an unconscious process of the same sort as the conscious process which results in my typing the whole sentence. What makes us want to say that in this case there is a kind of mental process is that the outcome of that process is one of two possible representations of an ambiguous figure, and that we have a model for what it is like to disambiguate some figures or sentences by a conscious process. But the model is inappropriately applied in this case, because it is not possible to bring to our awareness any such mental process. Furthermore, clearly this kind of case should be expected even if one thinks that the process is entirely nonmental. For given that it is advantageous to see objects as falling under certain kinds on the basis of a few cues about them, it will be possible to produce ambiguous figures, and since it is advantageous to be primed to see what one expects in one's environment on the basis of as few cues as possible, one would expect that the experiential upshot of seeing an ambiguous figure would be causally sensitive to one's expectations about what one is likely to see.

Objection 3. Many of our perceptual abilities obviously depend upon learning. This is clear, e.g., in the case of many pictorial cues to relative depth, such as interposition patterns. Learning is also clear in cases of perceptual adaptation, as in the case of subjects adapting to lenses which distort the image projected onto the retina. A simpler case in which learning is clearly important involves ambiguous figures such as the familiar duck-rabbit figure (Figure 2.6), which would clearly not present itself to us as either a duck or a rabbit unless we were familiar with and could recognize features of both ducks and rabbits. Someone unacquainted with animals altogether would not see such a drawing as representing anything. But if such perceptions depend upon learning, then it must be that at some time one came to recognize an object by an explicit process of detecting features and consciously bringing an object under a concept as a result. Similarly in the other cases. When one becomes skilled at this, the process takes place below the level of consciousness. But this is no reason to deny that it is a process of the same type.

Reply. First, that a skill or ability to recognize something is acquired does not show that the acquisition of it involved an explicit process of taking into account features of an object or scene and recognizing that the object or scene falls under a concept in virtue of having those features. But even if the process by which the skill is acquired did involve initially taking account explicitly of features of a scene in deciding that it fell under a concept, that does not require that we think of the skill once it is acquired as a matter of an explicitly represented inference or recipe that is followed that has dropped below the level of consciousness. Representations and skills are in different logical categories. This can be seen by noticing that in the exercise of any complex skill that involves explicitly represented parts, one must have the ability to carry out the parts. If each part in turn had to be broken down into a series of explicitly represented instructions, then since each instruction could be carried out only if one had the ability to do it, we would have an infinite regress. The parallel with acquiring a skill such as playing tennis is useful here. One can receive instruction in how to serve in tennis. But when one has acquired a good serve, one does not any longer go through those instructions, either consciously or unconsciously. The acquisition of a skill is the process of dropping the need for any explicit representation of the task below the level of representing the goal toward which the skill is applied. In the same way we can acquire skills in recognizing objects without supposing that there is any processing or inference which goes on below the level of consciousness, even if originally we learned to recognize an item with the help of explicit instruction.

Objection 4. If recognitional abilities are acquired, then this implies that past experience is taken into account in our present perceptual processing. This means that some physical trace of the past experience is left in the brain, which is a memory trace, and that when we see something what we see it as is a result of a very rapid unconscious search through these memory traces. This search can be conceived of as either a parallel search or a serial search. Moreover, it is clear that there is empirical evidence which bears on this question, so that it cannot be ruled out *a priori*. For example, in one experiment, subjects were given a list of items to memorize. Thereafter, they were shown an item and asked to say whether it was on the list. The amount of time it took subjects to answer was proportional to the number of items on the original list they were asked to memorize, thus bearing out the hypothesis that a very rapid but serial search through memory was being performed. This process is experimentally confirmed, and obviously too fast to be accessible to consciousness. Therefore there cannot be any in principle objection to unconscious inferences in explaining cognitive abilities.

Reply. All that is implied by the fact that recognitional abilities are acquired as a result of our experience is that they are causally sensitive to past experience. This is a genetic fact about them, not a fact about how the recognitional ability is realized. The mistake in the above argument occurs in the movement from 'physical trace' to 'memory' in the sense of a representational state. In the sense in which a physical trace is a memory, a tree remembers which years were wet and which were dry, because this leaves a physical trace in the rings in the tree's trunk. But it does not follow that the tree represents certain years as wet and other years as dry. The experiment designed to distinguish between serial and parallel processing in recognitional abilities requires careful treatment. This is not a good test case for the inference theory because in the experiment described the representation of the different items on the list are straightforwardly accessible to consciousness in the sense that once the list is memorized, the subject has a disposition to form a conscious thought that an item was on the list as a result. Thus these representations are not inaccessible unconscious representations of the sort that might be involved in basic perceptual recognitional abilities. It might be thought, nonetheless, that there is a process of unconscious reasoning going on, an unconscious comparison of the item the subject is shown with an unconscious mental image or representation of each successive item on the list. This must be rejected on my account because such a process is conceived of as involving states which are not simply dispositions to produce conscious mental states but just like a conscious process of inference except for being unconscious. The reply to this is that there is certainly no requirement that the experimental results be understood this way. They are perfectly compatible with the claim that there is no unconscious process of inference at all; the results tell us something about how our recognitional abilities are implemented, but do not require us to think of them as implemented in a process of unconscious inference. What the experiment tells us is something about how our dispositions to have certain conscious thoughts and our desire to perform a certain recognitional task interact to produce a conscious judgement about whether an item is or is not on a memorized list.

Objection 5. Toward any visual experience we can take a stance which we can call proximal perception.[20] This is the standpoint an artist takes toward his experience when he wants to paint so that the painting will look like the scene. Thus, in the case of the Ponzo illusion, it is possible to see or experience the scene, even if with some difficulty, simply as two lines on the page which are converging at the top of the page, and the two circles as at least more nearly the same in size. This shows that the input to the process that produces the appearance that the upper circle is larger is accessible to consciousness, and so that the input is actually a mental state. If the input is a mental state and the output is a mental state, then the process that takes us from the one to the other must be a mental process.

Reply. There are two mistakes in this objection. The first is that we are not licensed to infer from the fact that how things appear to us can change if we adopt the stance of proximal perception that things appear to us that way in any sense when we do not. So we are not licensed in drawing the inference that we see things that way all the time unconsciously and then infer unconsciously from the character of that experience to how things should be represented. On the other hand, if we are aware in some sense even when perceiving a road receding into the distance that the edges of the road appear to be converging toward the top of the visual field, then our perception of depth is not a matter of an unconscious inference from unconscious input to a conscious experience. In this case it might still be said that an unconscious inference takes place. But this is the second mistake. The fact that we make a transition from one mental state to another mental state does not require that the transition be mediated by a mental process. If it did, then since a mental process is itself a sequence of mental states, we would immediately have a vicious regress.

Objection 6. If you deny that the inference theory is coherent, then you will have to deny as well that we engage in unconscious mental processing in cases such as disambiguating sentences in natural languages. For example, consider the following sentence:

Bud and Pearl saw the Great Lakes while they were driving to Canada.[21]

We understand the antecedent of 'they' in this sentence to be Bud and Pearl rather than the Great Lakes without any conscious awareness of disambiguating it. But it is overwhelmingly plausible that we do this on the basis of our knowledge that interpreting 'they' as referring to the Great Lakes would require an interpretation someone could intend only if he were seriously confused about the nature of large bodies of water. But if your criticism of the inference theory is correct, you are committed to saying that we do not arrive at this interpretation by any mental process whatsoever.

Reply. That we disambiguate this sentence on the basis of our knowledge about the relative plausibility of someone who uttered it intending 'they' to refer to Bud and Pearl rather than to the Great Lakes is not incompatible with my account. This knowledge is clearly not ruled out by the connection principle because if one points out to someone that 'they' has two interpretations, one can explain with little difficulty why it is implausible that someone would utter such a sentence intending 'they' to refer to the Great Lakes rather than Bud and Pearl. What my account denies, however, is that when we disambiguate such expressions on the basis of our knowledge, what we do is to go through a very rapid unconscious inference in which we entertain each of the interpretations and reject one on the basis of its implausibility. Rather, our dispositional knowledge causally conditions how we understand the sentence. But this does not require that there be an extremely rapid unconscious inference.

Objection 7. The sorts of inference theories you have considered here are unsophisticated. More sophisticated theories (which provide detailed accounts of how the incoming signal is processed stage by stage to generate a 3-D image from the 2-D array of input at the retina) are not subject to these objections.

Reply. This objection mistakes my criticisms for empirical criticisms of the inference theories I have considered which claim that these inferences are too coarse-grained to provide an adequate account of how our perceptual mechanism works. The objections that I have raised do not depend upon how detailed or sophisticated the inferences postulated are but only on their being genuine mental processes just like conscious processes except for being independent of our conscious mental lives.

Notes

1 A prominent recent defender of the theory of unconscious inferences in perceptual processing among psychologists is Irvin Rock (1983, 1984), whom I will use for purposes of illustration. Among Philosophers, Jerry Fodor is well-known for defending this position (1983).

2 I make no pretence in what follows to provide an exhaustive account of the kinds of experimental evidence bearing on the perception of size and motion that psychologists have accumulated and strategies for explaining it in terms of unconscious inferences they have employed. That would be an enormous undertaking. My aim is to provide enough of a sketch of the kinds of evidence available and the kinds of explanation which have been offered to fix our subject matter and give substance to the criticisms and diagnosis that I will offer.

3 For example, the central criticism I make will apply to all computational theories of cognitive capacities which (a) treat computations as operations over genuine representations and (b) treat them as independent of our conscious mental lives.

4 In this sketch of an inference account of visual perception of size constancy, we have taken for granted that the visual system can determine the distance of an object from the observer. The explanation of how it does this can be expected to take into account many different facts, such as recognition of familiar objects whose sizes we know, information about the convergence of both eyes on an object to keep it in focus, the tendency of the eye to accommodate for the distance of an image to keep it in sharp focus, retinal disparity, motion parallax and pictorial information. The explanation of how the visual system determines distance can be given in terms of unconscious inferences from perceptual cues about the relative distances of objects in the environment. For our purposes, nothing essential is left out in concentrating on the stage of processing which moves from distance information and visual angle to relative size.

5 It is striking that this account of how the inference theory would apply to the perception of motion can be given just from a description of the perceptual problem. This should make us suspect that in some cases the empirical content of the inference theory does not exceed the description of the problem itself.

6 As Irvin Rock puts it at one point, "According to this theory, apparent movement is a solution to the problem posed when object A disappears in one place in the scene and another object, B, suddenly appears in another place. After all, this sequence is quite similar to real motion, particularly when it is rapid" (1984, 195). And "Thus, in an apparent-movement display, when the conditions mimic those of real, rapid motion, entailing sudden disappearance of an object in one place and its reappearance in another, our perceptual system makes the plausible inference that the object has moved." (1984, 196)

7 The point of this paragraph is not to endorse this alternative explanation, which may be disputable, but to show that empirical findings can apparently bear on the correctness of the inference theory. For this purpose it is not necessary to show that theory is false, but only that it could be.

8   The connection principle is not new; most classical philosophers apparently held it in one form or another. For example, Descartes apparently held that no state is a mental state unless it is a conscious mental state. Thus: "As to the fact that there can be nothing in the mind, in so far as it is a thinking thing, of which it is not aware, this seems to me to be self-evident. For there is nothing that we can understand to be in the mind, regarded in this way, that is not a thought or dependent on a thought. If it were not a thought or dependent on a thought it would not belong to the mind *qua* thinking thing; and we cannot have any thought of which we are not aware at the very moment when it is in us" (1647/1985, 171-72). Thomas Nagel is a contemporary adherent along with Searle: "Not all mental states are conscious, but all of them are capable of producing states that are" (1979c, 188).

9   The first formulation, that every mental state is or is potentially a conscious mental state, suggests a picture of the relation between conscious and unconscious mental states that makes it difficult to see how the connection principle could be a conceptual truth, for it suggests that unconscious mental states are just like conscious mental states except for being unconscious. In a metaphor that Searle uses himself, this is the conception of unconscious states as like fish below the surface of the sea, which have only to be brought to the surface. On this conception, it is puzzling why we must think of an unconscious mental state as essentially tied to a conscious mental state. Perhaps we must think of it as the sort of thing which could become conscious, that is, as falling under a mental type such as belief, which a conscious mental state could also fall under, but this leaves it open to think of it as the sort of thing which for a particular individual is completely inaccessible to him. The second formulation can be read in either of two ways. On the first reading it is simply the claim that the type under which an unconscious mental state falls must also be a type under which a conscious mental state can fall. On the second reading, it is the claim that necessarily every unconscious mental state of a given individual is a potential conscious mental state for that individual. Both of these readings are distinct from the last form because neither says anything about "the ontology of the unconscious" and neither entails that what it is for a state to be an unconscious mental state is for it to be capable of causing a conscious mental state. The last formulation is too weak, for reasons which I give below.

10 The question is really more general than this, if there can be creatures with mental states which are not persons. For convenience, however, I will continue to speak of persons.

11 To say that we have a special kind of knowledge of our own conscious mental states is not, however, to claim that we are incorrigible or infallible about them. It is therefore not an objection to this distinction that no certainty attaches to our pronouncements or beliefs about even our conscious mental states.

12 It might be objected at this point that we can first identify a body as a particular person's body by reference to its effects on his conscious mental life, and then identify his unconscious mental states in terms of their being causally located in his body. But this does not avoid any problems, since if a body is identified initially by its contingent relations to a person's conscious mental states, then there can be no in principle bar to more than one person bearing those relations to that body.

13 We must think of it also as a disposition to produce behaviour in conjunction with one's other beliefs and desires.

14 The dispositions which we identify as unconscious mental states are dispositions of the person whose states they are. Thus, although it may be true that the wall is in a certain sense disposed to cause a visual experience in me, that disposition is not my unconscious mental state because it not a disposition of me. The wall could cease to exist without the visual experience or the perceiver ceasing to exist.

    Note that the conception of unconscious mental states presupposed in much of the argument, as states just like conscious mental states only unconscious, has now been abandoned in favour of conceiving of unconscious mental states as being, as it were, mental by courtesy of their power to produce conscious mental states.

15 The Freudian theory, however, as traditionally conceived, violates the connection principle for other reasons, for it conceives of unconscious process as just like conscious processes, rather than just as dispositions to produce conscious mental states.

16 Joseph Tolliver has suggested helpfully that one could think of this as a secondary qualities theory of unconscious mental states.

17 This is in fact the way that inference theorists represent the inferences that they attribute to a perceiver or his perceptual system. Here is an example given by Rock (1983, 274): "*Major premise:* An object's visual angel is inversely proportional to distance. *Minor premise:* Visual angle is 1 degree (producing a particular perceived extensity); distance is 50 feet (producing a particular perceived distance). *Conclusion:* Object is equivalent to one that would yield a visual angle of 25 degrees at 2 feet (or 5 degrees at 10 feet, etc.)." As I note in the text, this cannot be correct, because strictly speaking the "conclusion" is supposed to be a visual experience.

18 Another aspect of this disconnection between the usual procedures for attributing concepts to someone and the procedures of the inference theory is that the attribution of beliefs and assumptions in the inference theory is radically indeterminate. There are clearly many different sets of premises which could be attributed that would have the same conclusions. But since the attribution of such inferences is not constrained by any evidence that the perceiver has the concepts needed to entertain them, or by the perceiver's awareness of such inferences, any inference which produces the right result

compatibly with the constraints on the input and the constraint that the perceptual experience be such that it is by and large veridical in the perceiver's environment is as good an any other. There is no objective ground to choose between them.

19 One might attempt to defuse this objection by arguing that as we go down levels we get to dumber and dumber homunculi so that we really are achieving some explanatory progress. However, in this particular case, we have a homunculi that has conceptual resources which may be more sophisticated in some ways than those of the perceiver, and there is no reason to think as we go down levels the lower levels will involve any less sophisticated concepts.

20 I borrow the term from Rock (1983, 1984).

21 Adapted from an example by George Miller.

References

Anstis, S.M., and R.L. Gregory (1964). The after-effect of seen motion: The role of retinal stimulation and eye movements. *Quarterly Journal of Experimental Psychology*, 17, 173-74

Descartes, R. [1647] (1985). *Fourth Replies*. Translated by John Cottingham, Robert Stoothoff and Dugland Murdoch. In *The Philosophical Writings of Descartes*. Cambridge: Cambridge University Press

Fodor, J. (1983). *The Modularity of Mind*. Cambridge: MIT Press

Gibson, J.J. (1950). *The Perception of the Visual World*. Boston: Houghton Mifflin

Helmholtz, H. von. [1867] (1962). *Treatise on Physiological Optics*, Vol. III. Edited and Translated from the 3rd German edition by J.P.C. Southall. New York: Dover Publications

Ludwig, K. (1993). A dilemma for Searle's argument for the connection principle. *Behavioral and Brain Sciences* 16: 194-5

Nagel, T. (1979a). *Moral Questions*. Cambridge: Cambridge University Press

————. (1979b). What is it like to be a bat? In T. Nagel (1979a), *Moral Questions*. Cambridge: Cambridge University Press

————. (1979c). Panpsychism. In T. Nagel (1979a), *Moral Questions*. Cambridge: Cambridge University Press

Penrose, L.S., and R. Penrose (1958). Impossible objects: A special type of visual illusion. *British Journal of Psychology* 49: 31-33

Rock, I. (1983). *The Logic of Perception*. Cambridge: MIT Press

————. (1984). *Perception*. New York: Scientific American Library

Rock, I., and S. Ebenholtz (1959). The relational determination of perceived size. *Psychological Review* 66: 387-401

Rock, I., and S. Ebenholtz (1962). Stroboscopic movement based on change of phenomenal rather than retinal location. *American Journal of Psychology* 75: 193-207

Searle, John R. (1990a). Consciousness, explanatory inversion, and cognitive science. *Behavioral and Brain Sciences* 13: 585-96

———. (1990b). Who is computing with the brain? *Behavioral and Brain Sciences* 13: 632-40

Sigman E., and I. Rock (1974). Stroboscopic movement based on perceptual intelligence. *Perception* 3: 9-28

3

A Feedforward Network for Fast Stereo Vision with Movable Fusion Plane

Paul M. Churchland

Introductory epistemology courses often begin by addressing the problem of "our knowledge of the external world." Typically the problem is posed in the form, "How is one justified in believing a certain class of sentences?" (such as those about the arrangment and character of proximate physical objects). Two major assumptions are thus made surreptitiously central right at the outset. First, to pose the question in this way is to assume that our *representations* of the world are basically sentential or propositional in character. And it is also to assume that the relational features from which an account of *virtuous cognitive activity* is to be drawn must be the various relations that typically connect sentences to each other and to the world – relations such as entailment, coherence, probability, truth and so forth. Thus are we launched on a long tradition of epistemological discussion.

The most recent and in many ways the most useful instance of this tradition is the attempt by classical AI to construct artificial cognitive systems. It is especially useful because, unlike the representational / computational stories earlier composed by philosophers of science and inductive logicians, the stories produced (or reproduced) in AI were quickly implemented on large and powerful machines where their virtues – and their shortcomings – could be made dramatically evident. Where philosophers had spent months or years, pencils in hand, trying to discover failures and counter-examples in some intricate computational scheme, AI researchers could see its wheels fall off much more swiftly, indeed, often in milliseconds. We have learned from the machine-implemented experiments of classical AI, much more firmly than from the scratch-pad experiments of philosophy, how difficult it is to account for the acquisition, administration and deployment of knowledge if we restrict ourselves to the classical representational and computational assumptions of the preceding paragraph.

For this we should be grateful, since a sister discipline invites research down a different path in any case. Empirical neuroscience suggests that a very different style of representation and computation is the basis of cognition in humans and animals generally. In a nutshell, the high-dimensional activation vector – that is, the pattern of activations across a large population of neurons – appears to be the biological brain's basic mode of (occurrent) representation. And the basic mode of computation appears to be the vector-to-vector transformation, effected by passing the input vector through a large matrix of synaptic connections. Such matrices of artfully tuned synaptic weights constitute the brain's chronic or abeyant representations of the world and its general behaviour. (See Churchland 1989 for an accessible summary of how these ideas bear on epistemology and the philosophy of science, and Churchland and Sejnowski 1992 for a summary of how they bear on cognitive neurobiology.)

The present paper is one instance of this general theme. The issue is stereo vision – the binocular capacity for perceiving the relative and even the absolute positions of distinct objects in three-dimensional space. The aim is to provide an account of that capacity that is faithful both to the functional capacities of human and animal stereo vision, and to the anatomical and physiological realities of the human and animal brain. Computational accounts of stereo vision are not new, but they typically ignore certain important features of our stereoptic competence, and they make little attempt to be neurophysiologically realistic. I hope to repair both defects below.

Stereo algorithms typically divide into two parts or stages. The first stage divines correlations between the picture elements of the left and right images. The second stage processes those correlations in some iterative, co-operative or competitive fashion. The first stage can be very fast, but it can also leave much about depth unsettled and ambiguous. The second stage can be very effective in reducing those ambiguities, but it may also consume more time than is biologically plausible.

The present paper explores just how much of the task of locating objects in 3-space can be performed by a purely feedforward network pursuing a purely correlational strategy. The basic message is that it is more than is commonly assumed. The ambiguities of correspondence that frustrate earlier correlational approaches are dramatically reduced if 3-D reconstruction is more realistically confined to the close vicinity of a movable plane-like locus, and if inputs to the system display a more realistic variety of gray-scale values. Evolutionary and developmental considerations join these modelling results in suggesting that a very fast and relatively simple network of this kind should underlie such recurrent processes as may later be deployed in more advanced creatures or at later developmental stages.

Serious computational models for stereo vision must be able to solve random-dot stereograms (Julesz 1971). The classical success in this regard is the co-operative/competitive algorithm of Marr and Poggio (1976). But serious models must also solve the problem in realistic time. Here the Marr/Poggio model is problematic, since it must cycle through many iterations before finally settling into a solution configuration. Given an appropriate vergence, however, humans achieve binocular fusion very swiftly. In hopping one's fixation around a dinner table, one can successively fuse at least five different objects at five different depths in less than one second. So fusion can be achieved within 200 msec., and, being part of a larger process that includes successive foveal acquisitions and focussings, the fusion process itself likely consumes considerably less than 200 msec.

A single-pass feedforward network has a major speed advantage over iterative/settling networks. Can a purely feedforward network solve the problem of 3-D structure? Within broad limits, the answer is yes, and such networks show psychophysical and "physiological" features characteristic of human stereo vision as well.

1. Some Behavioural Desiderata

A central feature of human stereo vision, under-represented in previous models, is the shallow plane-like locus – "Panum's fusional area" – within which binocular fusion is achieved. This preferred plane, normal to the line of sight, is movable, by means of changes in binocular vergence, from infinity to mere centimeters in front of the face. Objects momentarily located much before or behind that plane are not perceived with anything like the clarity or resolution of objects within it (Figure 3.1).

This selective resolution is typically hidden from us by two facts. At vergences close to zero – i.e., at fixations close to infinity – objects beyond 50 meters are *all* well-fused because binocular disparities are

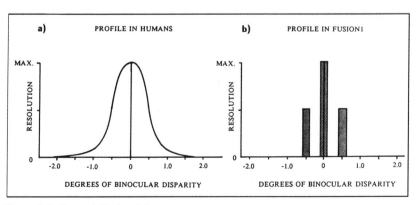

Figure 3.1: Panum's Fusional Area.

negligible beyond that distance. And at vergences closer to hand, where binocular disparities are large, we are able repeatedly to reset our vergence in order to fixate previously unfused objects. A rough analogy here is the unexpectedly small area of foveal resolution and the poor quality of visual resolution outside that area. The swift fall-off tends to be hidden from us because we are so skilled and so swift at relocating that favoured area upon objects of interest to us. As with the area of maximal foveal resolution, so with the plane of maximal binocular fusion.

The models reported below were motivated primarily by the desire to recreate these two features: a high-resolution fusion plane movable by vergence changes, and the swift computational achievement of depth-appropriate binocular fusion of objects located at that plane. This approach reduces the magnitude of the classical "correspondence problem" by recognizing that, despite expectations (e.g., Hubel 1988, 153), the brain does not solve the problem globally, but only locally. The problem gets solved anew, for a specific plane of fixation, with each vergence change. Successful fusion does reach somewhat beyond and in front of the preferred plane, but that is a minor complexity we shall address below. Despite appearance and tradition, this is not the central feature of binocular vision.

2. Network Architecture and Training

To serve easy comprehension, we examine a sequence of four similar networks. Unrealistic simplifying assumptions are progressively relaxed as we proceed. The first network takes only binary, black/white inputs at the retina. The second and third take various grey-scale inputs. And the fourth takes as inputs *changes* in grey-scale values across the retina.

The gross organization of the first network – FUSION1.NET – is schematically depicted in Figure 3.2. Two 60 × 60 pixel "retinas" project to a layer of hidden units, which projects in turn to a cyclopean output layer – the tuned "fixation" units – of 60 × 60 pixels. Each retina also projects directly to that output layer. Finally, there is a bias unit that projects to every unit beyond the input layer. (This unit and its projections are left out of most diagrams for reasons of clarity. Its job is merely to help simulate the intrinsic activation levels found in real neurons.) In total, this initial net has 21,601 units and 50,400 connections.

Random-dot stereo pairs (Figure 3.3) are simultaneously presented to each retina. Vergence changes in pair-presentation to the network are managed by sliding the two input images sideways and farther apart for increasing vergence, or closer together for decreasing ver-

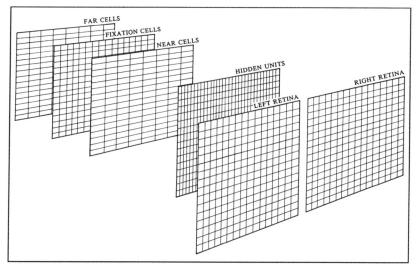

Figure 3.2: The principal cell populations of FUSION1.NET.

gence, before they are coded into the two retinas. The stereo pair in Figure 3.3 portrays a large square surface raised above a flat background, with a second and smaller square surface raised again above the first. See also Figure 3.4.

The job of the output layer is to code, at each appropriate pixel, the occurrence of either a correspondence or a disparity between the activation levels of the corresponding left and right pixels on the two retinas. Unitary physical objects at the fixation distance should therefore

Figure 3.3: A random-dot stereo pair in which three distinct surfaces are camouflaged. Vergence = 2.0°.

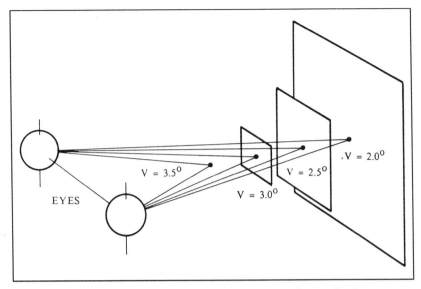

Figure 3.4: Three planes located at three distinct vergences or fixation depths.

be coded at the output layer with an appropriately shaped area of uniformly black pixels. Areas of merely random – that is, of accidental – correspondences should appear as a salt-and-pepper mixture of white (for disparity) and black (for correspondence) pixels. Constructing a net equal to this task required two things: finding the right pattern of connectivity, and finding the right configuration of "synaptic" weights. The task was first addressed with very small networks in order to reduce the time of construction and training. Training proceeded by presenting vector pairs, of various correspondences and disparities, at the input layer. Back propagation of the performance error apprehended at the output layer was used to modify the many connection weights.

The earliest prototypes had each processing unit fully connected to all of the units in every successive layer. But training fairly quickly confirmed that only the *topographic* projections between layers were functional relative to the task at hand. The weights of non-topographic connections tended to fall to zero in the course of training: those connections were slowly "pruned out" by the learning algorithm.

This sanctioned the construction of a more streamlined net, all of whose layer-to-layer projections were topographic to begin with (see Figure 3.5). It remained only to configure the remaining weights to yield the desired correspondence/disparity codings at the output layer. In contrast to their more profligate predecessors, topographically organized networks learn a successful weight configuration

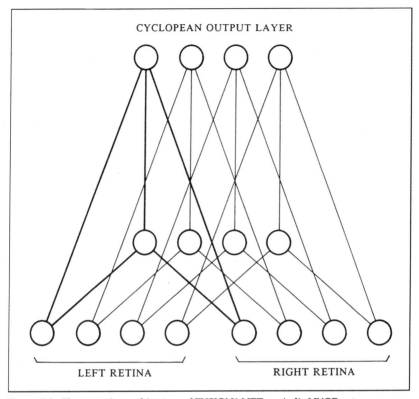

CYCLOPEAN OUTPUT LAYER

LEFT RETINA   RIGHT RETINA

Figure 3.5: The repeating architecture of FUSION1.NET: periodic NXOR nets.

almost immediately: typically in less than 2,000 presentations. More-over, the speed with which the correct weights are learned is indepen-dent of the size of the network: a large network learns exactly as swiftly as a small one.

None of this is surprising if one looks closely at the architecture of the successful network (Figure 3.5 portrays the relevant pattern in miniature). Taken globally, the all-topographic connections constitute a repeating series of mutually independent, negative-exclusive 'or' (NXOR) subnets. (A single NXOR – or IFF – subnet is highlighted at the left end of Figure 3.5.) Each tiny subnet realizes the inverse or neg-ative "exclusive 'or'" (XOR) function: it gives a minimal output acti-vation if its two inputs are disparate, and a maximal output activation if its two inputs are identical. An NXOR net is thus the simplest pos-sible correspondence/disparity detector. Its characteristic connection weights are typically learned in less than 2,000 presentations of the rel-evant input-output examples. And if trained simultaneously on input vectors of 7,200 elements (3,600 for each retina), then the 3,600 NXOR

68   Paul M. Churchland

subnets that make up FUSION1 train up just as swiftly as one: they are all learning simultaneously and independently.

The story to this point ignores the two low-resolution layers flanking the central high-resolution output layer of tuned "fixation" cells portrayed in Figure 3.2. We shall return to those additional layers after the following section.

3. Basic Network Performance

Thus trained, the network quickly reaches 100 percent accuracy in its output coding of left/right retinal correspondences and disparities. Confronted with the random-dot stereogram of Figure 3.3, presented initially at a vergence of 2.0°, the resulting pattern of activation levels at the output layer of tuned "fixation" units is as portrayed in Figure 3.6b. A background surface of uniform depth is correctly detected. A central region of 30 × 30 pixels is coded as noise, indicating only random correspondences discovered at that fixation depth.

The noise level, of course, is 50 percent, since that is probability of accidental correspondences across black/white (B/W) random-dot stereo pairs. This may be thought to be high, but remember that it occurs at the single-pixel level. The probability of accidental correspondences across areas larger than a single pixel shrinks exponentially with area. A noise level of 50 percent may therefore be tolerable, especially in a visual system whose pixels are small relative to the objects typically perceived. But we shall see in section VI how a feedforward system can reduce that noise level dramatically.

If the network's vergence is now increased to 2.5° (i.e., turned inward by one pixel, as portrayed in Figure 3.4), the background

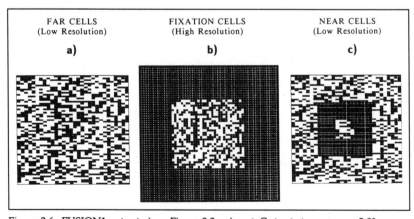

| FAR CELLS (Low Resolution) | FIXATION CELLS (High Resolution) | NEAR CELLS (Low Resolution) |
| a) | b) | c) |

Figure 3.6: FUSION1 output given Figure 3.3 as input. Output at vergence = 2.0°.

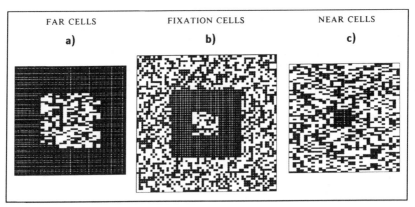

Figure 3.7: FUSION1 output given Figure 3.3 as input. Output at vergence = 2.5°.

region no longer presents a systematic correspondence to each retina, and is coded at the output layer as noise (see Figure 3.7b). It is now the central 30 × 30 that presents systematic correspondences to the network, and it now gets recognized in the output layer as a large square region of uniformly black pixels. It too, however, shows a central 10 × 10 region of noise, indicating only random correspondences at that fixation depth.

A further increase of vergence to 3.0° (i.e., to a fixation point one notch closer still) finds uniform correspondences within that central 10 × 10 square. This is recognized in the output layer as a 10 × 10 square of uniformly black pixels. At this vergence, all of the surround is now coded as noise (see Figure 3.8b).

What the network has done is successively to verge or fixate at three different depths, there to discover the shape, angular size and location

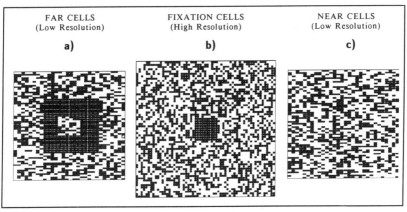

Figure 3.8: FUSION1 output given Figure 3.3 as input. Output at vergence = 3.0°.

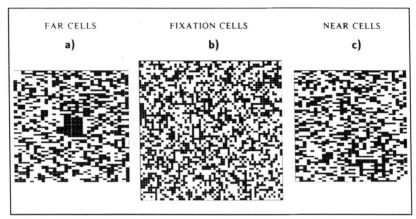

Figure 3.9: FUSION1 output given Figure 3.3 as input. Output at vergence = 3.5°.

of the camouflaged object at each depth (see Figure 3.4). The recovery of that information occurs very swiftly. As simulated in a very modest serial machine (an 8MHz 80286 AT clone), the network completes the global computation in 31 seconds. More importantly, a non-fictive network with biological transmission times (~15 msec. per layer) would complete the relevant computation in only 30 msec. This leaves ample time for several distinct planar fusions within a single second, a requirement on realistic models noted earlier.

But something important is still missing. As described to this point, the network has no *simultaneous* representation of objects and their relative positions throughout a *range* of different depths. One might even hold this capability to be definitive of true or full stereopsis. The deficit is repaired in the next section. Before we address it, however, note the following point. Stereopsis, it is often said, is what breaks camouflage. The preceding network, we have just agreed, still lacks true stereopsis. And yet it breaks the camouflage of random-dot stereograms easily. It is evident that what defeats camouflage, first and foremost, is *depth-selective fusion*. Full stereopsis, as strongly defined above, is not necessary, and it may be a somewhat later evolutionary and/or developmental achievement. (For more on this, see Pettigrew 1990).

4. The Full-Stereo Network: Near and Far Cells

If we take a single row of pixels from the middle of both the left and right retinal images of Figure 3.3 and then superimpose the one over the other, as in Figure 3.10, we can see at a glance the activational correspondences and disparities to which the output layer of "fixation" units has been trained to respond. As far as the fixation units are concerned, the relevantly corresponding left and right retinal units are those lying on the vertical lines. You will notice that the 15 pixels at each end of the row all show perfect activational correspondences, while the central 30 pixels show only random correspondences. It is precisely these relations that are portrayed in the central row of Figure 3.6b.

However, you will also notice, in the central region of Figure 3.10, a *second* set of systematic correspondences between the left-cell and right-cell activation levels, this time along the diagonal lines. At this vergence (2.0°), those diagonal correspondences are not detected by the output layer, although a vergence increase of .5° would shift the entire upper pattern one pixel to the left and thus bring those displaced match-ups into detectable position, as represented in Figure 3.7b.

But we want a system that will find those secondary correspondences *without* the necessity of a vergence change. A simple addition to the network will provide it. Consider a net whose output cells include a subpopulation – say, 25 percent – whose connections are identical to those of the fixation cells, save that the "corresponding" left and right retinal cells are exactly one pixel *closer together*. That subpopulation – call them "near cells" – would detect the secondary correspondences at issue while the main population of fixation cells was busy detecting the primary correspondences. Let this larger net have also a second subpopulation of output cells – again, 25 percent of the total – whose connections embrace left and right retinal cells one pixel *farther apart* than those embraced by the central population of fixation cells. These units – call them "far cells" – will simultaneously detect

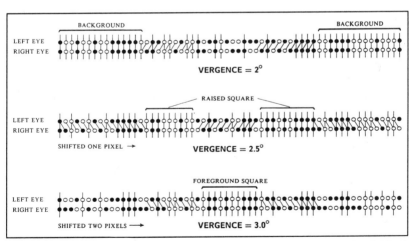

Figure 3.10: Horizontal row #30 of the stereo pair in Figure 3.3: the left and right horizontal pixels successively superimposed, showing the left and right correspondences at three different vergences.

correspondences that betray the presence of objects slightly *behind* the primary fusion layer.

Collectively, these three populations of output cells will simultaneously detect the angular size, shape and position of objects at three successive depths. The fixation cells provide a high-resolution image of correspondences at precisely the current fixation depth, and the near and far cells provide a lower-resolution image of further correspondences respectively just in front of and just behind that preferred plane. This is the architecture of the net portrayed in Figure 3.2, and its performance finally meets the definition of full stereopsis expressed in the previous section. Let us examine its performance on the problem addressed earlier.

Consider again the stereogram of Figure 3.3 and its presentation to the net at a vergence of 2.0°. This vergence fixates the background surround, as is reflected in the output pattern of Figure 3.6b. The near cells, however, clearly detect the central 30 × 30 square (although with central noise), as shown in Figure 3.6c. The far cells detect nothing at that vergence (see Figure 3.6a), since there is nothing unitary to detect beyond the 60 × 60 background. The near-cell image is of lower resolution than that of the tuned cells, since it has only half as many cells. But it is easily sufficient to convey roughly what the fixation-cell layer can expect to find if the vergence is increased by one pixel.

When the same stereogram is presented to the net at a vergence of 2.5°, the fixation cells do indeed detect (Figure 3.7b) the raised square earlier promised by the near cells. The near cells now detect a unitary 10 × 10 pixel object that is closer still (Figure 3.7c), while the far cells pick up the background surround (Figure 3.7a)

If we now increase the vergence to 3.0°, the far cells detect the 30 × 30 raised square (Figure 3.8a), the fixation cells detect the 10 × 10 raised square (Figure 3.8b), and the near cells detect nothing at all (Figure 3.8c), since there are no unitary objects in front of the second raised square.

A final increase of vergence to 3.5° leaves both the near and the fixation cells detecting nothing (Figures 3.9c and b), with only the far cells beckoning the entire system back toward smaller vergences with the promise of a small 10 × 10 reward (Figure 3.9a). This metaphor illustrates an important functional possibility for the near and far cells. They can serve to indicate when and how one's vergence is *close* to finding a systematic and hence interesting set of correspondences. They can serve to tell the high resolution fixation cells when they are getting "warm" in their never-ending vergence-determined hunt for unitary objects. In a noisy environment and without such help, hunting for the right vergence would be like looking for a needle in a haystack.

Plainly, it is both possible and desirable to add further layers of near and far cells, tuned to disparities even greater than +1 and -1 pixel, to give an approximation to the curve of Figure 3.1a that is closer than that of Figure 3.1b. This may well happen naturally in the course of neural development. The developing topographic projections from left and right will form retinotopically corresponding connections in area 17, but there will be residual imperfections. Some of the connections will be out of perfect register by a pixel or two or more to either side of fixation. These residual "mistakes" can end up functioning quite usefully as the near and far cells. These provide a pilot for the guided relocation of one's vergence, and the beginnings of true depth perception.

Adding near cells and far cells to the basic network entails no penalty whatever in computational time. The larger (non-fictive) network will deliver its more informative output vector just as swiftly as did the smaller. Nor is there a penalty in training time, since the additional connections simply constitute yet more NXOR nets, to be trained simultaneously with all of the others. Both performance time and training time are completely independent of the size of the network.

In closing this section, I should mention that, despite the three output layers portrayed in Figure 3.2, there is no suggestion that these cell populations are physically segregated in real cortex. They are segregated in the model only for our convenience in determining what their collective output is. Finally, note well that the near and far cells are "near" and "far" not absolutely, but only relative to the current location of the plane of current fusion as determined by the creature's current vergence. That preferred plane belongs always to the fixation cells, but it moves. In fact, all three layers detect objects at continuously various distances, depending on where current vergence happens to be. They are not entirely fixed even relative to one another, since the external distances they respectively fuse differ only slightly at close fixations, but differ substantially at more distant fixations. This may be the basis of a familiar illusion, to be discussed below.

5. Some Stereo Ambiguities and Illusions

False or ambiguous fusions show up in many forms, but a prototypical instance of the phenomenon is the "wallpaper illusion." An identically repeating pattern of narrow vertical picture elements offers the visual system multiple opportunities for systematic fusion: any vergence that fixates each eye on some vertical element will find systematic fusion, whether or not the foveated elements are strictly identical for each eye. If the repetition is qualitatively perfect, if the spatial frequency is high,

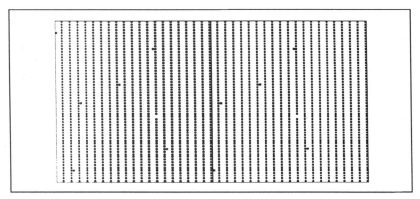

Figure 3.11: A stereo pair with ambiguous fusion: the "wallpaper" illusion. Note the residual noise.

and if the scene comprehends the entire field of view, one can even lose track of the true distance of the apprehended surface. One becomes lost, as it were, in a maze of alternative possible fusions. How does the network perform on such ambiguous stimuli? Much as humans do. Starting at V = 0, the stereogram of Figure 3.11 was presented to the net at seven successive vergences. The correspondences and disparities discovered at three critical vergences are depicted in Figure 3.12. The net found near-universal correspondences at vergences of 0°, 1.5° and 3.0°. It found only incomplete and variously periodic correspondences at all others. Each of these preferred vergences therefore indicates a plausible objective surface at the relevant distance. For those same vergences, the stereogram of Figure 3.11 will produce the same three fusions in your own case.

Ambiguous scenes like this are relatively rare in real life, but even when we do encounter them we are rarely much fooled. Humans have

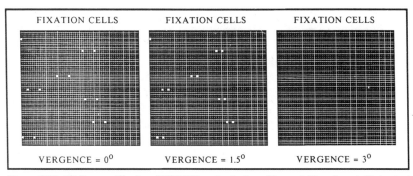

FIXATION CELLS	FIXATION CELLS	FIXATION CELLS
VERGENCE = 0°	VERGENCE = 1.5°	VERGENCE = 3°

Figure 3.12: Wallpaper illusion: FUSION1 output given Figure 3.11 as input. Output at three critical vergences that produce local fusional maxima. Note the perfect or total fusion at Vergence = 3.0°.

access to a variety of independent and non-binocular visual cues for distance, and it takes a carefully contrived situation to circumvent them all. Even then there usually remains a residual binocular cue that serves to disambiguate the correct fusion from the illusory ones. Repeating wallpaper is rarely perfect. The printing of each stripe displays occasional imperfections, the paper itself has a fibrous texture that is noisy (i.e., non-repeating), and there may be scattered flecks of dust or paint on its surface. This entails that one of the many possible fusions will be unique in having its disparities fall absolutely to zero, in contrast to the several false fusions which must inevitably fail to fuse those residual non-repeaters.

The pair of Figure 3.11 deliberately contains seven such imperfections. And you will notice in Figure 3.12 that the fusions found at V = 0° and V = 1.5° are both incomplete: they reveal the scattered splotches as doubled-up fusional anomalies. This is also how they appear to humans when the same stereo pair is fixated at the appropriate vergences. Only at V = 3.0° do those imperfections finally get fused along with everything else, which firmly distinguishes the correct fusion and the real surface from all of the illusory ones, in the net as well as in your own case.

Consider a further illusion. If you are able to free-fuse stereo pairs both in direct and in crossed-eye mode, then you know that the 3-D structure discovered by the visual system is completely inverted from one to the other. A foreground surface in one mode becomes a background depression in the other. With the net, if we reverse the left and right images and re-present them at an appropriately higher vergence, the net also finds an inverted 3-D structure. Additionally, the absolute size of the squares, and the absolute distances between them, are judged much *smaller* by the network in the crossed mode than they are in the uncrossed mode, just as they are by the human visual system.

This reflects the ever-present role of vergence in judgments of absolute size and distance. This size illusion shows up in the wallpaper illusion as well: the fused stripes are judged to be larger when presented at smaller vergences, both by humans and by the net. In the model, these "size" determinations are made by a network auxiliary to the main one, a net whose sole input is the vergence of current pair-presentation, and whose six outputs are the absolute distances of each of the three external planes grasped by the three output layers, and the absolute width of an object one pixel across at each of those three distances. There is no expectation that this auxiliary net has a structure corresponding to anything real in humans, but it does illustrate that the relevant computations can quickly and easily be performed by a feedforward system.

6. Grey-Scale Inputs

It is time to address a serious failing of FUSION1. Specifically, it processes only bimodal inputs: each input pixel is either fully white or fully black. In its universe there are no intervening shades of grey to provide a stiffer test for a detector of correspondences and disparities. This problem is an artifact of the experimental situation initially addressed, namely, the classic black and white random-dot stereograms of Julesz (1971). On inputs like these the net performs well, but its particular architecture will not support a correspondence detector that works over a continuous range of input brightnesses, as real images will display. Since stereoptic mammals excel at detecting grey-scale correspondences and disparities, FUSION1.NET cannot be physiologically correct.

It is detailed in the preceding pages because it was indeed the first net learned in response to the training examples, because it does illustrate how the correspondence problem can be solved locally with a movable fusion plane, because it is fast, and because it illustrates the strong empirical predictions to be expected from such models. And because from here it is only a small step to a much better one.

There is a further form of NXOR network, one whose gross organization is similar to the one employed above and whose iteration by a factor of 3,600 will produce another large network – FUSION2.NET – with all of the powers observed in FUSION1.NET, plus two more. First, FUSION2 will detect grey-scale correspondences across the entire range of brightnesses, and code them as such at the output layer. And second, it shows a much lower noise level in the unfused surround. Since we are now dealing with many different levels of brightness across the seen image, the frequency of accidental correspondences beyond the fused object will be much lower than the robust 50 percent displayed in the binary B/W stereograms.

The elemental net in Figure 3.13b – a "grey-scale" (NXOR) net – is a modification of a Perceptron-style XOR net. It functions by means of a mutual inhibition of the left and right pathways. Figure 3.14b shows its activation profile, in contrast to the profile (Figure 3.14a) for the basic NXOR units of FUSION1 (Figure 3.13a). Notice that it responds robustly and equally to left-right correspondences at all grey-scale levels.

FUSION2 contains twice as many hidden units as FUSION1, but it requires a similar deployment of topographic projections and it has a more uniform pattern of connection weights. Indeed, they are so utterly uniform that they suggest the possibility of an endogenous rather than a learned configuration. Further, it matters none to the network's behaviour what the value of the weights at the hidden units

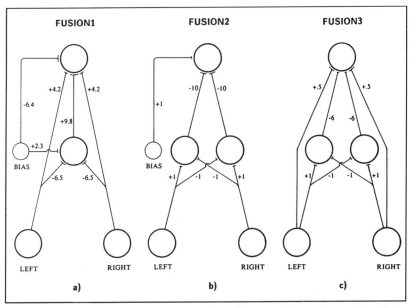

Figure 3.13: Three types of elemental subnets (correspondence detectors): (a) for FUSION1; (b) for FUSION2; (c) for FUSION3.

happens to be, so long as that value is uniform across the hidden-unit population: their only job is to provide an equal level of mutual inhibition. The weights onto the output units are non-critical as well, so long as they also are uniform, and fairly large. Variation here controls only how fussily close in grey-scale value a left-eye and right-eye pixel must be in order that the network count them as "the same."

The behavioural profile of FUSION2 includes all the features of FUSION1, so the problem-solving examples already discussed are

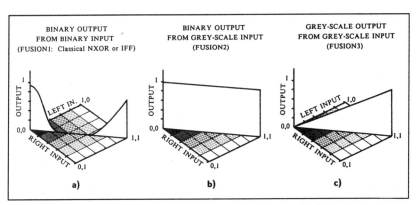

Figure 3.14: Input/output profiles of the three types of elemental subnet.

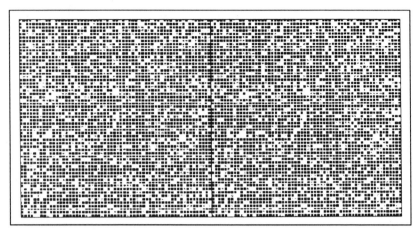

Figure 3.15: A gray-scale random-dot stereo pair hiding the same three planes portrayed in Figure 3.3. The pixels display ten different levels of brightness. (Fully faithful reproduction here is difficult.)

equally illustrative of the powers of FUSION2. The next figure illustrates its principal advantage over FUSION1. If FUSION2 is presented with the ten-level, grey-scale, random-dot stereogram of Figure 3.15, then its near, fixation and far cells yield the outputs portrayed in Figure 3.16. Note in particular the substantially reduced noise in the unfused areas. With ten grey-scale levels now in action, false correspondences at the single-pixel level have fallen to 10 percent. Fifty grey-scale levels would reduce it to 2 percent. And real objects with less random grey-scale distributions across their surfaces would reliably push it near zero.

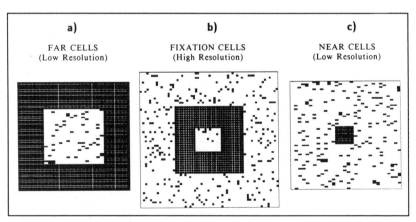

Figure 3.16: FUSION2 output given Figure 3.15 as input. Vergence = 2.5°. The gray-scale sensitive FUSION2 successfully identifies the three planes. Note the low noise level in the unfused areas, compared to FUSION1's noisy output in Figure 3.7.

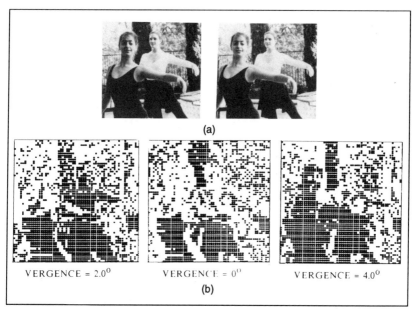

(a)

VERGENCE = 2.0⁰   VERGENCE = 0⁰   VERGENCE = 4.0⁰

(b)

Figure 3.17: Processing real images. (a) A complex gray-scale scene with rich 3-D structure. (b) FUSION2 output at three vergences, fixating the fore-ground dancer, the background dancer and infinity respectively.

It is evident, therefore, that a binocular system with grey-scale inputs
and a vergence-controlled plane of selective fusion confronts a much
smaller ambiguity problem than is confronted, for example, by the classic Marr/Poggio model. In contrast to that model, FUSION2 makes no
attempt to reconstruct the 3-D structure of the entire visual world, and
FUSION2 has the statistics of grey-scales working for it rather than
against it. A creature with such a system might navigate the real visual
world quite successfully. Figure 3.17a shows a photographic stereo pair
of a real-world scene and Figure 3.17b shows the result of feeding it into
FUSION2 with a 60 × 60 coding at 10 grey-scale levels. The net is clearly
handicapped by its low resolution and coarse grey-scale. (In particular,
it is reporting some false correspondences of the dancers' uniformly
bright or dark outfits. Coding at 20 grey-scale levels would reduce this.)
But the network is performing appropriately.

You will notice that the dancers are still identified at the output layers
as areas of uniformly activated (black) pixels, and one might wonder
if it is really necessary for the network thus to *lose* the retinal information concerning the original brightness levels of the detected grey-scale
correspondences. Wouldn't it be better, and isn't it possible, to have a
network that gives as outputs the original grey-scale values found to
be in left/right correspondence, while somehow suppressing all of the

surrounding disparities as uniform black? That would allow each dancer, when fused, to be portrayed at the fixation layer, in salient isolation, in the same full grey-scale glory she shows in the input pair. And her companion would appear similarly in the near- or far-cell layers. It is indeed possible, and a minor change in our Perceptron NXOR will bring it about. Delete the bias unit and add a projection from each of the two input units to the output unit, with a weight of +.5, as in Figure 3.13c. That does it (see Figure 3.14c). Let this third elemental net be iterated some 7,200 times in the same fashion as the earlier nets to yield FUSION3.NET. On the face of it, this arrangement is hard to resist. After all, fused objects do not *look* uniformly black when we view them. We see them in full grey-scale detail.

Despite appearances, this network is not what we want, and the reasons tell us something very important about human stereopsis. With FUSION3, we are now asking one net to do two jobs: detect depth *and* portray the brightness levels in detailed scenes. FUSION3 answers the call, but at a perilous price. If the input to either eye is occluded, the entire system is rendered totally blind. Such a system has no monocular vision at all. An isolated eye will not drive the output layer to represent anything. No matter what its monocular input might be, the output layers will remain uniformly inactive. The disparities, which of course dominate during a monocular shut-down, all produce inaction at the output units, and the few accidental correspondences between the active and inactive retinas will all be at a brightness value of zero, which also produces inaction at the output. Even if only part of one retina's field of view is occluded, the corresponding area of the output layer is rendered blind.

All of this contrasts starkly with human vision, where it is not remotely true that simply putting your hand over one eye shuts down the entire visual system. Neither is it true that scene elements beyond the fusion plane are ruthlessly suppressed. They are diffuse, perhaps, because they are in degraded register, but they do not mostly *disappear* (view again Figure 3.3). The cells responsible for scene portrayal in area 17 do not behave at all as in FUSION3.

On the other hand, while *scene portrayal* does not disappear under monocular occlusion, the human sense of stereoptic depth does disappear entirely in that condition. And any partial monocular occlusion also produces a complete loss of stereoptic discrimination within that occluded area. The perils that do not threaten our vision in general are precisely characteristic of our stereopsis in particular.

This means that scene portrayal and depth coding are two distinct tasks, tasks presumably performed by distinct subpopulations of the cells in area 17. Depth is obviously not coded in the form of a brightness value or a special colour. The suggestion here is that depth has its own coding: in proprietary cells distributed among the more basic two-dimensional "scene" cells that do code brightness values and colours. Those scene cells are mostly binocular, in that they are driven by either or both eyes, but they are not specifically stereoptic in their function. That job is reserved for the specially tuned fixation, near and far cells, which have nothing to do with the brightness levels of scene portrayal proper. This returns us to the slightly simpler virtues, and the more realistic architecture, of FUSION2. (Both scene cells and stereo cells, note, may be driven by distinct terminal end branches of the very same projections arriving from 4Ca.) FUSION2, of course, is also monocularly blind (as is FUSION1), but this is not a defect in a dedicated *depth*-detector. It is inescapable.

Fused objects, certainly, do not look uniformly black, but this complaint misses the point of Figures 3.6 to 3.9 and 3.16. Fused objects do look uniformly *distant*, and that is what the black pixels in those figures indicate, viz., "object here at current fixation depth." For multiple objects at different depths, the various classes of tuned cells do their job with minimal noise levels, thanks to the now very low levels of false correspondence purchased with grey-scale sensitivity. In areas where disparities are zero, the fixation cells and only the fixation cells are active: outside that area they are mostly quiescent, leaving the field clear for the differently tuned near and far cells to "speak" of different depths. In areas where the disparities are +1, all and only the near cells are active: outside that area they are mostly quiescent. And in areas where the disparities are -1, all and only the far cells are active: outside that area they are mostly quiescent. More extreme disparities elsewhere can be picked up by "even-nearer" and "even-farther" cells, should the network be so provided.

The overall result is a two-dimensional cortical representation of a scene's grey-scale structure – by the *scene* cells – that is simultaneously and unambiguously coded for appropriate depths in various of its subareas – by the *stereo* cells. Figure 3.18 portrays how the stereogram of Figure 3.3 may be simultaneously coded by both the scene cells and by the various tuned cells in area 17 when vergence fixates on the first and larger of the two raised squares. That 30 × 30 central area will thus be unique in having zero binocular rivalry in the activation of all of the local scene cells. It will therefore be maximally coherent in its scene portrayal and it will show maximal activity in all of the tuned fixation cells within that area. At that vergence, the other areas will display one-half a degree's worth of binocular rivalry and representational confusion in their scene cells. But the small central square of that cortical representation will show maximum activity in the near cells that it contains, and the background surround will show systematic activity in the far cells. Objects in those two confused regions will be perceived clearly only if a vergence change relocates the fusion plane so as to reduce the local scene-cell disparities to zero.

AREA WITH NEAR CELLS ACTIVE

AREA WITH FIXATION CELLS ACTIVE

AREA WITH FAR CELLS ACTIVE

Figure 3.18: A schematic portrayal of the "Cyclopean" coding at area 17. Vergence = 2.5°. The "scene cells" portray 2-D scene structure (with no binocular rivalry in the fused areas but with increasing rivalry in the unfused areas) while the various "stereo cells" (near, fixation and far) code for the relative distances of the scene areas in which they are active.

7. Delta Grey-Scale Inputs

It is time to address a serious failing of FUSION2, at least as so far described. Should there happen to be even a small systematic difference in the brightness levels of the left and right stereo images, such as might occur with differential processing of a left/right photographic pair, or with sunglasses placed over one eye, or simply with a temporary difference in left/right pupil size, then a net like FUSION2 will find nothing but disparities. Stereo depth perception will entirely disappear. But in humans it disappears in none of these conditions. We are relatively insensitive to left/right brightness differences.

There is a further failing in the story. The mammalian retina is relatively poor at projecting detailed grey-scale information forward to the lateral geniculate nucleus (LGN). What the ganglion cells code in exquisite detail is not grey-scale values at various points across the retina, but rather *differences* in grey-scale values across adjacent points on the retina. This information does go forward. But absolute grey-scale values do not. A net faithful to the biology must therefore tell a better story about input coding.

Fortunately, repairing this latter defect repairs the former as well. We need a network whose input units code the difference in grey-scale levels between each pixel and its immediate neighbour. A 120 × 60 input vector of this character is quickly calculated from the grey-scale stereogram of Figure 3.15. But what network will process it appropriately? The answer is: FUSION2, as wired and as weighted originally. If the delta-grey-scale vector is fed into FUSION2, the result is exactly as depicted in Figure 3.16. It performs appropriately on all of the previous examples as well.

This should not be surprising. What interests FUSION2 is correspondences and disparities. But it does not care if they are correspondences in grey-scale levels or correspondences in differences-between-adjacent-grey-scale levels. It tots them all up just the same. And to the same effect. This is because the transform from a grey-scale (GS) vector to a delta-GS vector preserves all the structural information in the former, except the absolute values of the pixels. This means that FUSION2 can still recover all of the 3-D information it did before, but with an acquired immunity to the earlier problem of Left/Right differences in brightness levels. This is because the delta-GS vector remains the *same* across fairly large differences in brightness levels. FUSION2 is thus an appropriate net for the job, but we must assume that its inputs correspond not to the activation levels of our rods and cones, but rather to the activation levels of the retinal ganglion cells to which those more peripheral cells project. This is anatomically more realistic in any case.

Finally, notice that a net whose inputs are delta-GS values must suddenly fail to find stereo information, even in a scene containing clear colour contrasts, if the images presented to it are isoluminant across their entire surfaces. FUSION2 fails utterly in this condition. So does human stereopsis. As Gregory (1977) has shown, when the picture elements within a stereo pair are distinguished only by different colours at isoluminance, human stereo discrimination vanishes.

8. Anatomical and Physiological Predictions

All units above FUSION2's input layer are binocular cells. Since the first binocular cells in mammalian cortex appear in area 17 just beyond layer 4Ca, the model requires that there be topographic projections (perhaps multisynaptic) from both retinas to some retinotopic subset of the binocular cells in area 17. These must correspond to the "hidden" units of the model. The model further requires that those cells project topographically to a second retinotopic population of binocular cells corresponding to the various "tuned" cells: the fixation, near and far cells. These cells are likely in a distinct layer of area 17, in which case the projection requirement could be met by short interlayer connections roughly normal to the cortical layers.

Since each input projects both an excitatory and an inhibitory connection to the hidden layer, a realistic model will require an inhibitory interneuron to intervene in the crossing projections of Figure 3.13b. (The terminal end-branches of a single axon rarely have different polarities.) Further, according to FUSION2 the hidden units must be intrinsically quiescent cells. Strictly speaking, they are also binocular cells, since their activity is binocularly controlled. But notice that they will show an increase in activation only upon stimulation of a single eye, since the effect of any stimulation from the other eye is always to *inhibit* the cell. This opens the possibility that the cells in layer 4Ca of area 17 are in fact the binocular hidden units of an architecture like FUSION2, despite their common reputation as monocular cells. The clear test is whether a monocularly activated cell in 4Ca can have its activation reduced by stimulating the corresponding field in the other eye. (If not, we must look beyond 4Ca for the relevant cells.) Pettigrew (1979, 1990) reports precisely this result:

A little studied but important feature of stereoscopic visual systems is the presence at the earliest stages of processing of an inhibitory field in the otherwise unresponsive eye opposite to the eye μwhich provides the monocular excitation. Thus, at the level of the lateral geniculate nucleus (LGN) or lamina IV of striate cortex, a concentrically-organized excitatory field in the "dominant" eye has a corresponding, horizontally-elongated inhibitory field in the other eye. (1990, 285)

If the 4Ca cells do behave in the fashion required by FUSION2, then we must expect the various tuned cells in other layers of area 17 to correspond to the output units of the model. Here the model requires that the output cells be intrinsically active, that they receive converging topographic projections from layer 4Ca, and that these be short, strongly inhibitory connections somewhat diagonal to the layers.

9. Concluding Remarks

I close by addressing two points. The first concerns a final virtue of the network described. And the second concerns its residual failings.

Consider a particularly striking feature of human stereopsis: the ability to fuse scenes clearly through quasi-transparent surfaces such as a dusty car windshield, a screen door, or a chain-link fence. Here the scene elements at different depths do not cluster together to form discretely localized objects. Rather, they are interleaved or superimposed more or less uniformly throughout the entire scene. Such cases pose special difficulties for co-operative-competitive algorithms such as that of the classical Marr/Poggio model, since there are no large clusters of adjacent co-depth elements selectively to "find" each other. Instead, competition is spread evenly and everywhere.

The feedforward network of FUSION2, however, has no difficulty at all with such scenes. Since each correspondence-detecting "NXOR" subnet operates independently of every other, the overall net is quite

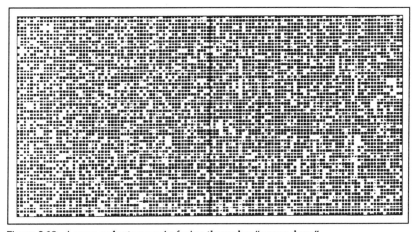

Figure 3.19: A gray-scale stereo pair: fusion through a "screen door."

insensitive either to the grain or to the scattered distribution of such correspondences as the scene may contain. At the proper vergence, FUSION2 will pick them up just the same as if they were clustered tightly together, and it will do so successfully even when the scene elements are noisy at both the near (transparent) and the distant planes. To see this, find the noisy foreground "screen" in the stereo pair of Figure 3.19, and then compare the performance of the network as displayed in Figure 3.20.

It must be mentioned that Ning and Sejnowski (1988) did find a nonstandard weighting for the original Marr/Poggio algorithm that would successfully handle sparse-element "transparent surface" stereograms. This was achieved by substantially reducing the weights that embodied all of the super-correlational conditions such as uniqueness and continuity. This weight reduction is equivalent to moving the network substantially in the direction of a purely feedforward configuration. And this capability was purchased at the expense of some loss of its original performance on dense-element pairs.

Finally, what is FUSION2 completely *unable* to do? It remains entirely unable to resolve the ambiguities that result from false or accidental correspondences. A central claim of this paper is that in real animals the noise level of such ambiguities is typically much lower than is supposed, but certainly they will happen and FUSION2 is helpless in the face of them. For example, despite all its grey-scale sophistication, FUSION2 still performs unimpressively when fed the original binary B/W random-dot stereograms: the "unfused" areas still show 50 percent noise, just as in FUSION1. Figure 3.3 is indeed a highly unusual

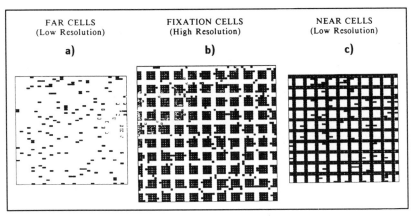

Figure 3.20: FUSION2 output given Figure 3.19 as input. Vergence was fixated on the plane behind the foreground grid.

visual input, but it remains problematic because the net's output layer is coding 50 percent of the outlying pixels as being at the same depth as the large raised square, whereas human observers typically do not see such a raised scatter of surrounding pixels when they fuse that square. It is therefore inescapable that human stereo vision involves mechanisms, perhaps recurrent mechanisms, beyond the simple mechanism of FUSION2. An obvious suggestion concerns the addition of inhibitory connections between the several populations of tuned cells. Such line-of-sight inhibition is a prominent feature of the original Marr/Poggio algorithm. This will certainly clean up the noise, but it runs the opposite risk of degrading or destroying genuine *signal* when the signal is small-grained and evenly distributed. A net thus strongly inhibited will do poorly on transparent surfaces like those portrayed in Figures 3.18 and 3.19. As well, such a net would doom us to seeing genuine ambiguities in only one way, whereas in fact we can usually alternate between competing perceptual "hypotheses," even where the ambiguities are stereoptic. Finally, mutual inhibition and recurrent settling among the various tuned cells is simply not necessary to achieve the desired end of reducing ambiguities, even in the tough case at issue. Let tuned-cell activity be fed forward to a yet higher layer of processing whose cells are collectively unimpressed by 50 percent fine-grained noise from the fixation cells, especially when in simultaneous receipt of uniform signal from the far cells in the same cortical area. This would be faster than iterative/recurrent disambiguation, and it need not lose useful information.

A modulatable set of inhibitory connections among the distinct tuned cells is also a possibility, but I shall pursue such speculations no further. It may be tactical mistake to take a model of stereopsis, any model of modest success, and keep asking what further mechanisms we have to add to it to make it do everything that the human visual system can do. Relative to the rest of the visual system, stereoptic circuitry is an evolutionary latecomer. It feeds into a visual system that has a great many preexisting capacities, many of which deal successfully with object recognition and with complex spatial information quite independently of stereo input. The occasional slack we observe in the performance of FUSION2 may be somehow taken up in the machinery of the pre-existing visual system, rather than in any specifically stereoptic additions to the peripheral correlational system portrayed in FUSION2. Such a peripheral system has its virtues, and its contribution to one's cognitive economy would be non-trivial. The anatomical and physiological predictions outlined in section 8 should allow us to determine whether or not they are real.

Acknowledgments

Thanks to V.S. Ramachandran for suggesting the wallpaper test; to Alexander Pouget and Terry Sejnowski for helpful comments concerning grey-scale processing; to Patricia Churchland for bringing the Pettigrew results to my attention; and to Richard Gregory for encouraging the project in the first place.

References

Churchland, P.M. (1989). *A Neurocomputational Perspective: The Nature of Mind and the Structure of Science* (Cambridge, MA: The MIT Press)

Churchland, P.S. and Sejnowski, T. (1992). *The Computational Brain* (Cambridge, MA: The MIT Press

Gregory, R.L. (1977). Vision with isoluminant colour contrast, *Perception* 6: 113-19

Hubel, D. (1988). *Eye, Brain, and Vision*. New York: W.H. Freeman

Julesz, B. (1971). *The Foundations of Cyclopean Perception*. Chicago: University of Chicago Press

Marr, D., and T. Poggio (1976). Co-operative computation of stereo disparity. *Science* 194

Ning, Q., and T.J. Sejnowski (1988). Learning to solve random-dot stereograms of dense and transparent surfaces with recurrent backpropagation In *Proceedings of the 1988 Connectionist Models Summer School*. Technical report. UCSD Institute for Neural Computation

Pettigrew, J.D. (1979). Binocular visual processing in the owl's telencephalon *Proceedings of the Royal Society of London* B204: 435-54

———. (1990). Is there a single, most-efficient algorithm for stereopsis? In C. Blakemore (ed.), *Vision: Coding and Efficiency*. Cambridge: Cambridge University Press

4

On the Failure to Detect Changes in Scenes across Saccades

John Grimes

Imagine yourself viewing a full-colour picture of a city park, a scene with trees, lawns, flowers, paths and roads. What if you were told that the image could be significantly altered – say, by moving a prominent tree or by removing a clearly visible parked car – *while you were actively studying the picture* and that you would not notice the change? Intuitively, this is hard to believe. Yet in our visual perception laboratory, this type of high technological sleight of hand is a daily occurrence: if the timing of the image manipulation is right, most people will miss seven out of ten such changes. Images can be manipulated such that conspicuous objects change their colour or brightness, increase or decrease in size, change identity or position, or sometimes even disappear entirely, all without the awareness of the subject studying the scene. Even when the viewer is told that such a change will occur, the alteration usually eludes the subject. How can large-scale alterations such as these be made to scenes without the viewer's awareness? What does the critical nature of the timing of the image manipulation reveal about the visual system? And what implications does this odd phenomenon have for theories of vision and visual perception?

Before an attempt to answer these questions can be made, it would be helpful to consider some of the subevents that occur when a person views a scene. There are several discrete levels of analysis that are useful to consider when a person views a picture, and factors at each of those levels have a direct influence on the person's overall perception. In the present case, I believe that the phenomenon occurs due to an interaction between different levels of the visual system. Specifically, I suspect that it is the combination of certain properties present at different levels of the visual system that interact in a way that opens a hole, as it were, in the perception of the visual world, and it is through this hole that image changes like those described above fall.

At perhaps the lowest functional level of analysis is the receptive surface within the eye, the retina itself. In particular, it is the organization of the receptor cells, termed *cones*, which has implications for scene perception. The cones are the visual receptor cells that are sensitive to colour and small visual details under normal lighting conditions. The other visual receptive cells, the *rods*, function only in low-illumination settings and are functionally colour-insensitive. It is with the cones that humans view normally illuminated pictures and scenes. In the human retina, the cones are arranged with a densely packed region in the centre of the retina surrounded by an increasingly sparse array of cones going out to the periphery. This central area, the *fovea*, is the region of highest spatial acuity of the retina, that is, it is the area most sensitive to fine or minute detail (Dowling, 1987). As the distance from the fovea increases, sensitivity to fine detail drops off rapidly. When you study the objects of a scene or read the words on this page, you are using the fovea to acquire the minute visual details.

The functional implication of a foveated retinal organization is that in order to study different areas of a visual scene via the high-acuity fovea, it is necessary to aim the fovea at each of the successive, individual areas. Humans move their eyes from one location to another using very rapid, point to point movements called *saccades*. In picture viewing, a typical saccade takes $1/200$ to $1/12$ of a second (5 to 80 msec) to occur. Upon termination of the saccade, the eye pauses for about 250 msec, and visual details are acquired from the picture during the *fixation*. Following the eye fixation, another saccade is launched, and the cycle repeats. One additional observation completes this second level of analysis. The human visual system is functionally blind during a saccade, although the cause or causes of this saccadic visual "suppression" is the topic of current debate. Retina-based explanations suggest that such blindness may rise from the rotational forces on the retina due to the speed of a saccade or that it may be caused by the velocity of visual details whipping across the retina during the eye movement. Either of these, as well as other unknown factors, may all play a role in saccadic suppression. For our purposes, however, the combination of a saccade followed by a fixation, with the accompanying brief period of suppressed vision during the saccade, can be considered the second functional level of analysis.

The sequence and locations of fixations comprise the next level of analysis. Although there is great variability among people in how they study a scene, an adult viewing a picture for the first time will generally alternate between two eye-movement patterns (Buswell, 1935). A long-distance saccade will launch the eye toward some object location, chosen from the low-resolution information available in peripheral vision, presumably to learn something about the object in that location. Upon arriving at the new location, a few fixations are generally made on and around the object, as individual features are sequentially targeted by the high-resolution fovea. A new, distant target is then selected and the eye makes another long, image-traversing saccade, and the process repeats. In this way, the important objects of a scene are quickly identified and studied in sequence (Noton and Stark, 1971).

The interaction between these two levels of analysis, the organization of cones on the retina and the resultant need to saccade to and sequentially fixate new locations, coupled with the functional blindness during these saccades, raises some questions about the next, higher level of analysis. Glossing over the biological complexities and visual processing issues of the many stages of the actual, physical visual nervous system, the next functional level of analysis could be considered the mental representation of the scene being studied. The final useful level of analysis is the conscious perceptual experience of the viewer. Note that the perceptual experience of a person viewing a scene is that of *a smooth, continuous scan across the image.* In most visual tasks, people are completely unaware of making discrete saccades and fixations. The experience is one of a "seamless comprehension" of the visual world. For example, I once overheard an experienced reading teacher instruct a child to let her eyes sweep across the line of text like a broom sweeps across the floor. In fact, it is nearly impossible to make what is called a "smooth pursuit eye movement" in the absence of a moving target (i. e. , when confronted with stationary text). When we read, it is not the "smooth" eye movements versus the "jerky" ones that separate an experienced reader from the beginner. On the contrary, in reading, adults will saccade to a single word, fixate it for ¼ of a second or so, saccade to another word, reverse directions to reread an earlier portion of the text, jump ahead again, and so on (McConkie, 1979). Despite all this discrete saccading and fixating about, however, the reader experiences the perception of a smooth, continuous scan across the line of text. Similarly, in picture viewing the phenomenological experience is of smoothly scanning the visual world, noting interesting objects and details instead of viewing a series of brief, disjointed snapshots of the visual world.

The discrepancy between the proximal stimulus, the image on the retina, and the mental representation is the crux of the interaction between the foveated retina and the functional blindness of the saccade. The discrete fixations are somewhat isolated snapshots of different parts of the visual world, separated by brief periods of non-vision. Given the divergent, discontinuous nature of the stimulation at the retina, why do we perceive such a stable, seamless visual experience? How do we go from these sporadic, individual samples of the visual world to the smooth, stable visual experience to which we are all accustomed? How is the information from the current fixation integrated with information from previous fixations into some type of global mental representation of the scene? Finally, why is it that obvious changes can be made to an image while a person studies it without his awareness as long as the change occurs during a saccade?

In the late 1970s, interest in questions such as these resulted in the development of a new research environment and experimental paradigm. The *eye movement-contingent display system*, developed by George McConkie and Keith Rayner, exploits the phenomenon of saccadic suppression as a tool for the investigation of various perceptual and cognitive aspects of reading (for details, see McConkie, Zola, Wolverton & Burns, 1978). The eye-tracking system developed by McConkie et al. links an "eye-tracker," a machine that monitors the position and movement of the eyes, to a computer controlling a text display. This allows the experimenters to change the text during saccades: as the eyes begin to move, their targeted destination is predicted, and the text in that location is changed before the eyes arrive. Therefore, the researchers could present different information to the reader on the current fixation than had been available during the prior one, without the reader being aware of the actual change itself. This experimental setting allows the study of the influence of various factors upon reading performance without directly disrupting the reading process.

One early study, for example, examined the fusion of letter details from the current fixation with letter details acquired on the previous fixation. In that study, McConkie and Zola (1979) were attempting to obtain evidence supporting a model of visual processing during reading that included an integrative buffer. This buffer was conceived of as a short-term memory store where the visual contents of the previous fixation were maintained until they could be fused with the contents of the current fixation, based upon an overlap of the visual details of the two fixations. McConkie and Zola hypothesized that if the visual details of the letters themselves were changed during a saccade, while the actual lexical and content structures of the text were preserved, then any disruption of the reading process could be attributed to a failure to fuse the visual letter details acquired from the two fixations. To that end, they had subjects read text in alternating case, as shown in lines 1 and 2:

1. ThE sPaCe ShUtTlE tHuNdErEd InTo ThE sKy On A cOlUmN oF sMoKe.
2. tHe SpAcE sHuTtLe ThUnDeReD iNtO tHe SkY oN a CoLuMn Of SmOkE.

While alternating case text is a bit unusual and difficult to read at first, one quickly becomes accustomed to it with practice. McConkie and

Zola had college students read this type of text from a computer screen while their eye movements were monitored. During *every* saccade, in some experimental conditions, the case of every letter was changed as the computer switched between the two lines of alternate text, as shown in the example. That is, the visual appearance of every letter and every word was dramatically different on each new fixation than on the previous fixation. McConkie and Zola hypothesized that the sudden presence of the altered text, with completely mismatched visual details, should have prevented or interfered with fusion in the integrative buffer, and would make reading much more difficult, if not impossible. Such disruption would have been accepted as evidence for the visual integrative buffer.

The first answer to their question about a visual integrative buffer model was obtained even before an actual subject had read the alternating case text. After serving as the first pilot subject for this investigation, Zola sat back from the eye tracking apparatus and announced that something must be wrong with the system because the text was not changing. Others in the room, whose eye movements were not coupled with the text changes, were astonished: *they* had clearly seen the case of the letters dancing up and down on the monitor as Zola read. Results from actual subjects later confirmed Zola's revelation. Not only did the experimental manipulation fail to produce any disruption of the reading process or of the eye-movement patterns, it failed to produce even the *awareness* that something unusual was going on. I recall one subject who became somewhat angry with me during the debriefing at the end of an experiment. Absolutely faithful to her perception of the world, she adamantly refused to believe that such a stunt could be pulled on her, preferring to believe instead that psychologists are tricky and that the debriefing was part of the experimental deception. Psychologists can be that tricky, of course, but there had been no deception in this case, just a perfectly normal human visual system with a puzzling property.

Needless to say, the observation that such obvious changes could be made to text without any indication of an effect on the subject's eye-movement parameters, reading comprehension, or perceptual experience was quite a surprise. (It was also compelling evidence against visual integrative buffer-based models of lexical processing during reading.)The basic paradigm has since been extended to demonstrate similar "failures" of perception in the course of studying other aspects of cognition and reading. In one series of studies, the text was shifted a few character positions to the left or right during a saccade so that the eye would land upon a different letter or word than the one intended. When such a shift occurred, the subjects would frequently make a small, corrective saccade of the same magnitude, but in the opposite direction of the original shift. They rarely indicated, however, any awareness that the text had been moved. In another experiment, one word replaced another during a saccade such that the meaning of the entire sentence was altered (e. g. , "The kids played on the *beach/bench* all afternoon"). In this experiment, the subjects tended to report one word or the other, but rarely indicated any awareness of the switch, the presence of two different words, or that the meaning of the sentence was ambiguous in any fashion. One final example, the classic "moving window" studies, involved a series of studies in which all of the letters outside a window surrounding the fixation point were replaced with Xs, as shown in lines 3 and 4:

3. XXX XXXXX XXXXXXX thundered inXX XXX XXX XX X XXXXXX XX XXXXX.
                              ^ fixation point
4. XXX XXXXX XXXXXXX XXXXXXXed into the sky XX X XXXXXX XX XXXXX.
                        ^ fixation point

When the subject made a saccade, the computer caused the window of unobscured text to move, too, so that unobscured text was always visible during the fixation. As long as the window of normal text extended approximately four letters to the left and seven or eight letters to the right of the fixation point, there was no effect on the subject's eye movements or upon subject awareness. Indeed, one long-standing lab anecdote has it that in an attempt to capitalize on the Cocktail Party effect, where one's name has an enhanced chance of catching one's attention, the words were replaced with the fellow's name (e.g., "TOM TOM TOM space shuttle TOM TOM TOM"). The results were the same. It was beginning to seem that people either had little or no access to, or made little use of, the actual peripheral visual information gleaned from prior fixations.

As the exploration of eye movements and cognition during reading continued using this paradigm, it became natural to wonder if this phenomenon would occur in a richer visual environment. In the reading studies, the changes all occurred to small green letters and words on a computer monitor. Would it also be possible to make such manipulations to full-colour, real-world scenes without the viewer's awareness? If so, what would be revealed about visual perception and what implications would this have for models of visual perception? What are the implications for humans in daily life?

To explore the issues raised by these questions, a new eye tracking system was established in Dr. George McConkie's lab at the University of Illinois to carry out similar investigations with full-colour, real world scenery (as opposed to line drawings). Interfacing a Fourward Technologies Generation V Dual Purkinje Image Eye Tracker with a Compaq 386-20 computer, an AT&T TrueVision Vista card and a Princeton Ultra-Sync Graphics monitor was no small task and would not have been possible without the ingenuity and perseverance of Gary S. Wolverton, our systems programmer. The system, as it stands today, samples eye position 1,000 times per second with positional accuracy of ¼° of visual angle (¼° is approximately the size one character position on our display screen). The high sampling rate allows the system to detect an eye movement while it is still in progress and switch between different full-colour, real-world images. To do this, the program that monitors and records eye position also controls the display card. Within 4 msec of the start of a saccade, the control program determines that a saccade is in progress and performs the image manipulation.

In our apparatus, the display card has two images stored in its memory, the original image and an altered version of the image. In most experiments, the altered version of the image is identical to the original except for one object or region. For example, in the altered version, an object can be different in size, colour or location (see Figures 4.1A through 4.2B). In other cases, objects, or parts of objects, may be deleted entirely. Similar to the way a television set replaces the image on the screen by rapidly drawing individual scan lines from top to bottom of the screen approximately 30 times each second, the display card in our system scans across the image in memory every ⅟₆₀th of a second (16 msec) and refreshes the image on the display screen with that information. When the control program indicates that a saccade is in progress and that a display change is due, the image scan is interrupted *at that instant* and the scan point is switched to the corresponding location in the second, altered image, and begins refreshing the screen with it instead. In this way, the image displayed on the screen can be completely switched between the two images within 16 msec of the detection of a saccade in progress. The switch happens so quickly and smoothly that a bystander simply viewing the monitor perceives the change as a single, instantaneous event.

Two things remained to be developed before the actual investigation could begin: a research paradigm that would put subjects in a situation where they would view these images normally, but still be prepared to respond should an image change be observed, and a high-quality set of scanned photographs with a set of edited alternates.

The aim of the research paradigm was to have the subject be receptive to detecting the image changes, without introducing artificial eye-movement behaviours or strategies due to the detection task itself. Without some sort of relatively normal task to perform, subjects tend to invent their own behavioural strategies, based on their perception

Figure 4.1A

as to the "real" point of an experiment. Many test subjects were run through variations of the general experimental task before an acceptable situation was devised. The paradigm we finally settled upon presents the subject with a series of computer-displayed images while his eye movements are monitored. The subject is told that the focus of the study is upon the eye movements that people make when they are studying pictures to commit them to memory. He is told that a series of 50 pictures will be presented, that his eye movements will be monitored while he studies each picture, and that after a short rest break, a recognition task will be administered. The subject is told to study the pictures carefully, as some of the distractors in the memory task are quite subtle. The subject is also told that "in a few of the pictures something will change. An object might become larger or smaller, change location or colour or something like that. "The subject is asked to press a button if he believes he sees anything of that nature happen. Before the actual study phase of the experiment, a practice block of trials is run to familiarize the subject with the eye tracker, the task and, in particular, to give experience detecting images with changes in them, as well as with the types of changes involved.

In a typical trial, the subject fixates a small target in the centre of the display screen and presses a button. The image appears and during an experimentally predetermined saccade the alternate image is written to the screen and stays there for the remaining duration of the 10-second study period. The subject presses the button if a change is noticed,

Figure 4.1B

and continues to study the image until it disappears. After a few seconds, the next trial begins, and so on. Two blocks of 25 trials each are presented, separated by a brief rest period. Following the conclusion of the second block, the subject answers several questions about his impression of the experiment. Finally, the subject is informed as to the nature and goal of the experiment, paid and sent home. (There is no memory test. That is merely a ruse used to make the subjects carefully study the images. Without this instruction, the subjects tend to stare fixedly at the screen, waiting for something to happen. Nothing happens when they do that, of course, as it is their saccades that trigger the display change in the first place. The threat of a memory test gives the subjects a task to perform and a goal to strive for, thereby lessening the chance that they will invent their own strategies to cause and detect the changes. This is important, in that, similar to the strategy necessary to detect the alternating letter cases mentioned earlier, these strategies are hardly natural, normal viewing patterns and tell us little about the perceptual processes that occur during normal viewing.)

The final element to be developed was the stimuli set. The stimuli for these studies consisted of a series of computer-scanned and edited magazine photographs. Once an image had been captured by a graphic scanner, the Macintosh program Adobe Photoshop (1991) provided a fantastic graphic editing environment where almost any conceivable alteration could be performed. It is relatively simple, for example, to take a scene of two men sitting on a bench, define their

Figure 4.2A. Luis Marden© National Geographic Society

heads as objects, and swap them. Photoshop also includes the tools to
seamlessly reintegrate the altered object back into the original scene,
so that any gaps or irregularities caused by such antics can be filled or
smoothed over. The results, as shown in Figures 4.1B and 4.2B, are
alternate versions of the original photographs without any telltale
signs of the manipulations themselves. In fact, when asked to choose
the original of such pairs, subjects were as likely to choose the alternative as the original.

Figure 4.2B. Luis Marden© National Geographic Society

In altering the various photographs, we initially contented our-selves with relatively small changes. A fork might disappear from a dinner scene, for example, or a book might change colour on the book-shelf in the background. Stimuli with such insignificant changes were then timidly tendered between many control images (images with no changes) to give the subject a sense of viewing a series of normal pic-tures, a few of which might have some image alteration. We wanted to avoid predisposing the subjects to expecting, and therefore, being overly sensitive to, image alterations. We wanted them to miss a few of the changes while detecting others so that we could estimate sensitivity ratios. We did not want the subjects to be able to report every change as it occurred, so we kept the changes subtle such that the detection task would not be too easy. We were concerned, as things turned out, about the wrong things.

The early subjects rarely, if ever, pushed the button to indicate the detection "that something in the image had changed." We checked the button. It worked. We ran the study in slow motion without a subject to be certain that the apparatus and the experimental control programs were working properly. They were. Then, we ran ourselves through the experiment and found, as Zola had found years before in the reading task, that even with full knowledge of what was going to change and when, it was still often difficult or impossible to detect anything unusual. Perhaps, we thought, the changes were too subtle. And so began a gradual exploration of just how bold an image manipulation would go undetected. After all, the strength of our visual experience is so powerful and seems so veridical that there must be some limit to what a person can overlook, even if the actual change does take place during the relative blindness of a saccade.

The images shown at the Vancouver conference, *Problems in Perception*, a subset of which is presented here as Figures 4.1A to 4.2B, represent some of our latest, and in certain cases, most outlandish, efforts. Our goal was to create a set of 40 images with object alterations that a bystander watching the experiment in progress could not possibly fail to observe. The following table (Table 4.1) is intended to give the flavour and magnitude of the image alterations presented to the subjects.

Image manipulations of this nature, it seemed, would surely always be detected by the subjects, saccadic suppression notwithstanding. After all, most people, if asked, would state a strong belief that they could detect manipulations such as these if they were made. Those same people would also predict that few could fail to notice such gross modifications occurring right before their eyes. Now, it seemed, we had an image set that people would take notice of. Now, we thought, we would see some detection of the changes.

Finally, all of the pieces were in place, and real subjects came in to participate in the experiment. They were given an introduction to the laboratory and our general line of research, and then familiarized with the eye-tracker and other apparatus. Following that, they were positioned in front of the eye-tracker; it was calibrated to the individual characteristics of their eyes; and the experiment began.

Ordinarily, sitting in a darkened room watching a subject press a button is fairly dull work. This experiment, in contrast, was a delight to conduct. Watching obvious image change after image change go undetected by the subjects makes one feel like the king of practical jokers. The subjects simply had little awareness of the image changes, and it was difficult to watch their oversights without considerable amusement. In one case, I had to send a subject's husband (too nearsighted to be a subject himself) from the room out of fear that his exclamations of amazement would clue his wife to the presence of the image manipulations. The subjects themselves revealed considerable surprise when, at the end of the experiment, they were informed that 80% of the images underwent some sort of alteration. Their typical estimates were that between 20% and 30% of the images contained some change. Complete surprise is perhaps a better way to express their reaction when informed of the actual number of display changes. In most of the

Image Manipulation Description
A prominent building in a city skyline becomes 25% larger.
Two men exchange hats. The hats are of different colours and styles.
In a crowd of 30 puffins, 33% of them are removed.
In a playground scene, a child is enlarged by 30% and brought forward in the depth of the picture by approximately 5 m.
In a marketplace, brightly coloured fruits switch places among their four respective baskets.
A celebrity, leaning upon an air conditioner, is rotated approximately 40 degrees to lean in the other direction.
Two cowboys sitting on a bench exchange heads.
A parrot, comprising roughly 25% of the picture space, changes from a brilliant green to an equally brilliant red.
The castle at Disneyland rotates around its vertical axis so that what was visible on the left is now present on the right, and vice versa.
The swimsuit of one of four people posing for a swimsuit advertisement changes from bright pink to bright green. The subjects begin viewing the picture while fixated on that person.

Table 4.1: A sample of the types of image changes presented to the subjects as they viewed the scenes.

cases, it seemed that the subjects truly did not perceive the stimulus changes (see Table 4.2 for the detection failure percentages). Overall, the subjects in this experiment detected 33% of the changes in the images. During post-experiment interviews, many of them volunteered information regarding the changes they detected, which fell into three general categories. The first class of reasons represents true detections that something had changed. In these cases, the subject

Image Manipulation Description	Percent Detection Failure
A prominent building in a city skyline becomes 25% larger.	100
Two men exchange hats. The hats are of different colours and styles.	100
In a crowd of 30 puffins, 33% of them are removed.	92
In a playground scene, a child is enlarged by 30% and brought forward in the depth of the picture by approximately 5 m.	83
In a marketplace, brightly coloured fruits switch places among their four respective baskets.	75
A celebrity, leaning upon an air conditioner, is rotated approximately 40 degrees to lean the other direction.	67
Two cowboys sitting on a bench exchange heads.	50
A parrot, comprising roughly 25% of the picture space, changes from a brilliant green to an equally brilliant red.	18
The castle at Disneyland rotates around its vertical axis so that what was visible on the left is now present on the right, and vice versa.	25
The swimsuit of one of four people posing for a swimsuit advertisement changes from bright pink to bright green. The subjects begin viewing the picture while fixated on that person.	58

Table 4.2: The percentage of subjects who missed each of the image changes presented in Table 4.1.

viewed the image, stored some information regarding it, and when conflicting information arrived on a later fixation, detected the difference and reported it. This was particularly true of image manipulations that involved changes of identity, for example, "The first time I looked at it, it was a cat, but when I came back, it was a dog." Another frequently mentioned observation was that "something jumped or flickered when I was looking at the picture, so I decided to press the button." This second category is also, unfortunately, easy to explain. In our eye-tracker display system, it takes 4 msec to detect a saccade with certainty and 16 msec from that point in time until the new, alternate image has been completely written to the screen. If the image change happens to occur during a very short saccade, such as the kind one makes when studying small details of the picture that are located close together, the eye can already be settled into the new fixation before the completion of the image manipulation. In these cases, the image change occurs during the fixation instead of during the saccade: the subject actually sees the change occur. Careful examination of the data has revealed that as many as half the detections reported may fall into this category. Failing any impartial, objective method to remove these detections from consideration, they have been included as legitimate detections in this type of experiment using this experimental apparatus. As will be discussed, however, this does not present as much of a problem as it may seem.

The third category was related to the second, but the subjects were less certain: "I felt like something was different, but I can't say what." This category seems to be a combination of cases where there was a true detection, cases where the subject actually saw the change occur, and cases where other factors may have played a role. Of the latter, perhaps the most common circumstance occurred when the subject pressed the button because of a feeling that something changed, without any concrete evidence that a change had really occurred. One subject said, "You feel like you're hallucinating. It looked like something happened, but you didn't really see anything. Sometimes you just push your button when that happens." In a related situation, subjects were occasionally observed playing indecisively with the button for a few seconds before eventually pressing it. When later questioned about this behaviour, the subjects said that they were vacillating in their decision about whether a change really took place, and had then just guessed that one had occurred. This type of detection tends to be indicated later in time than cases where the subject detects the actual change itself. Situations such as these typify the myriad reasons that the subjects might have pressed the button to indicate the detection of a change, when they may not have been certain that one had actually occurred.

At present, we lack a rationale to differentiate these marginal detections from the so-called "true" detections, but as mentioned above, this is cause for little concern. The reason underlying my lack of concern over the inability to segregate and explain each subclass of detections is that I consider these the least interesting cases. There are any number of reasons why a subject might detect the various display changes, many easily understandable given the nature and properties of the human visual system. What I find fascinating instead is that the subjects *missed 67% of the changes*. As with the detections, there are several categories of reasons that some image changes were missed by the subjects. One subject, for example, had the uncanny knack of looking at something as far as possible from the region undergoing a change. This scenario was true in some cases for all of the subjects. It is hardly surprising that the subjects were unable to detect a change to the image in this circumstance, especially if they had not directly fixated the change area before the change. Lacking direct evidence of the change, due to its occurrence during the eye movement, and having had no previous direct exposure to the information in that region, there is little reason that a subject would be able to detect such a change. Similar to the reasons for detecting the image changes, these are relatively uninformative observations.

More interesting are the cases in which the subject has fixated a region, which subsequently undergoes a change, and then refixates that region again, but fails to note the presence of any new information. In one notable instance, the image portrays a bridegroom, wearing a formal grey morning-coat with a matching grey silk hat, standing beside his new father-in-law, attired in a black tuxedo with matching top hat. In this trial, most subjects had already fixated both faces several times before the hats were switched between the two men, and yet no subject reported detection of the event. Another good example involves the image of four people in the forefront of a beach scene. Although all of the subjects began viewing the image directly fixated upon the woman wearing a bright pink swimsuit, only 50% responded when its colour changed to an equally bright green colour. Of the subjects who missed this image manipulation, some never came back to view the woman following the change (although her swimsuit occupied a substantial part of the picture). In most of the cases, however, the subjects refixated the woman without response. In these, and similar situations, the subject has had exposure to the visual information of an area, but for some reason either does not store, does not consolidate, or stores but does not make use of, the prior information and notice that something is now different. Or perhaps the visual system accepts and integrates the new information into some internal representation of the world without regard to what was viewed before, and without alerting the viewer.

Perhaps the oddest cases of all were those in which the subject was directly fixated upon the change region *before and immediately after* the change and still failed to detect the image manipulation. Among these instances, one of the most puzzling and striking involved an image of a boy holding up to the camera a parrot with brilliant green plumage. The parrot occupied approximately 25% of the scene and yet when its plumage changed to an equally brilliant red, 18% of the subjects missed it. Examination of the data revealed that of the 18% who missed it, two of the subjects were directly fixated upon the bird immediately before and after the change, *and still failed to respond.* Their eyes left a large, brilliant green parrot and landed, 20 msec later, upon a brilliant red parrot and yet nothing in their experience told them that anything unusual had happened. The data from this and related experiments are full of such events. These are the data that I consider truly interesting. Somehow the subject was either completely insensitive to, or was able to completely absorb, the sudden presence of the new visual information without any awareness or disturbance. How can these changes occur right in front of awake adults without their awareness? What is the nature of the internal visual representation and why does it accept the appearance of radically different information without a hiccup, just because the visual world happens to change during an eye movement? What mechanisms in the visual system can ignore, absorb or accommodate changes in the visual world of this magnitude? Is it not important to inform the viewer of such a change, just because it happened to have occurred during an eye movement? And finally, is this phenomenon just a scientific curiosity that has no place in, and teaches us nothing about, real everyday life? Or is it a real characteristic of the visual system that has implications for human vision and theories of visual processing?

One final anecdote will be offered as evidence of the presence and strength of this phenomenon. As part of my talk at the Vancouver conference, I presented a videotape containing a sample of my stimuli. I wanted the audience to see first-hand how glaring the changes were and to see how it would be quite unlikely for someone to fail to notice them without the eye-movement contingent display technology at work in the background. The tape itself consisted of pairs of images, the original followed by the altered version, edited together so that the switch between them occurred without any pause or glitch. The goal was to duplicate, within the limits of video technology, how the stimuli appeared in our lab. Each pair was followed by a report of the percentage of subjects who missed the switch. In preparing for the conference, my goal was to demonstrate the dismal performance of our subjects on some of the more amusing image manipulations. What I had not counted on were the characteristics of the auditorium and its video system. I found my images being projected onto a 5×8-meter screen. As I began to relate a few anecdotes reported by the subjects while the tape played, I gradually became aware of a stir in the audience. Following each image switch, the expected exclamation of amusement from the crowd was overheard. But mingled among those responses were frustrated cries of "What changed? I didn't see anything change," followed by hushed explanations from nearby people. The phenomenon was happening right there in the auditorium! It seems that the projection screen was large enough that people were required to make lengthy saccades while viewing it, and that for a handful of the audience, the image change occurred during one of those saccades *and they missed it*. My demonstration tape had much more of an impact than I had intended, and I had unwittingly shown that apparently this phenomenon can happen in the real world, outside the laboratory. It is difficult to convey in writing the impact that this event had on the audience at the conference. Perhaps it will suffice to say that it eliminated any questions regarding the reality of the phenomenon or its impact upon adults in the real world. The audience was convinced. My goal in relating this anecdote lies in the hope that if nothing else in this chapter has convinced the reader about the reality, power and oddity of this phenomenon, the reader will let the audience, their senses, and their experience serve as a proxy for the reader's own direct experience.

Discussion

The basic phenomenon, in the fewest words possible, is that large changes can be made to a full-colour image while a person is viewing it, and that person is very likely to miss these changes if they happen to occur during saccades. At the physiological level, visual information impinges upon the retina and streams through the various substages of the visual system, ultimately reaching the viewer's mental representation of the world. Interspersed throughout that stream, however, are periodic gaps in the visual information caused by the saccades. Given that most current explanations of saccadic suppression are retina-based, it seems reasonable to assume that these gaps are present in the stream of visual information from its beginning at the retina. In contrast, when a change in the visual world occurs *during* a fixation there is an alteration in the middle of one of those "information packets." A change of this nature could be detected by any number of visual processes, from as early in the visual system as the retina itself (Dowling, 1987) through many of the higher visual processing centres. Given this, the failure to receive the actual visual information that something in the world has changed occurs very early in the visual system, at the biological end where sensory transduction occurs. The information representing the change itself simply does not enter the visual stream, and therefore is not able to affect the final mental representation. Strong evidence for this claim would be provided if subjects displayed similarly abysmal detection performance when the image manipulation occurred during a blink, where the stream of visual information is completely disrupted at the retinal level. In either case, the failure to *acquire* direct evidence of the change probably occurs very early in the visual system. The visual stream contains information from the current visual context, a gap in that stream, and then information from a new visual context, with no flag or warning that anything in the visual context has changed (cf., Dennett, 1991, pp. 355-56).

In such a system, the failure to detect that the current incoming packet of visual information from the visual stream contains information discrepant from that transmitted by previous fixations must reside at higher levels of visual representation. Although there is much debate over the extent and nature of visual representation, it seems reasonable to accept the basic assumption that somewhere in the brain or in the mind there is a representation (or representations) of the visual world. Such a representation serves several purposes and reveals its presence in several ways – it serves to maintain information about the world across the visual gaps caused by saccades and blinks; it serves as the point of contact where stored experiences with the properties of objects of the world can be mated to objects in the current visual world; it serves as the interface for making plans to interact with the world and is where the visual feedback of our actions registers; and it serves to present new information regarding changes in the visual environment to our ongoing experience of that environment.

Similarly, there is readily available, observable evidence that not only does some type of internal representation of the visual world exist but that it can be used in our interactions with our environment. For example, one can point at something after closing one's eyes, as well as describe its visual properties, or navigate through a room with the eyes closed, once the room has been viewed briefly. Moreover, it is possible to saccade directly to something not currently in view, and that has not been directly fixated before, based solely upon its likely position given other information from the scene, and to reason about the external environment based on an internal visual representation, such as whether two colours will match or two objects will fit together in a given amount of space. Again, although the debate over the nature and properties of an internal visual representation rages, it seems clear that the visual world is represented internally in some way or other, and that these representations are used in our interactions with the external world.

It seems safe to assume, then, that there is a point, or points, of contact between the previous mental experiences of the person and the information gathered from the current environment. It is the interface between the environment and the conscious experience of the viewer. In the case of our sense of vision, it is where new information from the world impinges upon internal information, gathered from previous fixations and drawn from previous experiences. The current study, as well as the alternating case study and related studies mentioned above (McConkie & Zola, 1979), suggests that this representation is not based very strongly upon exact visual details, or at least that the visual details are not maintained across a saccade, and are therefore presumably of relatively little importance for that ongoing internal representation.

In light of the current data, perhaps the internal representation is based more on the information carried by the visual objects, rather than the details themselves (i. e. , not based upon the visual details of the image of a dog, but instead upon the observation that the image is of the dog). If so, the mind would only need to keep track of the salient information regarding objects and events in the world, not the entire "booming, buzzing confusion" (James, 1890). It would only need to store and interpret things important to the task at hand. In such a system, there is no need to store all of the visual details of the world in some internal memory; the world itself provides for the continuity of the details. It is more economical to store just the information contained within the details, rather than store the visual details themselves. Such an economy is sustainable because should the details be needed again for some reason, they are there, available for reacquisition. Given such a system, as long as the information within the scene remains intact, there would be little chance of detecting changes in the simple visual details of the scene.

In the study reported here, it was the express goal to perform image manipulations that *did not change the meaning of the scene*. One could certainly conduct a parallel study, where the visual details of the objects within the same scenes remained relatively unmolested, but the meaning of the scenes was altered. For example, Table 2 describes an image in which a child is enlarged by 30% and brought forward approximately five meters in the depth of the picture, and yet only

17% of the subjects detected it. If the child had been central to the theme of the picture, had been an active agent in the scene (involved in a fight, or some such activity), or been a child of some significance (either a young celebrity or the viewer's own child), would the detection rate have been so low? Similarly, if one of those two cowboys whose heads kept jumping about had been the viewer's brother, would the detection rate have been higher than 50%? The information-based view of the internal visual representation presented here would suggest so, because in such cases there is a change in the salient information of the scene. Studies such as this will be conducted in the near future to test such claims and hypotheses. Other studies will investigate the psychophysics of different types of manipulations, such as brightness changes or the perceptability of changes of different colours, size changes, etc. With the aid of the research environment described here, we hope to further study the various roles that visual details and scene information play in visual perception.

Acknowledgments

I would like to thank several people without whom this work would not have been possible. First and foremost, I would like to thank Dr. George McConkie and Dr. David Zola for their gentle guidance and leadership during my course of study, and for making it possible for me to play a role in the extension of their reading research paradigm to the field of visual perception of photographs. I would also like to thank Gary S. Wolverton for his technological ingenuity and tenacity in overcoming the numerous hurdles involved in the development of the laboratory system that made this work possible.

References

Adobe photoshop for the Macintosh: Version 2 [Computer program] (1991). Mountain View, CA: Adobe Systems Incorporated.

Buswell, G.T. (1935). *How People Look at Pictures.* Chicago: University of Chicago Press.

Dennett, D.C. (1991). *Consciousness Explained.* Boston: Little, Brown.

Dowling, J.E. (1987). *The Retina: An Approachable Part of the Brain.* Cambridge, MA: Belknap Press of Harvard University Press.

James, W. (1890). *The principles of psychology.* New York: Holt, Rinehart and Winston.

McConkie, G.W., Zola, D., Wolverton, G.S., and Burns, D.D. (1978). Eye movement contingent display control in studying reading. *Behavior Research Methods and Instrumentation,* 4: 529-44.

McConkie, G.W. (1979). On the role of and control of eye movements in reading. In P. A. Kolers, M. Wrolstad, and H. Bouma (Eds.) *Processing of Visible Language, I.* New York: Plenum Press.

McConkie, G.W., and Zola, D. (1979). Is visual information integrated across successive fixations in reading? *Perception and Psychophysics,* 25: 221-224.

Noton, D., and Stark, L. (1971). Scanpaths in saccadic eye movements while viewing and recognizing patterns. *Vision Research.* 11: 929-942.

5

On the Function of Visual Representation

Dana H. Ballard

1. The Recent History of Visual Representation

Vision is our most elaborate sense, and as such has challenged philosophers over many centuries to explain the mystery of its functioning. However, the advent of computer science has allowed a new perspective, namely that of a *computational theory*. Grounded in information theory, a computational theory seeks to describe what information is extracted from the image, but perhaps more importantly, how that information is computed and used. The elements of such a theory may be more readily appreciated in comparison to what might be termed the last pre-computational theory. In a series of books, Gibson (1950; 1979) argued for *direct perception*. The nub of this theory was that the environment is the repository for information necessary to act. Its information is expressed in terms of invariants that are implicitly contained in the optical array. The best known example is that of optic flow, the velocity patterns induced on the optic array by motion of the observer. This special kind of time-varying image contains information about significant behavioural events, for example, parameters related to the time to collision. The optic flow invariants illustrate the two most important tenets of this theory, namely: (1) The world is the repository of the information needed to act. With respect to the observer, it is stored "out there," and by implication not represented internally in some mental state that exists separately from the stimulus. (2) The information needed to act is computed directly (direct perception).

In the light of later work that meticulously counts the computational overhead, the second tenet seems a controversial claim. As pointed out by Geoff Hinton, it is likely that Gibson was trying to distinguish between the sequential computational model advocated for logical reasoning and the computation involved in perception; however, subsequent computational theories turn on the cost of computing these invariants.

Marr (1982) originated the first computational theory of vision. His emphasis focussed on representation of vision, or the data structures needed to support the information extraction process. Vision was the problem of determining "what is where." The what of vision was object-centered representations. These are useful, as object-centered descriptions are invariant with respect to the viewer. Finding out where objects are was judged to be difficult, as objects appear in viewer-centered co-ordinates. In other words, the object-centered and viewer-centered descriptions do not match. Thus computing such descriptions was claimed to be a very difficult task that could only be done in several stages. A series of representations was proposed, each with the objective of facilitating the computation of object-centered descriptions. These are summarized in Table 5.1.

The table shows that photometric data is converted into physical data, but more importantly that most of the representations of vision are retinotopically indexed, that is, accessed by spatial co-ordinates in a retinal co-ordinate system. In neurological terms, the visual maps are retinotopically indexed. Transisting neurons within these maps produces responses whose predominant variation is in terms of the retinal effective stimulus. As the first computational theory of vision, it was enormously valuable in defining the principal issues. One of its major successes was the definition of the 2½ dimensional sketch, a representation that is used by what has been termed "early vision." The kinds of explicit features used in the retinotopic maps of early vision – optic flow, texture, colour and disparity – have been observed in monkey cortex.

Despite these and other successes, there were major issues not addressed in the theory. The most important may have been the exclusion of the effects of the perceiver's behavioural context. The theory was essentially about passive vision. Another thing Marr did not include was the special features of human vision, such as its elaborate gaze control system that includes saccades, and the fovea, with its greatly enhanced resolution near the optical axis. To understand these

Data Structure	Index	Type
image	retinotopic	photometric features
primal sketch	retinotopic	photometric features
2½-D sketch	retinotopic	physical properties
object-centered representations	object-centered	physical properties

Table 5.1: Marr's Representational Structures

omissions from a single perspective, let us consider another of Marr's contributions. He defined three principal levels of analysis: the *task level*, which defines what is computed; the *algorithm level*, which defines how these things are computed; and the *implementation level*, which defines the machine- level details of the computation. In reality, however, the algorithm level interacts with the implementation level. In other words, the algorithms that are most efficient depend on the structure of the underlying machine. We argue that much of the work in vision has ignored a level of detail of the biological machine that has been termed the *embodiment* level (Ballard 1991a; Brooks 1986). Having a particular kind of body plays a major role in determining what is practical to compute. For example, without rapid eye movements, the retinal image becomes more valuable as a memory of the imaged scene, whereas with such movements it is far less useful.

Embodiment not only changes what is practical to compute but how the computation is done. The traditional view is that the products of vision are first computed and then used by cognition. The new view is that if the purpose of vision is the *sine qua non*, then even the earliest products of vision need be done only insofar as to subserve this purpose. The most radical view is that traditional image-like structures are never computed independently of a behavioural context.

In order to better understand these claims, we will discuss some of the issues arising from current computational vision models that seek to do without embodiment. Embodiment provides crucial context, so that doing without it leads to positing structures that represent information independently of context. This leads to what we term the *literalist view*. We will examine this view first from the point of internal consistencies. Next we will introduce a rival viewpoint, supported by embodiment: that of the *functional view*. We will attempt to show that functional explanations raise further difficulties for literalism.

2. The Literalist View

The main tenet of the literalist view is that much of the phenomena of vision result from *retinotopic* computations in the brain circuitry. In other words, the phenomena happen at the level of Marr's 2½-D sketch. In its strongest form, namely that there is a picture in the head, it probably has no proponents, but by only weakening the statement a little there are many proponents. For example, there is substantial support for the fact that visual illusions are the direct product of retinotopic computations (Grossberg 1973; Ramachandran 1987). And the support is increased by weakening the tenet a bit further to encompass the notion that the retinotopic representations compute physical properties of the external world (Poggio et al. 1992). A way to remember this is as "You See What You Think You See," i.e., there are retinotopic representations in the brain that directly correspond to your conscious percept.

It is easy to see the attraction of such a view: there is extensive neurological evidence that there are retinotopic representations in the brain that seem to represent precisely the products that participate in the illusion. And there are psychological studies that point to the fact that humans behave *as if* they had access to a retinotopic map of visual information (Kosslyn 1992). A couple of examples illustrate the strong form of the literalist view. One is from Yuille and Grzywacz (1988). Yuille models the observed phenomena of *motion capture*. In motion capture, random dots are "jiggled" against a background of a translating sine wave grating. The dots appear to move with the velocity of the grating and are thus said to be "captured" by the grating. To model this phenomenon, Yuille uses a retinotopic velocity space. The velocity of the dots in this space is ultimately made by his algorithm to conform to the velocity of the background. The point is that the velocity of the dots is explicitly represented in retinotopic space. From the literalist point of view, the dots are captured in our perception because they are captured in the representation. In a second example, vision in the blind spot of the retina has been studied by Ramachandran (1992). Subjects report being able to interpolate missing corners of squares when the missing corner interpenetrates the visual field of the blind spot. In other words, they see the figure as whole when the missing corner is invisible. How could they have this perception if there were not a retinotopic place in the cortex where this percept is explicitly created?

3. Problems with the Literalist View

While the idea of a retinotopic representation that looks like either the physics that we think we see or the way the world appears to be is appealing, problems start to arise when the details of this promise are confronted. As a case study in the difficulties with the literalist view, we will first turn to Churchland's stereo model (Churchland, this volume). Next we will argue that there is insufficient time to accomplish extensive propagation of the retina, a feature of some models. Then there is the difficult issue of what constitutes a perception. The "Nina" experiments with visual search challenge the classical definitions. Do people really see what they think they see? Experiments by Grimes (this volume) show that the amount of information captured during a fixation is much less than previously believed. Finally, we will conclude by offering a non-retinotopic version of "motion capture."

Case Study of Churchland's Stereo

The main point of this model is to suggest that previous models of stereo have failed to take into account that the measurements are referred to the fixation point (but see Ballard 1991a; Lehky and Sejnowski 1990)). Churchland points out that the computations are naturally conducted in relative terms with the disparity in the horopter as a surface that moves with the fixation point. He constructs a connectionist model that learns the correct responses by enjoying some pre-wiring together with the backpropagation-training algorithm. Leaving aside the difficulties with backpropagation as a supervised algorithm, let us consider the main issues from the literalist perspective. In the first place, disparity is not the same as depth, which depends on the fixation point geometry. The solution to this is the construction of an auxiliary network, which corrects the measurements. The auxiliary network represents the literalist view. A percept is captured by explicit circuitry. This of course leads to the possibility of an explosion of circuits to capture every percept. Churchland (this volume) seems to recognize this difficulty, but stops short of a solution:

> In the model, these determinations are made by a network auxiliary to the main one, a network whose inputs are the current pair-presentation, and whose six outputs are the absolute distances of each of the three external planes grasped by the three output layers, and the absolute width of an object one pixel across at each of those distances. There is no expectation that this auxiliary net has a structure corresponding to anything real in humans, but it does illustrate that the relevant computations can be quickly and easily performed by a feedforward system.

The difficulty with representing the percept veridically resurfaces in a discussion of the fact that the disparity code itself is not related to depth: "But something important is still missing. As described to this point, the network has no simultaneous representation of objects and their relative positions throughout a range of different depths. *One might even hold this capability to be definitive of true or full stereopsis* [emphasis mine]." The problem is: how can the model be a model of the percept if the internal representation is allowed to stray from a copy of the percept? Here Churchland finally gives in to the wisdom of representing information that could support the behaviour rather than the percept itself.

A final problem and its solution will serve as a summary of the difficulties of literal representation. In matching gray levels in the stereo algorithm, there is the problem that large areas of uniform gray levels are reported as matches, thereby confounding the algorithm, which desires punctate matches. The solution, apparently also used by biology, which devotes a large percentage of circuitry to encoding edges, is to match points of photometric change or edges, rather than the gray levels themselves. Of course, now one is faced with the inevitable: this solution means that the internal depth map is incomplete, having values only at the matched points. What can be done? Here the literalist versus non-literalist are finally at odds. The literalist solution is to interpolate so that the representation looks like the precept. The non-literalist seeks to find ways to use the representation as is to model the external behaviour.

If Illusions Survive Eye Movements Then Either the Circuitry Is Very Fast or the Perception Is non-Retinotopic.

One fact of primate vision is that of saccadic eye movements. The small size of the fovea places a premium on quickly placing the point of gaze on targets of interest. Probably as a consequence the primate visual system has a very fast, ballistic mechanism for moving the eyes quickly to targets. Speeds of up to 700%/second are reached, and as a consequence the visual input is extremely blurred during the movement. Under normal circumstances, fixation durations (the time between saccades when gaze is stabilized) are about 300 milliseconds. How do we account for illusions that survive saccadic eye movements? There are two possibilities. One is that there is sufficient time to perform the necessary computations to produce the illusion within each fixation. The other is that the retinotopic data is adjusted for the movements themselves (Anderson and Van Essen 1991; Duhamel et al. 1992). Both of these alternatives have potential difficulties. In the first, the best known algorithms require that the computations propagate over the retinotopic array. Given that normal cortical firing rates are about 10 hertz, there is only time for a single neuron to send 20 spikes during a fixation. Thus one cannot be confident that there is sufficient time for the information to propagate. In the second, there must be posited extensive machinery to handle the updating. As we will see in a moment, there are other complications.

Nina Searching – Do S's Have Perceptions or Don't They?

One subjective observation that fuels literalist intuitions is that of perception. Traditionally, visual perception has been given a primal status (Fodor 1983) in that, evoking Gibsonian terms, it seems immediate and cannot be overturned by our cognitive set. Hence the historical and persisting boundaries between perception and cognition. Recently, however, there have been several experiments that challenge both the sanctity of perception and the perceptual-cognitive dichotomy. We will present two examples here. In the first, we are able to catch the human system in an ambiguous state whereby according to its eye movements it is registering a stimulus; however, it cannot report a conscious percept. What is the status of the material that is on the retinal array but somehow not perceived by the subject? A special set of images is the "Nina" set. The face of a young woman is camouflaged by embedding it in a scene of comparable line drawings. Subjects are given the task of detecting the location of the Nina face in the figure and their eye movements are recorded. Analysis shows that subjects look at the correct location many times when they do not report it. From detection theory this is uninteresting: the subject did not have enough evidence to decide on the location of the face. Yet this scenario reveals a problem in separating the participation of the observer from the perception. Did the subjects have the perception of Nina or didn't they? If they did not, what grounds do we have for studying unconscious perception, since we can't really know when we are having one? Or alternatively, if we can't have perception without the background of mental set, then the presuppositions of most perception experiments could be called into question.

Grimes's Saccadic Experiments

The Nina experiments raise a fundamental scepticism about the boundary between perception and cognition that is supported by a second series of experiments by Grimes (this volume). These experiments study integration across eye movements. Subjects were instructed to look for changes in images and push a button if they detected any change. The changes, in the cases where there were any, were introduced only during the transit of a saccade. The images were of visually rich natural scenes. Surprisingly, subjects ignored huge changes in the image structure under these conditions. For example, in one image a huge green parrot, which dominates the scene, changes color to crimson. About 30 percent of the subjects do not report this change. In another example a prominent bunch of bananas switches orientation from pointing right to pointing left. None of the subjects report this change. One interpretation of these studies is that the content of the image is extensively linked to a semantic description. Subjects are insensitive to changes that affect that description in the subsequent fixation. As a corollary these experiments cast doubt on models that place a premium on integrating the content of the retinotopic array across fixations (Anderson and Van Essen 1991; Duhamel et al. 1992). If there were machinery for integrating across saccades one would expect that gross changes in the scene as introduced in the Grimes paradigm would be straightforward to detect. In contrast, it appears that the retinotopic information is not important from one saccade to the other.

Motion Capture without Retinopathy: Subspaces

To conclude our criticism of literalism *per se*, we offer an alternative explanation of motion capture. To be fair to Yuille's account, his explanation is in the form of a detailed computer model whereas ours is in the form of a thought- experiment and therefore much weaker. Nonetheless, consider that the brain architecture need not represent the details of the motion in the image, but only the coarse details. In this case, at an abstract level there are representations that denote "moving dots" and "motion to the left." Faced only with this information, the perceptual apparatus is designed to report "dots moving to the left." The conclusion follows from the non-retinotopic information, rather than the retinotopic information. Note that if the retinotopic information was computed veridically, as in the literalist explanation, there would still have to be a parser that analyzes the resultant picture in the head to produce the same report, so the introduction of the reporting structure adds nothing extra to the account.

4. The Alternative to Literalism: Functionalism

At the other end of the spectrum from the literalist view is the *functionalist view*. To remember it, let us term it "You Don't See What You Think You See." The principal tenet is that the machinery of the brain has to be accountable to the observed external behaviour, and that there are many ways to do this other than positing literal data structures.

The functionalist view depends critically on levels of abstraction. We are very comfortable with having to deal with many different levels of abstraction in biological systems. Sejnowski and Churchland (1990) identify seven different levels used in the study of the brain in computational neuroscience. However, in our models of human intelligence, we have not always been able to appreciate the need for such a hierarchy of abstraction. One reason may have been that the early work in the field has been dominated by tenets of artificial intelligence. One of the most important of these is that intelligence can be described in purely computational terms without recourse to any particular embodiment. From this perspective, the special features of the human body and its particular ways of interacting in the world have been seen as secondary to the fundamental problems of intelligence. That systems can appear dramatically different at different levels of abstraction can be best illustrated with an example from computer science. Consider the way virtual memory works on a conventional workstation. Virtual memory allows the applications programmer to write programs that are larger than the physical memory of the machine. What happens is that prior to the running of the program, it is broken up into smaller pages, and then at run-time the requisite pages are brought into the memory from peripheral storage as required. This strategy works largely because conventional sequential programs are designed to be executed sequentially, and the information required to interpret an instruction is usually very localized. Consider now two very different viewpoints. From the application programmer's viewpoint, it appears that a program of unlimited length can be written. But the system programmer's viewpoint is very different. The environment is very dynamic as individual pages are moved in and out of physical memory. This captures the difference between the cognitive level and the approach we are terming embodiment. At the symbolic level, which neglects the details of the machine, the world appears seamless and stable. It is only at the embodiment level that we find that this must be an illusion, as the human's real-time visuo-motor system has many creative ways to interact with the world in a timely manner.

Neural-level models of behaviour tend to make the opposite kind of error. These models offer a very concrete view of processing at very small spatial and temporal scales that obscure the coarser features of behaviour. For example, in vision, spatial scales of 20' and temporal scales of 2 to 50 milliseconds are important, whereas at the level of eye and hand movements, time constants are about an order of magnitude larger (see Table 5.2).

Time, Milliseconds	Processing Feature
2	shortest interspike interval
40	average attentional search time for each item
300	average eye fixation time
400	shortest reaction time

Table 5.2: Different Spatio-Temporal Scales

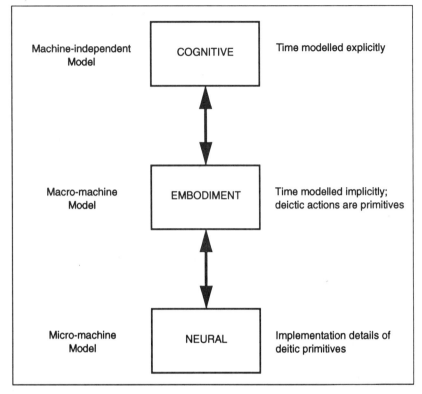

Figure 5.1: Embodiment as an Intermediate Level of Machine Architecture

In contrast to both of the above views, our central thesis is that intelligence has to relate to interactions with the physical world, and that means that the particular form of the human body is an important constraint in delimiting the aspects of intelligent behaviour. Thus embodiment is crucial and illuminating and, we argue, best handled by positing a distinct level of abstraction, as depicted in Figure 5.1.

Embodiment models may be seen as a level of abstraction properly between cognitive models and neural models. Embodiment models differ from cognitive models by implicitly modelling time, as opposed to the explicit models used at the cognitive level (e.g., Allen and Hayes 1989). Embodiment is distinguished from neural levels by using deictic primitives, as opposed to neural levels, which capture the implementation details of deictic models. The embodiment level specifies how the constraints of the physical system interact with cognition. One example is the movements of the eyes during the co-ordination of the hand in problem-solving tasks. Our purpose is to show that important features of cognition can be traced to constraints that act at this level of abstraction, and more importantly, that these features challenge the usefulness of the literalist interpretation of visual perception.

5. Embodiment Model

The main visual behaviour that the human has is the ability to fixate an environmental point. By fixating an environmental point, humans can use a special frame of reference centered at that point to simplify the task. This turns out to have a profound effect on the original "what is where" formulation of vision proposed by Marr. Technically, the ability to use an external frame of reference centered at the fixation point leads to great simplifications in algorithmic complexity (Ballard 1989). (This is a very different assertion than that of Marr 1982, who emphasized that vision calculations were initially in viewer-centred co-ordinates.) The fixation frame allows for closed-loop behavioural

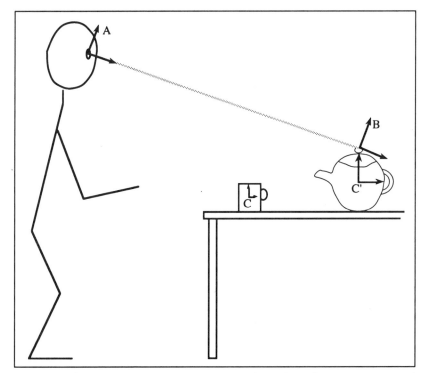

Figure 5.2: If vision is passive, computations must be performed in a viewer-centered frame (A). Instead, biological data argue for a world-centered frame (B). This frame is selected by the observer to suit information-gathering goals and is centered at the fixation point. The task of the observer is to relate information in the fixation point frame to object-centered frames (C), (C').

strategies that do not require precise three-dimensional information. For example, in grasping an object, we can first fixate the object and then direct the hand to the centre of the retinal co-ordinate system. In depth, the hand can be controlled relative to the plane of fixation. Informally, we refer to this behaviour as a "do-it-where-I'm-looking" strategy, but more technically it is referred to as a deictic strategy, after Agre and Chapman (1987).

The deictic strategy of using the perceptual system to actively control the point of action in the world has precisely the right kind of invariance for a large number of behaviours. One task that we have studied in detail (Ballard et al. 1992) is a block-copying task. In this task, subjects must copy a pattern of coloured blocks on a computer display by moving coloured blocks from a supply area with the computer mouse. By virtue of the fact that only one block can be moved at once, this task requires that the blocks be handled sequentially. However, our contention is that it can be further reduced to embodiment-level primitives. Let us consider the copying task at this more detailed level.

To copy the first block, its colour has to be determined. One way to do that is to fixate the block in question in the model area. Next a block of that color has to be located and picked up in the source area. Finally that block has to be moved and dropped in the workspace. Subsequent block moves are more complicated, as the relationship of the new block with the model has to be determined and then replicated in the workspace. In rough outline a cognitive program for a block move looks like:

Repeat until {the pattern has been copied}:
    Fixate(*A block in the model area with a given colour*)
    Remember(The colour)
    Fixate(A block in the source area with the same colour)
    PickUp(The block currently fixated)
    Fixate(*The appropriate location*)
    Remember(location)
    Fixate(Location in the workspace)
    Move(The block to the fixated location)
    PutDown(The block currently held at the current location)

In the model program, italics are used to denote a structure that has to be "bound" to the sensor data, whereas non-italicized arguments to the primitives denote structures that are already bound. Here binding is used in the same way as the value of a variable in a computer program is bound or assigned to that variable. These instructions make extensive use of deictic reference. It is assumed that the instruction

Fixate will orient the centre of gaze to point to a place in the image with a feature appropriate to the argument of the function. If multiple instances of the feature are present, then some tie-breaking scheme must be used. The deictic nature of these instructions is illustrated by *PickUp*, *Move* and *PutDown* which are assumed to act at the centre of the fixation frame, irrespective of its specific location in three-dimensional space. Fixate is actually also a deictic instruction if we include a mechanism for target selection, such as a focus of attention. A focus of attention may be thought of as an electronic fovea, in terms of its ability to select target locations. Thus *Fixate* becomes two instructions:

> AttendTo(*image-feature appropriate for target selection*)
> Fixate(Attended location)

The exact behaviour of these instructions depends on the particular embodiment, but the assumption at this level of modelling is that they can be designed to perform as described. We have shown that similar albeit simpler problems can be learned by a computer using these instructions (Whitehead and Ballard 1990).

Somewhat surprisingly, the above program, with only minor modifications, has proven to be an accurate model of human performance (Ballard et al. 1992). The principal result of the block-copying tasks, which is also suggested by the model program, is that for manipulating individual blocks, colour and relative location are acquired *separately*, even though they are notionally associated with the same retinal location. If this is true, then what was the representational status of a block's colour and location before they were bound by the task context? From the Triesman experiments (1982), it is obvious that binding is a problem.

6. Functional Uses of Retinotopic Representations

To develop our earlier metaphor, the embodiment level may be thought of as the operating system level and the cognitive level as the user program level (Dennett 1991; Ballard 1991b). At the embodiment level, stability may not be the issue but rather the function of a sequential program dedicated to achieving current goals. To accomplish this the algorithms that use the retinotopic array may need to appropriate it in many ways that could be at odds with stability. To emphasize this point, the primitives are articulated into neural-level representations. The motivation for such primitives is economy. The simplification of active viewing can also be understood with reference to the problem of relating internal models to objects in the world. One interpretation of the need for sequential, problem-dependent eye-movements is that the general problem of associating many models to many parts of the image simultaneously is too hard. In order to make the computation tractable within a single fixation, it has to be simplified into either one of location (one internal model) or one of identification (one world-object). A location task is to find the image co-ordinates of a single model in the presence of many alternatives. In this task the image periphery must be searched and one can assume that the model has been chosen *a priori*. An identification task is to associate the foveated part of the image with one of many possible models. In this task one can assume that the location of the material to be identified is at the fixation point. This dichotomy is exactly equivalent to the WHERE/WHAT dichotomy seen in the parietal and infero-temporal areas of visual cortex (Mishkin et al. 1983). Swain and Ballard (1991) have shown that both identification and location behaviours are much simpler than their combination, which has been termed "image understanding." The simplification of separating location and identification tasks has recently been extended to shape models as well (Ballard and Wixson 1992).

Using Colour for Identification

Colour can solve both the what and where problems using the colour histogram (Swain 1990; Swain and Ballard 1990; 1991). For the problem of object identification, the use of histogram matching provides a

		Models	
		One	Many
Image Parts	One	Manipulation: trying to do something with an object whose identity and location are known	Identification: trying to identify an object whose location can be fixated
	Many	Location: trying to find a known object that may not be in view	Image Understanding: trying to locate and identify all the structure in an image. Too Difficult?

Table 5.3: The biological organization of cortex into WHAT/WHERE modules may have a basis in computational complexity. Trying to match a large number of image segments to a large number of models at once may be too difficult.

very robust index that is insensitive to deformations of the object. A drawback of the matching process was sensitivity to lighting conditions, but recent extensions of this work by Funt and Finalyson (1991) have shown that a modified index is insensitive to such variations.

Using Colour for Location

For the problem of object location, Swain's algorithm uses feedback to the retinotopic representations of colour in the following way: the image colours are rated as to how helpful they are in selecting the current model. This rating is retinotopic and becomes a saliency map. Low-pass filtering of the saliency map followed by maximum detection is sufficient to locate the desired object.

Successful experiments have been conducted on a database of 70 articles of clothing. These are non-rigid and difficult to identify with current techniques. The experiments are preliminary and illustrate the concept of object location using top-down feedback. Interestingly, this is a very different proposal than that of Koch and Ullman (1985), who suggested a bottom-up technique that used coincidental feature alignment to define a salience measure. The main point, however, is that at the embodiment level the computation is dominated by the eye movement cycle. That cycle can be broken up into two kinds of tasks: (1) an identification task, whereby a property is extracted from the fixated location, and (2) a location task, whereby the eye is moved to a new location. Furthermore, as Figure 5.3 implies, the natural mapping of these algorithms onto the known cortical architecture uses the same architecture in fundamentally different ways. Thus the state of the cortex, instead of representing visual invariants, will vary with the demands of the location/identification cycle.

7. Programs with Small Numbers of Variables

Robot-Learning Example

Work done with a particular exocentric model of the use of gaze, combined with the concept of deictic representations, suggested that it would be efficacious if the human visual system solved problems in a minimal way. To explore this possibility, hand-eye co-ordination was studied for a sequential copying task. The strategy of memorizing the configuration to be copied in its entirety before moving blocks seemed to never be used. Instead, a variety of different programs were used to check the course of the copying task in the midst of moving individual blocks. These strategies point to the use of minimal memory solutions.

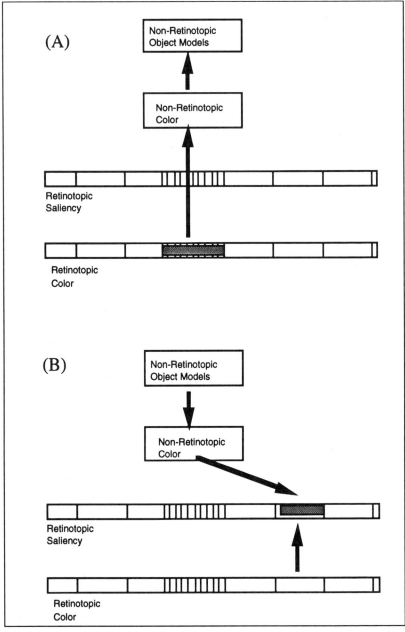

Figure 5.3: (A) Identification tasks can be modeled by using foveal features in a table-lookup scheme. (B) Location tasks can be modeled by comparing model features and retinal features in a saliency map. These two tasks use the same cortical architecture in different ways at different times.

The main observation is that although eye movements are used for the terminal phase of hand movements, they are used for other tasks prior to that phase. This implies that the underlying decision process that moves the eyes leaves key decisions until just before they are required. The results are compatible with the standard model of the brain as having a limited capacity for short-term memory, but they suggest a new interpretation of that memory. Rather than focus on the small number of items themselves, think of the number of behavioural programs that can be constructed with a limited number of memory registers. The limited number need only be a handicap if the entire task is to be completed from memory; in that case the short-term memory system is overburdened. In the more natural case of performing the task with ongoing access to the visual world, the task is completed perfectly. Detailed analysis of this case suggests that the subjects are using an economical representation scheme to represent or remember information about the task just before it is required. We refer to this scheme as *just-in-time representation*.

One way to reduce the burden of representation to just that essential for the task is to use *markers*, temporary variables that record partial computational results. This notion of markers has been championed by Agre and Chapman as a general method of object-centered computation. The notion is that markers provide a local context to resolve reference ambiguity. Agre and Chapman's focus was routine activity. They sought to model behaviour in terms of ongoing activity. Responses to the activity were in the form of rules that were activated by local context. The key points were that in routine activity, long causal chains were not necessary. It turns out that the fixation point strategy can be thought of as a kind of marker that has the right kind of transfer for learning many tasks. In our laboratory, Steve Whitehead has studied learning using a reinforcement paradigm (Whitehead and Ballard 1990). Whitehead has been studying block-stacking tasks. On each trial, the system, which is an abstracted model of our robot, is presented with a pile of coloured blocks. A pile consists of any number of blocks arbitrarily arranged. Each block is uniformly coloured. The system can manipulate the pile by picking and placing objects. When the system arranges the blocks into a successful configuration, it receives a positive reward and the trial ends. For example, one extremely simple block-stacking task is for the system to learn to pick up a light gray block. In this case, the successful configurations consist just of those states where the system is holding a gray object. The system learns to arrange arbitrary configurations of blocks into successful configurations. The key point here is that the marker encoding obviates the need for explicit co-ordinates.

7 Plus or Minus 2

How many markers are needed? In a study of chess-playing, it was found that subjects needed Miller's limit of 7 plus or minus 2 (Chase and Simon 1973). However, our studies suggest that the normal limit in everyday tasks might not use the full capacity of short-term memory. Instead, human decision tasks have to consider the following two constraints. If too few variables are used then the decision function becomes ambiguous, as shown in Figure 5.4. On the other hand, if too many variables are used, then the decision function becomes very difficult to learn, as its cost scales exponentially with the number of variables.

Back to Grimes

The 7 plus or minus 2 limit allows a succinct explanation of the Grimes result. How could subjects misperceive huge visual features on their retinae? The answer is that they can only be aware of the items that

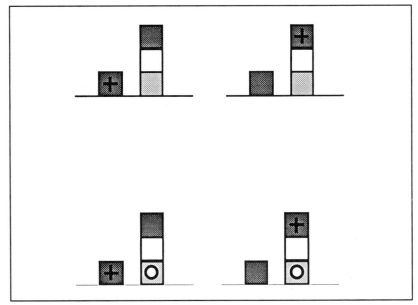

Figure 5.4: Encoding tasks with respect to deictic markers leads to ambiguities when the number of markers is too small. Here the task is to pick up the light gray block. On the top row the situation is ambiguous, with only one marker. On the left the desired action is to move the fixation frame to the light gray block (and then to the top), but in the right the desired action is to pick up the gray block. (Top) With only the context of a single marker, these two different situations cannot be disambiguated. (Bottom) An additional marker provides the context needed to disambiguate the situation.

they have explicitly kept track of, and this is a dynamic buffer of 7 plus or minus 2 variable bindings. If an image structure is, at the appropriate instant, not one of the bound variables, then no matter how salient it is, its changes will not be perceived.

Conclusion

A number of different avenues of investigation have suggested that much of the basic phenomenology of vision can be traced to "a picture in the head," retinotopic structures that represent phenomena of the world in a more or less veridical sense. While it is so far impossible to disprove this literal interpretation of experience, there are a variety of new results that challenge this literalism. These new results can be integrated under the heading of functionalism. Focussing on the tasks that humans have to do rather than subjective experiences, functionalism provides a new way of evaluating experimental data. In addition, the behaviour needs to be interpreted in terms of a human model that is both sufficiently abstract to suppress confounding neural-level detail, yet sufficiently concrete to include the crucial body mechanisms that mediate perception and action.

In regard to any dichotomy of putative brain function it is always possible that the brain can do both. In this case it is possible that the brain can simultaneously represent the visual invariants that correspond to the "perception" of seeing and the invariants that correspond to functional programs. However, the intent of this paper is to suggest that many of the phenomena that might have previously garnered a literal interpretation can be more succinctly explained by functional models, even though these functional models may challenge many of our intuitions about perception.

Acknowledgments

This research was supported in part by the Human Scientific Frontiers Program, the National Science Foundation (IRI-8903582) and the National Institutes of Health (1R24RRO6853).

References

Agre, P.E., and D. Chapman (1987). Pengi: An implementation of a theory of activity. *Proceedings, American Association for Artificial Intelligence (AAAI) 87*

Allen, J.F., and P.J. Hayes (November 1989). Moments and points in an interval-based temporal logic. *Computational Intelligence* 5(4): 225-38

Anderson, C.H., and D.C. Van Essen (1991). Dynamic neural routing circuits. In

A. Gale and K. Carr (eds.), *Visual Search 2* (Proceedings, Second International Conference on Visual Search, Durham University, Sept. 1990). New York: Taylor and Francis

Ballard, D.H. (1989). Reference frames for animate vision. *Proceedings, Internaional Joint Conference on Artificial Intelligence,* Detroit, MI

————. (1991a). Animate vision. *Artificial Intelligence* 48: 57-86

————. (January 1991b). Sub-symbolic modeling of hand-eye coordination. *Proceedings, Wolfson Lecture Series,* Wolfson College, Oxford

Ballard, D.H., M.M. Hayhoe, F. Li and S.D. Whitehead (March 1992). Hand-eye coordination during sequential tasks. *Proceedings, Philosophical Transactionss of the Royal Society of London B,* London

Ballard, D.H., and L.E. Wixson (October 1992). Object indexing. Working Paper, Computer Science Department, University of Rochester

Brooks, R.A. (1986). A robust layered control system for a mobile robot. *IEEE Journal of Robotics and Automation* RA-2: 14-23

Churchland, Paul (This volume). A feedforward network for fast stereo vision with movable fusion plane

Chase, W.G., and H.A. Simon (1973). Perception in chess. *Cognitive Psychology* 4: 55-81

Dennett, D.C. (1991). *Consciousness Explained.* New York: Little BrownDuhamel, J.-R., C.L. Colby and M.E. Goldberg (3 January 1992). The updating of the representation of visual space in parietal cortex by intended eye movements. *Science* 255: 90-92

Fodor, J.A. (1983). *The Modularity of Mind.* Cambridge, MA: MIT Press

Funt, B.V., and G.D. Finalyson (October 1991). Color constant color indexing. CSS/LCCR TR91-09, Centre for Systems Science, Simon Fraser University

Gibson, J.J. (1950). *The Perception of the Visual World.* Boston: Houghton Mifflin

————. (1979). *The Ecological Approach to Visual Perception.* Boston: Houghton Mifflin

Grimes, J. (This Volume). On the failure to detect changes in scenes across saccades

Grossberg, S. (1973). Contour enhancement, short-term memory and constancies in reverberating neural networks. *Studies in Applied Mathematics.* 52: 217-57

Koch, C., and S. Ullman (1985). Shifts in selective visual attention: Towards the underlying neural circuitry. *Human Neurobiology* 4: 219-27

Kosslyn, S.M. (1992). *Wet Mind: The New Cognitive Neuroscience.* New York: Maxwell Macmillan International

Lehky, S.R., and T.J. Sejnowski (1990). Neural model of stereoacuity and depth interpolation based on a distributed representation of stereo disparity. *Journal of Neuroscience* 10(7): 2281-99

Marr, D.C. (1982). *Vision.* San Francisco: W.H. Freeman

Mishkin, M., L.G. Ungerleider and K.A. Macko (1983). Object vision and spatial vision: Two cortical pathways. *Trends in Neuroscience* 6: 414-17

Poggio, T., M. Fahle and S. Edelman (1992). Fast perceptual-learning in visual hyperacuity. *Science* 256(5059): 1018-21

Ramachandran, V.S. (September 1987). Interactions between motion, depth, color and form: The utilitarian theory of perception. *Proceedings, Conference on Visual Coding and Efficiency*

————. (1992). Perceptual filling in of the blind spot and of cortical and retinal scotomas. *Investigative Ophthalmology and Visual Science* 33(4): 1348

Sejnowski, T.J., P. Churchland and C. Koch (1990). Computational neuroscience. *Science* 241(4871): 1299-1306

Swain, M.J. (November 1990). Color indexing. Ph.D. thesis and TR 360, Computer Science Department, University of Rochester

Swain, M.J., and D.H. Ballard (December 1990). Indexing via color histograms. *Proceedings, International Conference on Computer Vision*, Kyoto, Japan

Swain, M.J., and D.H. Ballard (1991). Color indexing. *International Journal of Computer Vision* (Special Issue) 7(1): 11-32

Triesman, A. (1982). The role of attention in object perception. *The Royal Society International Symposium on Physical and Biological Processing of Images*, London

Whitehead, S.D., and D.H. Ballard (1990). Active perception and reinforcement learning. *Neural Computation* 2: 409-19

Yuille, A.L., and N.M. Grzywacz (May 1988). A computational theory for the perception of coherent visual motion. *Nature* 333: 71-74

6

Filling In: Why Dennett Is Wrong

P.S. Churchland and V.S. Ramachandran

1. Introduction

It comes as a surprise to discover that the foveal area in which one has high resolution and high acuity vision is minute; it encompasses a mere 2° of visual angle – roughly, the area of the thumbnail at arm's length. The introspective guess concerning acuity in depth likewise errs on the side of extravagance; the region of crisp, fused perception is, at arm's length, only a few centimeters deep; closer in, the area of fused perception is even narrower. The eyes make a small movement – a saccade – about every 200 to 300 milliseconds, sampling the scene by shifting continuously the location of the fovea. Presumably interpolation across intervals of time to yield an integrated spatio-temporal representation is a major component of what brains do. Interpolation in perception probably enables generation of an internal representation of the world that is useful in the animal's struggle for survival.

The début demonstration of the blind spot in the visual field is likewise surprising. The standard set-up requires monocular viewing of an object offset about 13° to 15° from the point of fixation (Figure 6.1). If the object falls in the region of the blindspot of the viewing eye, the object will not be perceived. Instead, the background texture and colour will be seen as uniform across the region. This is generally characterized as "filling in" of the blind spot. The existence of the perceptual blind spot is owed to the specific architecture of the retina. As shown in Figure 6.2, each retina has a region where the optic nerve leaves the retina and hence where no transducers (rods and cones) exist. This region is the blind spot. Larger than the fovea, it is about 6° in length and about 4.5° in width.

Relying on two eyes, a perceiver – even a careful and discerning perceiver – will fail to notice the blind spot, mainly because the blind regions of the two eyes do not overlap. If light from a thimble, for example, falls in the blind spot of the left eye, it will nevertheless be detected normally by the right retina, and the viewer sees a thimble. Even in the monocular condition, however, one may fail to notice the

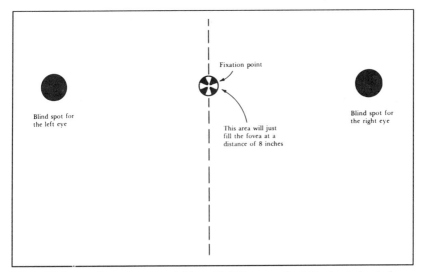

Figure 6.1: Instructions: close your right eye. Hold the page about 8 inches in front of you. Hold the page very straight, without tilting it. Stare at the fixation point. Adjust the angle and distance of the paper until the black spot on the left disappears. Repeat with the left eye closed. with permission, from P.H. Lindsay and D.A. Norman, *Human Information Processing*. New York: Academic Press, 1972

blind spot because objects whose borders extend past the boundaries of the blind spot tend to be seen as filled in, as without gaps.

What is going on when one's blind spot is seen as filled in – as without gaps in the scene? Is it analogous to acquiring the non-visual representation (belief) that Bowser, the family dog, is under the bed, on

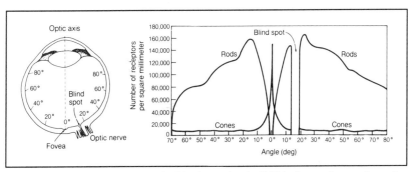

Figure 6.2: *Left*, the human eye. The blind spot (optic disk) is that region on the retina where the ganglion cells leave the retina and project to the lateral geniculate nucleus of the thalamus. *Right*, the packing density of light-sensitive cones is greatest at the fovea, decreasing sharply in the peripheral field. Rod density is greatest in the region that immediately surrounds the fovea, and gradually decreases in the more peripheral regions. Notice that the region of the blind spot is in the peripheral field, and is larger than the foveal area.

the basis of one's visual perception of his tail sticking out? Or is it more akin to regular visual perception of the whole Bowser in one's *peripheral but non-blind field?* That is, is the representation itself a visual representation, involving visual experiences? In *Consciousness Explained* (1991) Dennett favours the first hypothesis, which he sums up in his discussion of filling in: "The fundamental flaw in the idea of 'filling in' is that it suggests that the brain is providing something when in fact the brain is ignoring something" (356).

We understand Dennett to mean that in the monocular condition the person may represent that there is a non-gappy object – say, a vertical bar – in his visual field, but not because his brain generates a non-gappy *visual* representation of the vertical bar. In explicating his positive view on filling in, Dennett invites us to understand filling in of the blind spot by analogy to one's impression on walking into a room wallpapered with pictures of Marilyn Monroe:

> Consider how your brain must deal with wallpaper, for instance... Your brain just represents *that* there are hundreds of identical Marilyns, and no matter how vivid your impression is that you see all that detail, the detail is in the world, not in your head. And no figment gets used up in rendering the seeming, for the seeming isn't rendered at all, even as a bitmap. (355)

If, as instructed, we are to apply this to the case of filling in of the blind spot, presumably Dennett's point is that no matter how vivid one's impression that one sees a solid bar, one's brain actually just represents that there is a solid bar. Dennett's claim, as he clarifies later, is that the brain ignores the absence of data from the region of the blind spot. In what follows, we shall show that contrary to Dennett, the data strongly imply that at least some instances of filling in do indeed involve the brain "providing" something.

One preliminary semantic point should be made first to forestall needless metaphysical tut-tutting. Hereafter in discussing whether someone's perception of an object – say, an apple – is filled in, we shall, *as a convenient short-hand*, talk about whether or not "the apple is filled in." In availing ourselves of this expedient, we do *not* suppose that there might be a little (literal) apple or a (literal) picture of an apple in someone's head which is the thing that is filled in. Rather, we refer merely to some property of the brain's visual representation such that the perceiver sees a non-gappy apple.

Very crudely speaking, current neurobiological data suggest that when one sees an apple, the brain is in some state that can be described as representing an apple. This representation probably consists of a pattern of activity across some set of neurons, particularly those in visual cortex, that have some specific configuration of synaptic weights and a specific profile of connectivity (P.M. Churchland 1989). Given this general characterization of a representation, the question we want to address can now be rephrased: does filling in an apple-representation consist in the visual cortex generating a representation which more closely resembles the standard case of an apple-representation of an apple in the peripheral visual field? Or does it consist, as Dennett (1992) suggests, in a non-visual representation rather like one's non-visual representation of the dog under the bed?

Our approach to these questions assumes that *a priori* reflection will have value mainly as a spur to empirical investigation, but not as a method that can be counted upon by itself to reveal any facts. Thought-experiments are no substitute for real experiments. To understand what is going on such that the blind spot is seen as filled in (non-gappy), it will be important to know more about the psychological and neurobiological parameters. In addition to exploring filling in of the blind spot, other versions of visual filling in, such as the filling in experienced by subjects with cortical lesions, can also be studied. Although a more complete study would make an even wider sweep, embracing modalities other than vision, for reasons of space we narrow the discussion to visual filling in.

2. Psychophysical Data: The Blind Spot

To investigate the conditions of filling in, Ramachandran (1992) presented a variety of stimuli to subjects who were instructed to occlude one eye and fixate on a specified marker. Stimuli were then presented in various parts of the field in the region of the subject's blind spot. If a bar extends to the boundary on either side of the blind spot, but not across it (Figure 6.3), will the subject see it as complete or as having a gap? Subjects see it as complete. If, however, only the lower bar segment or only the upper bar segment is presented alone, the subject does not see the bar as filled in across the blind spot (Figure 6.4). What happens when the upper bar and the lower bar are different colours (e.g. upper red, lower green)? Subjects still see the bar as complete, with extensions of both the red and green bar, but they do not see a border where the red and green meet, and hence they cannot say just where one colour begins and the other leaves off. (For the explanation of non-perception of a border in terms of semi-segregated pathways for functionally specific tasks, see Ramachandran 1992.)

Ramachandran also found that spokes extending to but not into the blind-spot boundary were filled in, demonstrating that filling in can be very complex. Suppose there is a kind of competition between completion of a black bar across the blind spot and completion of an illusory contour lengthwise across the blind spot. Will the illusory contour or

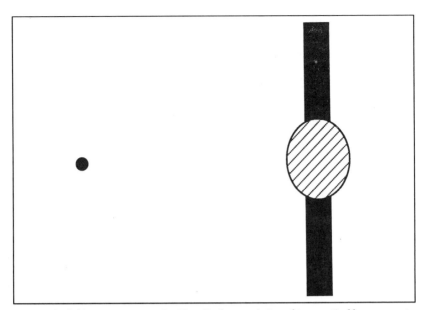

Figure 6.3: Subjects are presented with a display consisting of two vertical bar segments, separated by a gap of about 5°, and this gap is positioned to coincide with the subject's blind spot. Fixation is to the right for left-eye viewing. Subjects report seeing an uninterrupted bar.

the real contour complete? Ramachandran discovered that in this test, the illusory contour typically completes (Figures 6.5A and 6.5B.

Ramachandran next explored the relation between subjective completion of a figure and that figure's role in illusory motion (Figure 6.6). The basic question is this: does the brain treat a filled-in bar like a solid bar or like a gappy bar? In the control case, the upper gappy bar is

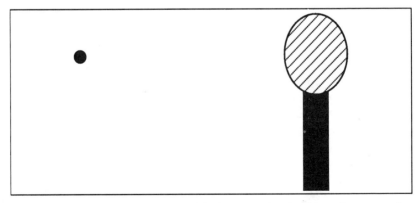

Figure 6.4: If only the lower segment of the bar is presented, subjects do not complete across the blind spot.

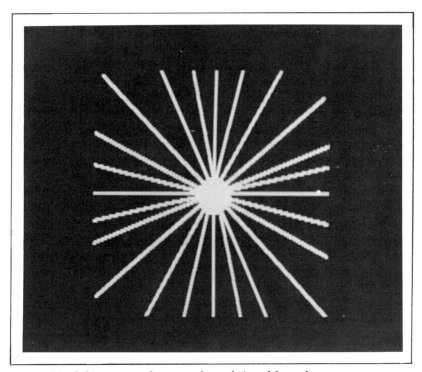

Figure 6.5A: Subjects reported perceptual completion of the spokes.

replaced with lower gappy bar (delay about 100 to 200 msec.) Because the gap in the upper bar is offset with respect to the gap in the lower bar, subjects see illusory motion in a diagonal direction from left to right. In the experimental (monocular) condition, the gap in the upper bar is positioned so that it falls in the subject's blind spot, and the subject sees a completed bar. Now when the upper bar is replaced by the lower bar to generate illusory motion, subjects see the bar moving vertically, *non-diagonally*, just as one does if a genuinely solid bar is replaced by the lower bar. This experiment shows that the brain treats a completed bar just as it treats a genuinely non-gappy bar in the perception of illusory motion.

According to Dennett's characterization of filling in (1992, 356), the brain follows the general principle that says, in effect, just more of the same inside the blind spot as outside. Several of Ramachandran's results are directly relevant to this claim. If filling in is just a matter of continuing the pattern outside the blind spot, then in Figure 6.7, subjects should see an uninterrupted string of red circle, as a red circle fills the blank space where the blind spot is. In fact, however, subjects see an interrupted sequence; that is, they see two upper red circles, two lower red circles, and a white gap in between. In a different experiment, subjects are presented with a display of "bagels," with one bagel positioned so that its hole falls within the subject's blind spot (Figure 6.8). The 'more of the same' principle presumable predicts that subjects will see only bagels in the display, as one apparently sees 'more Marilyns'. So the blind spot should not fill in with the colour of

Figure 6.5B: An illusory vertical strip was displayed so that a segment of the illusory contour fell on the blind spot. Subjects reported completion of the illusory strip rather than completion of the horizontal lines.

Figure 6.6: To generate illusory motion, the upper bar is replaced by the lower bar. When the gap in the bar is located outside the blind spot, subjects see diagonal movement. When the gap coincides with subjects' blind spot, the movement appears to be vertical.

its surrounding bagel. In fact, however, this is not what happens. Subjects see bagels everywhere, *save in the region of the blind spot*, where they see a disk, uniformly coloured.

3. Psychophysical Data: Cortical Scotomata

A lesion to early areas of visual cortex (V1, V2; i.e., areas 17, 18) typically results in a blind area in the visual field of both eyes. The standard optometric test for determining scotomata consists in flashing a

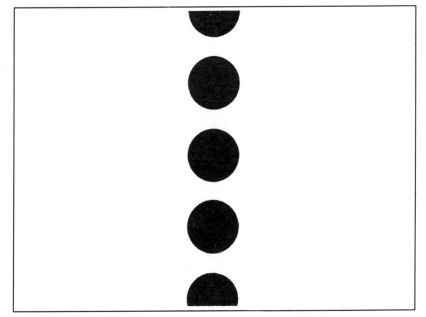

Figure 6.7: If the display is positioned so that a circle falls in the blind spot, subjects report a gap, not completion.

point of light in various locations of the visual field. Subjects are instructed to indicate, verbally or by button-pressing, when they see a flash. Using this method, the size and location of a field defect can be determined. Ramachandran, Rogers-Ramachandran and Damasio (1992) explored the spatial and temporal characteristics of filling in of the scotoma in two patients (BM and JR).

BM had a right occipital pole lesion caused by a penetrating skull fracture. He had a paracentral left hemifield scotoma, 6° by 6°, with clear margins. JR had a right occipital lesion caused by hemorrhage and a left visual field scotoma 12° in width and 6° in height. The locations of the lesions were determined by magnetic resonance (MR) scanning. Both patients were intelligent and otherwise normal neurologically. Vision was 20/20. BM was tested six months and JR eight months after the lesion events. Neither experienced his scotoma as a gap or hole in his visual field, but each was aware of the field defect. For example, each noticed some instances of "false" filling in of a real gap in an

Figure 6.8: The display consists of yellow bagels and a fixation marker. The hole in one bagel (labelled *b*) coincides with the subject's blind spot. Subjects report seeing a yellow *disk* at this location, indicating that the yellow bagel filled in.

object. Additionally, they noticed that small, separable components of objects were sometimes unperceived, and noticed as missing. For example, one subject mistook the Women's room for the Men's room because the 'WO' of 'WOMEN'S' fell into the scotoma. Seeing 'MEN'S', the subject walked directly in and quickly discovered his mistake.

In brief, the major findings of Ramachandran, Rogers-Ramachandran and Damasio are as follows. (1) A 3° gap in a vertical line is completed across the scotoma, the completion taking about 6 seconds. The duration was determined by asking the patients to press a button when the line segment was completely filled in. Even with repeated trials, the latency remained the same.

(2) One patient (JR) reported that his perception of the filled-in line segment persisted for an average of 5.3 seconds after the upper and lower lines were turned off. The delay in completion as well as the persistence of "fill" is intriguing, and it is not seen in non-traumatic blind-spot filling in.

(3) When the top and bottom segments of the line were misaligned horizontally by 2°, both patients first reported seeing two misaligned segments separated by a gap. After observing this for a few seconds, they spontaneously reported that the upper and lower line segments began to drift towards each other, moving into alignment, then slowly (over a period of about 10 seconds) the line segments filled in to form a single line spanning the scotoma (Figure 6.9). The realignment and visual completion took 6.8 seconds on average.

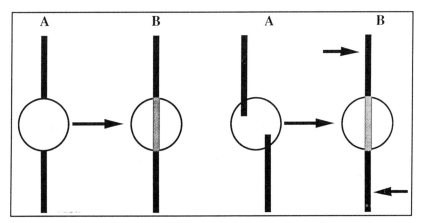

Figure 6.9: Schematic illustration of the stimuli shown to patients. The circle represents (roughly) the region of the patient's scotoma; fixation was approximately center field. *Left*, two bar segments were displayed on either side of the scotoma. The bar was vividly completed; the process of completion took about 4 to 5 seconds. *Right*, the vertical bar segments were misaligned in the horizontal plane. After a few seconds of viewing, patients reported the lines moving toward each other until they became colinear. They then gradually began to complete across the scotoma.

(4) When viewing dynamic 2-D noise (e.g. "snow" on a television screen), one patient reported that the scotoma was first filled in with static (non-flickering) noise for 7 or 8 seconds before the random spots began to move and flicker. When the noise was composed of red pixels of randomly varying luminance, JR reported seeing the red colour bleeding into the scotoma almost immediately, followed about 5 seconds later by the appearance of the dynamic texture.

(5) When a vertical column of spots (periodicity > 2°) was used instead of a solid line, both patients clearly saw a gap. When the spacing was reduced (periodicity < 0.3°), patients reported seeing completion across the scotoma of a dotted line. These conditions were repeated using X's instead of spots, and the results were comparable (Figure 6.10). Presenting a wavy, vertically oriented sinusoidal line (0.5 cycle/degree) with a gap matching the height of the patient's scotoma, both patients reported clearly seeing a non-gappy sinusoidally wavy line.

(6) Each patient reported seeing illusory contours filled in across his scotoma. The experiment was similar to that performed with normal subjects (see again Figure 6.5), save that the display was positioned so that the scotoma lined up with the gap in the stimuli. First, two horizontal line segments bordering the scotoma were presented, and, as expected, they completed across the gap. Next, when an aligned array of horizontal lines were presented, the horizontal bars did not

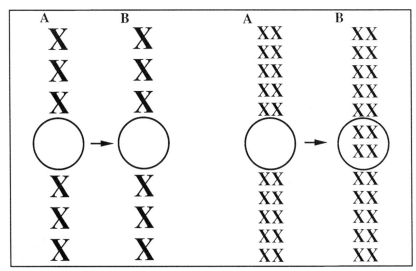

Figure 6.10: *Left*, a column of large X's was not completed across the scotoma. *Right*, a column of small X's did complete. If the column consisted of small horizontal lines segments, the results were similar.

complete across the gap, and instead patients saw the vertical illusory strip complete across the scotoma.

(7) Patients were presented with a checkerboard pattern, both fine (< 0.3°) and coarse (> 1.5°) grained, which were readily filled in. When the checkerboard texture was subjected to counterphase flicker (7.5 Hz flicker; 0.6 check width). BM completed the flickering checks. JR, however, reported that as soon as the pattern was made to flicker, he saw non-flickering stationary checks inside his scotoma, with the result that the margins of his scotoma became "entopically" visible. After about 8 seconds, JR saw the dynamic checks everywhere, including inside his scotoma.

(8) To determine whether these filling-in effects might be seen in patients with laser-induced paracentral *retinal* scotomata, the tests were repeated on two such patients. Ramachandran and colleagues found that (a) gaps in bars were not completed; (b) there was no motion or completion of misaligned bars; (c) the coarse checkerboard did not complete; (d) fine-grained 2-D random-dot textures were completed. This suggests that many of the completion effects are of cortical origin.

In the lesion studies, the time course for filling in, together with the subject's reports, indicate that the completion is a visual phenomenon rather than a non-visual judgment or representation. For example, when their spontaneous reports were tested with comments such as "you mean you *think* that the checkerboard is uniform everywhere," the patients would respond with emphatic denials such as "Doctor, I don't merely *think* it is there; I *see* that it is there." Insofar as there is nothing in the visual stimulus corresponding to the filled-in perception, it is reasonable to infer, in contrast to Dennett, that the brain is "providing" something, not merely "ignoring something." The visual character of the phenomenon also suggests that in looking for the neurobiological mechanism, visual cortex would be a reasonable place to start.

4. Psychophysical Data: Artificial Scotomata

Ramachandran and Richard Gregory (1991) discovered a species of filling-in readily experienced by normal subjects, and conditions for which can easily be set up by anyone. The recipe is simple: adjust the television set to "snow" (twinkling pattern of dots), make a fixation point with a piece of tape, roughly in the middle of the screen, and place a square piece of grey paper, about 1 centimeter square and roughly isoluminant to the grey of the background, at a distance of about 8 centimeters from the fixation point (in peripheral vision). Both eyes may be open, and after about 10 seconds of viewing the fixation point, the square in peripheral vision vanishes completely. Thereafter, one sees a uniformly twinkling screen. Insofar as this paradigm yields filling in that is reminiscent of filling in of the blind spot and cortical scotoma, it can be described as inducing a kind of artificial blind spot. Hence Ramachandran and Gregory called it an "artificial scotoma" (Figure 6.11).

By using a computer to generate visual displays, many different arrangements of background texture and artificial scotomata can be investigated. In exploring the variety of conditions for filling in of an artificial scotoma, Ramachandran and Gregory found a number of striking results, several of which we briefly outline here:

(1) Subjects tended to report filling in from outside the grey square to the inside, with a time scale of about 5 to 10 seconds.

(2) Once subjects reported filling in to be complete, the background twinkles were then turned off. Subjects now reported that they *continued* to see twinkling in the 'scotomic' square for about 3 to 4 seconds after the background twinkles disappeared.

(3) Suppose the background screen is pink, twinkles are white. The 'scotomic' square is, as before, grey, but within the square, dots are moving not randomly but coherently, left to right. Subjects report seeing a completely pink screen after about 5 to 10 seconds, but report

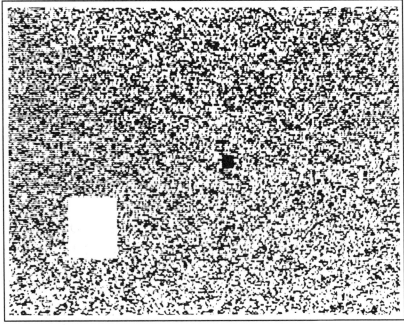

Figure 6.11: Display for artificial scotoma conditions consists of a background texture, fixation point and small segment in the peripheral field with a different texture, roughly isoluminant to the background.

that the dots in the square continue to move coherently from left to right. After a few more seconds, however, they report seeing uniformly random twinkles everywhere. Note that the artificial scotoma is in peripheral vision, where resolution is much poorer than in the foveal region (see again Figure 6.2). The twinkles that are filled in look just the same as the twinkles elsewhere in the peripheral field.

(4) If the screen is covered in text, the peripheral square comes to be filled in with text (Figure 6.12).

(5) If a smaller square with black borders is inscribed within the region of the grey square, subjects report that the inner area does not fill in with background texture.

Many other experiments in artificial scotomata are now underway in Ramachandran's laboratory, and those few cited here mark only the first pass in exploring a salient and intriguing visual phenomenon. For our purposes here, it is perhaps enough to note that so far as we can determine, the results from artificial scotoma experiments do not confirm Dennett's (1992) hypothesis that for phenomena such as filling in, "we can already be *quite* sure that the medium of representation is a

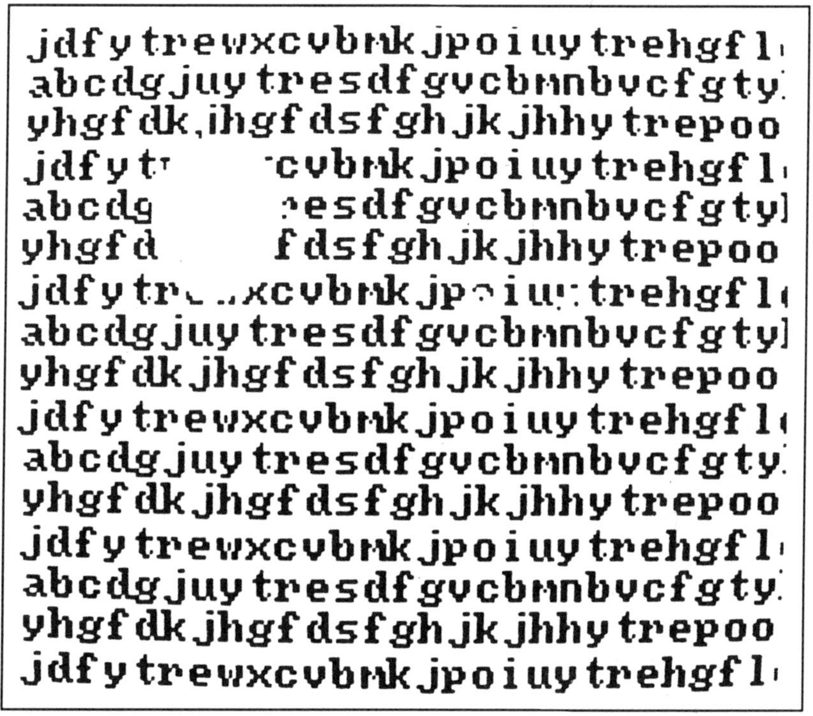

```
jdfy trewxcvbrik jpo i uy trehgf l ı
abcdg juy tresdf gvcbrinbvcf g ty.
yhgf dk,ihgf ds f gh jk jhhy trepoo
jdfy tʳ      ·cvbrik jpo i uy trehgf l ı
abcdg        ·esdf gvcbrinbvcf g ty]
yhgf d       f ds f gh jk jhhy trepoo
jdfy trʟ ..xcvbrik jpↄ i uⁱ: trehgf l ı
abcdg juy tresdf gvcbrinbvcf g ty]
yhgf dk jhgf ds f gh jk jhhy trepoo
jdfy trewxcvbrik jpo i uy trehgf l ı
abcdg juy tresdf gvcbrinbvcf g ty.
yhgf dk jhgf ds f gh jk jhhy trepoo
jdfy trewxcvbrik jpo i uy trehgf l ı
abcdg juy tresdf gvcbrinbvcf g ty.
yhgf dk jhgf ds f gh jk jhhy trepoo
jdfy trewxcvbrik jpo i uy trehgf l ı
```

Figure 6.12: The filling in of the artificial scotoma can be complex. In this condition, subjects report that the text fills in.

version of something efficient, like color-by-numbers [which gives a single label to a whole region], not roughly continuous, like bitmapping" (354).

5. Psychophysics and the Krauskopf Effect

Krauskopf (1963) discovered a remarkable filling-in phenomenon. In his set-up, a green disk is superimposed on a larger orange disk. The inner boundary (between green and orange) is stabilized on the retina so that it remains on exactly the same retinal location no matter how the eyes jitter and saccade, but the outer boundary moves across the retina as the eyes jitter and saccade. After a few seconds of image stabilization, the subject no longer sees a green disk; instead, the entire region is seen as uniformly orange – as filled in with the background colour.

Using the Krauskopf image stabilization method to explore additional aspects of the filling-in phenomenon, Thomas Piantanida and his colleagues have found more remarkable filling-in results. It is known that adaptation to yellow light alters a subject's sensitivity to a small flickering blue light; more exactly, flicker sensitivity is reduced in the presence of a yellow adapting background. *Prima facie* this is odd, given that 'blue' cones are essentially insensitive to yellow light (it is the 'red' and 'green' cones that are sensitive to yellow light). Piantanida (1985) asked this question: is blue flicker sensitivity the same if yellow adaptation is obtained by subjective *filling in of yellow* rather than by actual yellow light illuminating the retina?

To get a perception of yellow in an area where the retina was not actually illuminated with yellow light, Piantanida presented subjects with a yellow bagel, whose inner boundary was stabilized on the retina (using a dual Purkinje eye-tracker) and whose outer boundary was not stabilized. The finding was that the yellow background achieved by image stabilization was *as effective* in reducing 'blue' cone flicker sensitivity as an actual yellow stimulus. This probably means, therefore, that the reduction in flicker sensitivity as a function of perceived background is a cortical rather than a retinal effect. The most likely hypothesis is that cortical circumstances relevantly like those produced by retinal stimulation with yellow light are produced by yellow filling in, and hence the adaptation effects are comparable.

There is a further and quite stunning result reported by Crane and Piantanida (1983) that is especially relevant here. They presented subjects with a stimulus consisting of a green stripe adjacent to a red stripe, where the borders between them were stabilized, but the outside borders were not stabilized. After a few seconds, the colours began to fill in across the stabilized border. At this point, some observers described what they saw as a new and unnamable color that was somehow a mixture of red and green. Similar results were obtained with yellow and blue. Produced extraretinally, these visual perceptions of hitherto unperceived colours resulted from experimental manipulation of filling-in mechanisms – mechanisms that actively do something, as opposed to simply ignoring something. Dennett says of the blind spot, "The area is simply neglected" (355). He says that "the brain doesn't have to 'fill in' for the blind spot since the region in which the blind spot falls is already labelled (e.g. 'plaid' or 'Marilyns' or just 'more of the same')" (355). Part of the trouble with Dennett's approach to the various filling-in phenomena is that he confidently prejudges what the neurobiological data at the cellular level will look like. Reasoning more like a computer engineer who knows a lot about the architectural details of the device in front of him than like a neurobiologist who realizes how much is still to be learned about the brain, Dennett jumps to conclusions about what the brain does not need to do, ought to do, and so forth.

In sections 6 and 7 below, we discuss neurophysiological data that conflict with Dennett's claim that "There are no homunculi, as I have put it, who are supposed to 'care about' information arising from the part of the visual field covered by the blind spot, so when nothing arrives, there is no one to complain" (357). And again: "The brain's motto for handling the blind spot could be: Ask me no questions and I'll tell you no lies" (356). While Dennett's idea may seem to have some engineering plausibility, it is really a bit of *a priori* neurophysiology gone wrong. Biological solutions, alas, are not easily predicted from reasonable engineering considerations. What might, from our limited vantage point, have the earmarks of sound engineering strategy, is, often as not, out of kilter with the way Nature does it.

6. The Blind Spot and Cortical Physiology: The Gattass Effect

There are upwards of 20 cortical visual areas in each hemisphere of monkeys, and probably at least that many in humans. Many of these areas are retinotopically mapped, in the sense that neighbouring cells have neighbouring receptive fields; i.e., neighbourhood points in the visual field will be represented by neighbouring cells in the cortex. In particular, visual area V1, has been extensively explored (Figure 6.13). The receptive field size of V1 cell is about 2 to 3°, and hence are much smaller than the size of the blind spot (about 6° x 4.5°).

Ricardo Gattass and his colleagues (Fiorani et al. 1990; Gattass et al. 1992; Fiorani et al. forthcoming) were the first to try to answer the

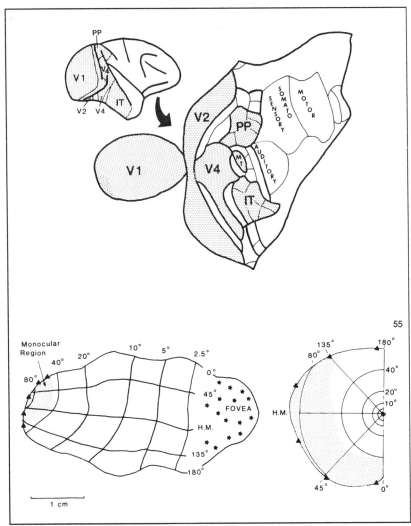

Figure 6.13: *Upper*, visual areas in the cerebral cortex of the macaque, as seen in a lateral view of the right hemisphere, and (*arrow*) in an unfolded two-dimensional map. The primary visual cortex (V1) is topographically organized. Lines of eccentricity (semicircles in the visual field drawing on *lower right*) map onto contours that run approximately vertically on the cortical map (*lower left*). Lines of constant polar angle (rays emanating from the center of gaze in the visual field) map onto contours that run approximately horizontally on the cortical map. The foveal representation (asterisks) corresponding to the central 2° radius, occupies slightly more than 10 percent of V1. The monocular region (stipple) in the visual field occupies a very small region of the cortical map. From D.C. Van Essen and C.H. Anderson, 1990. Information processing in primate vision. In S.F. Zornetzer, J.L. Davis and C. Lau (eds.), *An Introduction to Neural and Electronic Networks*. San Diego: Academic Press.

following question: how do V1 cells corresponding to the region of the blind spot for the right eye respond when the left eye is closed and a stimulus is presented to the open right eye (and vice versa)?

For ease of reference hereafter, by 'Gattass condition' we denote the set-up in which the experimenter records from single cells in V1 in the general area corresponding to the optic disk when the stimulus is presented to the contralateral (opposite side) eye. Call the V1 region corresponding to the optic disk of the contralateral eye, the *optic disk cortex*, 'ODC'. The optic disk is that region of retina where no transducers exist, corresponding to that part of the visual field where the blind spot resides. Remember that if a cortical region corresponds to the optic disk for the contralateral eye, it will correspond to the normal retinal area for the ipsilateral (same side) eye. See Figure 6.14 for projection patterns.

The seemingly obvious answer to Gattass's question – and the answer Gattass and colleagues expected – is that the ODC cells will not respond in the monocular condition to stimuli presented in the contralateral blind spot. That is, one would predict that the cells in that region are responsive only to stimuli from the non-blind region of the ipsilateral eye. This is not what they found. Applying standard physiological mapping techniques to monkeys, and using the conventional bars of light as stimuli, they tested the responses of ODC cells (left hemisphere) with the left eye closed. As they moved the bar of light around and recorded from single cells, they found that neurons in the ODC area responded very well. That is, cells corresponding to the blind spot gave consistent responses to a bar of light passing through the blind sector of the visual field. The response data did, however, show that the ODC was somewhat less neatly mapped by contralateral stimuli (i.e., in the blind spot) than by ipsilateral stimuli (i.e., in the non-blind field).

For some cells, an excitatory receptive field – presumably an interpolated receptive field – located *inside* the ODC could be specified. Exploring further, they found that sweeping bars on only one end of the blind spot yielded poor responses or none at all. In other cells, they discovered that the sum of responses to two bar-segments entering either end of the blind spot was comparable to the response for a single non-gappy bar. This indicates that some cells in the Gattass conditions exhibit discontinuous receptive fields, presumably via interpolation signals from other neurons with neighbouring receptive fields. To study the relevance of neighbouring relations, Gattass and colleagues masked the area immediately surrounding the optic disk during stimulus presentations to the blind spot region of the visual field. They discovered responses of the ODC neurons were abolished in the masked

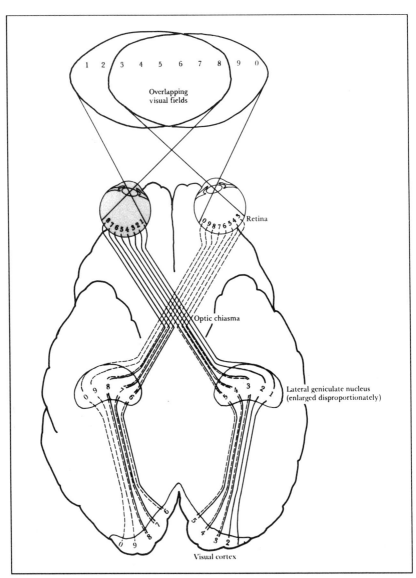

Figure 6.14: Schematic illustration of the projection pathways from the retina to the cortex, showing which parts of the visual field are represented in specific parts of the lateral geniculate nucleus (LGN) and the visual cortex. Notice that the left *hemifield* projects to the right lateral geniculate nucleus (contralateral), which in turn projects to the right hemisphere. The blind spot of the left eye corresponds approximately to the region coded as '3', which is part of the central region where the fields of the two eyes overlap. By tracking '3' from the field, to the retina, to the LGN and the cortex, one can track the pathway for a particular stimulus in the blind region of the left eye. With permission, from P.H. Lindsay and D.A. Norman, *Human Information Processing*. New York: Academic Press, 1972.

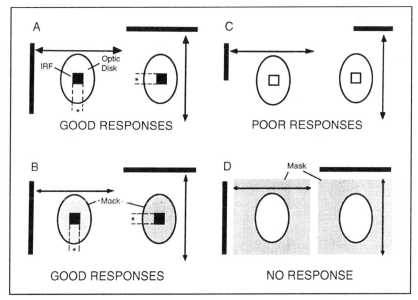

Figure 6.15: Summary of responses of cortical neurons in the ODC region to bars and masks of varying sizes. IRF: Interpolated receptive field. Asterisks indicate locations where stimulation with long bars elicited responses. (From M. Fiorani, M.G.P. Rosa, R. Gattass and C.E. Rocha-Miranda (forthcoming), Visual responses outside the "classical" receptive field in primate striate cortex: A possible correlate of perceptual completion. *Proceedings of the National Academy of Science.*

condition (Figures 6.15, 6.16A and 6.16B). Fifteen out of 43 neurons (mostly from layer 4cα) were found to exhibit interpolation properties across a region of the visual field at least three times the size of the classical receptive field.

7. Artificial Scotomata and Cortical Physiology: The Gilbert Effect

How do cortical cells respond when their receptive field corresponds to the area of an artificial scotoma, such as the kind Ramachandran and Gregory studied? (For ease of reference, hereafter call these cortical neurons "artificial scotoma" [AS] cells.) Or when the area of both retinae from which they receive projections is lesioned? (Hereafter, call these cortical neurons "retinal lesion" [RL] cells.) These questions have been addressed by Charles Gilbert and colleagues of Rockefeller University. Recording from V1 in monkeys, they discovered that the receptive fields of cortical cells surrounding the cortical RL cells expanded in several minutes so that collectively they covered that part of the visual field normally covered by the RL cortical cells (Gilbert and Wiesel 1992).

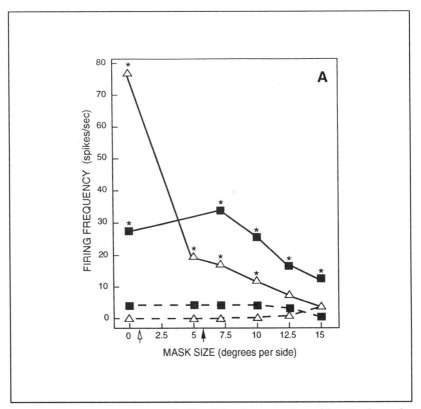

Figure 6.16A: Mean response rate of a V1 cell for 10 presentations of the stimulus under different masking conditions. Triangles and filled squares linked by continuous lines show response to ipsilateral and contralateral eye, respectively, in paired trials. The lower (dotted) lines show the mean spontaneous activity where each eye is opened separately. The size of the ipsilateral classical receptive field is shown by an outlined arrow, and the diameter of the optic disc by a filled arrow. *Proceedings of the National Academy of Science.*

A similar result was found in the artificial scotoma experiments in cats (Pettet and Gilbert 1991). The cortical cells in V1 surrounding the AS cortical cells very quickly expanded their receptive fields to include the area normally in the domain of the AS cells. The receptive field expansion was on the order of three-to fivefold. It was observed as soon as tests could be made (2 minutes), and it was reversible, in that once the experimental condition was removed and a standard, non-scotomic stimulus was presented, normal mapping of cortical cells was restored. Although the neurobiological basis for this modification/interpolation in receptive field properties has not yet been determined, it is conjectured that lateral interactions within the cortex are probably crucial.

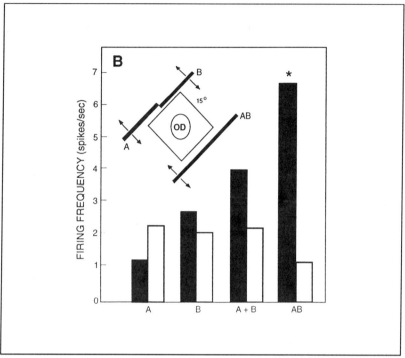

Figure 6.16B: Black bars: mean response frequency of the same neuron to stimulation over a mask 15° per side. Open bars show the mean spontaneous activity in paired trials without stimulation. (From M. Fiorani, M.G.P. Rosa, R. Gattass and C.E. Rocha-Miranda (forthcoming), Visual responses outside the "classical" receptive field in primate striate cortex: A possible correlate of perceptual completion. *Proceedings of the National Academy of Science.*

The Gattass effect together with the Gilbert effect are important evidence that the receptive fields of cortical cells are dynamic and can be modified on very short time scales. What precisely this means in terms of the neurobiological mechanisms of visual experience will require many more experiments. In any case, it is unlikely that the results are irrelevant to determining whether the brain merely ignores the blind spot or whether there is an active process related to filling in. As we try to track down the neurobiology of visual awareness, the discoveries in neuroscience are important clues to the nature of visual processing and to that component of the processing relevant to visual awareness.

Do the results from Gattass et al. and Gilbert et al. mean that, contrary to Dennett's assurances, filling in *is* rendered as a bit-map? No. The choices here are not exhausted by Dennett's alternatives "bit map or colour-by-number." We suspect that neither the bit-map metaphor nor the colour-by-numbers metaphor is even remotely adequate to the kind of representation and computation in nervous systems. Indeed, the very lability of a neuron's response properties and receptive field properties means the bit-map metaphor is misleading. In order to understand more clearly how to interpret the results from Gattass and colleagues, and from Gilbert and Wiesel, much more needs to be known about interpolation in neural networks and about the interaction of neurons within a mapped region and between regions. The fact is that very little is known at this point about the detailed nature of neural computation and representation, though we are at a stage where computer models highly constrained by neurobiological and psychophysical data can yield important clues (Churchland and Sejnowski 1992).

8. Conclusion

In *Consciousness Explained*, Dennett quite properly debunks the idea that the brain contains a Cartesian Theatre wherein images and the like are displayed. But the hypothesis that filling in (perceptual completion) may sometimes involve the brain's interpolating ("contributing something rather than ignoring something") certainly need have no truck whatever with Cartesian Theaters, either implicitly or explicitly, either metaphorically or literally, either *sotto voce* or *viva voce*. Given the data from psychophysics and neurophysiology, we hypothesize that (1) the brain has mechanisms for interpolation, some of which may operate early in visual processing; (2) brains sometimes visually represent completions, including quite complex completions and (3) such representation probably involves those interpolation mechanisms.

How did Dennett come to embrace a conclusion so manifestly contrary to the data, some of which was readily available when his book was published? And why does "filling in" play such an important role in *Consciousness Explained*? According to our analysis, the answer derives from the background behaviourist ideology that is endemic to Dennett's work from the very beginning – from his first book, *Content and Consciousness* (1969) through *Brainstorms* (1978), *Elbow Room* (1984), *The Intentional Stance* (1987) and *Conciousness Explained* (1991).

Simplified, the heart of Dennett's behaviourism is this: the conceptual framework of the mental does not denote anything real in the brain. The importance of the framework derives not from its description of neural or any other reality; rather, it is an organizing instrument that allows us to do fairly well in explaining and predicting one another's behaviour, the literal unreality of qualia, etc., notwithstanding. How is it that the framework manages to be a useful instrument, despite the unreality of its categories? Because, according to Dennett, even though there is nothing *really* in the brain that corresponds to visual awareness of red, there is *something or other* in the brain which, luckily enough, allows us to get on pretty well in making sense of people's behaviour on the pretense, as it were, that the brain really does have states corresponding to awareness of red. As for filling in, Dennett's rhetorical strategy hoists it as *paradigmatic* of a mental thing that we mistakenly assume to be real.

Dennett's discussions regarding the dubiousness of selected old-time intuitions often fall upon receptive ears because some categories such as "the will" and "the soul" probably do not in fact correspond to anything real, and because neuroscience is bound to teach us many surprising things about the mental, including that some of our fundamental categories can be improved upon. The sweeping behaviourism and instrumentalism, however, does not follow from these observations about revisability of psychological concepts – nor even from the eliminability by cognitive neuroscience of *some* concepts that turn out to be the psychological counterpart of "phlogiston," "impetus," and "natural place." Thus one may readily concur that qualia cannot be little pictures displayed in the brain's Cartesian Theatre and that the self is not a little person tucked away in the folds of frontal cortex. These debunking treats are, however, just the teaspoon of sugar that helps the medicine go down. And the medicine, make no mistake, is behaviourism. The elixir is *Gilbert Ryle's "Ghost-Be-Gone"* (Ryle 1949). Taken regularly, it is supposed to prevent the outbreak of mental realism. Drawing on AI's conceptual repertoire of the "virtual machine," Dennett has systematically argued *against* the neural reality, and *for* the merely instrumental utility, of mental categories generally. Dennett's engaging exposition and brilliantly inventive metaphors tend to mask the fact that this less palatable message is indeed the main message (see also McCauley, forthcoming).

This brief excursion through Dennett's behaviourism and instrumentalism may help explain why he is found defending assorted theses that are highly implausible from a scientific perspective: the brain does not fill in; there is nothing whatever ("no fact of the matter") to distinguish between a misperception and a misrecollection; there is no time before which one is not aware of, say, a sound, and after which one is aware; human consciousness is a virtual machine that comes into being as humans learn to talk to themselves, and so forth (Dennett 1991).

Scientific realism, in contrast to Dennett's instrumentalism, (P.M. Churchland 1979;1989) proposes that we determine by empirical means by converging research from experimental psychology, neuropsychology and neuroscience – what hypotheses are probably true and hence what categories truly apply to the mind-brain. Some categories may be largely correct, for example 'visual perception'; some, for example 'memory', 'attention' and 'consciousness' appear to be subdividing, budding, and regrouping; and some may be replaced by high-level categories that are more empirically adequate. At this stage, it is reasonable to consider sensory experiences to be real states of the brain, states whose neurobiological properties will be discovered as cognitive neuroscience proceeds (P.S. Churchland 1986;1989; P.M. Churchland 1989).

Perhaps Dennett's main achievement consists in showing the Cartesian dangers waiting to ensnare those who refer to perceptual filling in by means of the expression "filling in." If so, then the achievement is primarily semantic, not empirical. Furthermore, his aim could be satisfied merely instructing us on the dangers, without requiring also that the very description "filling in" be expunged as untrue of what goes on in the brain. In any case, one might well wonder whether Dennett overestimates the naïveté amongst scientists. To judge from the literature (see references below), those who scientifically study perceptual completion phenomena understand perfectly well that filling in involves no Cartesian Theatres, ghosts, paint, little pictures, putty knives or homunculi. At the very least, they are no more addled by metaphor than is Dennett when he refers to the brain as "editing multiple drafts." Taken as a linguistic prohibition rather than an empirical hypothesis about the mind-brain, Dennett's thesis that "the brain does not fill in" sounds uncomfortably like a quirky edict of the "word-police."

Acknowledgements

For helpful discussion at many stages, we thank Paul Churchland, Francis Crick, Peter Dayan, Bo Dahlbom, Ricardo Gattass, Read Montague, Diane Rogers-Ramachandran, Adina Roskies and Oron Shagrir.

References

Churchland, P.M. (1979). *Scientific Realism and the Plasticity of Mind.* Cambridge: Cambridge University Press

————. (1989). *A Neurocomputational Perspective.* Cambridge, MA: MIT Press

Churchland, P.S. (1986) *Neurophilosophy.* Cambridge, MA: MIT Press

————. (1988). Reduction and the neurobiological basis of consciousness. In A.J. Marcel and E. Bisiach (eds.), *Consciousness in Contemporary Science.* Oxford: Oxford University Press. 273-304

Churchland, P.S. and T.J. Sejnowski (1992). *The Computational Brain.* Cambridge, MA: MIT Press

Crane, H.D., and T.P. Piantanida (1983) On seeing reddish-green and yellowish-blue. *Science* 221: 1078-79

Dennett, D.C. (1969). *Content and Consciousness*. London: Routledge and Kegan Paul

———. (1978). *Brainstorms*. Cambridge, MA: MIT Press

———. (1984). *Elbow Room*. Cambridge, MA: MIT Press

———. (1987). *The Intentional Stance*. Cambridge, MA: MIT Press

———. (1991). *Consciousness Explained*. New York: Little, Brown

Fiorani, M., R. Gattass, M.G.P. Rosa and C.E. Rocha-Miranda (1990). Changes in receptive field (RF) size of single cells of primate V1 as a correlate of perceptual completion. *Society for Neuroscience Abstracts* 16: 1219

Fiorani, M., M.G.P. Rosa, R. Gattass and C.E. Rocha-Miranda (in press). Visual responses outside the "classical" receptive field in primate striate cortex: A possible correlate of perceptual completion. *Proceedings of the National Academy of Sciences*.

Gattass, R, M. Fiorani, M.G.P. Rosa, M.C.F. Pinon, A.P.B. Sousa and J.G.M. Soares (1992). Changes in receptive field size in Vl and its relation to perceptual completion. In R. Lent (ed.),*The Visual System from Genesis to Maturity*. Boston: Birkhauser

Gilbert, C.D., and T.N. Wiesel (1992). Receptive field dynamics in adult primary visual cortex. *Nature* 356: 150-52

Krauskopf, J. (1963). *Journal of the Optometric Society of America* 53: 741

Lindsay, P.H. and D.A. Norman (1972). *Human Information Processing*. New York: Academic Press

McCauley, R.N. (forthcoming). Why the blind can't lead the blind: Dennett on the blind spot, blind sight, and sensory qualia. *Behavior and Philosophy*.

Pettet, M.W., and C.D. Gilbert (1991). Contextual stimuli influence receptive field size of single neurons in cat primary visual cortex.*Neuroscience Abstracts* 431.12

Piantanida, T.P. (1985) Temporal modulation sensitivity of the blue mechanism: measurements made with extraretinal chromatic adaptation. *Vision Research* 25: 1439-44

Piantanida, T.P., and J. Larimer (1989). The impact of boundaries on color: stabilized image studies. *Journal of Imaging Technology* 15: 58-63

Ramachandran, V.S. (1992) Blind spots. *Scientific American* 266: 86-91

Ramachandran, V.S. (forthcoming). Filling in gaps in perception.*Current Directions in Psychological Science*.

Ramachandran, V.S., and R.L. Gregory (1991). Perceptual filling in of artificially induced scotomas in human vision. *Nature* 350: 699-702

Ramachandran, V.S., D. Rogers-Ramachandran and H. Damasio (in press) Perceptual "filling in" of scotomas of cortical origin.

Ryle, G. (1949). *The Concept of Mind*. New York: Barnes and Noble

Van Essen, D.C., and C.H. Anderson (1990). Information processing in primate vision. In S.F. Zornetzer, J.L. Davis, and C. Lau (eds.),*An Introduction to Neural and Electronic Networks*. San Diego: Academic Press

7

Seeing is Believing – Or Is It?

Daniel C. Dennett

We would all like to have a good theory of perception. Such a theory would account for all the known phenomena and predict novel phenomena, explaining everything in terms of processes occurring in nervous systems in accordance with the principles and laws already established by science: the principles of optics, physics, biochemistry and the like. Such a theory might come to exist without our ever having to answer the awkward "philosophical" question that arises:

What exactly is *the product* of a perceptual process?

There seems to be an innocuous – indeed trivial – answer:

The product of a perceptual process is *a perception*!

What could be more obvious? Some processes have products, and the products of perceptual processes are perceptions. But on reflection, is it so obvious? Do we have any idea what we might mean by this? What are perceptions? What manner of thing – state, event, entity, process – is a perception? It is merely a state of the brain, we may say (hastening to keep dualism at bay), but what could make a state of the brain a *perceptual* state as opposed to, say, merely a metabolic state, or – more to the point – a *pre*-perceptual state, or a *post*-perceptual state? For instance, the state of one's retinas at any moment is surely a state of the nervous system, but intuitively *it* is not a perception. It is something more like the raw material from which subsequent processes will eventually fashion a perception. And the state of one's motor cortex, as it triggers or controls the pressing of the YES button during a perceptual experiment is intuitively on the *other* side of the mysterious region, an effect of a perception, not a perception itself. Even the most doctrinaire behaviourist would be reluctant to identify the button-pressing behaviour of your finger as itself the perception; it is a *response* to... what? To a stimulus occurring on the retina, says the behaviourist. But now that behaviourism is history we are prepared to insist that this peripheral response is mediated by another, internal response: a perception is a response to a stimulus, and a behavioural reaction such as a button-press is a response to a perception. Or so it is natural to think.

Natural or not, such ways of thinking lead to riddles. For instance, in a so-called computer vision system does any internal state count as a perception? If so, what about a simpler device? Is a Geiger counter a perceiver – *any* sort of perceiver? Or, closer to home, is thermoregulation or electrolyte balance in our bodies accomplished by a *perceptual* process, or does such manifestly unconscious monitoring not count? If not, why not? What about "recognition" by the immune system? Should we reserve the term "perception" for processes with *conscious* products (whatever they might be), or is it a better idea to countenance not only unconscious perceptual processes but also processes with unconscious *perceptions* as their products?

I said at the outset that a good theory of perception *might* come into existence without our ever having to get clear about these awkward questions. We *might* achieve a theory of perception that answered all our detailed questions without ever tackling the big one: what is a perception? Such a state of affairs might confound the bystanders – or amuse or outrage them, but so what? Most biologists can get on with their work without getting absolutely straight about what life is, most physicists comfortably excuse themselves from the ticklish task of saying exactly what matter is. Why should perception theorists be embarrassed not to have achieved consensus on just what perception is?

"Who cares?" some may say. "Let the philosophers haggle over these stumpers, while we scientists get on with actually developing and testing theories of perception." I usually have some sympathy for this dismissive attitude, but I think that in this instance, it is a mistake. It leads to distortion and misperception of the very theories under development. A florid case of what I have in mind was recently given expression by Jerry Fodor (in a talk at MIT, November 19, 1991): "Cognitive Science is the art of pushing the soul into a smaller and smaller part of the playing field." If this is how you think – even if this is only how you think *in the back of your mind* – you are bound to keep forcing all the phenomena you study into the two varieties: pre-perceptual and post-perceptual, forever postponing a direct confrontation with the product at the presumed watershed, the perception or perceptual state itself. Whatever occupies this mysterious middle realm then becomes more and more unfathomable. Fodor, on the same occasion, went on to say in fact that there were two main mysteries in cognitive science: consciousness and the frame problem – and neither was soluble in his opinion. No wonder he thinks this, considering his vision of how Cognitive Science should proceed. This sort of reasoning leads to viewing the curving chain of causation that leads from pre-perceptual causes to post-perceptual effects as having not only a maximum but a pointed summit – with a sharp discontinuity just where the corner is turned. (As Marcel Kinsbourne has put it, people tend to imagine there is a gothic arch hidden in the mist; see Figure 7.1.)

There is no question that the corner must be turned somehow. That's what perception is: responding to something "given" by *taking* it – by responding to it in one interpretive manner or another. On the traditional view, all the taking is *deferred* until the raw given, the raw materials of stimulation, have been processed in various ways. Once each bit is "finished" it can enter consciousness and be *appreciated* for the first time. As C.S. Sherrington put it: "The mental action lies buried in the brain, and in that part most deeply recessed from outside world that is furthest from input and output" (1934, p. 23).

I call the mythical place somewhere in the centre of the brain "where it all comes together" for consciousness the Cartesian Theater (Dennett 1991, Dennett and Kinsbourne 1992). All the work that has been dimly imagined to be done in the Cartesian Theater has to be done somewhere, and no doubt all the corner-turning happens in the brain. In the model that Kinsbourne and I recommend, the Multiple Drafts Model, this single, unified taking is broken up in cerebral space and real time. We suggest that the judgmental tasks are fragmented into many distributed moments of micro-taking (Kinsbourne 1988). There is actually very little controversy about the claim that there is no place in the brain where it all comes together. What people have a hard

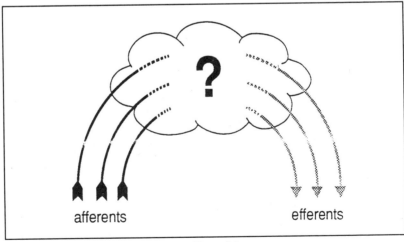

Figure 7.1

time recognizing – and we have a hard time describing – are the implications of this for other aspects of the traditional way of thinking. I want to concentrate here on just one aspect: the nature of "takings." An accompanying theme of Cartesian materialism, what with its sharp discontinuity at the summit, is the almost irresistible tendency to see a sharp distinction between, on the one hand, the items that presumably reside at the top, and, on the other hand, the various items that are their causes and effects. The basic idea is that until some content swims all the way up from the ears and retinas into this Theater, it is still just pre-conscious, pre-experienced. It has no moxie; it lacks the *je ne sais quoi* of conscious experience. And then, as the content completes its centripetal journey, it abruptly changes status, bursting into consciousness. Thereafter, the effects that flow, directly or indirectly, from the Audience Appreciation that mythically occurs in the Cartesian Theater count as post-conscious, and these effects, too, lack some special something.

Let's consider a garden variety case of this theme in slow motion, working backwards from peripheral behaviour to conscious perception. Suppose you tell me you believe in flying saucers. Let us further suppose that that behaviour – the telling – is an indirect effect of your once having been shown a highly detailed and realistic photograph of what purported to be a flying saucer. The behaviour of telling is itself an indirect effect of your belief that there are flying saucers – you are telling me what you actually believe. And that belief in turn is an effect of yet another prior belief: your belief that you were shown the photograph. And this belief that you were shown the photograph was originally supported by yet prior beliefs of yours about all the details in the photograph you were shown. Those beliefs about the particular details of the photograph and the immediate perceptual environment of your looking at it were themselves short-lived *effects* – effects of having seen the photograph. They may all have faded away into oblivion, but these *beliefs* had their onset in your memory at the very moment – or very shortly thereafter – that you had the conscious visual perception of the photograph. You believe you saw the photograph because you did see the photograph; it didn't just irradiate your retinas; you saw it, consciously, in a conscious experience.

It looks as if these perceptual beliefs are the most immediate effect of the perceptual state itself.[1] But they are *not* (it seems) the perception itself, because they are (it seems) *propositional*, not... um, *perceptual*. That at least is a common understanding of these terms. Propositional, or conceptual, representations are more abstract (in some hard-to-define way), and less, well, vivid and colourful. For instance, V.S. Ramachandran draws our attention to the way the brain seems to "fill in" the region of our blind spots in each eye, and contrasts our sense of what is in our blind spot with our sense of what objects are behind our heads: "For such objects, the brain creates what might be loosely called a logical inference. The distinction is not just semantic. Perceptual and conceptual representations are probably generated in separate regions of the brain and may be processed in very different ways" (Ramachandran 1992, 87). Just what contrast is there between perceptual and conceptual? Is it a difference in degree or kind, and is there a sharp discontinuity in the normal progression of perceptual processes? If there is, then one – and only one – of the following is the right thing to say. Which is it to be?

(1) *Seeing is believing.* My belief that I see such-and-such details in the photograph in my hand is a perceptual state, not an inferential state. I do, after all, *see* those details to be there. A visually induced belief to the effect that all those details are there just *is* the perception!

(2) *Seeing causes (or grounds) believing.* My belief that I see such-and-such details in the photograph in my hand is an inferential, nonperceptual state. It is, after all, *merely* a belief – a state that mustbe inferred from a perceptual state of actually seeing those details.

Neither, I will argue, is the right thing to say. To see why, we should consider a slightly different question, which Ramachandran goes on to ask: "How rich is the perceptual representation corresponding to the blind spot?" Answers to that eminently investigatable question are simply neutral with regard to the presumed controversy between (1) and (2). One of the reasons people tend to see a contrast between (1) and (2) is that they tend to think of perceptual states as somehow much richer in content than mere belief states. (After all, perceptions are like pictures, beliefs are like sentences, and a picture's worth a thousand words.) But these are spurious connotations. *There is no upper bound on the richness of content of a proposition.* So it would be a confusion – a simple but ubiquitous confusion – to suppose that since a perceptual state has such-and-such richness, it cannot be a propositional state, but must be a perceptual state (whatever that might be) *instead.*

No sane participant in the debates would claim that the product of perception was either literally a picture in the head or literally a sentence in the head. Both ways of talking are reckoned as metaphors, with strengths and shortcomings. Speaking, as Kinsbourne and I have done, of the Multiple *Drafts* Model of consciousness leans in the direction of the sentence metaphor, in the direction of a language of thought. (After all, those drafts must all be *written*, mustn't they?) But our model could just as readily be cast in picture talk. In Hollywood, directors, producers and stars fight fiercely over who has "final cut" – over who gets to authorize the canonical version of the film that will eventually be released to the public. According to the Multiple Cuts Model, then, nobody at Psychomount Studios has final cut; films are made, cut, edited, recut, re-edited, released, shelved indefinitely, destroyed, spliced together, run backwards and forwards – and no privileged subset of these processes counts as the Official Private Screening, relative to which any *subsequent* revisions count as unauthorized adulterations. Different versions exist within the corridors and cutting rooms of Psychomount Studios at different times and places, and no one of them counts as the definitive work.

In some regards the Multiple Cuts version is a more telling metaphor – especially as an antidote to the Cartesian Theater. There are even some useful elaborations. Imagine cutting a film into its individual frames, and then jumbling them all up – losing track of the "correct" order of the frames. Now consider the task of "putting them back in order." Numbering the frames in sequence would accomplish this, provided that any process that needs access to sequencing information can then extract that information by comparing frame numbers. There is no logical necessity actually to splice the frames in order, or line them up in spatial order on the film library shelf. And there is certainly no need to "run" them through some projector in the chosen temporal order. The chosen order can be unequivocally secured by the numbering all by itself. The counterpart in our model of consciousness is that it *does not follow* from the fact that we are equipped to make sequence judgments about events in our experience that there is *any* occurrence in real time of a sequence of neural representations of the events in the order judged. Sometimes there *may* be such a sequence occurring in the brain, but this cannot be determined simply by an analysis of the subjective content of experience; it is neither a necessary nor sufficient condition for a like-ordered subjective sequence.

In other regards, however, the Multiple Cuts version of our model is altogether too vivid, what with its suggestions of elaborate *pictorial* renderings. We should be leery of metaphor, but is there any alternative at this point? Are there any non-metaphorical ways of talking that capture the points that need making? How about the terms being popularized by the connectionists: "vector coding and vector completion"? This new way of talking about content in cognitive science is appealing partly because whatever it is, vector coding is obviously neither pictures nor words, and partly, I suspect, because none of the uninitiated dare to ask just what it means!

Let me tell you what it means, so far as I can tell. Think of an enormous multi-dimensional hyperspace of possible contents – all the possible contents a particular organism can discriminate. A vector, if I may indulge yet again in metaphor, can be considered a path leading into a particular quadrant or subspace in this hyperspace. Vector completion is just the process of pursuing a trajectory to an ultimate destination in that hyperspace. Most of the hyperspace is empty, unoccupied. When something (some *sort* of thing) has been encountered by an organism, it renders the relevant portion of the organism's hyperspace *occupied*; recognizing it again (or being reminded of it by another, similar one) is getting back to the same place, the same co-ordinates, by the same or a similar path. Vector completion creates a path to a location in content-hyperspace.

"Vector completion" talk is just as metaphorical as "language of thought" talk or "pictures in the head" talk; it is simply a *more abstract* metaphorical way of talking about content, a metaphor which neatly evades the talk of pictures versus sentences, while securing the essential informational point: to "discriminate" or "recognize" or "judge" or "turn the corner" is simply to determine some determinable aspect of content within a space of possibilities.

Vector-completion talk is thus like *possible-world semantics;* it is propositional without being sentential (see, e.g., Stalnaker 1984). It provides a way of asserting that a particular "world" or "set of worlds" has been singled out from all the possible worlds the organism might single out for one purpose or another. Acknowledging that perception or discrimination is a matter of vector completion is thus acknowledging something so uncontroversial as to be almost tautological. Vector completion is a cognitive process in the same way growing old is a biological process; short of dying, whatever you do counts.

Almost tautological, but not quite. What the connectionists argue is that as long as you have machinery that can traverse this huge state-space efficiently and appropriately (completing the vectors it *ought* to complete most of the time), you don't have to burden the system with extra machinery – scene-painting machinery *or* script-writing machinery. A highly particular content can be embodied in the state of a nervous system without having any such further properties – just so long as the right sort of transitions are supported by the machinery. Given the neutrality of vector-coding talk, there is no particular reason for the machinery described to be connectionist machinery. You could describe the most sentential and logistic of representation-systems in vector-coding terms if you wished. What you would lose would be the details of symbol-manipulation, lemma-proving, rule-consulting that carried the system down the path to completion – but if those features were deemed beneath the level of the intended model, so much the better. But – and here is the meat, at last – connectionist systems are particularly well-suited to a vector-coding description because of the way they actually accomplish state transitions. The connectionist systems created to date exhibit *fragments* of the appropriate transitional behaviour, and that's a promising sign. We just don't know, yet, whether whole cognitive systems, exhibiting all the sorts of state transitions exhibited by cognizing agents, can be stitched together from such fabrics.

One of the virtues of vector-coding talk, then, is its neutrality; it avoids the spurious connotations of pictures or sentences. But that very neutrality might actually prevent one from thinking vividly enough to dream up good experiments that reveal something about the actual machinery determining the contents. Ramachandran has conducted a series of ingenious experiments designed to shed light on the question of how rich perceptual representations are, and the metaphor of pictorial filling-in has apparently played a large role in guiding his imaginative transition from experiment to experiment (Ramachandran and Gregory 1991, Ramachandran forthcoming). I have been sharply critical of reliance on this "filling-in" metaphor, (Dennett 1991, 1992), but I must grant that any perspective on the issue that encourages dreaming these experiments up is valuable for just that reason, and should not be dismissed out of hand, even if in the end we have to fall back on some more neutral description of the phenomena.

One of the most dramatic of these experiments is Ramachandran and Gregory's "artificial scotoma" which the brain "fills in" with "twinkle." According to Ramachandran (1992), it can be reproduced at home, using an ordinary television set. (I must confess that my own efforts to achieve the effect at home have not been successful, but I do not doubt that it can be achieved under the right conditions.)

Choose an open channel so that the television produces "snow," a twinkling pattern of dots. Then stick a very tiny circular label in the middle of the screen. About eight centimeters from the label, tape on a square piece of gray paper whose sides are one centimeter and whose luminances roughly matches the gray in the snow... If you gaze at the label very steadily for about 10 seconds, you will find that the square vanishes completely and gets "replaced" be the twinkling dots... Recently we came up with an interesting variation of the original "twinkle" experiment. When a volunteer indicated that the square had been filled in with twinkling dots, we instructed the computer to make the screen uniformly gray. To our surprise, the volunteers reported that they saw a square patch of twinkling dots in the region where the original gray square had been filled in. They saw the patch for as long as 10 seconds. (Ramachandran 1992, 90)

In this new perceptual illusion, the illusory *content* is *that there is twinkling in the square*. But, one is tempted to ask, how is this content *rendered?* Is it a matter of the representation being composed of hundreds or thousands of individual illusory twinkles or is it a matter of there being, in effect, a label that just says "twinkling" attached to the representation of the square?

Can the brain represent twinkling, perceptually, without representing individual twinkles?

This is a good mind-opening question, I think. That is, if you ask yourself this question, you are apt to discover something about how you have been tacitly understanding the issues – and the terms – all along. Real twinkling – twinkling in the world – is composed of lots of individual twinkles, of course, happening at particular times and places. That's what twinkling is. But not all representations of twinkling are composed of lots of representations of individual twinkles, happening at particular times and places. For instance, this essay frequently represents twinkling, but never by representing individual twinkles. We know that during the induction phase of this experiment, over a large portion of your retina, there are individual twinkles doing their individual work of getting the twinkle-representation machinery going, by stimulating particular groups of cells at particular times and places. What we don't yet know is whether, when neurally represented twinkling "fills in" the neurally represented square area – an area whose counterpart on the retina has no individual twinkles, of course – this represented twinkling consists of individual representations of twinkles. This is part of what one might want to know, when the question one asks is: *how rich* is the neural representation? It is an empirical question, and not at all an obvious one. It does not follow from the fact that *we see the twinkling* that the individual twinkles are represented. They may be, but this has yet to be determined. The fact that the twinkling is remarkably vivid, subjectively, also settles nothing. There are equally stunning illusory effects that are *surely* not rendered in individual details.

When I first saw Bellotto's landscape painting of Dresden at the North Carolina Museum of Art in Raleigh, I marvelled at the gorgeously rendered details of all the various people walking in bright sunlight across the distant bridge, in their various costumes, with their differences in attitude and activity. (See Figure 7.2.)

I remember having had a sense that the artist must have executed these delicate miniature figures with the aid of a magnifying glass. When I leaned close to the painting to examine the brushwork, I was astonished to find that all the little people were merely artfully positioned single blobs and daubs of paint – not a hand or foot or head or hat or shoulder to be discerned. (See Figure 7.3.)

Figure: 7.2

Nothing shaped remotely like a tiny person appears on the canvas, but there is no question that my brain represented those blobs *as* persons. Bellotto's deft brushwork "suggests" people crossing the bridge, and my brain certainly took the "suggestion" to heart. But what did its *taking* the suggestion amount to? We may want to say, metaphorically, that my brain "filled in" all the details, or we may want to say – more abstractly, but still metaphorically – that my brain completed the vector: *a variety of different people in various costumes and attitudes.* What I doubt very much, however, is that any particular

Figure: 7.3

neural representations of hands or feet or hats or shoulders were created by my brain. (This, too, is an empirical question, of course, but I'll eat my hat if I'm wrong about this one!)

How can we tell, then, how rich the content of the neural representation actually is? As Ramachandran says, by doing more experiments. Consider for instance another of his embellishments on the artificial scotoma theme, in which the twinkling background is coloured pink, and there is a "conveyor belt" of spots coherently moving from left to right within the gray square region (Ramachandran forthcoming). As before, the square fades, replaced by pink, but the conveyor belt continues for awhile, before its coherent motion is replaced by the random jiggling of the rest of the background. Ramachandran concludes, correctly, that there must be two separate "fill in" events occurring in the brain; one for the background colour, one for the motion. But he goes on to draw a second conclusion that does not follow:

> The visual system must be actually seeing pink – i.e., creating a visual representation of pink in the region of the scotoma, for if that were not true why would they actually see the spots moving against a pink background? If no actual filling in were taking place they would simply have been unable to report what was immediately around the moving spots. (Ramachandran forthcoming, ms. 14)

Of course in some sense "the visual system must be actually seeing pink" – that is, the subject is actually seeing pink that isn't there. No doubt about it! But this does not mean the pink is represented by actually filling in between the moving spots on the conveyor belt – and Ramachandran has yet another experiment that shows this: when a "thin black ring" was suddenly introduced in the centre of the square, the background colour, yellow, "filled the interior of the ring as well; its spread was not 'blocked' by the ring." As he says,

> This observation is especially interesting since it implies that the phrase 'filling in' is merely a metaphor. If there had been an actual neural process that even remotely resembled 'filling in' then one would have expected its progress to be blocked by the black ring but no such effect occurred. Therefore we would be better off saying that the visual system 'assigns' the same color as the surround to the faded region.... (Ramachandran forthcoming, ms. 16)

In yet another experiment, Ramachandran had subjects look at a fixation point on a page of text which had a blank area off to the side. Subjects duly "filled in" the gap with text. But of course the words were not readable, the letters were not identifiable. As Ramachandran says: "It was as though what was filled in was the 'texture' of the letters rather than the letters themselves" (forthcoming, ms. 15). No rendering of individual letters, in other words, but rather a representation *to the effect that* there was no gap in the text, but just more of the same – more 12-point Times Roman, or whatever. The effect is, of course, perceptual, but that does not mean it is not conceptual, not propositional. The content is actually *less rich* than it would have to be, if the gap were filled with particular letters spelling out particular words (or non-words).

Let's now return to the opening question: what is *the product* of perception? This question may have seemed at first like a good question to ask, but it gets one off on the wrong foot because it presupposes that perceptual processes have a single kind of product. To presuppose this, however, is already to commit oneself to the Cartesian Theater. There are in fact many different ways of turning the corner, or responding to the given, and only a few of them are "pictorial" (or for that matter "sentential") in any sense at all. For instance, when something looms swiftly in the visual field, one tends to duck. Ducking is one sort of taking. It itself is not remotely pictorial or propositional; the behaviour is not a speech act; it does not express a proposition. And there is no reason on earth to posit an intermediary state that "represents" in some "code" or "system of representation."

Suppose a picture of a cow is very briefly flashed in your visual field, and then masked. You might not be able to report it or draw it, but it might have the effect of making you more likely to say the word "milk" if asked to name a beverage. This is another sort of corner-turning; it is presumably accomplished by activating or sensitizing a particular semantic domain centered around cows, so your visual system must have done its interpretive work – must have completed the *cow* vector – but its only "product" on this occasion may be just to turn on the cow-neighbouring portion of your semantic network.

The magician moves his hand just so, misdirecting you. We know he succeeded, because you exhibit astonishment when he turns over the cup and the ball has vanished. What product did he produce by this manipulation of your visual system? Astonishment now, but that, like ducking, is not a speech act. The astonishment is caused by failed expectation; you had *expected* the ball to be under the cup. Now what sort of a "product" is this unarticulated expectation? Is it a sentence of mentalese, "The ball is under the cup" swiftly written in your belief-box, or is it a pictorial representation of the ball under the cup? It's something else, propositional only in the bland sense that it is content-specific; it is *about the ball being under the cup*, which is not the same thing as being *about the cup being on the table* or being *about the magician having moved his hands away from the cup*. Those are *different* products of visual perception, vectors into different regions of your content hyperspace.

This state that you have been put into not only grounds your astonishment if the magician now turns over the cup, but also influences how you will perceive the next move the magician makes if he doesn't turn over the cup. That is, this "product" of perception can immediately go on to influence the processes producing the *next* products of perception, and on and on. Ramachandran illustrates this point with an experiment in which a field of yellow rings is shown to subjects in such a way that one of the rings has its inner boundary obscured by the blind spot. (See Figure 7.4.)

What will their brains do? "Fill in" with yet another ring, just like all the other rings, or "fill in" the center of the obscured ring with yellow, turning it into a yellow disk? The latter, it turns out; the solid yellow disk "pops out" as the exception in the field of yellow rings. But even this is not a demonstration of *actual* filling in; in this case, the

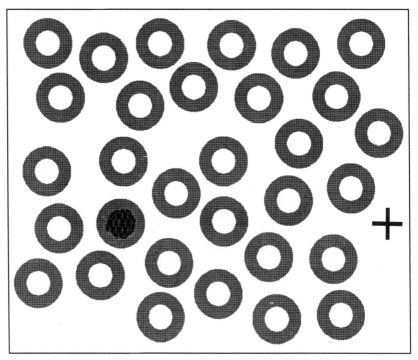

Figure: 7.4

brain has evidence that there is a yellow region with a circular perimeter, and it has no *local* evidence about whether or not the whole region is yellow. Not having any contrary evidence, it draws the inference that it must be "more of the same" – *more yellow*. This is a fine example of a micro-taking, for this *"conclusion"* amounts to the creation of the content *yellow disk*, which in turn becomes a *premise* of sorts: the odd-one-out in a field represented as consisting of yellow rings, which then triggers "pop out." It might have turned out otherwise; the micro-taking process first invoked for the blind-spot region might have had access to the global information about the multitude of rings, and treated this global content as evidence for a different inference: considered globally, "more of the same" is *more rings*. In that case there would have been no pop-out, and the field would have been seen, veridically, in fact, as a uniform field of rings. So the experiment very definitely shows us something about the order and access relations between a variety of micro-takings, but in neither case does the brain have to provide something in order to arrive at its initial judgment.

The creation of conscious experience is not a batch process but a continuous process. There is not one corner that is turned, once, but many. The order in which these determinations occur determines the order in which they can have effects (no backwards causation allowed!), but is strictly independent of the *order represented* in the contents thus determined. The micro-takings have to interact. A micro-taking, as a sort of judgment or decision, can't just be inscribed in the brain in isolation; it has to have its consequences – for guiding action and modulating further micro-judgments made "in its light." This interaction of micro-takings, however it is accomplished in particular cases, has the effect that a modicum of coherence is maintained, with discrepant elements dropping out of contention, and all without the assistance of a Master Judge. Since there is no Master Judge, there is no *further* process of being-appreciated-in-consciousness, so the question of *exactly* when a particular element was *consciously* (as opposed to unconsciously) taken admits no non-arbitrary answer. And since there is no privileged moment at which to measure richness of content, and since the richness of content of micro-takings waxes and wanes, the idea that we can identify *perceptual* – as opposed to conceptual – states by an evaluation of their contents turns out to be an illusion.

Notes

1 This is what I called the β-manifold in "Two Approaches to Mental Images," in Dennett (1978).

References

Dennett, D.C. (1978). *Brainstorms.* Cambridge, MA: MIT Press

———. (1991). *Consciousness Explained.* Boston: Little, Brown

———. (1992). Filling in versus finding out: A ubiquitous confusion in cognitive science. In P. van den Broek, Herbert L. Pick, Jr., and D. Knill, (eds.), *Cognition: Conceptual and Methodological Issues,* Washington, DC: American Psychological Association

Dennett, D.C., and M. Kinsbourne (1992). Time and the observer: the where and when of consciousness in the brain. *Behavioral and Brain Sciences,* 15, 2 (June): 183-201

Kinsbourne, M. (1988). Integrated field theory of consciousness. In A.J. Marcel and E. Bisiach, (eds.), *Consciousness in Contemporary Science,* Oxford: Oxford University Press

Ramachandran, V.S. (1992). Blind spots. *Scientific American,* 266 (May): 86-91

———. (forthcoming) "Filling in gaps in perception," in *Current Directions in Psychological Science.*

Ramachandran, V.S., and R.L. Gregory (1991). Perceptual filling in of artificially induced scotomas in human vision. *Nature* 350, 6320: 699-702

Sherrington, C.S. (1934) *The Brain and Its Mechanism.* Cambridge: Cambridge University Press.

Stalnaker, R. (1984). *Inquiry.* Cambridge, MA: MIT Press

8

Ships in the Night:
Churchland and Ramachandran on
Dennett's Theory of Consciousness

Kathleen A. Akins and Steven Winger

I. Dennett's Views on Filling In

In Daniel Dennett's exchange with P.S. Churchland and V.S. Ramachandran, much of the discussion circles around one general issue – the relationship between sub-personal neural representations and the phenomenology that we as persons experience. I sit in my chair enjoying a particular Brahms trio; inside my head, at numerous cortical and subcortical sites, a variety of neural processes occur; some of these processes, we think, are responsible for my experience. But what is the relationship between what I hear and what goes on? What kinds of neural representations – what kinds of neural processes, structures and contents – constitute this type of auditory event?[1]

A special case of this general issue arises for human vision, for the kinds of representations, processes and contents that underlie our ordinary visual experience of the world. When we look at the world, say, through the window to the trees and garden below, the information received through our eyes is transient (e.g., it is interrupted by blinks and saccadic eye movements), serial (we look, first, at one small point in visual space, say at the small pond on the right, then at another point, at the clump of irises beside it) and varies in its informational texture (e.g., from the fovea to the periphery, the eye receives information with diminishing spatial and frequency resolution). But the world we *perceive*, however, the world of which we are conscious, does not bear the mark of its representational origins; even given the fragmented and serial nature of visual information, somehow we come to experience objects and properties as stable across time, as unified, as existing independently of our perceptions and actions, and so on. Focusing on first one part of the garden, then another, we nonetheless perceive the landscape as a whole, existing through time in front of us; the garden does not come into existence, piece by piece as our eyes traverse the landscape, nor are the objects within it – the pond and the trees – seen as fragmented or disunified. Moreover, when we ask about our visual experience itself, we take our perceptions of the world to be panoramic: at any moment, it *seems* to us that the visual field encompasses a single, large arc of the world in front of us, one that is equally rich in detail across its entire broad field. In other words, we both perceive the world as permanent and stable and experience our visual phenomenology as everywhere rich in information and non-gappy. The particular case of our general question, then, is about the representations and processes that sustain this kind of conscious visual experience.

It is in the context of providing an answer to this question about visual experience that Dennett warns his readers against various forms of filling in. Most generally, he cautions us that, in constructing a theory of vision, we should not accept uncritically either our introspective understanding of what needs to be explained (our views about 'what it is like' to see) or our intuitive assumptions about the kinds of representational structures that must underlie visual experience. More specifically, he argues against three separate kinds of filling in. (What makes Dennett's discussion of filling in so confusing is that an answer to the general question about the relationship between representational vehicles, representational content and conscious experience is merely presupposed, taken as a background assumption. It is never explicitly stated. Here we will begin with a discussion of visual filling in; later, in part III, we will take up Dennett's implicit views on the broader question.)

(1) "Neural Pigment" and "Mental Figment" versus Neural Symbols

First, Dennett dismisses a naïve view about how our visual experiences must come about – the view that properties of the world are represented by like properties in the brain, and that these representations, in turn, give rise to phenomenological experiences with similar characteristics. Thus, a naïve person might imagine that viewing a red apple gives rise to a red coloured representation in the brain (a representation coloured with neural "pigment"), which results in a visual image *of* a red apple, an image which is itself "red" in some metaphorical sense (as Dennett would say, an image that is "coloured" with some mental property, "figment"). Less naïvely, one might imagine that looking at an armchair results in a two-dimensional picture of the armchair at various places in visual cortex, pictures that result in a visual experience of the armchair which is, itself, somehow chair-shaped or, more vaguely, "spatially extended". As Dennett points out, there is no reason why representational vehicles must themselves exhibit the properties represented – why color needs to be represented by coloured symbols, why the spatial relations of the world must be mimicked by the spatial relations between various symbols in the brain, and so on. Nor is there good reason to think that there are mysterious mental properties, "sort of" colours or "sort of" shapes that exist in a special mental medium. Thus, claims Dennett, we need not posit any visual filling in in the following sense – neural representations need not exhibit the properties of the world they represent nor does visual experience require a mysterious filling in with mental figment in visual experience.

As Dennett well knows, there are very few cognitive scientists who would argue, on general principles, that properties of the world must be represented by like properties in the brain; fewer still who would be keen to champion the existence of peculiar phenomenal properties in an equally strange mental medium. Dennett believes, however, that even though we all know better, the remnants of the naïve view continue to inadvertently shape our theories of visual processing and phenomenology – for example, when we assume that the order of occurrence for external events must be represented by the order of occurrence of neural events, which in turn give rise to a perception of the external events as occurring in a particular objective sequence. This brings us to (2) below, another example of how this intuitive view permeates our theoretical understanding of conscious experience.

(2) Judgments versus Visual Representations: Filling in versus Finding out

Put in telegraphic form, Dennett's second injunction against "filling in" in visual processing is as follows. *Given a "conclusion" by one visual module, in whatever representational form it may arise, there need be no transformation of that "judgment" into a "purely visual mode" of representation in order for us to have a paradigmatically visual experience.*

To understand what lies behind this view, consider something that we will call "Marr's Paradox". This is a paradox that seems to arise if one attempts to understand how conscious vision is related to the neural computational events posited by a typical model of visual processing – say, Marr's theory of vision.[3] (Marr, of course, had nothing to say about the origins of consciousness or about those of visual phenomenology either; nor did he wish to claim that his computational theory of vision constituted anything like a complete explanation of human vision. Without misrepresenting Marr's own claims, however, we can use Marr's theory to understand the perplexing nature of visual phenomenology.)

On Marr's theory, recall, the principal task of the system is *shape recognition*. The model contains four distinct representational stages. The purpose of each is to draw out or make explicit certain kinds of information contained in the original retinal image. On Marr's scheme, then, the four stages are as follows: (1) an image that represents light intensity at points in the retinal image, the representational primitives of which are intensity values at each point; (2) the Primal Sketch that makes explicit intensity changes and their spatial organization, the primitives of which are zero-crossings, blobs, terminations and discontinuities, edge segments, virtual lines, groups and boundaries; (3) the 2½-D sketch that makes explicit the orientation and depth of the visible surfaces, essentially a line drawing with dotted lines (discontinuities in object surface) and arrows (surface orientation); and (4) the 3-D Model that describes shapes and their spatial organization using hierarchically organized models, stick figures to which volumetric primitives (e.g., generalized cylinders) are attached. Each level of representation, on Marr's view, is to be entirely derivable from processes that act upon the lower level representations (as well as from fully general implicit assumptions). For example, the 2½-D sketch is derived from the Primal Sketch by incorporating the results of a number of processes. Among others, there are the processes that take, as their input, particular descriptions from the Primal Sketch and produce as their output the values for the representational primitives of the 2½-D sketch (relative distance, discontinuities of depth and surfaces, and surface orientation): stereopsis, structure from motion, shape from shading, optical flow and occlusion cues. Thus each new representational level (and the information that is thereby made explicit) is constructed from a series of inferential processes using lower level information.

Here we have the specific case of our general issue: exactly how do these representations and processes meet with our visual phenomenology? When we look at the garden outside the window, we do not see the blobs, boundaries and zero-crossings of the Primal Sketch. Nor do we see little dots and arrows affixed to cartoon outlines, the primitives of the 2½-D sketch; nor the stick figures with their affixed generalized cylinders, the primitives of the shape-recognition system. If any of Marr's representational stages "looks like" our conscious view of the world, it is surely the initial photographic display; cylinders and stick figures are a far cry from what we *see*. In other words, there is potential paradox at hand: starting with the photographic image, the more processing steps taken, each one serving to make explicit *more* information from the retinal image, the less like our visual phenomenology the representational primitives appear to be. So a mystery about visual processing and conscious phenomenology arises: how could the end results of visual processing actually *be* what we know as visual experience? What part in our rich and varied visual lives could the representational primitives of the higher processing levels (the stick figures, cylinders, dots and arrows) actually play?

Marr's theory of vision seems to present us with a paradox only because we start with two conflicting assumptions. First, we assume that it is the upper levels of visual processing – those levels at which the information contained implicitly in the retinal image is rendered explicit – that ought, *prima facie*, to give us some clue about the relation between neural representation and visual phenomenology. After all, if the raison d'être of representational stages, indeed of the processes of vision itself, is to weed out salient information from the retinal image, then surely the *results* of that process – that which is made explicit – support conscious experience. We also seem to assume, on intuitive grounds, that certain kinds of representations are more likely to support particular kinds of phenomenal experience – e.g., that the imagistic aspects of visual experience must arise from iconic representations, that felt judgments ("Aha! now I can make out the giraffe against the trees!") are the product of inferential processes, and so on. (Note that this assumption, while intuitively appealing to even sophisticated researchers, runs uncomfortably close to positing Cartesian figment.) However, given Marr's theory of visual processing, these assumptions cannot both be correct. If imagistic representations are required for imagistic experiences, then the upper representational levels of Marr's theory could not be what underlies visual experience; on the other hand, if it is the upper levels of visual processing that support conscious experience, then the relationship between experience and representational vehicles could not be anything like what our intuitions suggest. Iconic representations are not required for imagistic experience. This is the implicit contradiction that gives rise to our sense of paradox.

Marr's Paradox makes clear, then, that *neither of these assumptions is necessarily true* – both are merely contingent propositions. Moreover, because they are inconsistent, one of them must be false. Perhaps attempting to pair a single type of representational form selected from the latter stages of visual processing (e.g., one instance of a 3-D sketch) with a conscious visual experience (e.g., looking out at the garden) is *not* the way to understand the origins of visual experience. On the other hand, perhaps the relation between representations and experience does not require the similarity of representational and phenomenal properties that we intuitively assume. Indeed, a more interesting suggestion – one that Dennett makes – is that perhaps *both* assumptions are false: *perhaps many of the representational levels and, indeed, the inferential processes that produce them are all part of the representational basis of visual phenomenology.* Were this the case, what underlies our conscious visual experience would be nothing like what our conservative intuitions suggest.

Not many researchers working in mammalian vision continue to believe that Marr's computational theory is likely to be correct – and those who do, tend to think that Marr's model of shape recognition is but a small part of visual processing. Whether or not Marr's theory is adopted in the end, however, it is not clear that any other of the computational theories of vision currently on offer gives us any clear guidance in addressing the kinds of issues raised by Marr's paradox. To put the point another way, looking at the 26 known visual areas of the brain, whatever computational functions they turn out to perform, it seems plausible that, like Marr's 3-D hierarchical models for shape recognition (of sticks and attached cylinders) much of the representational machinery may not fit neatly into our preconceptions about conscious experience. Whatever the true computational story of vision, it will probably include multiple levels of representation, a variety of representational types and an abundance of processes that mediate between those different representational spaces – all properties that are unlikely to render intuitively transparent the relationship between visual representational vehicles, their content and our visual phenomenology. Indeed, it is Dennett's consideration of multiprocessor models of vision, both computational and physiological ones, that has led him to similar conclusions about representation and phenomenology.

More specifically, Dennett begins with the assumption that there is no Cartesian Theatre – that conscious perception occurs without any "central observer" who "views," from a particular place or vantage point, the results of the multiple visual processes. He then reasons that:

(a) There need be no collation of the individual results of the modular visual processes, *no gathering together of these perceptual conclusions into a single informationally cohesive "package."*[3]

(b) Given (a), and in light of the fact that vision involves inferential and imagistic processes throughout, our conscious visual perceptions of the world are not the products of picture-like neural representations alone nor of any other unified form of representation characteristic of vision; *in this sense, there are no strictly visual perceptions, no perceptions that result from a single form of visual representation.*

(c) Given both (a) and (b), *there need be no re-rendering of the individual results of modular processes into some standard perceptual form*: "once a judgment is made it need not be made again."

Putting these three conclusions together, Dennett denies that there is a second kind of filling in: *given a conclusion by one visual module, in whatever representational form it may arise, there need be no transformation of that judgment into a purely visual mode of representation in order for us to experience it as a visual experience.* There need be no filling in (in standard visual representational form) as opposed to finding-out.

(3) Stockpiled Knowledge versus "Need-to-Know" Access

The world in which we live is, to a large and often predictable extent, stable and unchanging (or so it seems to us, here in central Illinois); occasionally a fly goes by, the leaves on a tree flutter in the wind, or a person approaches. Given this overall stability, Dennett suggests, there is little need for a visual system to process and store detailed representations of the visual world's multitudinous objects and properties. Visual perception will work equally well (indeed, *better*, for reasons of limited storage and ease of access) if the eyes are moved from point to point as particular aspects of the world become of interest. Even then, incoming information may be only partially processed ("nothing of interest there"), other parts may be given a more thorough treatment ("let's just have a better look at that"), while only some small subset of these visual conclusions are likely to be stored for future use. Our representation of the visual world, Dennett speculates, is probably more gappy than our introspective access would ever lead us to suspect.

Still, if our representations of the world are so sparse, why does it seem to us that our visual experience is relatively seamless and extremely complex? Here, Dennett provides two answers. First, the absence of a stimulus must be recorded *as* an absence before it can be experienced as such. For an absence to be experienced or, more relevantly, remedied, there must be a judgment of the form "information of type x is missing." But the visual system, operating as it does on a need-to-know basis, makes no such judgments; hence *no attempt at all – either by inference or otherwise – is made to fill in the missing information of our normal gappy visual representations.*

Second, Dennett suggests that perceptual representations often have what one might call vague or abstract content – propositions of the form 'lots of brightly clothed people crossing the bridge' or 'a circle filled evenly with twinkles of the very same type' or simply 'a line that changes colour somewhere in between the red end and green end'.

Just as the Belloti painting does not represent specifically the finery of the people crossing the bridge, the visual representations themselves lack information about specific aspects of the world; but the representations *depict* the world *as* having complex properties, just as the Belloti painting gives the impression of many individuals, sumptuously attired. In other words, if the content of the representation is suitably abstract, sparsely detailed representational content need not be manifested, phenomenologically, as a sparsity in the perceived properties of the world. *Hence, again, there is no felt loss of information nor any need to fill in or find out the missing details given the abstract content of the representation.* (If something seems amiss here, worry not. We will come back to this point later.)

Hence, Dennett's third moral about filling in: *even though, in normal visual processing, the visual content is both gappy (piecemeal) and abstract, there is no reason to suppose that this information must be supplemented in order to produce our rich visual phenomenology.*

II. Gliding on Past

All three denials of representational filling in are offered by Dennett as general principles of conscious visual processing. Thus his view on the blind spot is offered merely as one speculative case, one instance in which these principles might be borne out. (Note that Dennett's explanation of the blindspot need not apply to the phenomenology of artificial scotomas. Whatever strategies the visual system has developed for *normal functioning* with the blindspot need not be the same kinds of strategies that are used in cases of breakdown – here, in the case of artificial scotomas, when suddenly the system fails to receive information of the usual kind.) What, then, according to Dennett, happens when the visual space occupied by the blind spot fills in? Dennett postulates that, at some level of visual function, the system infers, on the basis of information from surrounding areas in the neural map, what the blind spot ought to have contained. The exact content of such inferences depends upon the stage or area of representation at which the inference is made – a content consonant with the information processing tasks of the particular neural site. If the inference is made further up in visual processing, then, the judgment will necessarily have a content that is propositionally abstract (e.g., "small twinkles exactly like the surrounding ones") *for that is all the inference from the surrounding areas warrants, given the more abstract content of the representational primitives (or type of "content determinings," in Dennett's terminology).* And once such inferences are made, they will be neither confirmed nor disconfirmed directly, for there are no neurons that are capable of providing the requisite consistency check. As this is the normal case, the absence of confirmation is not judged *as* an absence. (Here it is clear why Dennett's explanation of the blind spot cannot be used to explain the phenomenology created by an artificial scotoma. With an artificial scotoma, there *are* neurons, below the level of pattern recognition, that are responsible for monitoring the blank area of visual space. Some story must be told then about why, when only noise is received from such lower level neurons – for visual neurons will continue to fire randomly in the absence of stimulation – the inference is not judged false.) The spot is labelled "just more of the same twinkling" and in virtue of that label alone, we experience the blind spot as filled with twinkles. There is no reason why the judgment must be reinterpreted into the correct form of visual representation (for there is none) nor painted into psychological space with some kind of mental figment (for there is none of that either), before the experience can occur. Dennett says, by way of summary,

> The brain doesn't have to "fill in" for the blind spot, *since the region in which the blind spot falls is already labeled* (italics ours) (e.g. "plaid" or "Marilyns" or "just more of the same"). If the brain received contradictory evidence from some region, it would abandon or adjust its generalization, but not getting evidence from the blind spot region is not the same as getting contradictory evidence. The absence of confirming evidence from the blind spot region is no problem for the brain; since the brain has no precedent of getting information from that gap in the retina, it has not developed epistemically hungry agencies demanding to be fed. Among all the homunculi of vision, not a single one has the role of co-ordinating information from that region of the eye, so when no information arrives from those sources, no one complains. The area is simply neglected. (Dennett 1991, 355)

The various ways in which Churchland and Ramachandran pass by Dennett's position should now be clear. First, Churchland and Ramachandran misconstrue Dennett's specific views about how the blind spot is handled during normal visual processing. On Churchland and Ramachandran's interpretation, Dennett simply denies that the brain provides or infers any information about the contents of the blind spot. For example, they cite him as saying, as evidence of this view: "The fundamental flaw in the idea of 'filling in' is that it suggests that the brain is providing something when in fact the brain is ignoring something" (Dennett 1991, 356). On the contrary, Dennett assumes that the visual system *is* providing something, namely, an inference with an abstract propositional content; what it ignores is the lack of any direct confirmation or refutation of that inference.

Admittedly, it would greatly surprise Dennett if the phenomenon of filling in for the blind spot turned out to be explainable solely in terms of very low-level visual processes – if, say, the visual map in V1 contained individual "healthy" neurons that represented the area of visual space covered by the blind spot, and that thereafter absolutely no further special "finagling" (judgments or inferences) occurred.[4] After all, the experiments make clear that the principles that govern filling in utilize higher level properties of the visual scene – continuity, shape, relational properties between shapes, and so on – in order to determine the contents of the blind spot. So if filling in occurs at the level of V1 alone, somehow the patterns of neural activity created must be such that they can sustain the orderly computational processes of pattern recognition that occur further down stream, at the higher levels of processing. How is it, one might well wonder, that the pattern of activity qua pattern is recreated over the entire cortical area of the blind spot if information from above (from pattern recognizers) is not used? Note that, by Dennett's lights, such filling in cannot come about by means of the feedback of information from the higher processing levels (i.e., through the information discerned by the higher levels about the patterns of neural activity surrounding the blind spot), for such "back-filling" would violate Dennett's rule that "once a judgment is made, it need not be made again." If the patterns of the surrounding areas have already been discerned and the inference that the blind spot contains pattern x has already been drawn, why would it be necessary to re-write this inference into the representational space of V1? It is simply concluded that pattern x occurs. It seems natural for Dennett to suppose, then, that inferences about the blind spot occur at higher processing levels, those at which the various complex properties of the retinal image are discerned, and those at which the content of the representational primitives is of a vague or abstract kind.

Churchland and Ramachandran, on the one hand, and Dennett, on the other, seem to agree, in other words, about the interesting empirical questions yet to be answered. Both want to know: "what is the level at which inferences about the blind spot occur?" and "how rich is the informational content of those judgments?" It is not their *philosophical* intuituions that here diverge but their *empirical* intuitions – namely, each party's best guess about where in the visual processing hierarchy such inferences are most likely to occur.

More importantly, Churchland and Ramachandran seem to miss Dennett's proposal that there need be no single form of visual representation across visual cortical areas – that our phenomenology might be supported by a large variety of representational types and inferential processes. For this reason, they also pass by his contention that we cannot use the standard dichotomies in marking the distinction between the kinds of representations that underlie visual experience and those that are involved in non-visual conceptual thought. We cannot say that what separates visual perception from non-visual thoughts are the standard distinctions between imagistic and sentential processes, between perceptual states and conceptual ones, and so on. Churchland and Ramachandran, however, seem to equate "genuine" visual experience with *neural activity in any visual sensory area*, i.e., any neural area the cells of which can be driven by, at least in part, visual stimuli. Instead, if Churchland and Ramachandran want to make contact with Dennett's point, they must argue that one of these distinctions serves to mark the relevant divide or that, while these particular dichotomies are false, nonetheless our visual experiences are underwritten by an as yet unspecified form of visual representation. Then Churchland and Ramachandran would need to show that visual processes of the hypothesized type are both necessary and sufficient for our visual experience of filling in (e.g., our experience of the artificial scotoma filling in with twinkles). The neurophysiological evidence that Churchland and Ramachandran present, in other words, does not address the issue at the right level of abstraction – at the level of *neural representational structure and content* as opposed to at the level of single-neuron activity. The issue at hand, once again, is this: what kinds of representations result in human visual experience?

Finally, because Churchland and Ramachandran do not address the question of what makes a particular kind of representation a visual one, they miss what, by Dennett's lights, would or would not count as empirical evidence in favour of filling in. Thus Churchland and Ramachandran cite the declarations of the experimental subjects, those who attest to the very visual feel of filling in as evidence for the genuinely visual nature of the representations. Yet such declarations, however sincere, do not meet with Dennett's argument. If the form of a visual event need not match the resultant phenomenology, then Dennett would deny that any conclusions about representations can be drawn from our introspective reflections (or from the sincere declarations of other people about their own experiences). Again, to counter Dennett's view, the following question must be raised: is it really true that conscious visual episodes, even those that seem very vivid and complex, could be the product of inferential processes or judgments alone? It is a positive answer to this question, we think, that lies behind Dennett's denial of filling in.

In these three ways, Churchland and Ramachandran's empirical data and Dennett's theory of consciousness pass each other by.

III. Docking the Freighter

If Churchland and Ramachandran have failed to distil the essence of Dennett's view, this is a position with which many readers of *Consciousness Explained* will sympathize. To a large extent, the authors' interpretative problems result from Dennett's indirect narrative style: as we said earlier, Dennett's solutions (or dissolutions) to specific puzzles about consciousness presuppose a certain relationship between sub-personal neural representations and the phenomenology that we each, as persons, experience, but no account of it is ever explicitly given.

What, then, is Dennett's answer to this central puzzle? Dennett's view, we suspect, is simply this: *it is the content of neural judgments, not their form or structure, that is transparent in conscious experience.* The very feel of our phenomenology, in all its apparent complexity and variety, in some sense *is* the representational content of a narrative stream, a stream that has been precipitated by particular probes or questions. When you listen to the Brahms trio, say, when you delight in the unexpected progressions and wonder at their subtlety and innovation, what you experience is the content of a series of conclusions: here, presumably, conclusions drawn in answer to your own sub-personal expectations or your conscious personal-level queries about harmonic progressions and musical form. The character of your phenomenological experience depends upon your (often sub-personal) judgments about "how things lie" – the state of the external objective world and, in other cases, the state of your own neural processes. In other words, on Dennett's view, "what it is like" is a matter of how things are judged to be.

This view, that the nature of phenomenological events is a function of the content of the relevant neural states, is both radical and puzzling. (In particular, how are we to understand this notion of "transparency"? In what sense does the content of neural events shine through to conscious experience?) It is also a view that, prima facie, does not sit easily with all of Dennett's other philosophical commitments (as we will discuss later). In support of this interpretation of Dennett's theory of consciousness, then, consider the following four examples from *Consciousness Explained*, in which Dennett's explanations of various properties of conscious experience seem to presuppose just this position.

First, in the Prelude, which is given as a preview to the main themes of the book, Dennett presents a theory of hallucinations. The problem with which Dennett begins is this: how could we have detailed and vivid hallucinations (or dreams) in the absence of the detailed sensory information about the world that normally informs visual experience? Psychoactive drugs do not contain within them any "script" or "video" of the hallucinations which they cause; white noise, by definition, does not contain the content of the hallucinations it often fosters. Dennett's solution is to suggest that, in the absence of orderly sensory input, the top-down hypothesis-generators of normal perception (primarily in vision and audition) begin to produce hypotheses which are then randomly confirmed or negated by noise on the input channels. While, under normal cognitive conditions, such random confirmations would be noticed and questioned by epistemic "demons" whose job it is to check for the consistency and plausibility of the confirmed hypotheses, in the case of hallucinations and dreams, such demons are uncharacteristically lax. They passively accept whatever random hypotheses are confirmed; they show a lack of "epistemic hunger." The conclusions are simply *seen* – or heard or smelled and so on, depending upon the sensory information of the hypotheses.

What is interesting here is that Dennett does not find it problematic that a hypothesis – a linguistic or quasi-linguistic entity – could give rise to *sensory* phenomenology simply in virtue of being *accepted*. How is it that an affirmative answer to the question "Am I hearing a Brahms trio?" could actually cause me to hallucinate, in its full auditory glory, a performance of a Brahms trio? Why would that produce a complex auditory hallucination?

As we saw above, Dennett does not believe that visual experiences must result from pictorial representations, nor, more generally, that each modality of sensory experience has a characteristic representational form. Moreover, in "Seeing Is Believing – Or Is It?", Dennett concludes that sentential or linguistic representations need not be impoverished in their content relative to more pictorial or imagistic forms of representation. As he puts it: *"There is no upper bound on the richness of content of a proposition"* (Dennett's italics) (This volume, p. 162). In other words, if linguistic hypotheses can cause visual sensations, and if there is no upper bound on the propositional content of sentence-like representations, there is no reason why mere hypotheses could not cause rich sensory events – for example, hearing a particular Brahms trio. No reason why not, that is, if one assumes that it is content alone that determines "what it is like."

Second, in Dennett's discussion of the representation of time in Chapters 5 and 6 of *Consciousness Explained*, he argues that no amount of evidence, either from the natural sciences (in the form of neurophysiological findings about the brain or psychophysical research) or from our own introspective reports, could serve to pinpoint the exact time of occurrence of a conscious event. In conscious awareness, says Dennett, we experience only the time as represented, not the time of the neural event as it actually occurs; we have access to the content of the representation as opposed to the properties of the vehicle itself. According to Dennett, "introspection provides us – the subject as well as the 'outside' experimenter – only with the content of the representation, not with the features of the representational medium itself" (1991, 354). Admittedly, one way to interpret this statement is to give it a very weak reading: perhaps Dennett is saying only that we lack access to the properties of representational vehicles qua vehicles just because, as a matter of fact, we do not know the bridge laws that connect the properties of our phenomenology to any of the other non-semantic properties of the representations.[5] Still, if it were the (practical or theoretical) absence of bridge laws that blocked our access to the non-semantic properties of neural representations, then our access to representational content ought to be equally impaired. To date, that is, there are few commonly accepted bridge laws that link content and experience (and even fewer known to those of us who are not psychophysicists) so *mutatis mutandis*, with introspection as our only guide, the content of our conscious experiences ought to be just as opaque to us as all of the other properties of neural representations. In other words, if Dennett insists that there is a difference in our introspective access between the content of a representation and the other properties of the representational vehicle, then Dennett is making the stronger claim: that representational content is somehow transparent to experience in a way in which the other properties of representational vehicles are not.

Assume, then, that any complex conscious event will require any number of content determinings or conclusions, and that each of these will occur at slightly different times at a variety of neural sites. All are necessary for the occurrence of the conscious event, yet together they have no single point of onset. But if *subjective* experience does not point to any particular moment in time as "the" time of onset, then there is, in principle, no means of pinpointing the exact time, within a given window of opportunity, as "the" one at which a given conscious experience begins.

Criticisms of this argument aside, note that Dennett is not led by this train of thought into anomalous monism (not even on his darkest days). He does not conclude from his view that we have access to *only* the time of conscious events as they are represented, nor that we therefore have *no basis at all* for selecting neural representational events with which to pair the events of phenomenal experience (and hence no means by which to discover regularities between types of phenomenal experiences and types of neural representational events). In theory at least, it is possible to choose, among the multitude of neural events that occur at roughly the right time, those neural representations which are relevant, to select whatever neural events give rise to a particular conscious perception or thought. And this we are able to do in virtue of matching the *content* of our phenomenological experiences with the content of neural events – by comparing what conscious events are about with what those neural events represent. Again, this is possible only on the presupposition that content both determines and is transparent in phenomenology.

Third, in Dennett's chapter in *Consciousness Explained* "Prosthetic Vision: What aside from Information Is Still Missing?" he describes experiments in which blind subjects were equipped with small video cameras mounted on eyeglass frames, plus a device that translated the low resolution images into an array of electrical "tingles" over the surface of the back. After several hours, the subjects could describe rudimentary shapes, read signs and even identify people's faces. But what of the feelings, asks Dennett, that the device produced? Did the electrical "tactors" succeed in producing prosthetic vision or was the electrical stimulation felt merely as "tingles," as tactile sensations of the usual kind? In reply, Dennett cites evidence for the transparency of the tingles, for the conclusion that the (visual) informational content of the video images informs the blind subjects' experience and thereby gives them visual experience: the subjects' felt point of view was directly ahead, the direction in which the camera was pointing, not directly behind; when the tactors were shifted from the back to the stomach, subjects were able to adapt almost immediately to the change; moreover, itches on the back were still felt *as* itches not "seen" as distal events. On the other hand, as Dennett admits, using the prosthetic device did not produce all of the phenomenological effects of normal vision in the experimental subjects – for example, *Playboy* pictures failed to be "interesting" to two blind male college students. Here, suggests Dennett, the problem might lie in the low spatial resolution of the images, the slow response rate of the "sluggish" tactile receptors and in the lack of neural connections from sensory cortex to areas responsible for emotional affect. He says:

> It is not clear how much would change if we somehow managed to improve the "baud" rate of prosthetic vision to match normal vision. It might be that simply increasing the amount and rate of information, somehow providing higher-resolution bit-maps to the brain, would suffice to produce the delight that is missing. Or some of it.... It might also be that some of the pleasure we take in visual experience is the by-product of ancient fossil traces of an earlier economy in our nervous systems...." (Dennett 1991, 342)

In other words, Dennett believes that insofar as the devices produce visual sensations, this is the result of the information common to both systems; and insofar as the subjects' phenomenology fails to mimic that of normal vision, informational differences or a difference in neural connections to "earlier economies" account for the discrepancy – and this regardless of how the sense of touch packages its informational content, regardless of the form of the representational vehicles.[6]

As a fourth and final example of the proposed view, consider Dennett's solution to one of the classical problems of consciousness and representation, namely, the nature of secondary qualities, of the "purely qualitative" sensations of color, warmth, hardness and so on. Consider the problem of colours. We know that any number of different conditions can cause the sensation of red: our perceptions of red objects are not caused, on each and every occasion of perception, by a specific wavelength (or combination of wavelengths) of reflected light. We also know that our neural representations of red objects are not themselves coloured red. But if neither external objects in the world nor the inner neural states which represent them are red, where is redness to be found? Given that red is neither "out there" nor "in the head," must it not exist, as Descartes thought, in yet another realm, in the non-material mind? (Here again we see the naïve theory of consciousness at work.)

Roughly put, Dennett's solution to this puzzle is to propose that colours really do exist as properties of objects in the external world – but as extremely complex, heterogeneous properties, those which the human visual system has evolved to "detect." Given the facts about the light-reflective surfaces of the world, the human visual system and its color categories have evolved to make use of those contingencies; indeed, to a large extent, one could say that our color categories have co-evolved with the surface reflectance properties of various other biological entities. The color red, for example, is just whatever set of light conditions is now capable of producing in human observers the sensation of red, and this is true no matter how large, unruly or disjoint such a set might be. So colours are properties in the world and our sensations of color are simply representations of those (admittedly) peculiar properties.[7]

Setting aside the issue of primary and secondary qualities, what we want to highlight is why Dennett considers this an adequate answer to the question at hand – to the problem of the *consciousness* of secondary properties. To the average reader, we suspect, his answer will seem to side-step the issue: Dennett does not explain here why the detection of the peculiar property of red gives rise to its particular phenomenology, nor does he say where the *psychological* property of redness resides. Rather, the pedagogical move is to assure the reader that our perceptions of redness are representationally – or rather, informationally – respectable. Note, however, that if informational content is "transparent" to consciousness under certain circumstances,[8] then Dennett's answer goes further towards providing an explanation than first appears. To understand the informational content of a representational state is to understand why a type of conscious perceptual event has its own particular feel. (This also explains Dennett's answer to Otto's objection that "[y]ou haven't said why pink should look like this!... Like the particularly ineffable, wonderful, intrinsic pinkness that I am right now enjoying" (Dennett 1991, 383). Dennett answers with an explanation of the affective qualities of conscious experiences (e.g., why we enjoy some of them and hate others) and by arguing against any "intrinsic" or "purely qualitative" aspects of colour sensations. In other words, the complete answer he gives to the problem of conscious colour states is in terms of their functional/informational properties – their informational ties to the world and their links to other cognitive/affective states.) Perhaps, then, this is the unspoken view that lies behind the text.

Despite the cautions of Churchland and Ramachandran (this volume), then, we think that Dennett's magic elixir for consciousness is not "Gilbert Ryle's 'Ghost-Be-Gone'." Instead, Dennett is a philosopher trying to float two separate projects that drift in different directions.[9] First, it is true that Dennett has a long-standing philosophical allegiance to both Ryle and Quine, and, just as Churchland and Ramachandran say, these strands in his philosophy seem to restrict the science of the mind's legitimate domain. From Ryle, Dennett inherits the view that our everyday ascriptions of psychological states cannot be construed as descriptions of internal processes.[10] According to Dennett's Intentional System Theory, ascriptions of beliefs and desires, made under the assumption of rationality, serve to capture only large-scale patterns of human behaviour. They do not describe internal cognitive events, nor do they reflect any underlying "true" ontology, the ontology of neurophysiological states. Rather, the ascription of such states provides us with *predictive powers* about human behaviour, powers that are not available to us using other kinds of generalizations (and this includes the generalizations of neurophysiology). Thus, the job of explaining beliefs and desires is viewed as outside the rightful domain of the neurosciences.

Similarly, one can see Quine's influence in the host of roughly Quinean indeterminacy claims that inhabit Dennett's writings – the indeterminacy of meaning, translation and intentional ascription, plus the indeterminacy of biological function, of the time and content of conscious events, and so on. In effect, such claims serve to limit the scope of scientific explanation. If there are certain questions for which, in principle, there can be no answers, then there is nothing that science

– or any other discipline for that matter – can contribute to their elucidation. (E.g., if there is no sense to be made of the time of onset of a conscious state, then there are no experiments to be done that might pinpoint time of occurrence.) Again, the science of the mind may seem denuded.

Despite these seemingly anti-scientific philosophical views, Dennett (like both Churchland and Ramachandran) is a true believer. We are creatures with cognitive powers and phenomenological experiences and science can – will – elucidate and explain these capacities. Moreover, science will do so whether the subject is our own (human) cognition and phenomenology, or whether it is that of the echo-locating bat (should the bat turn out to be conscious).[11] This is the domain of science, a domain it has even if – despite the fact that – at the outset of the investigation, introspection, folk psychology and our commonsense intuitions are not entirely helpful in delineating what body of facts needs to be explained. Even if, at the beginning, we are somewhat confused about exactly how we are.

This faith in scientific explanation motivates Dennett's views about the mind/brain described *at the "sub-personal" level*. For this – the neurofunctional or neurocomputational level – is the rightful domain of science. Here science can ask: what is the essential nature of our cognitive processes? How, in particular, do these processes work? Why is there consciousness at all? And what is the specific relationship of cognitive processes to our conscious phenomenology? Moreover, Dennett's answers to these questions, as given in *Consciousness Explained*, are actually quite theoretically staid. All tread along (or at least next to) the beaten path in cognitive science: they fall within the scope of the computational model of mind. He holds, for example, that cognitive processes are essentially computational processes – the brain is a "syntactic engine" which nonetheless manages "to approximate the impossible task, to mimic the behavior of the impossible object, the semantic engine" (Dennett 1987, 61); that consciousness arises out of the imposition of a culturally transmitted "virtual machine," a serial machine that "sits atop" the brain's more primitive parallel processes (Dennett 1991, 209-26); and finally, that (if our suggestion is correct) we experience what we do because the very shape and feel of a conscious experience is a function of the content of the virtual machine's relevant computational states.

In *Consciousness Explained*, then, we see Dennett attempting to honour his Quinean and Rylean views about persons while holding onto his faith in science as the means of investigating sub-personal neuro-computational processes. Whether Dennett can stay afloat on this divided structure, of course, remains to be seen. Often, we think, the two separate projects – Dennett's philosophical doctrines about persons (or entire intentional systems) and his scientific/philosophical explanations of sub-personal processing – tend to collide or split apart. This results, prima facie, in a number of inconsistencies, incoherencies or (often) large areas of theoretical unclarity. We will close then by mentioning three such problems that Dennett needs to resolve.

First, Dennett must reconcile the transparency of content with a subject's ability to misdescribe or make mistakes about the nature of his or her own phenomenological experience. On the one hand, Dennett claims that there is no appearance/reality distinction for phenomenological experience. Because any episode of conscious awareness emerges only as the result of a (personal or sub-personal) probe, there is no difference between how things seem to be and how they really are. As we said earlier, on Dennett's view, "what it is like" for the subject just *is* a matter of how things are judged to be. On the other hand, when we as subjects of experience make reports about our conscious lives, it is entirely possible that we are in some way mistaken about the nature of those internal events. By treating such reports as possible fictions in need of confirmation, Dennett's method of "heterophenomenology" presupposes a personal-level capacity for error (Dennett 1991, chap. 4). But in what ways could the subject be wrong about his phenomenology if the content of the experience is transparent to the subject and indeed, may have come about as the result of a conscious probe initiated at the personal level? What needs to made clear, then, is the distinction between personal-level and sub-personal judgments (what these are judgments about) and the relation of each kind of judgment to our capacity for – and immunity to – error.

Second, if content is transparent to consciousness, Dennett must explain why there seems to be no real difference in our phenomenological experience of neural events with abstract content (our representations of non-foveal visual space or our representations of the blind spot) and our experience of neural events that contain detailed information about properties of the world (this is a criticism very close to Churchland and Ramachandran's). That is, when the content of a representation is suitably abstract – "just more Marilyns" or "lots of people in brightly coloured costumes crossing a bridge" – why does it not *seem* abstract to the subject, or more to the point, seem *any different than* our visual experiences that are supported by more concrete representational contents? We don't say, for example "well I see one Marilyn on the wall and the others I see there, um, in a kind of abstract way"; nor do we report that while the very small portion of one Marilyn centered on the fovea seems crystal clear, all of the other Marilyns (and the other parts of the foveated Marilyn) seem completely "fuzzy" (although we may say that, at the very edges of peripheral vision, the world seems dim or blurred). On Dennett's theory of consciousness, one would think that seeing a wall of Marilyns would be a little like imagining a speckled brown hen – lots of spots, just not any particular spots anywhere in particular. Similarly, when we look at an (actual) bridge in the distance, and see lots of different people, each in bright and individual attire, the foveated portion of the visual scene provides the brain with specific (albeit partial) information about the individuals on that part of the bridge. For non-foveated vision and the blindspot, the visual system draws the conclusion "more brightly and distinctly attired people." But again it is hard to see why there is no apparent difference in our perceptions – no difference between how we see the people for whom we do have specific visual information and how we see those individuals about whom we have made only a vague generalization. (Indeed, here, the generalization cannot be literally "just more of the same" because our impression of is of *distinctly* attired individuals.) In short, Dennett needs to say more about the various forms of abstract content and about the relation of abstract content to conscious experience.

Finally – and most importantly – Dennett requires a notion of computational content that makes sense of his claim that content is transparent to consciousness, or more strongly, that content alone determines phenomenological experience. As we said above, Dennett adheres to a standard computational line about the semantics of subpersonal states. According to this familiar story, brains, as syntactic engines, have causal access to only the physical (or formal or syntactic) properties of mental representations. So computational systems manipulate symbols *in accordance with* their meaning or semantic properties but *by virtue of* their syntactic properties, through causal processes. Syntactic properties are what make the impossible object – the semantic engine – run. In turn, on Dennett's scheme, the content of symbols is determined by biological function: to understand what a particular state of a mechanism means is to step back and assess its natural function, both past and present – its present role in relation to inputs of the system, the mechanism's informational links with various other states, its connections to outputs of the system, and last, the evolutionary history of that mechanism or state. Thus the dual aspects of computational states, on Dennett's view of sub-personal events, their semantic and syntactic properties.

What kinds of properties are available to consciousness, then, according to Dennett? What is puzzling here is that according to the computational picture, content itself could not be transparent in a person's experience, for content is a *relational* property of states, one that often depends upon facts beyond the cognitive reach of the subject (say, upon the evolutionary history of a sensory mechanism). In a real sense, content could not be a legitimate or felt participant at all. On the other hand, Dennett claims that *none of the non-semantic properties of the representational vehicle are available to the subject in conscious experience.* Recall Dennett's statement, cited earlier, that "introspection provides us – the subject as well as the 'outside' experimenter – only with the content of the representation, not with the features of the representational medium itself" (1991, 354). Given Dennett's computational explanation of sub-personal processing, there would seem to be *no* properties of neural representations that could be felt in conscious experience.

A natural response to this dilemma is for Dennett to draw a distinction between the syntactic properties of representations and any other (non-semantic) properties that a representational vehicle might have. Let the syntax of the representational vehicle "go proxy" for content in the function of the syntactic engine. Let all of the other properties of representational vehicles, the "purely physical" or non-syntactic characteristics of representational states, remain hidden from view. In other words, the line drawn between that which finds its way into consciousness and that which does not is a distinction between two classes of non-semantic properties, between syntactic properties on the one hand and purely physical properties on the other. If Dennett wishes to maintain the computational party line, drawing this distinction might make for a plausible revision of his view.

In fact, Dennett's writings do not provide a stable answer to this problem nor does he fill in any of the details that would be necessary to flesh out this computational strategy.[12] To do so, he must provide an explanation of the difference between syntactic and non-syntactic (yet non-semantic) properties of representations. He must also give an explanation of why the difference has such profound consequences for human experience – why syntactic properties alone are transparent to consciousness. It is here, then, that we come to the most serious hurdle for Dennett's theory of consciousness: in order for Dennett to explain why syntactic properties alone are transparent to consciousness he must give a general explanation of the mysterious notion of transparency itself: what transparency amounts to given the prima facie profound difference between the syntactic properties of neural representations and the phenomenal properties of individual experiences, and why in general transparency occurs. In other words, if we are correct about Dennett's implicit views on content and consciousness, the heart of the explanation of phenomenal experience has yet to be given. So, we will close by simply noting that Dennett needs to sort through these issues – and note that this, we suspect, will be a rather lengthy project.

Acknowledgments

This paper was presented in an earlier draft in November 1992 at the McDonnell-Pugh Seminar Series in cognitive science at Oxford. For their comments and helpful criticisms, we would like to thank Patricia Churchland, Daniel Dennett, Martin Davies, Denis Robinson and David Rosenthal.

Notes

1 It is very hard to speak of the relationship between neural processes and conscious events without speaking of the neural states as "giving rise to," "underlying" or "supporting" conscious events – that is, without the appearance of dualist sentiments. Despite appearances, this is not a philosophical commitment we intend to express.

2 This example, "Marr's Paradox", was first given by Kathleen Akins in a review of Michael Tye's book *The Imagery Debate* forthcoming in *The Philosophical Review*.

3 Note here that Dennett does not consider any other reasons, except the demands of the fictitious Cartesian Theatre, why the regular integration of visual information might be necessary. Nor does he explain his notion of a "probe," those judgments which constitute the individual acts of consciousness. As probes are judgments about the contents of individual modules at particular times, probes are surely agents of integration. But Dennett does not say how such "gathering together" occurs.

4 It is helpful to note here that, at the retina, there are no transduction cells in the area of the blind spot and hence no ganglion cells to carry the outgoing signal for this area of visual space either. So, at the first level of cortical processing, the lateral geniculate nucleus (LGN), there is a map of visual space but one from which the blind spot is simply omitted. There is no hole in the map, an area which contains only silent neurons or none at all; rather, those neurons that are activated by stimulation *around* the blind spot sit *side-by-side* in the neural map of the LGN. At the next cortical level, however, at V1, there *are* neurons in the neural map that cover the blind spot (from Churchland and Ramachandran, this volume; see also Fiorani et al. 1990; Gattas et al. 1992; Fiorani et al. [forthcoming]) – although, as Churchland points out, it is not clear what kind of information their signals contain.

5 We owe this objection to Martin Davies.

6 We cannot resist pointing out that somehow Dennett has missed the following point: that if the "very same" information about a woman's shape were obtained through more *normal* tactile means (yes, even through the back), the desired effects might well occur in the blind subjects – and this despite the sluggish response and low spatial resolution of the tactile transducers. So it seems highly unlikely that the human sense of touch lacks the sort of "ancient fossil traces" of links to "earlier economies" that are required for the experience of pleasure.

7 Although Dennett attributes this view to Akins (1989), Dennett and I draw somewhat different metaphysical conclusions about secondary properties. Although this is not the place to attempt to develop a complete account of properties, suffice it to say that, on my view, transducers with standard nomological causal properties need not "capture" (be responding to) a property in the world, not even a heterogeneous property. *Transducer mechanisms need not be used as property detectors* – the mere existence of such a transducer does not "create" a property in the world, nor are the outputs of such systems necessarily used either as representations of properties per se or as "content determinings" in Dennett's terminology. On my view, in order to claim that a sensory state is used as a representation of a secondary property (or that such a secondary property exists), a lengthy ontological story must be told about how organisms are able to use certain sensory states as representations of objects and their properties.

8 Namely, on Dennett's view, when it is incorporated into the working of the serial virtual machine.

9 Call this the "Multiple Air Mattress Theory of Consciousness."

10 Dennett also adopts Ryle's deep suspicion of "introspection" as a legitimate means of access to whatever neural processes actually do occur. In fact, Ryle held, in *The Concept of Mind*, that we do have conscious experience of our own thoughts, but that this process cannot be explained as "introspection" or "inner perception" or as any other kind of monitoring of one's current mental state. Rather, what we enjoy is "retrospection," a process that occurs only when we chance to ask ourselves what we have been thinking. As such, it is open to all the normal failures of any other kind of recollection or memory. Ryle says that "aside from the fact that even prompt recollection is subject both to evaporations and to dilutions, however accurately I may recollect an action or feeling, I may still fail to recognize its nature.... Chronicles are not explanatory of what they record." This is a theory that sounds for all the world like Dennett's own Multiple Drafts model – just as Churchland and Ramachandran would have it.

11 Dennett's clear support for the neurophysiological investigation of the "alien" consciousness of other animals might seem to contradict our interpretation of his view. After all, if it is only the representational *content* that is

transparent to conscious experience, and if this content is not affected by the way in which it is neurally packaged, how could the study of the vehicles of content – the packaging – lead to an increased understanding of another subject's phenomenology? What could neurophysiology possibly add to "outer" investigation, to purely behavioural discriminatory tests (e.g., to tests of whether the bat can discriminate between a freely fluttering insect and an inert meal worm tossed into the air by an experimenter)? Moreover, our understanding of computational states suggests that if any feature of neural events is a reasonable candidate for offering insight into phenomenology, it is surely the *structure* of the subject's present representations and the form of the representational system as a whole, its representational relations. Even Thomas Nagel, for all his reasoned objections to the possibility of third-person access to consciousness, sometimes speaks as if neural structure might give us insight into certain "structural" aspects of consciousness. And Dennett himself says: "we learn about the bat's world by learning the systematic structure of bat perception and behavior, not by imagining bat worlds or imagining our minds turned into bat minds." (1991, 442).

The answer to this apparent contradiction lies in Dennett's understanding of neural function, of what neural mechanisms in the brain are designed, by and large, to do. Throughout *Consciousness Explained*, Dennett speaks of individual processors as performing the common task of "content discrimination." It is the product of such discriminations or "determinings" that are subject to continual revision, that are discerned intermittently by probes, that compose the serial narratives constructed out of the probe's findings, and so on. (Note how well this conception of things sits with the low-level task of Marr's theory of vision, namely the task of making explicit information from the original visual image.)

Two things follow from this view. First, if "content determining" is the central task of (most) neural processors, then, at least theoretically, behavioural discriminatory tests are capable of finding out the processing results of (most) brain functions. We watch the bat to see its discriminatory capabilities. Neurophysiological investigation, on the other hand, merely offers a more direct route to discerning which content determinings are going on. "Looking in the head" while monitoring the informational input to the brain is often a speedier and more reliable scientific methodology. Second, if one views brain function in this way, one might also reasonably assume that the logical relations between the content determined will be mimicked by the structural relations between the vehicles of representation – that the systematicity of the content qua content will be mirrored by the structural systematicity of neural representational vehicles. So on this view, to look into the brain, by neurophysiological means, and see the relevant structures (the structure of the processing results as opposed to the structure of the processes themselves) *is* to look into the brain and see the appropriate content determining – the two ride together, like a numeral and its number. On this view of neural functioning, then, it is natural to equate structure with content. And we suspect that this is what Dennett does in this and like passages.

Note that if the raison d'être of brain processes is not content discrimination (if one cannot always classify the processing answers in this way) or if the processes themselves are part of conscious phenomenology, then no such convenient equation between content and structure can be made.

12 For example, in the case of prosthetic vision given above, Dennett suggests that perhaps the absence of cortical links, from somatosensory cortex to "earlier economies" accounts for the lack of pleasure taken in the nude photographs. In other words, he seems to believe that the *functional facts on the basis of which we would ascribe certain content to normal visual "images"* (here, the cortical connections to earlier economies) are themselves responsible for a certain phenomenology – for feelings of pleasure. Then again, perhaps not. Perhaps these informational links from visual cortex to sub-cortical sites result in sub-cortical representations, the syntax of which finds its way into experience as felt pleasure. We think, though, that there is little point to this kind of speculation, for it is not clear that Dennett has a settled or considered view on the matter.

References

Akins, K. (1989) On Piranhas, Narcissism and Mental Representation: An Essay on Intentionality. Ph.D. dissertation. AnnArbor, MI: University of Michigan
———. (forthcoming) Review of *The Imaginary Debate* by Michael Tye. *The Philosophical Review*
Dennett, D.C.D. (1987) Three kinds of intentional psychology. In D. Dennett, *The Intentional Stance*. Cambridge, MA: MIT Press
———. (1991) *Consciousness Explained*. Boston, MA: Little, Brown
Fiorani, M., M.G.P. Rosa, R. Gattass and C.E. Rocha-Miranda (1990). *Society for Neuroscience Abstracts* 16: 1219
Fiorani, M., M.G.P. Rosa, R. Gattass and C.E. Rocha-Miranda (forthcoming). Visual responses outside the "classical" receptive field in primate striate cortex: A possible correlate of perceptual completion. *Proceedings of the national Academy of Sciences*
Gattas, R., M. Fiorani, M.G.P. Rosa, M.C.F. Pinon, A.P.B. Sousa and J.G.M. Soares (1992). Changes in receptive field size in V1 and its relation to perceptual completion. In R. Lent (ed.), *The Visual System from Genesis to Maturity*. Boston: Birkhauser
Ryle, G. (1949) *The Concept of Mind*. London: Hutchison

9

Lewis on What Distinguishes Perception from Hallucination

Brian P. McLaughlin

Since the advent of possible-worlds semantics for counterfactuals, counterfactuals have been used with increasing frequency in analyses of various capacities. This trend is deplorable. I say this not because of difficulties with the semantics of counterfactuals (though I think there are such), but because the counterfactuals associated with capacities are typically, at best, criteria for them, not analysans for them. I will not attempt to defend this general claim here, however. In this paper, I will focus exclusively on whether a specific capacity can be analyzed in terms of counterfactuals, namely the capacity to see. I focus on this capacity for three reasons. First, I am especially interested in psychological capacities. Second, we know more about the physical and neurophysiological causal processes normally involved in the exercise of the capacity to see than we know about those involved in the exercise of most other psychological capacities; that makes the capacity to see a nice test case for the project of analyzing psychological capacities in terms of counterfactuals. And third, David Lewis (1986a) has offered what may appear to be a fairly compelling counterfactual analysis of the capacity to see.

In what follows, I will first argue that Lewis's analysis fails for the reasons counterfactual analyses of capacities can be expected to fail. Then, I will propose a non-counterfactual account of the capacity to see. The account has the merits of Lewis's but avoids the problems I raise for it.

1. Lewis's Analysis Of Intransitive Seeing

Lewis tells us that his analysandum is seeing. More specifically, he says:

(1) My analysandum is seeing in a strong sense that requires a relation to the external scene. Someone whose visual experience is entirely hallucinatory does not see in this strong sense. I take it that he can be said to see in a weaker,

198

phenomenal sense – he sees what isn't there – and this is to say just that he has a visual experience. (2) My analysandum is seeing in the intransitive sense, not seeing such-and-such particular thing. The latter analysandum poses all the problems of the former, and more besides: it raises the questions whether something is seen if it makes a suitable causal contribution to visual experience but it is not noticed separately from its background, and whether something is seen when part of it – for instance, its front surface – makes a causal contribution to visual experience. (1986a, 276)

In the relevant sense of seeing, one is seeing if and only if one is exercising the capacity to see (that capacity the possession of which distinguishes the sighted from the blind). Exercising the capacity to see thus seems to be Lewis's analysandum.

Lewis (1986a) remarks that "it is not far wrong to say simply that someone sees if and only if the scene before his eyes causes matching visual experience" (1986a, 273).[1] But he notes that this simple proposal fails. There are extraordinary circumstances in which the scene before a subject's eyes causes a matching visual experience but the subject hallucinates, rather than sees, by having the experience. He cites the following three such situations:

The Brain Before the Eyes. ...I hallucinate at random, I seem to see a brain before my eyes, my own brain looks just like the one I seem to see, and my brain is causing my visual experience. [Moreover] my brain is before my eyes. It has been carefully removed from my skull. The nerves and blood vessels that connect it to the rest of me have been stretched somehow, not severed. It is still working and I am still randomly hallucinating....

The Wizard. The scene before my eyes consists mostly of a wizard casting a spell. His spell causes me to hallucinate at random, and the hallucination so caused happens to match the scene before my eyes....

The Light Meter. I am blind; but electrodes have been implanted in my brain in such a way that when turned on they will cause me to have a visual experience of a certain sort of landscape. A light meter is on my head. It is connected to the electrodes in such a way that they are turned on if and only if the average illumination exceeds a certain threshold. By chance, just such a landscape is before my eyes, and its illumination is enough to turn on the electrodes. (1986a, 277-78)

Lewis calls cases in which the scene before a subject's eyes is a cause of a matching hallucinatory experience cases of "veridical hallucination." In the above cases, the subject veridically hallucinates, rather than sees. Thus, the initial simple proposal fails to state a sufficient condition for seeing.[2]

To put it mildly, a striking feature of each of the above cases of veridical hallucination is that the scene before the subject's eyes fails to
cause the subject's experience by the (or a) physical-neurophysiologi-
cal causal process normally involved in human vision. The normal
causal process involves, in outline, light from the infra-red to ultraviolet spectrum being reflected and/or emitted from parts of a scene to
the subject's eyes and the lenses of the eyes focussing the light on the
retinas, where a pattern of retinal cell stimulation occurs that sends
electro-chemical impulses along the optic nerve to the visual cortex,
where a pattern of brain cell stimulation occurs with the upshot that
the subject has a visual experience. The external (to the body) stages
of the normal causal process are present in the cases described above,
but not all the internal stages are. Moreover, in the Brain before the
Eyes case, the normal external causal process plays no causal role in
producing the visual experience; for the experience is not produced by
light from the scene. And while light from the scene plays a causal role
in the Light Meter case, it is not the light supplied to the subject's *eyes*
that plays a causal role.[3]

It is easy enough, however, to imagine cases of veridical hallucination in which light supplied to a subject's eyes by parts of a scene
plays a causal role in the production of an hallucinatory visual experience that matches the scene. The subject may have taken a powerful
hallucinogenic drug which so affects him that normal retinal images
trigger processes of random hallucination; and a visual hallucination
so produced might, purely by chance, match the scene before the subject's eyes. Things can go badly wrong anywhere in the internal causal
process leading to experience and, thereby, render the experience hallucinatory; and the hallucinatory experience might, purely by chance,
match the scene.

Of course, in cases of veridical hallucination in which the external
stages of the causal process are the normal ones, the normal internal
causal process will be absent. When the scene before a subject's eyes
causes a matching visual experience by means of the normal external
and internal causal processes, then the subject sees. Will it do, then,
simply to require that the causal process from scene to experience be
the normal one? No. As Lewis points out, it is possible for a subject to
see without the normal internal causal process occurring. One can, he
notes, see without a natural eye, that is, without an eye made of cells
and tissue and with which one has been naturally endowed. One can
see with a prosthetic eye.

The Prosthetic Eye. A prosthetic eye consists of a miniature television camera
mounted in, or on, the front of the head; a computer; and an array of elec-

trodes in the brain. The computer receives input from the camera and sends signals to the electrodes in such a way as to produce visual experience that matches the scene before the eyes. When prosthetic eyes are perfected, the blind will see. (1986a, 279)

Such a device might be instrumental in the production of visual experiences in essentially the same way a natural eye is. The light meter described earlier would not, of course, be instrumental in the production of visual experiences in the right way to count as a prosthetic eye. But there could be a prosthetic device that co-operates with light and the brain in such a way as to discharge the proper function of an eye in the visual system.[4] Suffice it to note, then, that I share Lewis's view that "prosthetic seeing" is seeing. Some of us now walk with prosthetic legs, perhaps some of us will someday see with prosthetic eyes. In prosthetic seeing, as Lewis notes, the normal internal causal process is absent. That process is not required for seeing. One can see by means of an abnormal causal process.[5]

Another striking feature of the above cases of veridical hallucination is that in each, the match between the subject's experience and the scene is only momentary. Is that relevant? Lewis points out that it is not. Whether a subject sees by having a visual experience does not depend on whether the experience is part of a long run of experiences matching scenes before the eyes. As Lewis rightly notes: "Veridical hallucinations are improbable, a long run of them is still more improbable, but that does not make it impossible. No matter how long they go on the sorts of occurrences I've classified as cases of veridical hallucination still are that and not seeing" (1986a, 280). Moreover, he also notes that "a process that permits genuine seeing might work only seldom, perhaps only this once" (1986a, 281).

> *The Loose Wire.* A prosthetic eye has a loose wire. Mostly it flops around; and when it does the eye malfunctions and the subject's visual experience consists of splotches unrelated to the scene before his eyes. But sometimes it touches the contact it ought to be bonded to; and as long as it does, the eye functions perfectly and the subject sees. Whether he sees has nothing to do with whether the wire touches the contact often, or seldom, or only this once. (1986a, 281).

It is not required for a subject to see that she have an experience that is part of a long run of experiences matching the scenes before her eyes.

Lewis goes on to tell us that while it is irrelevant whether a case of matching is one of a series of such cases over an interval of time, it *is* relevant whether the case is isolated or part of a range of cases. For it matters whether the subject *would* have experiences that match the scene before the eyes in a wide range of alternative situations. He says:

> What distinguishes cases of veridical hallucination from genuine seeing... is that there is no proper counterfactual dependence of visual experience on the scene before the eyes. If the scene had been different, it would not have caused correspondingly different visual experience to match that different scene. Any match that occurs is a lucky accident... In genuine seeing... just as the actual scene causes matching visual experience, so likewise would alternative scenes. Different scenes would have produced different visual experience, and thus the subject is in a position to discriminate between the alternatives. (1986a, 281)

The capacity to see is a discriminative capacity. Lewis proposes to analyze the exercise of that capacity in terms of there being a pattern of counterfactual dependence of visual experience on the scene before the subject's eyes.[6] Thus, Lewis says:

> This is my proposal: if the scene before the eyes causes matching visual experience as part of a suitable pattern of counterfactual dependence, then the subject sees; if the scene before the eyes causes matching visual experience without a suitable pattern of counterfactual dependence, then the subject does not see. (1986a, 281)

To begin to elaborate, what, according to Lewis, counts as a "suitable" pattern of counterfactual dependence? Ideally, he says, the subject's visual experience would depend counterfactually on a wide range of possible scenes before his eyes. Moreover, the dependency would be such as to ensure a match between visual experiences and scenes. Let $S1$, $S2$... be propositions specifying possible scenes before the subject's eyes. Let $V1$, $V2$... specify visual experiences. Then, the V's would depend counterfactually on the S's in that a large family of counterfactuals of the following form would be true: 'If Si were before the subject's eyes, the subject would have Vi', where each Vi would match the Si on which it counterfactually depends. How large a family of such counterfactuals is required for seeing? How close a match between experiences and scenes is required? Lewis says that these are vague matters. He tells us:

> The difference between veridical hallucination and genuine seeing is not sharp, on my analysis. It is fuzzy; when the requirement of suitable counterfactual dependence is met to some degree, but to a degree that falls short of the standard set by normal seeing, we may expect borderline cases. And in-

deed it is easy to imagine cases of partial blindness, or of rudimentary prosthetic vision, in which the counterfactual dependence is unsatisfactory and it
is therefore doubtful whether the subject may be said to see. (1986a, 283)[7]

A suitable pattern of counterfactual dependence will include sufficiently many family members, each member involving a sufficiently
close match between experience and scene. But intuitions will vary
somewhat concerning how many members and how close a match are
sufficient.[8]

Lewis's proposal explicitly invokes the notion of causation. He says,
however, that:

> To make the explicit mention of causation redundant, we need not only a
> suitable battery of scene-to-visual-experience counterfactuals but also some
> further counterfactuals. Along with each counterfactual saying that if the
> scene were S the visual experience would be E, we need another saying that
> if the scene S were entirely absent, the visual experience would not be E.
> (1986a, 247)

According to Lewis (1986c), given that the scene S and experience E
are entirely distinct, if E counterfactually depends on S in such a way
that if S had been entirely absent, then E would not have occurred,
then S is a cause of E.[9] To borrow a term from Robert Nozick (1981,
178), Lewis's proposal, reformulated so as to replace mention of causation with counterfactuals, is a "tracking" account of seeing. A visual
experience E tracks the presence of a scene S before the subject's eyes
just in case (i) if S were before the subject's eyes, the subject would
have E and (ii) if S were not before the subject's eyes, the subject
would not have E. Borrowing some further terminology from Nozick,
let us say that the first conditional expresses an *adherence* condition
and the second, a *variation* condition. On Lewis's tracking proposal, a
suitable pattern of counterfactual dependence will consist of a (sufficiently) large number of pairs of adherence and variation conditions.

Let us call this pattern of counterfactual dependence "the multi-
tracking condition"; and let us call the wide pattern of adherence
counterfactuals which include explicit mention of causation, simply
"the multi-adherence condition." By Lewis's lights, the multi-tracking
condition implies the multi-adherence condition, but not conversely.
For Lewis (1986c) acknowledges that one event can cause another
(distinct event) even if the latter is not counterfactually dependent on
the former. Having noted the distinctness of these two proposals, I
should add that the difference between them will not matter at all in
what follows.

2. Some Issues Set Aside

A host of questions immediately arise that bear on whether Lewis's proposal succeeds in stating a necessary condition for seeing. To note just some: (a) Can a subject see without eyes, either natural or prosthetic? (b) Can a subject see without having a visual experience? (c) Can a subject's experience completely fail to match the scene before the eyes yet the subject see by having the experience? (d) Can a subject see by having a visual experience if the subject's experiences track scenes elsewhere than before the subject's eyes?[10]

Lewis does not raise question (a). He does, however, raise questions (b) to (d), only to set them aside. He says:

> I shall not dwell on the question whether it is possible to see even if the scene before the eyes does not cause matching visual experience. Three sorts of examples come to mind. (1) Perhaps someone could see without having visual experience. He would need something that more or less played the role of visual experience, either because it played the role quite imperfectly [as happens in cases of "blind sight," 275, n.4] or because it is not what normally plays the role in human beings (or in some other natural kind to which the subject in question belongs). (2) Perhaps someone could see in whom the scene before the eyes causes non-matching visual experience, provided that the failure of match is systematic and that the subject knows how to infer information about the scene before the eyes from this non-matching visual experience. (3) Perhaps someone could see in whom the scene elsewhere than before the eyes causes visual experience matching that scene, but not matching the scene before the eyes (if such there be). I do not find these examples clear one way or the other, and therefore I shall consider them no further. (1986a, 276)

Nor will I "dwell on the question whether it is possible to see even if the scene before the eyes does not cause matching visual experience." I, too, set (a) to (d) aside. These issues are orthogonal to my central concerns here.

3. Capacities And Counterfactuals

A capacity can be possessed without being exercised. A television may have the capacity to receive 300 channels, but not be receiving any because it is shut off; likewise, someone with the capacity to play the piano need not be exercising that capacity. The capacity to see is no exception. One can possess the capacity to see and yet not be exercising it; one might be fast asleep.

Capacities typically have counterfactual conditions associated with their exercise. Again, the capacity to see is no exception. Lewis's multi-tracking condition consists of counterfactuals that seem associated with the exercise of the capacity to see, and thus with (intransitive) seeing. But it is important to note that typically, a capacity can be exercised but its associated counterfactuals fail to hold due to factors extraneous to the exercise of the capacity; and typically, the counterfactuals can hold for reasons other than that the capacity is being exercised. The counterfactual conditions associated with a capacity are thus typically neither necessary nor sufficient for the exercise of the capacity. The counterfactuals are associated with the capacity in that they are *criteria* for the exercise of the capacity. Capacities are not exercised *because* their associated counterfactuals hold; the counterfactuals can hold when the capacity is not being exercised. Rather, the counterfactuals normally hold at least partly *because* the capacity is being exercised. I say "at least partly" since, as I mentioned, factors other than that the capacity is being exercised may be required for the counterfactuals to hold. But when the additional factors, if any, are normally present when the capacity is being exercised, the counterfactuals are criteria for the exercise of the capacity. Once again, the capacity to see is no exception. Lewis's multi-tracking condition is, I believe, at best, a criterion for whether a subject is exercising the capacity to see, and thus for whether the subject is seeing. The condition bears on whether a subject is seeing only in that it normally holds (at least partly) *because* the subject is seeing. The subject does not see because the counterfactuals hold. Lewis thus reverses the order of explanation.

Now as I indicated at the outset, I will not try to make a case for this general view of capacities and their associated counterfactual conditions. I will simply try to make the case for the capacity to see. However, the general morals will, I hope, be apparent.[11]

Four sections remain. In the next section, section 4, I will argue that both Lewis's multi-tracking condition and his multi-adherence condition fail to be necessary for seeing: they can fail to hold due to factors extraneous to the subject's exercising the capacity to see, and thus can fail to hold even when the subject is exercising that capacity. In section 5, I will consider a counterfactual proposal by Bruce LeCatt (1982) intended as a "modest correction" of Lewis's proposal and argue that it too fails to state a necessary condition for seeing. In section 6, I will argue that neither Lewis nor LeCatt succeed in stating a sufficient condition for seeing: the counterfactual conditions they propose can hold for reasons other than that the subject is exercising the capacity to see, and thus can hold even when the subject is not exercising that capacity. Finally, in section 7, I will offer a non-counterfactual proposal that has, I believe, the virtues of Lewis's proposal but avoids the problems I raise for it.

4. Is Lewis's Condition Necessary For Seeing?

The following case, presented by Lewis himself, shows, I believe, that neither the multi-tracking condition nor the multi-adherence condition is necessary for seeing:

> *The Censor.* My natural or prosthetic eye is in perfect condition and functioning normally, and by means of it the scene before my eyes causes matching visual experience. But if the scene were any different my visual experience would be just the same. For there is a censor standing by, ready to see to it that I have precisely that visual experience and no other, whatever the scene may be. (Perhaps the censor is external, perhaps it is something in my own brain.) So long as the scene is such as to cause the right experience, the censor does nothing. But if the scene were any different, the censor would intervene and cause the same experience by other means. If so, my eye would not function normally and the scene before my eyes would not cause matching visual experience. (1986a, 285)

In this case, neither the multi-tracking condition nor the multi-adherence condition hold. Moreover, despite the fact that the subject's experience is caused by and matches the actual scene before the eyes, the subject's experience does not even track that particular scene. Nonetheless, the subject sees by having the experience; or at least the case can be fleshed out in such a way that the subject sees.

Suppose the subject was seeing by means of the normal causal process. At some point, the censor came on the scene and began to monitor the process.[12] As yet, the censor has not had to intervene since the scene has been of the right sort to produce the visual experience the censor wants the subject to have. Parts of the scene continue to reflect visible light to the subject's eyes by a normal path; the eyes continue to be stimulated in a normal way; and the subject's "natural eye[s] [are] in perfect condition and functioning normally, and by means of [them] the scene before the subject's eyes causes matching visual experience." In short, the scene before the eyes continues to produce the subject's visual experience by the normal causal means. The causal process from scene to experience is the normal one, though it occurs in abnormal circumstances, namely circumstances in which a censor is monitoring it. Since the censor come on the scene, the multi-tracking condition and the multi-adherence condition no longer hold. But despite the failure of these conditions, the subject continues to see. Or so I claim.

Unsurprisingly, Lewis is well-aware that someone might take the censor case to be a counter-example to the necessity of his proposed condition. He says of the case that it is

> a hard one. It closely resembles cases of genuine seeing, and we might well be tempted to classify it as such. According to my analysis, however, it is a case of veridical hallucination. The scene before the eyes causes matching visual experience without any pattern of counterfactual dependence whatever, suitable or otherwise. (1986a, 285)

But Lewis stands by his analysis, saying:

> The decisive consideration, despite the misleading resemblance of this case to a genuine case of seeing, is that the censor's potential victim has no capacity at all to discriminate by sight. Just as in any other case of veridical hallucination, the match that occurs is a lucky accident. (1986a, 286)

I find this response to the Censor case implausible. As I indicated, I think the Censor case is a counter-example to Lewis's proposal.

To begin to respond to Lewis, then, it may indeed be a "lucky accident" that the scene before the subject's eyes is the right sort to prevent the censor's intervention. But given that the censor does not intervene, it is not a lucky accident that the scene produces a matching visual experience. For it does so by means of the normal causal process for seeing. The subject, to use Lewis's own phrase, is "a potential victim," not an actual victim of the censor. But Lewis tells us that "the censor's potential victim has no capacity at all to discriminate by sight." The capacity to see *is* indeed a discriminative capacity. If the subject lacked the capacity to discriminate by sight, the subject would indeed not be seeing. But Lewis is mistaken in claiming that the potential victim lacks the capacity to discriminate by sight. In fact, as I have fleshed out the case, the potential victim is exercising that capacity. In having the experience in question, the subject exercises his capacity to discriminate scenes before his eyes by matching experience; the experience discriminates the actual scene from the other possible scenes before his eyes. Moreover, were the scene before the subject's eyes to change and the censor to intervene, the subject may very well retain his capacity to discriminate by sight. What the censor would do if the scene changed is prevent the subject from exercising the capacity, not eradicate the subject's capacity.[13] The censor would prevent the subject from exercising the capacity by causing "the same experience by other means," means that would not be means by which the capacity to see can be exercised. But since the actual scene before the subject's eyes is the right sort, the censor in fact does nothing to interfere with the process; the censor does not intervene; the censor stands idly by. And the subject sees.

Consider the following censor case:

> *The Grand Canyon at Sunset.* One year ago, while seeing, Jack had the misfortune of being targeted by a censor. The scene before Jack's eyes was not the right sort to prevent the censor's intervention. Since then, Jack's days have been visually just alike. The censor has been producing in him a visual experience with a content that might be entitled "The Grand Canyon at Sunset." (The censor is external and his intervention has not damaged Jack in any way. Jack's eyes and brain remain intact.) This evening, as luck would have it, Jack is standing before the Grand Canyon at sunset, and the scene is just right. The censor stops intervening, and the scene produces a visual experience by the normal means for human seeing. The censor remains ready and able, however, to intervene again should the scene before Jack's eyes change in any visible way.

It appears to be Lewis's position that as soon as the censor came onto the scene, Jack lost the capacity to see, and that Jack lacks that capacity even on the evening in question. Lewis would allow, of course, that Jack would regain the capacity to see were the censor to go on his way and leave Jack alone. But for Lewis, whether the Censor is actually producing the experience in question or instead just standing by ready to intervene if necessary and produce it by other means makes no difference to whether Jack sees, or even to whether Jack has the capacity to see. Whether the censor is actually intervening or just standing by ready to intervene if necessary, Jack does not see since he lacks the capacity to see. So far as whether Jack is seeing, the evening in question is no different from all the rest since the censor came on the scene. Whether Jack is an actual victim or only a potential victim of the censor, Jack lacks the capacity to see and thus does not see. On Lewis's view, the difference between the evening in question and all the rest is only that on the evening in question, Jack veridically hallucinates, rather than non-veridically hallucinates.

But whether Jack is an actual victim or only a potential victim seems to me to make the difference as to whether or not Jack is exercising the capacity to see. Moreover, Jack retained the capacity to see all along.[14] It is just that the censor prevented him from exercising it until the evening Jack stood before the Grand Canyon; but on that evening, Jack exercised the capacity. It would be perfectly coherent to say that the censor lets Jack see on the evening in question. Indeed, it might be the censor's intention to let Jack see only when exactly that one sort of scene is before Jack's eyes. Lewis would, I believe, have to say that the censor could not possibly carry out such an intention; there is no way that the censor could let Jack see only when that scene is before his eyes. I find that extremely unintuitive. I see no reason to believe it. It seems to me perfectly possible that the censor allows Jack to see only when that one scene is before his eyes.

Censor cases illustrate that one might not only have, but actually exercise, a capacity to discriminate by sight, even when the multi-tracking and multi-adherence conditions do not hold. For such cases illustrate that those conditions can fail to hold due to factors that are *extraneous* to the exercising of the capacity.

So I claim. Lewis disagrees. And there is one reason he disagrees that I have yet to mention, namely: "the censor's idleness is an essential factor in the causal process by which matching visual experience is produced, just as the censor's intervention would be in the alternative process" (1986a, 286). I agree that the censor's intervention would be a factor in the causal process by which the experience would be produced were the scene before the eyes to change. But the censor's idleness does not seem to be an essential factor, or even a factor, in the actual causal process from scene to experience. I say this not because I doubt that omissions can be causes,[15] but simply because the censor's idleness seem to be extraneous to the causal process in question. As the situation is depicted, the censor's idleness consists in the censor's refraining from producing the experience in question by other means. I do not see how the censor's so refraining counts as a factor in the process from scene to experience, let alone an essential factor. The censor's idleness is an effect of the scene before the subject's eyes, and so of a stage of the causal process leading to visual experience. The experience and the censor's idleness are thus dual effects of a common cause. Lewis does not elaborate on the point in question in any detail. He does, however, say:

> We cannot uniformly ignore or hold fixed those causal factors which are absences of interventions. The standard process might be riddled with them. (Think of a circuit built up from exclusive-or-gates: every output signal from such a gate is caused partly by the absence of a second input signal.) (1986a, 286)

These remarks suggest that Lewis may have been thinking of censors who are part of an internal mechanism whose operation is involved in the exercise of the capacity to see. But that is not the sort of censor case I have presented. I am concerned with a censor who is not part of any such mechanism.[16] I am concerned with external censors. The presence of an external censor will, as Lewis recognizes, falsify the relevant counterfactuals.

Perhaps, however, an external censor's idleness is in some sense a causal condition for the scene's producing the experience. We should note that the censor's idleness does not *enable* the scene to produce the experience: the scene would have produced the experience even if the censor were entirely absent. But it seems right to say that the censor's idleness permits the scene to cause the experience; and perhaps that makes the censor's idleness a causal condition for the scene's causing the experience, despite the fact that it is not an enabling condition for the scene's causing the experience. I grant this much, then: the censor's idleness counts as his *letting* the scene cause the visual experience. The censor could have prevented the scene from causing the experience, but he did not. If that makes the censor's idleness a causal condition for the scene's causing the experience, so be it. My point is that there is a process that (1) the censor idleness is not a stage of and that (2) counts as an exercise of the capacity to see. The censor lets the scene cause the experience by the normal process for seeing. And the censor's idleness is no part of that process.

Consider a billiard ball's rolling across a billiard table and hitting another billiard ball. Suppose that there was a bystander determined and able to ensure that the first ball hit the second (at just the right velocity and angle and at just the right time it in fact did so) should the ball have strayed from its actual path. The ball did not stray; so the bystander stood idly by. The presence of the bystander affects what counterfactuals hold. It is not true that if the first ball had not been rolling in such-and-such a direction and with such-and-such a velocity, it would not have hit the second ball. For the bystander would have ensured that the first ball hit the second, had the ball not been taking that path across the billiard table. However, while the bystander affects such counterfactual dependencies, his presence is extraneous to the causal process consisting of the ball rolling across the table and hitting the other ball; the bystander stands by, not interfering. The bystander lets the one ball hit the other. The censor is likewise extraneous to the causal process from scene to experience. The censor is a bystander who lets the scene before the eyes cause the experience by the normal causal route. Indeed, I think it is right to say that the censor lets the subject see that one scene.

Here it appears that Lewis and I have a fundamental disagreement. The censor example seems to me a clear and clean counter-example to his proposal. The moral I draw from it is that a subject can have the capacity to discriminate by sight, and even be exercising that capacity, yet the counterfactuals in question fail to hold due to factors extraneous to the exercise of that capacity. The occurrence of a causal process that constitutes the exercise of the capacity is *not*, by itself, enough to ensure that the counterfactuals hold. In addition, surrounding circumstances must be right. That is what the censor case illustrates. Lewis disagrees. He tells us that the censor's idleness is an essential factor in the causal process itself. While that would be true of censors who are a part of some mechanism whose operation is involved in the exercise of the capacity to see, it is not true of external censors. If Lewis insists that it is true of external censors too, then he would say exactly the same about the bystander's idleness in the billiard case and the causal process involved there. I say that the censor and bystander let the respective causal processes occur but are not factors in the processes, let alone essential factors in them. Perhaps Lewis would insist that bystanders are essential factors in the causal processes in question. But I see no reason to believe that.

Moreover, it is worthwhile noting here that Lewis's views about causation and causal processes have changed somewhat in recent years in a way that bears on the issue of whether the censor's idleness is a factor in the causal process from scene to experience. The changes have come both in response to a certain powerful intuitive consideration concerning cases of causal pre-emption and in response to technical problems his counterfactual theory of causation faces because of certain cases of causal pre-emption.[17] The problems and the intuitive consideration are directly relevant to our present concern. For the Censor case, as Lewis notes,

> is one of causal preemption. The scene before [the subject's] eyes is the actual cause of [the subject's] visual experience: the censor is an alternative potential cause of the same effect. The actual cause pre-empts the potential alternative cause, stopping the alternative chain that would otherwise go to completion. (1986a, 285-86)

Lewis (1986d) has acknowledged that because of certain cases of causal pre-emption, it appears that we cannot understand causation as he once thought we could. He once thought (see 1986c, 167):

> An event *c* is a cause of an event *e* iff there is chain of events from *c* to *e*, each event in the chain being causally dependent on its predecessor. (*e* causally depends on *c* iff [*c* and *e* are wholly distinct, and if *c* had not occurred *e* would not have occurred].)

Causation cannot be understood in this way because there are causal processes from one event to another in which not every stage is counterfactually dependent on its immediate predecessor, due to the presence of a potential alternative cause that is pre-empted by some stage of the process. I will discuss some of the technical problems raised by causal pre-emption in section 5. In what remains of this section, I want to present Lewis's intuitive consideration in favour of not requiring that events in a causal process counterfactually depend on their immediate predecessors. For the intuitive consideration bears in a striking way on the issue of whether the censor's idleness is a factor in the causal process from scene to experience.

Here is how Lewis presents the intuitive consideration:

> Suppose we have processes – courses of events, which may or may not be causally connected – going on in two distinct spatiotemporal regions, regions of the same or of different possible worlds. Disregarding the surroundings of the two regions, and disregarding any irrelevant events that may be occurring in either region without being part of the process in question, what goes on in the two regions is exactly alike. Suppose further that the laws of nature that govern the two regions are exactly the same. Then can it be that we have a causal process in one of the regions but not the other? It seems not. Intuitively, whether the process going on in a region is causal depends only on the intrinsic character of the process itself, and on the relevant laws. The surroundings, and even other events in the region, are irrelevant. Maybe the laws of nature are relevant without being intrinsic to the region (if some sort of regularity theory of lawhood is true) but nothing else is. (1986d, 205)

Partly in the light of this intuitive consideration, Lewis says that in cases of causal pre-emption "what spoils the [counterfactual] dependence is something extraneous: the presence alongside the main process of one or more pre-empted alternatives. Without them, all would be well. Hold fixed the laws but change the surroundings, in any of many ways, and we would have dependence" (1986d, 206). Indeed, as we saw above, something as extraneous to a causal process as a bystander standing idly by letting the causal process occur rather than producing the relevant effect by other means can "spoil the counterfactual dependence."

Partly in response to the above intuitive consideration and the phenomena of causal pre-emption, Lewis has introduced the notion of quasi-dependence, a kind of non-counterfactual dependence, and claimed that quasi-dependence suffices for causation. In introducing this notion, he says:

> suppose some process in some region does not itself exhibit this pattern of dependence [i.e., counterfactual dependence]; but suppose that in its intrinsic character it is just like processes in other regions (of the same world, or other

worlds with the same laws) situated in various surroundings. And suppose that among these processes in other regions, the great majority – as measured by the surroundings – do exhibit the proper pattern of dependence. This means that the intrinsic character of the given process is right, and the laws are right, for the proper pattern of dependence – if only the surroundings were different, and different in any of many ways... Suppose that there exists some actually occurring process of the kind just described, and that two distinct events c and e are the first and last in that process. Then let us say that e *quasi-depends* on c. (1986d, 206)

Lewis goes on to say "we could redefine a causal chain as a sequence of two or more events, with either dependence or quasi-dependence at each step. And as always, one event is a cause of another iff there is a causal chain from one to the other" (1986d, 206). We can now see that the censor's idleness makes the causal process one of quasi-dependence, rather than one of counterfactual dependence. But whether a causal process is one of quasi-dependence depends on the circumstances in which it occurs, not on its intrinsic nature and the laws that govern it. Moreover, it is important to recognize that processes of quasi-dependence are full-blooded causal processes; quasi-dependence is full-blooded causation. A causal process by which a guillotine cuts off someone's head is one of quasi-dependence if there is an executioner standing by with an axe ready and able to do the job if the guillotine fails to. The severing of the victim's head quasi-depends, in Lewis's sense, on the cutting action of the guillotine blade.[18]

Lewis acknowledges that this revised account of causation is "less purely a counterfactual analysis" than his "original analysis" (1986d, 207). But he says "the extended analysis may well be preferable" (1986d, 207). I agree.[19] The departure from a purely counterfactual analysis of causation is surely preferable if, as it appears, that is what it takes to count, say, the cutting action of a guillotine as a cause of the severing of a head in a case in which there is an axe-welding potential executioner standing by. The fact that there is a bystander standing idly by letting a process unfold rather than producing the relevant effect by other means should not disqualify the process as causal. The bystander at the billiard table, the censor and the potential executioner are all such bystander cases. In each such case, the bystander is extraneous to the causal process he lets occur.

My main reason for presenting Lewis's discussion of the intuitive consideration and of the notion of quasi-dependence has been to bolster my case that the censor's idleness is extraneous to the causal process from scene to experience, not a factor in the process, let alone an essential factor. Still, it should be noted that even if Lewis were to endorse the revised account of causation unequivocally, he could consistently continue to maintain that the subject is not exercising the capacity to see in censor cases. But my position is this: in censor cases (in which the censor is external), "what spoils the [multi-tracking or multi-adherence condition] is something extraneous: the presence alongside the main process of one or more pre-empted alternatives. Without them, all would be well. Hold fixed the laws but change the surroundings, in any of many ways, and we would have dependence" (1986d, 206). An exercise of the capacity to see, just like an exercise of any capacity, is a causal process. I take censor cases to show that whether the multi-tracking condition or the multi-adherence condition holds depends not just on whether the subject is exercising the capacity to see, and so not just on whether an appropriate causal process is occurring, but also on whether the surroundings are right. In censor cases, the surroundings are not right. Thus, the counterfactual conditions in question do not hold. But still the subject sees. That, at any rate, is my position. I will attempt to develop my case for the plausibility of this position in the remaining sections.

5. Lecatt's Proposal

Bruce LeCatt, at least, shares my intuition that the Censor case is one of seeing. He (1982) claims that the case is a counter-example to Lewis's proposal. But, unlike me, he holds that "a fresh start is uncalled for... the makings of a conservative correction are not far to seek" (1982, 159). LeCatt makes explicit appeal to causation, rather than appealing to variation counterfactuals, and cleverly appeals to the notion of a step-wise counterfactual dependency to handle adherence counterfactuals.

The notion of a step-wise counterfactual dependency is this. Suppose an event $c1$ is a cause of an effect e and that $c2$ is a potential cause of e that is pre-empted by $c1$. Suppose further there is some event, i, such that i is intermediate between the effect e and the effect of $c1$ that cuts off the potential causal chain from $c2$ to e. Then e will be counterfactually dependent on i, and i will be counterfactually dependent on $c1$. Thus, there will be a two-step counterfactual dependence of e on $c1$; and so e will be stepwise counterfactually dependent on $c1$.[20]

Here, then, is how LeCatt invokes the notion in a case in which there is one censor: there will be some stage of the causal process intermediate between (i) the experience and (ii) the stage of the process from scene to experience that the censor monitors. When the intermediate stage in question occurs, the alternative causal process from the censor to the experience has already been cut off. There may be a suitable pattern of counterfactual dependence of the subject's experience on what goes on at the intermediate stage in question; and what goes on at the intermediate stage may, in turn, be suitably counterfactually dependent of the scenes before the subject's eyes.[21] So, the experience is step-wise counterfactually dependent on a wide range of alternative scenes. If there is a second censor, then, again, there will be an intermediate stage, and a stepwise pattern of counterfactual dependence of experience on the scene before the eyes; and so on, for any finite number of censors.

LeCatt's conservative correction of Lewis's proposal is, then, this:

> if the scene before the eyes causes matching visual experience as part of a suitable pattern of counterfactual dependence, or as part of a suitable pattern of stepwise counterfactual dependence, then the subject sees; if the scene before the eyes causes matching visual experience without a pattern of either sort, the subject does not see. (1982, 161)

LeCatt claims that his weaker condition will hold in censor cases provided that (1) there are only finitely many censors monitoring the process, (2) there is no causal action at a distance involved in the process from scene to experience, and (3) no censor is part of the causal mechanism that produces the experience (1982, 161-62). For in such cases, there may be no appropriate intermediate stage of the causal process for a stepwise dependence. What, then, about censor cases in which one or more of (1) to (3) hold? He says that such cases "are too different from what could really happen; let us doubt any intuitions we may have [about them] and let them fall where they may" (1982, 162).

Lewis (1986b) has responded to LeCatt by saying:

> my case of the censor is a case of excellent stepwise dependence and no dependence simpliciter at all. LeCatt suggests, and I agree, that it is the stepwise dependence that accounts for any inclinations we have to judge the case of the censor a positive case of seeing. He further claims that this judgment is correct; but there I do not agree, and I insist that the essential feature of seeing is altogether missing. (1986b, 290)

Here is where I stand. I agree of course with LeCatt, against Lewis, that the Censor case is one of seeing: the essential feature of seeing, the capacity to discriminate by sight, is *not* missing; indeed, it is being exercised. I agree with Lewis, however, that the pattern of stepwise dependence LeCatt proposes does not suffice for seeing; I will say why in section 6. Finally, I disagree with Lewis's contention that "it is the stepwise dependence that accounts for any inclinations we have to judge the case of the censor a positive case of seeing" (1986b, 290) For, as I noted, I judge the case as positive because the censor is standing idling by as parts of the scene before the subject's eye supply light to it in the normal way and the "eye is in perfect condition and functioning normally and by means of it the scene before [the] eyes causes matching visual experience" (1986a, 285) The causal process from scene to experience is the normal one for seeing; despite the presence of the censor in the surroundings, the subject sees.

Will LeCatt's proposal, then, handle all the censor cases worth considering? Consider again the cases LeCatt tells us should not concern us: cases in which there is either (1) infinitely many censors, or (2) action at a distance, or in which (3) the censor is part of the mechanism. I will not discuss cases of type (3), except to note that I disagree with LeCatt's claim that such cases "are too different from what can really happen" (1986,161) to be worth considering. A censor need not be conscious or intelligent; it can be a mechanical device. A censor that is part of the mechanism would act as a kind of *filter*, allowing only just the right sort of prior causal process to proceed without interference. There may be nomologically possible censor cases of this sort that are cases of genuine seeing and in which LeCatt's stepwise dependence fails to hold. I will not consider them, however, since in such cases the causal process from scene to experience is not the normal one for seeing. I will now briefly comment on (1) and (2). After that, I will describe a censor case in which there is no action at a distance, only one censor is involved, the censor is not part of the mechanism, there is no stepwise dependence but the subject sees by means of the normal causal process.

As concerns (1), I cannot see why it would matter whether there were one censor standing idly by or infinitely many censors standing idly by. I cannot see that it makes any difference whether there are infinitely many censors lurking in the surroundings, if they do nothing to interfere with the process. Infinitely many censors that are extraneous to the process from scene to experience will not disqualify a case as one of seeing. Whether one censor or infinitely many censors let the scene before a subject's eyes cause a matching visual experience by the normal causal process, the subject sees. Or so it seems to me. And I cannot see what reason LeCatt could give for saying such cases would be disqualified, beyond the question-begging reason that in such a circumstance there would be no pattern of stepwise dependence.

As concerns (2), I find myself at a loss imagining cases in which there is action at a distance from the scene to the experience; like LeCatt, I lack any trustworthy intuitions about such cases. But it seems possible (though not nomologically possible) for there to be a causal process from scene to experience some stage of which is produced by its immediate predecessor via causal action at a distance (so that there is a spatio-temporal gap in the process). And we can easily describe a censor case in which there will be no stepwise counterfactual dependence for that reason: for the spatio-temporal gap may start at the stage where the censor monitors the process but end right at the stage at which the censor would intervene to produce the experience.[22] To be sure, such a process would not be the normal causal process (or even a nomologically possible causal process). But I fail to see why no such gappy causal process could be one by means of which someone sees. A censor standing *idly* by waiting to take advantage of the gap if necessary would not disqualify a case as one of seeing. But since in such cases the causal process is not the normal sort, I will not discuss them further. Before considering censor cases in which there is only one censor, no action at a distance and in which the censor is external to the mechanism, some background is useful.

Lewis (1986d) has distinguished two kinds of cases of pre-emption, "early" and "late." Of the former, he says:

> In early pre-emption, the process running from the pre-empted alternative is cut off well before the main process running from the pre-empting cause has gone to completion. Then somewhere along the main process, not too early and not too late, we can find an intermediate event to complete a causal chain in two steps from the peremption cause to the final effect. The effect depends on the intermediate, which depends in turn on the pre-emption cause. (1986d, 200)

In contrast, in cases of late pre-emption,

> the alternative process is doomed only when the final effect itself occurs. The alternative is cut off not by a branch process that diverges from the main process at a junction event before the effect is reached, but rather by a continuation of the main process beyond the effect. (1986d, 203)

Imagine that there is a terminator attempting to kill a certain victim. The terminator will persist in his attempt until he sees the victim dead. Were someone else to kill the terminator's intended victim before the terminator succeeded in doing so, this would be a case of late pre-emption. The death of the victim will not be stepwise dependent on the act that actually kills the victim. For there will be no intermediate point between the act and the death at which every alternative causal process from the terminator would have already been cut off.[23]

Late pre-emption cases lead Lewis to concede that even a chain of stepwise counterfactual dependence is not required for causation. Indeed, the fact that the notion of a stepwise dependence will not handle cases of late pre-emption is one reason Lewis invoked the notion of quasi-dependence discussed in the previous section.[24] The death of the victim in a terminator case will be only quasi-dependent, in Lewis's terminology, on the act that causes the death. (Quasi-dependence, you will recall, is full-blooded causation.)

There are censor cases involving late pre-emption in which the subject sees, but in which there is no stepwise dependence of experience on the scene before the eyes. The censor is bound, determined and able to ensure that the subject has a certain visual experience. Only the occurrence of that experience would make the censor desist from attempting to produce it. However, the actual scene, S, beats the censor to the punch and produces the experience by the normal causal means. The subject sees, I contend, despite the failure of LeCatt's condition. LeCatt's proposal fails to state a necessary condition for seeing.

Unlike LeCatt, I think that a fresh start is called for. It is a mistake to try to analyze the exercise of the capacity to see in terms of counterfactual dependencies. I will defend this claim further in the following section.

6. Is Lewis's Condition Sufficient For Seeing?

Recall the following example of veridical hallucination cited earlier: "*The Wizard.* The scene before my eyes consists mostly of a wizard casting a spell. His spell causes me to hallucinate at random, and the hallucination so caused happens to match the scene before my eyes " (Lewis 1986a, 277). In the postscript to Lewis (1986a) (viz., Lewis 1986b), Lewis correctly notes that this case is in fact a counter-example to his proposal. Speaking of the Wizard case, he says:

> I thought it a clear negative case, and cited it in my favor, without ever noticing that my own conditions classified it as positive! For the actual scene with the hallucinogenic wizard *does* cause matching experience; and we *do* have a wide range of alternative scenes – namely, ordinary scenes without the wizard – that would cause matching experience in a normal way. (1986b, 289)

The Wizard case, as Lewis acknowledges, shows that the multi-tracking condition fails to suffice for seeing. Thus his multi-adherence condition and LeCatt's stepwise dependence condition fail to suffice as well; for they are implied by the multi-tracking condition.[25] The case vividly illustrates that it is not enough that the counterfactuals in question hold, it matters *why* they hold. In the Wizard case, virtually all the counterfactuals hold because the subject *possesses* the capacity to see, but *not* because the subject is *exercising* that capacity. And since the subject is not exercising that capacity, the subject is not seeing. Lewis has a different diagnosis of the case. While he acknowledges that the Wizard case is a counter-example to the sufficiency of his proposal, he tries to mitigate the severity of the counter-example by arguing that the case counts as negative because of secondary considerations that influence our judgments about whether a subject sees. Let us look at the secondary considerations.

There are, Lewis says, three such considerations. The first is whether the causal process by means of which the scene before the subject's eyes causes a matching visual experience is the normal one. Lewis correctly counts this as a secondary consideration since, while it influences our judgements about how to classify a case, the absence of the normal causal process is not enough on its own to disqualify a case as one of seeing.[26]

The second secondary consideration has to do with the fact that the counterfactual dependencies in question will really be probabilistic. Lewis tells us that

what we have are not counterfactuals saying that if there were such-and-such scene then there would definitely be such-and-such matching experience; but rather that there would be a chance distribution over experiences giving significant probability (and much more than there would have been without the scene) to matching experience. Other things being equal, the better the chances of matching experience, the better the case of seeing. Here I have in mind the actual chance given the actual scene, as well as the chances there would be given other scenes. *Ex hypothesi* the actual experience matches the actual scene. And that is enough, if I am right that a counterfactual with a true antecedent is true iff its consequent is, to give us a non-probabilistic counterfactual for that one, actual scene: if there were that scene, there would be that matching experience. But there will be a probabilistic counterfactual as well: if there were that scene, then there would be so-and-so chance of that matching experience, and maybe also some chance of other experiences. If the actual chance of match is substantially below one, then despite the non-probabilistic counterfactual, we have a consideration that detracts somewhat from the claim of the case to be judged positive. (1986b, 286)

The probabilistic counterfactual, on Lewis's view, concerns the objective chance of that experience immediately after the scene occurs. So, the second consideration is whether the objective chance of a matching experience is very low immediately after the occurrence of the scene.[27] I agree that this is a secondary consideration, it can influence our judgements about a case, but it is not on its own enough to disqualify a case as of one of seeing.

Lewis calls the third secondary consideration "the island effect." Here is how he presents it:

> There are good scenes that would produce matching experience, and bad scenes that would not. An ideal pattern would have no bad scenes, but that is too much to demand; so I settled for the requirement that there be a wide range of good scenes. Note that scenes may be close together or far apart; they may differ from one another more or less. So a good scene might be surrounded by other good scenes, with no bad ones nearby. The nearest bad scene to it might differ quite substantially. Or at the opposite extreme it might be a tiny island, surrounded by a sea of bad scenes. Suppose the actual good scene is such an island. My requirement that there be a wide range of good scenes may be satisfied only in virtue of some distant continent. (Or in virtue of many other islands, widely scattered.) It's a narrow escape: the subject sees, on my analysis, but had the scene been just a little different then he wouldn't have done. For any scene just a little different would have been a bad scene. (1986b, 288)

I agree that the island effect is a secondary consideration. I will return to the island effect later.[28]

Finally, referring to all three considerations, abnormal process, low probability of match, and the island effect, Lewis tells us: "the secondary considerations *can* have decisive weight, if they all push together as hard as they can. Nothing less would do, I think" (1986b, 289). He would *not*, he tells us, judge a wizard case as negative unless all three secondary considerations were pushing together as hard as they can.

Now the original Wizard case is, by stipulation, a case of veridical hallucination. But Lewis's point is that he would count a case in which a wizard produces a matching visual experience by casting a spell as one of veridical hallucination only if all three considerations were pushing together as hard as they can. Of course, in such a circumstance, the abnormal process consideration will be pushing awfully hard. While the absence of the normal causal process is not enough to disqualify a case as one of seeing, I, for one, find it difficult to see how a wizard could cause a visual experience by casting a spell, and the subject count as seeing by having the visual experience. The reason is that it is difficult for me to see how such a process could be an exercise of the capacity to see. However, Lewis would, I take it, count a subject as seeing by having a visual experience produced by a wizard casting a spell if the experience matches and is caused by the scene before the subject's eyes, and a wide pattern of counterfactual dependence holds in which there is *not both* a low probability of match and the island effect. For he thinks that all three considerations must be pushing together as hard as they can to disqualify a wizard case as one of seeing.

But must the island effect be present to so disqualify a wizard case? Lewis tells us that he would not judge a wizard case negative "if the scene with the wizard were in the midst of other scenes that would somehow, with significant probability, also produce matching experience" (1986b, 289). Why not? Suppose that only a very precise way of casting the spell will work, a way that requires every visible detail of the scene before the subject's eyes to be just right; if any part of the scene is not just right, the spell will not take and the subject will see by the normal means. (It does not matter whether the wizard is part of the scene.) If the scene is just right, the spell will take, and the subject will randomly hallucinate. However, if the scene were to change, the spell would be broken. All the visible details of the scene matter to sustaining the spell. But, it is essential to note, they do not matter because the subject must see them for the spell to continue. For as soon as the spell takes, the subject ceases to see. The visible details of the scene do not contribute to sustaining the spell by means of the suject's seeing them. Rather, they contribute to sustaining the spell in the following way: they produce certain types of retinal images in the subject's eyes. The subject has been primed by the wizard in such a way that as long as a scene that produces the specific types of retinal images in question is before the subject's eyes, the spell continues, and the subject continues to randomly hallucinate.[29] The spell will thus be broken by any change of scene that will case retinal images not of the types in question. It could happen that while randomly hallucinating under such a spell, a subject has an hallucinatory experience that, purely by chance, matches the scene before his eyes. That would be a case of veridical hallucination in which a wide range of tracking relations hold and in which there is no island effect.[30]

Are, then, the absence of a normal causal process and a low probability of match alone enough to disqualify a case as one of seeing? In a word, "No." There are positive cases in which there is an abnormal process and a low probability of match. Consider one of Lewis's own examples of a positive case of seeing:

The Loose Wire. A prosthetic eye has a loose wire. Mostly it flops around; and when it does the eye malfunctions and the subject's visual experience consists of splotches unrelated to the scene before his eyes. But sometimes it touches the contact it ought to be bonded to; and as long as it does, the eye functions perfectly and the subject sees. Whether he sees has nothing to do with whether the wire touches the contact often, or seldom, or only this once. (1986a, 281)

Here the process is not the normal one. Moreover, given Lewis's own account of objective probability, if the wire is flopping immediately after the occurrence of the scene, the objective chance of match for any scene may be very low. In this case the first two considerations are pushing awfully hard, but I agree with Lewis that if the wire makes the right contact in time, the subject will see.[31] The case will be one of seeing by abnormal causal means and with a low chance of match between scenes before the eyes and experiences. Thus the fact that there is abnormal process and low chance of match is not enough to disqualify a case as one of seeing. Those conditions are present in the Loose Wire case.

It is worthwhile noting, moreover, that there need not be a low probability of match in the wizard case described above, except where the specific scene or very small group of scenes are concerned that would produce the sorts of retinal images that contribute to inducing and sustaining the spell. There is a low probability of match for that scene or that very small group of scenes since they will produce retinal images that trigger random hallucinations. However, every other normally visible scene may have a very high probability of producing a matching visual experience. Thus, there are wizard cases of veridical hallucination in which there is no island effect, and in which the low probability of match consideration is hardly pushing at all, let alone as hard as it can. There are wizard cases that fail to count as cases of seeing, but in which the only secondary consideration that comes into play pushing as hard as it can is that of whether the causal process is the normal one. This consideration alone is, however, as I noted, not what leads us to disqualify such cases as ones of seeing. The reason we disqualify such cases as ones of seeing is, rather, that the subject is not exercising his capacity to discriminate scenes by visual experience. That is not happening in wizard cases, even when the island effect is not present and the low probability of match consideration is barely pushing at all.

The difference between the Loose Wire case and the Wizard case is a difference in the causal processes at work. In the Loose Wire case, when the wire contacts what it ought to be bonded to, the prosthetic eye functions just like a natural eye. In contrast, in a wizard case (with or without the island effect), the internal causal process would not count as an exercise of the capacity to see; the causal process is one by which the subject randomly hallucinates. The fact that given the context in which the process occurs, a wide pattern of counterfactuals hold does not change that. For, as I noted, the pattern holds because the subject possesses the capacity to see, *not* because the subject is exercising that capacity. In wizard cases, the scene before the subject's eyes produces a matching visual experience by means that are mostly different from the means by which other scenes would produce matching visual experiences. Other scenes would produce the experience by means of processes that count as exercises of the capacity to see. But the actual spell-inducing scene does not produce the experience by such a process.

Suppose that a certain visual experience E tracks a certain scene S: if S were before the subject's eyes, the subject would have E; and if S were not before the subject's eyes, the subject would not have E. If the causal means by which S produces E are largely independent of the causal means by which other scenes would produce matching experiences, it is hard to see why it would matter to whether a subject sees when having E as a result of S that other experiences of the subject would track other scenes. To dramatize this, suppose that one could sufficiently dismantle the mechanisms (structures) whose operations would be involved in the production of a matching visual experience for any of the other scenes besides S, so that the other scenes would no longer produce matching experiences. Suppose further that the dismantling would not affect the mechanism by means of which S would produce E. Then, it is very hard to see why it would be relevant that the other scenes would produce matching experiences when the relevant mechanisms are intact. The point is that whether there is a wide pattern of counterfactual dependence of visual experiences on scenes is relevant to whether someone sees because it is evidence (though defeasible evidence) that any of a wide range of scenes would produce a matching experience by essentially the same causal means. A wide pattern of dependence is evidence (though defeasible evidence) that there is a mechanism (or structure) capable of operations that will support the counterfactuals. And that matters because it is evidence that the mechanism is a constitutive basis for the capacity to see.

In wizard cases, as we noted, the means by which the scene produces a matching visual experience are significantly independent of the means by which other scenes would produce matching experiences. Given the way the scene is producing the subject's experience in a wizard case, the fact that other scenes would produce matching experiences is no reason to think that the subject is seeing. For the other scenes would produce matching experiences by significantly independent causal means. Wizard cases shows that the counterfactuals can hold, yet *not hold because* the subject is exercising the capacity to see.

7. A Modest Alternative Proposal

My strategy for offering an alternative proposal is to spell out what it is the capacity to see is the capacity to do. I have argued that Lewis's proposal is mistaken in its attempt to analyze the exercise of the capacity to see as a pattern of counterfactual dependence. In order to spell out the nature of our capacity for vision, I will draw on Lewis's insight that the capacity to see is a discriminative capacity.

Consider, then, the following fill-in-the-blank question:

Q. The capacity to see is the capacity to _____.

Subtleties aside, the capacity to see is the capacity to discriminate scenes before one's eyes by having visual experiences that match the scenes. In broad outline, the proper function of an eye in the exercise of the capacity to see is to respond to scenes before it by activating dispositions to have visual experiences that match the scenes.[32] As I noted earlier, I agree with Lewis that it is possible for a prosthetic device to discharge that function. Here, then, is my alternative proposal:

If a subject has a visual experience and in having it exercises the capacity to discriminate a suitable range of scenes before her eyes by having matching visual experiences, then the subject sees; if it is not the case that a subject has a visual experience such that in having it the subject exercises the capacity to discriminate a suitable range of scenes before her eyes by having matching visual experiences, then the subject does not see.

If the notion of a suitable range of scenes is spelled out simply by requiring that there be a lot of different scenes, then Lewis would allow that my proposal is correct but insist that it implies his proposal. I deny that. For his multi-tracking and multi-adherence conditions do not hold in the censor cases described earlier, while my proposed condition does. Lewis would disagree, of course, that mine holds in censor cases. But I will not cover that ground again. Suffice it to note that whoever is right, he cannot fault my proposal for getting censor cases wrong; at most, he could fault me for misapplying my own condition.

Whether or not my proposal implies Lewis's, his proposal does not imply mine. For, as he acknowledges, his proposed condition holds in wizard cases but mine does not. In wizard cases the subject does not exercise his capacity to discriminate a suitable range of scenes before his eyes.

Moreover, my proposal puts the pattern of counterfactual dependence Lewis cites in its proper place. The pattern of dependence is a criterion for whether the subject is seeing in that it normally holds because the subject is seeing. I hope, however, to have made a case that it is a mistake to think that when a subject sees she does so because the pattern of dependence holds; that reverses the order of explanation. Lewis takes the subject to be seeing because the counterfactuals hold. I take the counterfactuals to hold, in typical cases in which they hold (wizard cases are atypical), because the subject is exercising a capacity to discriminate scenes before her eyes. When the subject is exercising the capacity to discriminate scenes before her eyes, and the surroundings are right (there are no censors), then the pattern of counterfactual dependence will hold.

Is the above proposal, then, correct? That depends, in part, on the answers to questions (a) to (e) set aside earlier. And there are further issues. To note just one, what counts as a suitable range of scenes? There is a problem with Lewis's suggestion that this be handled simply by claiming that there must be a lot of different scenes, and that it is a vague matter how many that is. The problem can be raised by considering, once again, the island effect. If we allow scenes that differ only in invisible respects to count as different scenes, then the island effect is always with us. Any scene we are able to discriminate by sight will be an island in a sea of scenes we cannot discriminate by sight. If we say instead that there must be plenty of visibly different scenes, the question arises as to which scenes are visibly different. We have gone in a tight circle if we say simply: the ones that can be visually discriminated by the subject. Lewis appealed to the idea that there must be plenty of scenes to avoid having to appeal to the idea of visible differences in scenes (1986a, 282-83). But then, as I noted, the island effect will always be with us; for there will be an astronomical number of invisibly different scenes separating any two visibly different scenes. There is a difference between island-effect cases in which the island scenes are only invisibly different from the seas of scenes that separate them and island-effect cases in which the island scenes are visibly different from the seas of scenes that separate them. Yet Lewis treats them the same.

Here is a suggestion: we might say that a scene is visible for a subject iff it would satisfy (to at least some minimal extent) the content of some visual experience the subject has the capacity to have.[33] When a subject can discriminate the vast majority of scenes that are visible for the subject, the subject sees. But if there are many scenes that are visible for the subject that the subject cannot discriminate, that detracts from the case being one of seeing. The island effect that would detract from a case being one of seeing is the one in which the scenes a subject can discriminate by matching visual experiences are islands separated by seas of scenes that satisfy the contents of visual experiences the subject can have. The island effect that would not detract from a case being one of seeing is the one in which the scenes in the seas separating the islands do *not* satisfy the contents of any visual experiences the subject has the capacity to have.[34]

A consequence of the above suggestion is that a subject capable of only a narrow range of visual experiences need only discriminate a narrow range of scenes in order to see. Suppose, then, that a subject has the capacity only for a single sort of visual experience. If in having that experience the subject exercises her capacity to discriminate the one sort of scene that answers to the content of the experience, would the subject see? Or should we require a subject to have the capacity to have at least some minimal range of different visual experiences to be able to see? I am inclined to think the latter, though intuitions will no doubt vary on how low a range is minimal. And it matters, I think, how rich the content of the experiences are; the richer the content, perhaps the fewer the number of types of experiences the subject *must* be able to have to see.

In any case, I will not pursue these issues further here. It is my hope that my proposal can be refined into a correct one, but I leave that task for another occasion. For present purposes, the points I want to underscore are these: (1) my proposal has the merits of Lewis's proposal while avoiding the difficulties I raised for his proposal; and (2) the difficulties I raise for Lewis's proposal are of the same sort that any would-be counterfactual analysis of a capacity can be expected to face. Let us eschew counterfactual analyses of psychological capacities.

Acknowledgments

An earlier draft of this paper was presented at the University of Alabama, and at a plenary session of the New Jersey Regional Philosophical Association. The penultimate draft was discussed by Ernest Sosa's epistemology seminar at Brown University. I wish to thank Professor Sosa and the students in his seminar. I wish also to thank Kent Bach, Fred Dretske, Dick Grandy, David Lewis, Vann McGee, David Sanford and Gene Witmer.

Notes

1 Lewis tells us that a visual experience matches an environmental scene to the extent that the scene satisfies the content of the experience (1986a, 274). He sketches a view of the contents of visual experiences that appeals to the

contents of certain beliefs (1986a, 274-75). Visual experiences indeed have contents, but I think Lewis's view of their contents is mistaken. I will not pause to criticize his view here, however. For his analysis of intransitive seeing does not presuppose any of the details of the view. It will do for present purposes simply to think of the content of a visual experience as, roughly, the way things look to the subject of the experience in virtue of her having the experience. A visual experience will "match" a scene to the extent that the way things look to the subject is the way the scene in question is. A scene can satisfy the content of an experience more or less, and so an experience can match a scene more or less. When Lewis speaks simply of an experience matching a scene, he means that the experience fairly closely matches the scene, even if not perfectly. (See note 8 below.)

2 It may also fail to state a necessary condition; but see section 2.

3 I discuss the Wizard case in section 6.

4 In section 7, I outline what I take to be the proper function of eyes in the visual system. Here I simply reply on our intuitive grasp of the role of eyes.

5 But can one see when the normal external causal process is absent? One can, I would claim, see without light from the infra-red to ultraviolet spectrum playing any causal role in the production of one's experience. But can one see, for example, without any part of any scene supplying light to one's (natural or prosthetic) eyes? Lewis does not address this issue, except to note that there is a sense in which we see in pitch darkness; for, he says, we can see that it is pitch dark, and so see (1986a, 283). He says nothing at all, however, about whether one can see scenes of objects without the objects in the scene supplying light to one's eyes. I think that in pitch darkness we can tell that it is pitch dark by looking. But what happens, I am inclined to think, is that we look and do not see, and so conclude that it is pitch dark. I thus am inclined to think that we do not exercise the capacity to see in pitch darkness; the presence of light is a precondition for the exercise of the capacity. But is this necessarily true? Can the external medium of sight be something other than light? I will not pause to address such questions; for doing so would take me far afield of my central concern here. My central concern is not with the essential external (to the body) preconditions for the exercise of the capacity to see, but with whether the exercise of the capacity to see admits of a counterfactual analysis. I will follow Lewis in speaking simply of the scenes before a subject's eyes. (See note 10 below.)

6 Goldman (1976; 1978) has appealed to a similar pattern of counterfactual dependence in his account of transitive seeing. Lewis (1986a, 276) cites Goldman (1976).

7 It is worthwhile noting that the partial blindness case is different from the other cases to which Lewis alludes. Consider someone who is legally blind, but not totally blind. In a circumstance with bad light, it may well be indeterminate whether or not the person sees by having a visual experience, yet be definite that the person is not hallucinating. The distinction between the

sighted and the blind is fuzzy and offers borderline cases different from the borderline cases of seeing rather than visually hallucinating.

8 Concerning the issue of the extent of match between experiences and scenes, it worthwhile noting that a perfect match is surely not required for seeing. There are among us, the near-sighted, the far-sighted, and the partially blind. Some mismatches are our common lot: we are subject to illusions, both non-psychological (straight sticks look bent at the water line) and psychological (the Mueller-Lyer arrows look different lengths). Also, it is possible to lack depth perception or chromatic colour perception yet see, although with poor visual acuity. And various sorts of systematic mismatches are acceptable: we can see wearing glasses that produce left-right reversals or up-down reversals. But can one see when one's experience fails entirely to match the scene before one's eyes? Lewis sets this issue aside; so will I. See section 2.

9 Lewis cautions, however, that the counterfactual expressing the dependence must not be a backtracker. See his example of the Screen (1986a, 284-85).

10 There is also a question of clarification that immediately arises: what it is for a scene to be before a subject's eyes? Must, for instance, parts of the scene supply light to the eyes? As I mentioned in note 5, except for his remark about seeing in pitch darkness, Lewis does not address this question; nor will I.

11 Colin McGinn (1984) has argued, on essentially the same grounds I mention in this section, that capacities typically cannot be reduced to counterfactual dependencies. I acknowledge my debt to him here. McGinn has, however, suggested that Lewis's counterfactual account of the capacity to see may prove to be right (1984, 539; 552). One of my aims is to argue that Lewis's account is not an exception to the rule that capacities do not reduce to counterfactual conditions.

12 Let the censor be external to the subject's brain. I do not wish to consider cases in which a censor is part of some internal mechanism whose operations is involved in the production of the visual experience; such cases raise special concerns.

13 This is not, of course, to say that the censor could not intervene in such a way as to make the subject lose his capacity to see altogether. The censor might intervene in such a way as to severely damage the subject's eyes, for instance. The point is that the censor might intervene without damaging any of the mechanisms whose joint operation counts as the subject's exercising the capacity to see. So, if that is the way the censor intervenes, then the subject does not lose his capacity to see, he is just prevented from exercising it.

14 Likewise, Jack retains the capacity to have various other visual experiences, though the censor is preventing him from exercising those capacities as well.

15 See Lewis (1986d), pp.189-93, for a discussion of whether omissions are causes.

16 See note 12 above.

17 They have come in part as well in response to certain problems of "redundant causation" involving what Lewis calls "Bunzl events."

18 If you are inclined to think that the executioner would not cause the very same severing, see Lewis's discussion of the firing squad case in Lewis (1986d), p.198. Suffice it to note here that a head severing is not so "fragile" an event that it could not have been slightly different in time or manner of occurrence.

19 This is not to say that I endorse the revised account. I wish I knew of an account of causation I could endorse.

20 Cf. Lewis (1986d), pp.200-201.

21 LeCatt does not elaborate on the relevant notion of suitability for the counterfactual dependencies. Visual experiences will not match the intermediate stage and the intermediate stage dependent on the scenes before the eyes will not be occupied by visual experiences. But LeCatt's idea, presumably, is that a suitable pattern of two-step dependence will be such that given that it holds, there is a wide pattern of stepwise dependence of visual experiences on scenes before the eyes, where the experiences match the scenes.

22 See Lewis's discussion of action at a distance in Lewis (1986d), p. 202.

23 Bystander cases – cases in which something lets a causal process occur – are arguably a frequently occurring kind of pre-emption case; they can involve early or late pre-emption.

24 Another reason is, as we noted, the intuitive consideration. Lewis (1986d, 208-12) also says that appeal to quasi-dependence may be the best response to problems of redundant causation posed by certain Bunzl events.

25 This claim of implication assumes, of course, that (a non-backtracking) counterfactual dependence among distinct events suffices for causation. But regardless of whether that is sufficient for causation, and so regardless of whether the implications hold, the Wizard case is a counter-example to the sufficiency of both Lewis's multi-adherence condition and LeCatt's stepwise dependence condition. In the Wizard case, these conditions hold, yet the subject veridically hallucinations.

26 By contrast, the fact that a scene produces a matching experience by means of the normal causal process is enough to make a case a positive one. Or so I have claimed.

27 For a discussion of Lewis's views on objective chance, see Lewis (1986f). Here I will simply use Lewis's notion of objective chance, without questioning it.

28 I think that there are two kinds of island effects. The presence of one counts against a case being positive (though it alone might not be enough to disqualify a case), while the presence of the other does not. I postpone discussing this matter until section 7, however.

29 Let us suppose that the relevant types of retinal imates are not so specific
    that the sorts of retinal changes that would result from tiny eye movements
    or occasional blinking would break the spell.
30 I wish to thank Jason Kawall for helping me to clarify this example.
31 At the point at which the wire makes the right contact, the objective chance
    of match might become very high. On Lewis's theory of objective chance,
    the objective chance of an occurrence can increase over time (1986f, 90-92).
    At some stage of random hallucinatory processes the objective chance of a
    matching visual experience will be extremely high. What matters is the
    objective chance, immediately after the occurrence of the scene, of a match-
    ing experience ensuing, not the objective chance of that at some later time.
    Now it is true that the objective chance of match will go up dramatically for
    every scene when the wire makes the proper contact; that typically will not
    happen at any stage of a process leading to veridical hallucination. But see
    the discussion of the wizard case in the following paragraph.
32 Must an organ respond to light from scenes to count as an eye, that is, to
    count as an organ of sight? I am disinclined to think it must, but I will not
    pursue the issue here.
33 Unlike Lewis, I would allow that a subject can have the capacity to have a
    certain visual experience, even if there is a censor standing by who would
    prevent the subject from having that experience. For there is a difference
    between having the capacity to have a certain experience and being able to
    exercise it in a given circumstance.
34 One might worry about circularity here too. Perhaps the notion of the con-
    tent of a visual experience cannot be fully analyzed without ultimately
    appealing to the notion of seeing. I leave that an open question. I should
    note, however, that I agree with Lewis that circularity is typically unavoid-
    able. Our concepts come in families; they are not ordered. But we can take
    certain members ofa family as primitive and try to explain the others in
    terms of them.

References

Goldman, A. (1976). Discrimination and perceptual knowledge. *Journal of Philos-
    ophy* 73: 771-91
————. (1977) Perceptual objects. *Synthese* 35: 257-84
LeCatt, B. (1982). Censored vision. *Australasian Journal of Philosophy* 60: 158-62
Lewis, D. (1986a). *Philosophical Papers: Vol. 2*. Oxford: Oxford University Press
————. (1986b). Veridical hallucination and prosthetic vision. In Lewis (1986a),
    273-86. Reprinted from *Australasian Journal of Philosophy* 58 (1980): 239-49
————. (1986c). Postscript to "veridical hallucination and prosthetic vision." In
    Lewis (1986a), 287-90
————. (1986d). Causation. In Lewis (1986a), 159-72. Reprinted from the *Journal
    of Philosophy* 70 (1973): 556-67

————. (1986e). Postscripts to "causation." In Lewis (1986a), 172-213

————. (1986f). A subjectivist guide to objective chance. In Lewis (1986a), 83-113

McGinn, C. (1984). The concept of knowledge. *Midwest Studies in Philosophy* 9: 536-42

Nozick, R. (1981). *Philosophical Explanation.* Cambridge, MA: Harvard University Press

10

Intentionality and the Theory of Vision

Frances Egan

Vision is the process of extracting from two-dimensional images information about the three-dimensional structure of the world. The computational study of vision treats it as an information-processing task involving the construction and manipulation of a series of representations that encode salient information about the distal scene. David Marr's theory of vision is among the most developed computational theories of vision,[1] and a target of considerable attention from philosophers of mind in search of empirical support for their work. Interpreters of Marr have typically assumed that his theory is intentional (see, e.g., Burge 1986, Davies 1991, Kitcher 1988, Morton 1993). One aim of this paper is to argue that an intentional construal of Marr's theory is a mistake. My argument relies on general features of computational methodology; if I am right, then it follows that computational theories of cognition are not intentional.

One way that a theory may be intentional is by including among its explanatory apparatus intentional states like beliefs and desires. No one, as far as I know, has claimed that Marr's theory is intentional in this sense, and it would be implausible to do so in part because the core of the theory concerns processes which are, to use Zenon Pylyshyn's term, *cognitively impenetrable*, that is, not subject to revision in light of what the subject comes to believe. Accordingly, the states posited by the theory fail to exhibit the complex functional roles characteristic of the propositional attitudes. They are *sub-doxastic* states.

The claim that Marr's theory is intentional is more plausibly understood as maintaining that visual processes are characterized essentially by reference to the *distal contents* of the representational tokens that form the inputs and outputs of these processes. This is the thesis I wish to deny. I shall argue that the hypothesized processes are characterized *formally* in the theory, without essential reference to the distal contents of the representations over which they are defined. In doing so I assume an additional burden – explaining the role that representational content plays in computational vision theories, if not to characterize the hypothesized processes.

Before proceeding with the main argument I shall give a brief sketch of Marr's theory.

1. An Overview of Marr's Theory

Marr argued that an information-processing system should be analysed at three distinct levels of description. The "topmost" level – what he called the *theory of the computation* – is a specification of the function computed by the system. The *algorithmic level* specifies a representation and algorithm for computing the function, and the *implementation level* describes how the representation and algorithm are realized physically. While all three components are necessary for a complete understanding of an information-processing system, Marr stressed the importance of the theory of the computation, arguing that a process is more readily understood by examining the nature of the problem to be solved than by studying the hardware that implements the solution.

The goal of the visual system is to derive a representation of three-dimensional structure from information contained in two-dimensional images. Marr's theory divides this task into three distinct stages, each involving the construction of a representation, tokens of which serve as inputs to subsequent processes. At each stage the processing is aided by additional assumptions, assumed to be innate, concerning very general features of the subject's environment. For example, the process of *stereopsis*, which yields information about depth, measures the disparity between a pair of retinal images. First, however, points in one image must be matched with their counterparts in the other. The matching process is facilitated by two physical constraints: *uniqueness*, which means that each item may be assigned only one counterpart in the image, since items to be matched can only be in one place at a time; and *continuity*, which means that disparity varies smoothly almost everywhere, since matter is cohesive. These constraints force a unique solution to the matching problem. The mechanism responsible for stereopsis is assumed to incorporate assumptions reflecting the uniqueness and continuity constraints.[2]

A final point concerning Marr's methodology is worth noting before proceeding to the main argument. Marr proposed separating the visual system into components (*modules*) that could be analyzed individually:

[T]he idea that a large computation can be split up and implemented as a collection of parts that are as nearly independent of one another as the overall task allows, is so important that I was moved to elevate it to a principle, the *principle of modular design.* This principle is important because if a process is not designed in this way, a small change in one place has consequences in many other places. As a result, the process as a whole is extremely difficult to debug or to improve, whether by a human designer or in the course of natural evolution, because a small change to improve one part has to be accompanied by many simultaneous compensatory changes elsewhere. (1982, 102)

Marr's theory posits a module responsible for stereopsis, another for computing structure from apparent motion, a third for computing shape from contour information, etc. Each of these modules incorporates assumptions reflecting physical constraints in the manner described above.

The claim that Marr's theory is intentional is more often taken for granted than explicitly argued. Tyler Burge, for example, finds the claim "sufficiently evident" as not to require explicit argument.[3] Recall that the claim that the theory is intentional is to be understood as maintaining that the hypothesized visual processes are characterized essentially by reference to the distal contents of the representational tokens that form the inputs and outputs of these processes. An intentional construal of the theory is compelling mainly because, as Burge puts it, "the top levels of the theory are explicitly formulated in intentional terms" (1986, 35), Burge's argument can be formulated as follows: The top two levels – the theory of the computation and the specification of the representation and algorithm – characterize what the components of the visual system do (the theory of the computation) and how they do it (the representation and algorithm) by appeal to the distal contents of the representations over which the component processes are defined. Hence, the top two levels of the theory are intentional. Since all three levels are essential to a complete understanding of the visual system, Marr's theory is intentional.

To defend the claim that Marr's theory is not intentional I must show that neither the theory of the computation nor the representation and algorithm characterize the visual system in essentially intentional terms.

2. Representation and Algorithm

Let us examine the intermediate level of the theory first. Marr's theory of vision is a *computational* theory.[4] It is therefore committed to the existence of a fully specifiable formal account of the processes it attempts to characterize; otherwise the described processes are not guaranteed to be programmable. The intermediate level of the theory – the specification of a representation for the input and output of a process and an algorithm for the transformation of one into the other – is, in an important sense, the heart of a computational account. The algorithm is the detailed formal specification of how the component processes of an information-processing system accomplish their specified tasks. The processes are described at this level by rigorous proofs, and the algorithms that characterize the processes are defined over formal (i.e., mathematical) structures.[5]

A concrete example will perhaps make the point clear. The first stage in the derivation of a representation sufficient for recovering three-dimensional structure is the construction of the *primal sketch*, which makes explicit information about intensity changes in the retinal image. The primal sketch is constructed out of various sorts of primitives – blobs, bars, edges, terminations and virtual lines. Marr is careful to point out that these primitives, considered individually at the lowest level of scale, do not reliably co-vary with salient features of the distal scene, and so do not have "physical reality." Only if discontinuities are present at several channels reflecting different scales of the image are they likely to be physically significant.

Marr and Hildreth (1980) describe in some detail how the visual system detects intensity changes and how this information is represented in a way that facilitates subsequent processing. A sudden intensity change in the image produces a peak or trough in the first directional derivative of intensity and a *zero-crossing* in the second directional derivative. (A zero-crossing is a point where the value of a function changes its sign.) The problem of detecting intensity changes in the image can therefore be reduced to the task of finding the zero-crossings in the second derivative of intensity, and the authors propose a set of filters which do this at different scales.

The information in the zero-crossings from multiple channels is contained in the *raw primal sketch*, which Marr describes as a binary map specifying the locations of zero-crossing segments[6] and the local orientation, type and extent of the intensity change at points along these segments. Structures such as bars, blobs and virtual lines, each with characteristic attributes of orientation, width, length, position and contrast, are then defined on the array. (A bar, for example, is a parallel segment pair.) The raw primal sketch is the input representation for most of the modular processes characterized by the theory.

The point I wish to emphasize is this: the processes characterized by the intermediate level of Marr's theory are explicated *at that level* by formal proofs, and the algorithms describing such processes are defined over mathematical structures. While there is perhaps no harm in informally describing what these processes do as detecting edges, or other salient features of the distal scene,[7] this is not how the processes are characterized at the level of the representation and algorithm. The process that culminates in the construction of the primal sketch, for example, detects zero-crossings in the second directional derivative of intensity; the primal sketch is a representation of zero-crossings and more complex structures defined over them.

3. The Theory of the Computation

I turn now to the top-most level of Marr's theory. The theory of the computation is generally thought to be an intentional specification of the functions computed by the various modules of the visual system. This level is often identified with Pylyshyn's semantic level (Pylyshyn 1984) and Newell's knowledge level (Newell 1982), and the algorithmic level with Pylyshyn's symbolic (or syntactic) level and Newell's symbol level.[8] Thus the top level, it is supposed, is intentional, characterizing states of the system by their representational contents.

The construal of Marr's top level as essentially an intentional or semantic description of the device is a mistake. It is more plausibly seen as a *function-theoretic* description of the device. Marr explicitly points out that the theory of the computation is a *formal* characterization of the function(s) computed by the various processing modules. The following diagram (Figure 10.1 from Marr 1982, 338) depicts (top) the mathematical formula that describes the initial filtering of the image (where ∇^2 represents the Laplacean, G a Gaussian, $I(x, y)$ the image and $*$ the operation of convolution), and (below) a cross-section of the retina which implements the computation.

The point to note is that the function computed by the retina ([a] in the diagram) is characterized formally. Marr says the following:

I have argued that from a computational point of view [the retina] signals $\nabla^2 G * I$ (the X channels) and its time derivative $\delta/\delta t$ ($\nabla^2 G * I$) (the Y channels). From a computational point of view, this is a precise specification of what the retina does. Of course it does a lot more – it transduces the light, allows for a huge dynamic range, has a fovea with interesting characteristics, can be moved around, and so forth. What you accept as a reasonable description of what the retina does depends on your point of view. I personally accept $\nabla^2 G$ [(a) in the diagram] as an adequate description, though I take an unashamedly information-processing point of view. (1982, 337)

$\nabla^2 G$ is a function that takes as arguments two dimensional intensity arrays $I(x, y)$ and has as values the isotropic rates of change of intensity at points (x, y) in the array. The implementation of this function is used in Marr and Hildreth's (1980) model to detect zero-crossings.

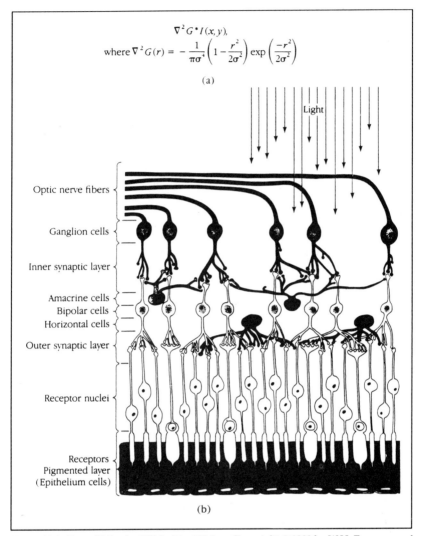

$$\nabla^2 G * I(x, y),$$

$$\text{where } \nabla^2 G(r) = -\frac{1}{\pi\sigma^4}\left(1 - \frac{r^2}{2\sigma^2}\right)\exp\left(\frac{-r^2}{2\sigma^2}\right)$$

(a)

(b)

Figure 10.1: From *Vision* (p. 338) by David Marr. Copyright © 1982 by W.H. Freeman and Company. Reprinted with permission.

Marr grants that the formal specification of the function computed by the retina may not make what the retina does *perspicuous*. Nonetheless, from an information-processing point of view, the formal specification is "adequate."[9]

Marr consistently stresses the importance of the theory of the computation, arguing that the nature of the information-processing task itself – the function computed by the system – needs to be understood independently of attempts to characterize the mechanisms supporting the computation. His preoccupation with the theory of the computation is primarily methodological: "Unless the computational theory of the process is correctly formulated, the algorithm will almost certainly be wrong" (1982, 124). The correct characterization of the algorithm used by a process depends upon the prior precise (i.e., mathematical) specification of the function computed by the process. There is no point looking for an algorithm before knowing what job it has to do.

So to correctly characterize the algorithm for a process, the computational theorist must first characterize the function computed. And a necessary first step in characterizing the function is discovering environmental constraints that make the computation tractable. The solutions to information-processing problems solved by perceptual mechanisms are often underdetermined by information contained in the input to the mechanism; the solution is achieved only with the help of additional information reflecting very general features of the subject's normal environment. It is reasonable to assume that the perceptual mechanisms of evolved creatures will exploit this environmental information, as, for example, the mechanism responsible for stereopsis solves the matching problem by incorporating assumptions reflecting the uniqueness and continuity constraints.

4. The Role of Content in Computational Vision Theory

I have argued that neither the theory of the computation nor the representation and algorithm characterizes the visual system in intentional or semantic terms. Since the implementation level provides a physiological description of the neural hardware that realizes visual processes, none of the three component levels of Marr's theory characterize the visual system in intentional terms. It follows that Marr's theory is not intentional.

In claiming that Marr's theory is not intentional I am not denying that some of the postulated states have representational contents. Structures in the raw primal sketch, which contains information from several distinct $\nabla^2 G$ channels and provides the input to most of the modular processes characterized by the theory, are reliably correlated with such salient distal properties as object boundaries or changes in illumination, and so can be interpreted as representing such properties. The important point, however, is that the postulated structures have no content *considered independently of the particular environment in which the subject is normally situated*. To call such structures "representations" is not to imply that they have intrinsic or essential content, but simply to claim that they are possible candidates for interpretation. In some radically different environment, structures in the raw primal sketch may be correlated with *different* distal properties, or with *no* objective feature of the world. In the latter case, the raw primal sketch would not be assigned a content in an interpretation appropriate to that world, much as individual zero-crossings are not distally interpretable in our world. In any event, whatever content may be plausibly assigned to a particular structure in an particular environment is extrinsic to the computational description of a process, and not part of the computational theory proper.

A computational theory is an environment-independent characterization of a mechanism. Of course, the process of theory construction cannot proceed without considering the environment in which the mechanism is normally deployed. The assumption that the cognitive mechanisms of evolved creatures are adapted to their environment will constrain computational accounts in important ways. Characterizing the function computed by a device requires discovering valid environmental constraints that allow the processing to proceed as efficiently as possible. However, this environmental information does not play an *individuative* role in the theory – the *same* mechanism could occur in a world where the relevant environmental assumptions were false, although in such an environment we might expect the mechanism (and perhaps the organisms containing it) to be short-lived. Two mechanisms that compute the same function (in the mathematical sense), using the same algorithm, are, from a computational point of view, the same *type* of mechanism, whether or not their states have the same representational contents in the environments in which they are normally deployed.

It might be claimed that the fact that the perceptual mechanisms of evolved creatures will typically be adapted to their normal environment provides a rationale for taking the contents that are assigned to representational structures in the actual world to be individuative of and essential to the postulated structures themselves. But while the fact that a mechanism is adapted to the actual world might provide a rationale for taking an interpretation appropriate to the actual world to be in some sense *privileged*, it does not justify construing this interpretation as part of the individuative apparatus of a computational theory. It would do so only if the fact that a mechanism is adaptive (relative to its normal environment) is itself an essential feature of a computational mechanism. But clearly it is not. As noted above, a computationally characterized device may be adaptive in one environment and maladaptive in another. It is precisely because a computational theory provides an environment-independent characterization of a device that we can see why *this* mechanism would not have been adaptive if the environment had been different, and why it might cease to be adaptive if the environment changes.[10]

What, then, *is* the role that representational content plays in computational accounts of cognitive mechanisms, if not to provide an essential characterization of the hypothesized mechanisms? In Egan (1992) I suggested that intentional interpretations of computational processes serve an explanatory function analogous to that served by models in the physical sciences. The analogy, while not exact, is nonetheless useful, in part because it underscores the difference between the interpretation of a computational mechanism and the theory proper, which, I have argued, is to be identified with the formal characterization of the processes, provided primarily by the top two levels of the theory.

It is at once natural and misleading to think that the interpretation of the postulated structures resides at a specific level of description, and hence should be considered part of the computational theory. It is natural because, while the designated task of the top two levels is to provide a formal characterization of the postulated processes, nonetheless, the formal account may be given an informal exposition in terms of an interpretation appropriate to the actual world. For example, the stereopsis module can be described as calculating the depth of objects in the visual field from information about the disparity of points in the two retinal images. Of course, the formal characterization of this process is much more complex, and makes no reference to such distal properties as *depth*. An intentional characterization of an essentially formal process can serve an expository function played by explanatory models of physical theories, viz., explicating a formal account which might otherwise not be perspicuous. It is therefore natural to assume that the intentional characterization is an essential part of the computational theory of a process. Yet it is misleading because while both the theory of the computation and the specification of the algorithm provide an environment-independent characterization of the mechanism, the assignment of contents to computational structures, we have seen, is not environment-independent.

While an intentional characterization of a computational process can facilitate the explication of a formal account, it also serves a more important explanatory function. The questions that define a psychological theory's domain are usually couched in intentional terms. An intentional specification of the postulated computational processes demonstrates that these questions are indeed answered by the theory. Vision, for example, is the recovery of information about the three-dimensional structure of the world from information contained in two-dimensional images. It is only under an interpretation of some of the states of the system as representations of distal properties that the computational processes postulated by Marr's theory are revealed as *vision,* and the theory can be seen to answer the question it was initially set. In other words, only when the states are interpreted as carrying information about the distal scene is it apparent that a device that computes the functions characterized formally by the theory of the computation will, in its normal environment, solve the problem of vision. Thus we can see why the contents assigned to computational states in the actual world, while not an essential part of the theory's individuative apparatus, are, in an important sense, *privileged.* Our primary interest in Marr's theory, after all, is that it reveals how a system that lives in this world can see.

An intentional charaterization of a computational process serves a third explanatory function. As previously noted, Marr's theory respects the principle of modular design, treating the visual system as an isolable component of the organism's larger cognitive apparatus, itself consisting of a collection of independently characterizable modules. The ascription of content to states postulated by modular computational theories will help to tie the various independent accounts together, and contribute to an understanding of each module's role in the overall cognitive economy of the organism. Interpreting the inputs and outputs of modular processes seems unavoidable if we hope to explain how they interact to produce complex behaviour, and how each component contributes to the organism's successful interaction with its environment.

I suspect that few will disagree that an intentional interpretation can serve the explanatory functions outlined above. But why aren't these three explanatory functions enough to make the computational theory intentional?

The first explanatory function is purely expository. Although an intentional characterization of a process can make a formal account more perspicuous, the formal account suffices to individuate the process. The third function – helping to tie independent computational theories together – is motivated by explanatory considerations external to a computational theory itself. The second function, however, may appear to undermine my claim that computational theories are not intentional.

I have argued that an intentional characterization of a computational mechanism is needed to demonstrate that the questions that antecedently define the theory's explanatory domain are answered by the theory. But it might seem that a computational theory, when divorced from a particular intentional interpretation, cannot properly be characterized as a theory of *cognition.*[11] There is a sense in which this is true; however, it does not undermine my point that computational theories are not intentional.

A computational theory provides a formal characterization of the function computed by a mechanism, but only in some environments can this function be characterized as a *cognitive* function (that is, a function whose arguments and values are epistemically related, such that the outputs of the computation can be seen as rational or cogent given the inputs). In some environments the constraints that enable a cognitive interpretation will not be satisfied. For example, recall the *continuity* constraint – disparity varies smoothly, because matter is cohesive – that facilitates the matching process essential to stereopsis. In environments where this constraint is not satisfied, the stereopsis module would compute the same formally characterized function, *but it would not be computing depth from disparity.* The function would presumably have no cognitive (i.e., rational) description is this environment. By prescinding from the actual environment, a computational theory provides a completely general description of a device that affords a basis for predicting and explaining its behaviour in any environment, even in environments where what the device is doing cannot comfortably be described as *cognition.* A computational theory, *when accompanied by an intentional interpretation*, allows us to see how a mechanism that computes a mathematical function can, in a particular context, subserve a cognitive function like vision, but the interpretation is not part of the theory itself.

A computational theory explains a cognitive capacity by subsuming the mechanism that has that capacity under a more general computational description. Explaining a pre-theoretically identifiable function as an instance of a more general class of devices that have an independent characterization is an explanatory strategy familiar from other domains, particularly biology. The ability of sharks to detect prey is explained by positing within the shark the existence of an *electric field detector,* a device whose architecture and behaviour is characterized by electromagnetic theory. Electromagnetic theory does most of the explanatory work in the biological explanation of the shark's prey-detecting capacity. Of course the explanation appeals to other facts, for example, that animals, but not rocks or other inanimate objects in the shark's natural environment, produce significant electrical fields, but no one would suggest that such facts are part of *electromagnetic theory.* Similarly, by specifying the class of computational devices a mechanism belongs to and providing an independent (i.e., non-cognitive) characterization of the behaviour of this class, a computational theory bears the primary explanatory burden in the explanation of a cognitive capacity. The intentional interpretation also plays an explanatory role – it demonstrates that the cognitive capacity has been explained – but playing an essential role in the cognitive explanation does not thereby make it part of the *computational theory.*

Does it follow that computational theories are not cognitive? It depends. If a theory must give a cognitive characterization of a mechanism (according to which computing a cognitive function is a necessary property of the mechanism) to be a cognitive theory, then computational theories are not cognitive. If bearing the primary explanatory burden in a cognitive explanation is sufficient, then some computational theories (in particular, Marr's theory of vision) are cognitive.[12]

5. An Alternative Proposal: Narrow Content

I take it to be a virtue of my account that it construes a computational theory as an environment-independent characterization of a mechanism. So construed, a computational theory can explain a mechanism's behaviour (or capacity to produce behaviour) in counterfactual environments. However, interpreting a computational theory as a *formal* characterization of a mechanism is not the only way to secure this advantage. It has recently been suggested (Segal 1989, 1991, McGinn 1989) that the representational states postulated by Marr's theory are plausibly interpreted as having *narrow* content, that is, content that supervenes on the internal, physical states of the subject, and hence is shared by physical duplicates in counterfactual environments where the normal causes of their representational states vary. Furthermore, it is claimed, these states are characterized and individuated in the theory by reference to their narrow contents. I shall conclude by considering the narrow content proposal.

According to Segal (1991), narrow contents are abstractions over the distal properties reliably correlated with Marrian structures in every possible environment to which the subject would be adapted. More specifically, the extension of a hypothesized structure of type T includes the normal cause of T in every possible environment in which the creature interacts successfully with those normal causes, on the basis of Ts.

I shall not argue that the hypothesized structures do not have narrow contents. Since I have suggested that interpretations of computational theories are in some respects analogous to models of physical theories, I am prepared to acknowledge the existence of "non-standard interpretations." Rather I wish to stress two points: (1) the processes described by Marr's theory are characterized *formally* in the theory, not by reference to any contents, narrow or wide; and (2) the explanatory purposes that I have argued are served by the ascription of content to the hypothesized structures would not be well-served by narrow contents of the proposed sort.

The problem with narrow contents is that they are too *non-specific* to play either an individuative or a genuine explanatory role. In Segal's account, narrow contents include within their extensions the normal cause of a structure's tokening in each environment in which the subject's behaviour in respect of that cause is successful. But who knows what combination of different causes and different laws will produce successful behaviour in wildly counterfactual environments? In particular, one might wonder how the theorist of vision is to know that a narrow content she has proposed is non-specific enough to include within its extension a normal cause in some wildly counterfactual environment.[13] But there must *be* some way of specifying such contents if they are to play an essential role in characterizing a computational process.

Furthermore, it is difficult to square the narrow content proposal with Marr's work. He shows no apparent interest in ascribing nonspecific contents to the structures postulated by the theory. He does point out that individual primitives in the raw primal sketch do not reliably co-vary (in the actual world) with salient distal properties, but his remarks in this context are more plausibly construed as cautioning against interpreting these structures at all, rather than as advocating the ascription of non-specific contents (of the proposed sort) to them.[14]

Most importantly, the ascription of narrow content appears to serve no explanatory function not already served by the formal characterization of a process. (A computational theory must provide a formal characterization if it is to demonstrate that the described process is programmable.) The most important explanatory function served by an intentional interpretation of a computational process is demonstrating that the questions that antecedently defined the theory's domain are answered by the theory. But it is difficult to see how this function could be served by non-specific contents of the proposed sort, given that the questions themselves are couched in environment-specific terms. For example, we want a theory of stereopsis to tell us how the visual system computes depth from disparity. But *depth* is an environment-specific property. As we have seen, the stereopsis module would compute a different (distal) property in other environments; hence, the narrow content that would be ascribed to the output of the module is a more general property. It appears that we still need environment-specific contents to connect the computational theory with its pre-theoretic intentional explananda. Finally, it is unlikely that narrow contents will serve any expository function, since non-specific contents of the proposed sort are hardly themselves perspicuous.

6. Conclusion

I have argued that Marr's theory of vision is not intentional – visual processes are not characterized essentially by reference to the distal contents of the structures that form the inputs and outputs of these processes. My argument relies on features of computational methodology that are not specific to the theory of vision. In articulating the levels methodology Marr took himself to be characterizing a practice that can be extended to other cognitive domains. If the foregoing account of Marr's theory is correct, and the levels methodology correctly characterizes computational practice, then it would follow that computational theories of cognition are not intentional.[15]

Notes

1 For the most detailed exposition of Marr's theory see Marr 1982. The theory has been developed considerably by Marr's co-workers since his death.

2 It is important to note that these assumptions are not assumed to be explicitly represented in the visual system. The assumptions are incorporated in the mechanism only in the following sense – the mechanism operates in such a way that if the assumptions are true of the subject's normal environment it will succeed in recovering information about the environment from information in the image.

3 Burge employs the claim as a crucial premise in his argument that Marr's theory of vision is not individualistic (Burge 1986). For criticism of Burge's argument see Segal 1989, 1991 and Egan 1991.

4 It is unfortunate that Marr used the term "theory of the computation" (and sometimes "computational theory") to denote the topmost level of analysis, the specification of the function computed by the system. Following standard usage, I shall use "computational theory" to refer to the analysis of a cognitive process as an information-processing task (which will comprise all three levels of description), reserving "theory of the computation" for Marr's topmost level.

5 These processes are often given only an informal exposition in Marr 1982, which Marr describes as an "introductory book" (p.330). The explanatory burden is carried by the technical papers, where the details of the algorithm are explicitly spelled out.

    The correct specification of the algorithm can be seen as *the* goal of a computational account of a process. The other two levels of analysis – the specification of the function computed (the theory of the computation) and the description of the physical implementation – are important primarily inasmuch as they characterize the constraints on the choice of an algorithm. The selection of an algorithm is constrained by environmental considerations (see next section) and by the available hardware.

6 Marr and Hildreth define *zero-crossing segment* as a "linear segment *l* of zero-crossings in the second directional derivative operator whose direction lies perpendicular to *l*" (Marr and Hildreth 1980, 195). Zero-crossing segments are sometimes referred to as "edge segments."

7 Marr himself sometimes slips into this way of talking in his informal exposition (primarily in Marr 1982), although he does caution against imparting "physical reality" to the representational primitives: "... the term *edge* has a partly physical meaning – it makes us think of a real physical boundary, for example – and all we have discussed so far are the zero values of a set of roughly band-pass second-derivative filters" (Marr 1982, 68).

8 McClamrock (1991) explicitly identifies Marr's hierarchy with Pylyshyn's. Although I think he has misconstrued Marr's top level, McClamrock offers an interesting perspective on the levels methodology, recasting it as distinguishing three natural classes of questions which arise for any information-processing system.

9 Therefore, if one insists on seeing the theory of the computation as specifying an intended interpretation of a computational process, then the intended interpretation is *mathematical*. Understood this way, Marr's theory is intentional in a broader sense, inasmuch as it characterizes the visual system as computing a series of functions defined on mathematical entities. This is not the sense in which interpreters of Marr have taken his theory to be intentional.

10 Therefore, a computational theory of a mechanism will contribute to an understanding of organism/environment interaction, that is, to an explanation of an organism's success in its normal environment, although the computational theory is itself "success-neutral." (Burge 1986 credits Bernard Kobes with coining this term. Burge 1986 and Kobes 1990 both argue that computational theories are *not* success-neutral.)

11 This point was suggested to me by David Davies.

12 My account may appear to be open to the following objection: identifying a computational theory with a formal characterization of a device is analogous to equating a physical theory with its formal structure alone, and treating the interpretation of its variables as extraneous to the theory. But a formal expression such as '$F = ma$' is not an expression of physics unless the variables in it are given meaning (e.g., 'm' stands for mass).

However, identifying a computational theory with a formal characterization of a device is *not* analogous to equating a physical theory with its mathematical formalism. A computational description of a device is a perfectly meaningful sentence. To say that a mechanism computes the $\nabla^2 G$ function is to characterize it as computing a well-defined mathematical function.

13 It is appropriate for *philosophers* to speculate on such matters. See Davies (1992).

14 Marr repeatedly points out that these structures, unlike those in the full primal sketch, are not *physically meaningful*, suggesting an important contrast between the structures which are suitable candidates for (wide) distal interpretation and those which are not.

15 Thanks to Robert Matthews, Gabriel Segal and Alastair Tait for helpful discussions on these issues.

References

Burge, T. (1986). Individualism and psychology. *Philosophical Review* 95: 3-45

Davies, M. (1991). Individualism and perceptual content. *Mind* 100: 461-84

———. (1992). Perceptual content and local supervenience. *Proceedings of the Aristotelian Society* 66: 21-45

Egan, F. (1991). Must psychology be individualistic? *Philosophical Review* 100: 179-203

———. (1992). Individualism, computation, and perceptual content. *Mind* 101: 443-59

Kitcher, P. (1988). Marr's computational theory of vision *Philosophy of Science* 55: 1-24

Kobes, B. (1990). Individualism and Artificial Intelligence. In J. Tomberlin (ed.), *Philosophical Perspectives*, Vol. 4: *Action Theory and Philosophy of Mind*. Atascadero, CA: Ridgeview Publishing, 429-59

Marr, D. (1982). *Vision*. New York: Freeman Press

Marr, D. and E. Hildreth (1980). Theory of edge detection. *Proceedings of the Royal Society* B200: 187-217

McClamrock, R. (1991). Marr's three levels: a re-evaluation. *Minds and Machines* 1: 185-96

McGinn, C. (1989). *Mental Content*. Oxford: Basil Blackwell

Morton, P. (1993). Supervenience and computational explanation in vision theory. *Philosophy of Science 60: 86-99*

Newell, A. (1982). The knowledge level. *Artificial Intelligence* 18: 87-127

Pylyshyn, Z. (1984). *Computation and Cognition*. Cambridge, MA: MIT Press

Segal, G. (1989). On seeing what is not there. *Philosophical Review* 98: 189-214

———. (1991). Defence of a reasonable individualism. *Mind* 100: 485-93

11

Success-Orientation and Individualism in Marr's Theory of Vision

Sarah Patterson

Do the contents of our perceptual states supervene on our physical and functional constitution? In other words, are perceptual contents individualistically individuated? These questions might be taken in two ways, as asking about the perceptual contents we attribute to one another in everyday contexts, or as asking about the contents attributed in a psychological theory of our perceptual processes. Tyler Burge answers both questions negatively. I shall be concerned with the second question, with David Marr's computational theory of vision and Burge's reasons for regarding it as non-individualistic.

Burge discusses Marr's theory when arguing that psychology does not and need not attribute individualistic intentional states, in response to claims that psychological states ought (for various metaphysical and methodological reasons) to be individualistically supervenient (Burge 1986).[1] Like him, I find these general arguments for individualism unpersuasive; I share the view that one should begin (though not necessarily end) with the practice of a science in deciding what its explanatory kinds should be. But I disagree with Burge's interpretation of Marr, and with the view that psychology ought to be non-individualistic, which that interpretation is enlisted to support.

Burge's interpretation centres on what he calls the success-orientation of Marr's theory (Burge 1986, 34). In Burge's view, explanation in the theory of vision and in psychology generally presupposes success and is geared to explaining it. In psychological theory, "states and events are individuated so as to set the terms for specific evaluations of them for truth or other types of success," allowing us to judge directly whether cognitive states are veridical (1986, 25). This is due to the fact that psychological theory aims "to frame explanations that account for these successes, and correlative failures" (1986, 25). Furthermore, it is because psychology is success-oriented that it is non-individualistic. Burge describes the non-individualism of psychology as grounded in two natural assumptions: that there are psychological states that represent an objective world; and that "there is a scientific account to be given that presupposes certain successes in our interaction with the world... and that explains specific successes and failures by reference to these states" (1986, 43-4). He uses Marr's theory of vision to illustrate this view of psychology, presenting it as guided by the assumption that perceivers succeed in representing specific aspects of their physical environment. In my view this is a misinterpretation; the success-orientation of Marr's theory is not such as to show it to be non-individualistic. I shall also take issue with Burge's argument that the success-orientation of psychology in general motivates the non-individualistic individuation of psychological states.

Burge's Interpretation of Marr's Theory

A Thought-Experiment

On Burge's reading, the theory of vision treats a creature's visual system as solving perceptual problems specific to the environment the creature inhabits. He states that:

> the methods of individuation and explanation are governed by the assumption that the subject has adapted to his or her environment sufficiently to obtain veridical information from it under certain normal conditions... If the regular, law-like relations between perception and the environment were different, the visual system would be solving different information-processing problems; it would pass through different informational and intentional states; and the explanation of vision would be different. (1986, 35)

The thought-experiment described in the third section of his paper (Burge 1986, 42-43) illustrates this approach. In the actual environment, the perceiver encounters mainly shadows; in the counterfactual environment, cracks are the norm. Since the regular, law-like relations between perception and the environment differ between the two cases, different information-processing problems are solved. In the actual case, the visual system solves the problem of representing shadows; in the counterfactual case, the problem solved is that of representing cracks.

Burge's analysis would block two possible ways in which an individualist might seek to attribute the same intentional contents across different environments. One way to do this would be to accept neither the content attributions Burge makes in the actual case nor those he makes in the counterfactual case. Instead, the proposal would be to ascribe representations applying to both cracks and shadows in both environments. (This is the type of response which Martin Davies 1991, 463 calls revisionary. It can be seen in Matthews 1985 and Segal 1989.) This would be consistent with the assumption of success, but not with the idea that the problems successfully solved are specific to the local environment – that a change in the law-like relations between perception and the environment makes for a change in problem solved. Another way the individualist might respond is to accept the content attributions Burge makes in the actual case, but apply them in the counterfactual case; that is, to attribute shadow representations in both the actual and counterfactual cases. (Davies refers to this type of response as conservative, for obvious reasons.) But this proposal would be inconsistent with the "governing assumption" that the subject has adapted to his or her environment sufficiently to obtain veridical information from it; shadow representations do not apply veridically to cracks.

If Burge's reading of the theory is right, its commitment to assuming specific successes dictates its non-individualistic individuation of visual content. His reading is founded on three points he makes about the theory, illustrated by examples. The first is that the theory makes physical assumptions; in Burge's words, it "makes essential reference to the subject's distal stimuli and makes essential assumptions about contingent facts regarding the subject's physical environment" (1986, 29). The second point is that the theory assumes success; it presupposes that perception is veridical under normal conditions and aims to explain how it is that visual processes succeed in recovering information about objective properties of the environment (1986, 29-30). The third point is that the theory individuates content causally; "the information carried by representations – their intentional content – is individuated in terms of the specific distal causal antecedents in the physical world that the information is about and that the representations normally apply to" (1986, 32).

These three points are the topic of the next section. I will outline the basis for the points in Marr's theory, the relationship between them and their contribution to Burge's argument that the theory is non-individualistic. The second point, the assumption of success, will be seen to be of central importance. This will be illustrated by showing the role the assumption plays in defending the non-individualistic argument against a certain type of objection. Thus the following section will illustrate the way in which the claim that Marr's theory is success-oriented motivates the view that it is non-individualistic.

Burge's Three Points

Marr aims to explain visual perception by explaining how the visual system is able to construct a description of the shape and spatial arrangement of viewed objects from retinal stimulation. The basic information-processing problem is that of taking a 2-dimensional image and working out the 3-dimensional shapes responsible for producing it so that object recognition can proceed. Marr sees this as the problem of mapping one representation (the image) onto another (the 3-D model). This mapping is achieved through the construction of a sequence of intermediate representations, the primal sketch and the 2½-D sketch (Marr 1982, 37; Table 1-1 summarizes key features of these four representations). The theory describes the structure of the representations (including the representational primitives) and the computational processes or strategies by which they are derived.

One of the hallmarks of Marr's approach is that he gives a "bottom-up" account of perception; the derivation of the final 3-D model is driven primarily by input, by the information available in the image (cf. Marr 1982, 100). Since "the surface structure [of distal objects] is strictly underdetermined from the information in images alone,... the secret of formulating the processes accurately lies in discovering precisely what additional information can safely be assumed about the world that provides powerful enough constraints for the process to run" (1982, 265-66; Table 3-3, 267 summarizes these assumptions).[2] Burge illustrates the role of physical assumptions with Marr's accounts of edge detection and of stereo matching (Burge 1986, 30-32). Stereo matching is the process of identifying positions in the slightly different images received by the right and left eyes which correspond to a single distal object. Edge detection is the process of detecting intensity changes in the image that are due to a single distal phenomenon, such as a change in reflectance, illumination or depth (Marr 1982, 70). The computational procedures Marr proposes generally succeed in edge detection and stereo matching because the external environment usually conforms to various physical constraints. The theory exploits regularities in the environment in two senses; the procedures it proposes serve their purpose because the regularities obtain, and discovery of such regularities can guide the theorist in proposing procedures. A critical part of Marr's method is to look to the environment for regularities or constraints which can be exploited to allow descriptions of distal objects to be constructed. Hence Burge's first point, that the theory makes physical assumptions.

Burge's second point is that the theory assumes success. In his view, it is because the theory is geared to explaining the success of vision that the discovery of environmental regularities is critical. Echoing Marr,[3] he writes that "the critical move is the formulation of general physical facts that limit the interpretation of a visual problem enough to allow one to interpret the machinations of the visual system as providing a unique and veridical solution, at least in typical cases. The primary aim of referring to contingent physical facts and properties is to enable the theory to explain… the success or veridicality of various types of visual representation" (1986, 32). So the fact that physical assumptions are made supports the claim that the theory is success-oriented, that is, it presupposes success and is geared to explaining it. Since the motivation for making physical assumptions is to explain the assumed success of vision, Burge uses the same examples to illustrate the role of physical assumptions and the assumption of success.

The theory's assumption of success is not only the motivation for making physical assumptions, it is also the basis for its causal individuation of content, according to Burge. He describes this latter as a "natural corollary" of the assumption of success, and adds that "the individuation of intentional content of representational types, presupposes the veridicality of perception" (1986, 32-33).

This third point, that content is individuated causally, is critical to Burge's argument that the theory of vision is non-individualistic (as he notes, 1986, 32). Burge's argument (1986, 34) might be summarized as follows:

1. The theory is intentional.
2. The intentional primitives of the theory and the information they carry are individuated by reference to contingently existing physical items or conditions by which they are normally caused and to which they normally apply.
3. So if these physical conditions were regularly different, the information conveyed and the intentional content of visual representations would be different.
4. Relevantly different physical conditions might regularly cause the same non-intentionally, individualistically individuated physical regularities in the subject's eyes and nervous system.
5. In such a case the subject's visual representations would carry different information and have different intentional content (by [3]).
6. Assuming that the theory identifies some perceptual states in terms of their informational or intentional content, individualism is false for the theory of vision.

Step 2 of this argument is essentially the third point Burge makes about the theory, that "the information carried by representations –

their intentional content – is individuated in terms of the specific distal causal antecedents in the physical world that the information is about and that the representations normally apply to" (1986, 32). Since this point is so crucial, it is important to examine the argument for it. Burge supports this claim by citing the way in which Marr chooses representational primitives for the primal sketch and for the 3-D model representation (1986, 35). He is at pains to show that Marr's primitives represent specific physical properties as such (1986, 38). Not only does 'physical edge' (to use Burge's example) give the extension of the edge primitive, it also gives its intension; it captures how the extension is specified by the primitive. So Burge rejects "descriptive" or "relational" intensions such as 'the normal distal cause of this representation' which pick out edges in the actual environment, but might pick out something else in another; the primitives not only in fact pick out physical edges, they could only pick out physical edges. This is intended to block the move of the individualist who assigns a relational content to such primitives, a content which applies to different distal objects in different environments while remaining invariant itself.

The question of whether the primal sketch does in fact represent distal, physical objects or properties has received some discussion recently. Marr usually describes the primal sketch as a representation of the image rather than the physical world (e.g., 1982, 37, 51-53, 71, 366), one that makes explicit important information about image intensity changes and their geometrical distribution and organization (1982, 37). Hence some commentators have challenged Burge's non-individualist use of the primal sketch on the grounds that its primitives refer to the internal image, not to the external world. Egan takes this to show that this part of the theory is not intentional, and therefore cannot serve Burge's argument (Egan 1991, 108), while Sterelny says that "we can give an individualist description of the primary sketch" because we can interpret its primitives as referring to features of the retinal image, which is invariant between duplicates (1990, 90). But Marr also says that the primal sketch primitives must correspond to real physical changes on the viewed surface (1982, 44), and that one must be cautious in using the word 'edge' because "it has a partly physical meaning – it makes us think of a real physical boundary, for example" (1982, 68); he speaks of constructing descriptions that "have physical meanings" (1982, 75). Segal says that the theory is not clear about whether the primitives have distal or proximal interpretations (1989, 209). Burge, of course, claims that the edge, bar and blob representations specify physical edges, bars and blobs (1986, 33).

Though Burge's interpretation of the primal sketch is not as straightforward as he implies, there are two reasons why this issue does not seem crucial for an individualist to contest. First, though it might support an *ad hominem* objection to Burge's use of the primal sketch, it does not suffice for an individualist interpretation of Marr's theory. Since Marr does explicitly describe the primitives of the 2½-D sketch as representing properties of the external world such as surface orientation, distance from viewer and discontinuities in depth and surface orientation (1982, 37), Burge could avoid these objections by basing his argument on the higher-level representation (cf. Burge 1986, 33, Example 4).

There is a more important reason, however, why it would be a mistake to think that allowing the primitives a physical interpretation makes the anti-individualist conclusion inescapable. It may seem to do so if one argues as follows: if the contents of psychological states are specified using terms that refer to parts of the physical environment, those contents are determined by that environment and hence are not supervenient on individual constitution. This reasoning, however, involves a slide between two senses of 'determined' – what might be called the descriptive and the modal senses. Even if the contents of mental or psychological states are descriptively determined by the environment in the sense that those contents are identified using terms that refer to objects in the environment, this does not entail that those contents are modally determined by the environment in the sense that they would vary with environment while individual constitution remained the same. (One way in which descriptive determination could occur without modal determination is by ascription of contents identified by terms referring to the actual environment in counterfactual or twin environments, as in the conservative response described earlier.) So even if we grant that Marr ascribes visual representations that specify the physical objects and properties which in fact normally cause them, we need not necessarily grant the stronger claim that visual contents are individuated by reference to their normal physical causes. The claim about individuation is a modal claim, as the inference drawn from it in step 3 of Burge's argument shows. But the fact that primitives' causes and contents in fact coincide does not entail the modal claim that the primitives' causes are essential to their contents.

How is the modal claim to be made out? Burge states that "the intentional kinds of the theory presuppose contingent facts about the subject's physical environment" (1986, 33), and supports this claim by showing that Marr's choice of representational primitives is motivated by assumptions about that environment. In discussing the primal sketch, Burge notes that such assumptions "are used to identify the physical significance of – the objective information normally given by – certain types of patterns in the image"; he gives as examples edge, boundary, bar and blob detectors (1986, 33). Similarly, Marr posits representations of generalized cones (objects generated by moving a cross-section along an axis) as primitives for the 3-D model, because physical assumptions plus information provided by earlier stages can be used to detect whether viewed surfaces approximate such cones, and because such representations are useful for object recognition (Burge 1986, 33-34; Marr 1982, 215-25, 314).

Certainly these examples indicate that Marr's rationale for claiming that we construct certain representations presupposes contingent facts about our physical environment. Marr exploits environmental regularities in finding in the image patterns that are likely to be the result of discontinuites in the viewed surface, and hence may be usefully and feasibly marked in the primal sketch. And he notes regularities in our environment which make it feasible and useful to construct representations of generalized cones (cf. Sterelny 1990, 93). But it does not follow that the contents of our visual representations essentially depend on those regularities, so that their contents would differ in environments in which those regularities did not obtain. Though Marr tries to design his program so that tokens of the symbol meaning 'blob here' are normally caused by blobs, and though he exploits environmental regularities in doing so, it does not follow that the tokens' having that type of cause is essential to their having that content, so that they could not mean 'blob here' in environments in which they were not normally caused by blobs. It does, however, illustrate Marr's use of physical assumptions in designing programs intended to succeed in detecting and representing what he assumes we succeed in detecting and representing. So even though the appeal to Marr's use of physical assumptions does not suffice to establish the modal claim, it suggests that the assumption of success may supply the requisite modal force.

If Marr were to assume that we would have detected and represented different things had our physical environment been different – that is, if he assumes success in representing specific features of the local environment – then the representational contents he attributes, and the rationale he gives, will depend on the environment in the requisite modal sense. So it is not surprising that Burge derives the causal individuation of content from the assumption of success: "in view of the success-orientation of the theory, this [causal] mode of individuation is grounded in its basic methods" (Burge 1986, 34); "[t]he intentional content of representations of edges or generalized cones is individuated in terms of *specific* reference to those very contingently instantiated physical properties, *on the assumption that those properties normally give rise to veridical representations of them*" (Burge 1986, 35;

first emphasis in original, second emphasis mine). If perceptual success under normal conditions is assumed, it follows that perceptual contents must apply to their normal distal causes.[4] Thus the assumption of success is crucial to the claim that the presence of a certain environmental cause is essential to the content of visual representations, and hence to Burge's anti-individualist argument.

The assumption of success plays a crucial role in supporting inferences from the contents actually ascribed to those that would be ascribed in counterfactual cases. Appeals to Marr's choice of representational primitives cannot establish the crucial claim about content individuation unless the assumption of success is in place, since the assumption is needed to supply the modal force which the examples lack. So the assumption of veridicality is not only central to Burge's presentation of Marr's theory but also provides essential support for the claim that the theory individuates perceptual content non-individualistically. It is because it is allegedly part of the methodology of the theory to presume veridical perception of specific features of the local environment that there is a constitutive relationship between that environment and perceivers' visual contents. But the assumption of success supplies the desired modal force only if it is a genuine methodological assumption about how a creature's interactions with its environment are to be described and explained. Hence it is important to look more closely at the role of success in Marr's theory and methodology.

Success

It is surely true that Marr's theory is oriented towards explaining how we succeed in solving the problem of seeing. He begins his book by describing vision as "the process of discovering from images what is present in the world, and where it is" (1982, 3), and goes on to explain how the process of discovery is able to exploit regularities in the physical world.

It seems that Marr does assume the success or veridicality of visual perception, and that his choice of computational theories is guided by this assumption. Surely, then, Burge is right that the theory presupposes success, and that its explanations of that success presuppose contingent facts about the environment. His conclusion seems to follow directly: if vision is a process of discovering what is present in the world, what is discovered and represented by the visual system will differ in worlds in which different things are present.

This is rather too swift, however. Marr does assume that we are largely successful in discovering what is where by looking, and he aims to explain how we do this. But this need not mean that he would (or should) automatically make the corresponding assumption about inhabitants of a different environment. This might follow if success in representing the local environment were automatically assumed without argument, as a matter of methodology; but this, I shall argue, is not the case.

I shall do so by setting the assumption of success in the context of Marr's methodological views. Marr is perhaps best known for his distinction between three levels of explanation of information-processing systems. The first, level 1, is that of the abstract computational theory; level 2 is that of representation and algorithm, and concerns computational implementation; level 3 deals with physical implementation. Level 1 (which Burge 1986, 28, refers to as the theory of the computation of the information) concerns the goal of the computation, why it is appropriate and the logic of the strategy by which it can be carried out (Marr 1982, 25). Marr says that "in the theory of visual processes, the underlying task is to reliably derive properties of the world from images of it," and the strategy is to employ physical constraints or assumptions (1982, 23; cf. the earlier discussion of Burge's first two points).

To understand the significance of perceptual success for Marr, one must appreciate the importance he attaches to level 1, the level of computational theory. The realization that perception must be analyzed at this level if it is to be understood at all is the basic foundation of his approach to vision; in fact, to explain vision as an information-processing task simply is to understand it at this level (1982, 19). He insists that "real progress can only be made... by precisely formulating the information-processing problems involved in the sense of our level one" (1982, 347). Level 1 analysis is critically important because "the nature of the computations that underlie perception depends more upon the computational problems that have to be solved than upon the particular hardware in which their solutions are implemented. To phrase the point another way, an algorithm is likely to be understood more readily by understanding the nature of the problem being solved than by examining the mechanism (and the hardware) in which it is embodied" (1982, 27).

Focussing on problems rather than mechanisms is central to Marr's view of computational psychology.[5] He typically motivates his own problem-based approach by contrasting it with what he calls "mechanism-based thinking". The first insists on a precise formulation of the computational problem, allowing "the information-processing basis of perception to be made rigorous" (1982, 19); the second is "thinking in similes" which is "too imprecise to be useful" (1982, 347). The first aims for true understanding, providing a theory which explains what must be computed to solve the problem and why; the second aims for mimicry, and "can easily degenerate into the writing of programs that do no more than mimic in an unenlightening way some small aspect of performance" (1982, 347; cf. 345). In the first paradigm, "it becomes possible to construct... theories stating that what is being computed is optimal in some sense or is guaranteed to function correctly" (1982, 19); in the second, "there was frequently no way to determine whether a program would deal with a particular case other than by running the program" (1982, 28). With the computational approach, "the ad hoc element is removed, and heuristic computer programs are replaced by solid foundations on which a real subject can be built" (1982, 19).[6]

Marr's slogan might be "Study problems, not mechanisms." He sums up his view in a passage which is worth quoting at length:

> If we believe that the aim of information-processing studies is to formulate and understand particular information-processing problems, then the structure of those problems is central, not the mechanisms through which their solutions are implemented. Therefore, in exploiting this fact, the first thing to do is to find problems that we can solve well, find out how to solve them, and examine our performance in the light of that understanding. The most fruitful source of such problems is operations that we perform well, fluently, and hence unconsciously, since it is difficult to see how reliability could be achieved if there was no sound, underlying method.
>
> Unfortunately, problem-solving research has for obvious reasons tended to concentrate on problems that we understand well intellectually but perform poorly on, like mental arithmetic and cryptarithmetic geometry-theorem proving, or the game of chess – all problems in which human skills are of doubtful quality and in which good performance seems to rest on a huge base of knowledge and expertise.
>
> I argue that these are exceptionally good grounds for *not* yet studying how we carry out such tasks. I have no doubt that when we do mental arithmetic we are doing something well, but it is not arithmetic, and we seem far from understanding even one component of what that something is. I therefore feel we should concentrate on the simpler problems first, for there we have some hope of genuine advancement.
>
> If one ignores this stricture, one is left with unlikely looking mechanisms whose only recommendation is that they cannot do something we cannot do. (1982, 347-48).

Marr enjoins us not only to study problems rather than mechanisms, but to study problems we can solve well, and to look to operations that we perform well as a source of such problems. Problems we solve well should be sought out because their structure can be exploited in understanding how we solve them. Marr does not say explicitly why this is so, but his talk of the rigour made possible by the computational approach suggests a reason. Since the nature of the problem determines the nature of the solution, the theorist can work from a clearly formulated, soluble problem towards a solution which can be proven to succeed, rather than proposing mechanisms and testing them in a hit-and-miss fashion. Not only is it possible to formulate theoretical goals and evaluate theoretical efforts with greater precision, but problem-driven efforts are likely to lead to genuine understanding rather than to mimicry. Since the theory is dictated by the nature of the problem, we understand how it solves it; and since there are many ways to fail but few to succeed, any solution to a problem our nervous system solves has a good chance of illuminating the manner in which our nervous system solves it.[7]

In the passage quoted above, Marr describes operations performed well as "the most fruitful source," but only a source, of problems we can solve (1982, 347). Significant work is required to formulate the problems, solution of which underlies our fluent performance of these operations. Since success is more elusive than failure, here again it is easier to say which problems must be solved to carry out a task well than to say which must be solved to do it poorly. So it is harder to formulate the problems whose successful solution underlies poor performance (in mental arithmetic, say) than to formulate those which must be solved for good performance. Moreover, if an operation is performed well, fluently and unconsciously, performance is likely to be controlled by relatively self-contained, specialized processes exploiting constraints specific to the domain. In Marr's words, there is probably "a sound, underlying method" dictated by the problem in question and hence recoverable by exploiting its structure. If good performance is hard to attain and requires a huge base of knowledge and expertise, the processes which produce it are unlikely to be tailored to the task and hence will not easily be discovered by reflecting on the problems in question. In the first case, the nature of the task indicates the problems which must be solved to succeed in it, which in turn constrain the nature of the processes which solve them; in the second, the relationship between task, problems and processes is much looser.

What is the moral of these methodological reflections? Marr is interested in operations we perform successfully and problems we succeed in solving, because the nature of these operations and problems can be exploited in arriving at an explanation of how we solve them. Moreover, this fact makes it possible to produce accounts which are both perspicuous and robust. Level 1 theories provide an explanation of our competence instead of merely mimicking our performance; and the theorist can prove that the hypothesized processes are capable of solving a general problem, instead of simply matching our performance over a limited range.

On this reading, Marr's success-orientation – his interest in seeking out and explaining our successes – is due to his belief that successful operations yield more readily to explanation, and that progress will best be made by formulating and solving the problems whose solution underlies our success. Given his methodological views, there is evidently a sense in which his interest in vision presupposes that seeing is something that we do well, that perception and numerous subroutines of perception are veridical in normal circumstances. His project is success-oriented insofar as he aims to show how we are able to extract veridical information about distal objects from retinal stimulation; he must do this if he is to explain how we succeed in doing what he assumes we can do. But the fact that Marr's enquiry presupposes and is oriented towards success in this sense will not do the work Burge's argument requires. Since Marr's project is to explain the actual reliability of vision, his project presupposes that vision is in fact generally reliable. He explains how we are able to see what (he assumes) we can see, by designing processes and representations which exploit regularities in our environment to extract reliable information from it. However, this does not entail that a methodological presumption of reliability would be made in counterfactual environments; and this is precisely the result which Burge's argument requires. The anti-individualist claim is that Marr assumes not only that we in fact succeed in solving the information-processing problems posed by our actual environment, but also that we would succeed in solving different information-processing problems if that environment were different (cf. Burge 1986, 35). But the moral of the excursion into Marr's discussion of his methodology is that he takes it to be a substantial empirical task to determine which information-processing problems we succeed in solving, and that he relies on the evidence of our performance in discovering which problems they are. Summing up the "methodology or style" of his approach, Marr writes, "In the study both of representations and of processes, general problems are often suggested by everyday experience or by psychophysical or even neurophysiological findings of a quite general nature. Such general observations can often lead to the formulation of a particular process or representational theory, specific examples of which can be programmed or subject to detailed psychophysical testing" (1982, 331; cf. 325, 327).

Let me mention some instances of such observations. When at the beginning of his enquiry Marr raises the broad question of what kind of information vision really delivers and what representational issues are involved, the piece of evidence that inspires his answer is War-rington's study of patients with parietal lesions (1982, 35). Patients with right parietal lesions were able to recognize common objects as long as they were seen from familiar angles. Those with left parietal lesions could perceive the shapes of objects even from unconventional perspectives, but could not recognize the objects. Marr interprets these results as showing that the ability to perceive the shape of objects can be dissociated from the ability to recognize objects from their shapes. This revealed the problem domain of vision: vision solves the problem of building a description of the shape and positions of objects from images, and it can do so independently of object recognition.[8]

Observations of the behaviour of patients with parietal lesions indi-cated the overall information-processing problem solved by vision; but the many subproblems which must be solved to achieve this goal also have to be formulated. Commenting on Julesz's discovery that stereo disparity alone could produce a sensation of depth in random-dot stereograms, Marr writes, "From a theoretical point of view, obser-vations like Bela Julesz's are extremely valuable because they enable us to formulate clear computational questions that we know must have answers because the human visual system can carry out the task in question" (1982, 102). Throughout the book Marr uses observations of our responses to different stimuli to reveal the cues our visual sys-tem responds to and the kinds of information visual processes are able to extract from images. These results play a crucial role in Marr's choice of representations and of processes.[9] Marr sees our visual abili-ties as a sign of problems successfully solved, and in that sense his the-ory of vision assumes success and is oriented to explaining it. But, the question of which problems we solve successfully when we see is still a substantial question for Marr, one that he answers through detailed observations of our performance.

Specificity of Success

I have been presenting Burge as viewing the theory of vision as non-individualistic because he interprets it as committed to assuming spe-cific successes; and I have been arguing that though Marr seeks out success, he does so by gathering data on our performance. At this point the defender of Burge may point out that an assumption of suc-cess in *any* environment is not necessary to establish his conclusion; all that is required is that our visual systems might have operated well and fluently in significantly different physical environments, and that in such cases the theorist would conclude that we were solving signif-icantly different information-processing problems. In Burge's words,

"If theory were confronted with a species of organism reliably and successfully interacting with a different set of objective visible properties, the representational types that the theory would attribute to the organism would be different, regardless of whether an individual organism's physical mechanisms were different" (1986, 34). As long as performance consistent with success is interpreted as evidence for success in perceptually representing the specific environmental features with which the subject normally interacts, success may wait on performance rather than being assumed.

The thought-experiment illustrates the strategy. Recall that in the actual environment, representations are normally caused by small shadows, while in the counterfactual one the normal causes are cracks. Burge stipulates that "the relevant visible entities [cracks and shadows] are very small and not such as to bear heavily on adaptive success" (1986, 42). So the perceiver's performance appears equally suited to both environments. To attribute misperception in the counterfactual case would be absurd, Burge claims; and if normal objective causes are specifically represented, contents that subsume cracks and shadows are ruled out.

But this thought-experiment attributes representational contents which are much more specific than those Marr posits in early vision. It is important not to read too much into terms like 'edge' as labels for primitives. The physical phenomena which can legitimately cause edge tokens – to which edge tokens apply – are very varied; they are not just the edges of physical objects. The role of these primitives in the theory is to indicate the presence of intensity changes in the image that are due to a single physical phenomenon: a change in reflectance, illumination, depth or surface orientation (1982, 70). Edges in this sense can be the boundaries of shadows, highlights, light sources or reflections; they can be creases, scratches or regions of change in curvature. To say that the edges signalled by edge tokens are physical is to say that they are due to physical phenomena, not that they are the edges of physical objects. They could not be; this level of processing is simply not sophisticated enough to detect such edges. So one should not take the term 'edge' to imply that the primal sketch specifies the edges of physical objects, let alone that it specifies them as such; its extension is much broader.

Of course this does not prevent the primitives of the primal sketch from specifying objective physical phenomena; when an edge token is constructed to mark a place in the image which does not correspond to an edge in the outside world, a mistake is made. This can happen; edge representations are not defined so as to apply to anything that causes them. But the fact that the extension of these primitives does not include anything that actually does (or counterfactually might) cause them should not lead one to exaggerate the specificity of their extensions. The edge, bar, boundary and blob primitives of the primal sketch provide no support for the postulation of crack or shadow representations in early vision.

A defender of Burge might protest that this is a complaint about the specific example, on which the conclusion does not depend; the non-individualistic character of the theory guarantees that an example faithful to Marr can be constructed.[10] I doubt that it can. If the differences between the environments are too fine-grained, they will not be plausibly represented by primitives of the type that Marr cites. If they are too coarse-grained – if there are differences in surface orientation, size, shape, distance or the other properties which are explicitly represented at the level of the 2½-D sketch – investigation of the perceiver's behaviour in other environments will indicate misperception. The difficulty is that either the environmental difference is one to which the perceiver is not able to respond, and her performance in psychophysical tasks will provide no reason to suppose that it is explicitly represented, or it is one to which the perceiver is able to respond, and the response will be indicative of misrepresentation.[11] If a subject's performance strongly suggests that she systematically misperceives certain aspects of her environment, this is good evidence that she does; there is no assumption of success which would impose contents individuated in terms of normal causes to avoid misperception. Nor is there a commitment to attributing fine-grained, environmentally specific abilities, such as the ability to solve the problem of detecting cracks or shadows, because cracks or shadows are prevalent in the environment. Burge appears to avoid the difficulty only by replacing Marr's more conservative estimate of perceivers' abilities with an unwarranted assumption of highly specific perceptual success.

Concluding Remarks

On Burge's reading of Marr, the nature of the perceiver's environment is constitutive of the information-processing problems the perceiver solves, since it is assumed that the perceiver succeeds in representing specific features of the environment. I have been arguing that Marr is interested in seeking out operations we perform successfully and explaining our successes, but that this success-orientation does not dictate that environment is essentially constitutive of visual content. Marr seeks out success because it is a fruitful source of solvable computational problems. But he looks to our performance to discover the nature of our problem-solving abilities, and the successes he attributes are not as specific as Burge's argument requires. Marr's concern with success is not such as to show his theory non-individualistic. Indeed, as the previous paragraph argued, there is reason to think that the visual representations Marr actually attributes to us to would be appropriate to our duplicates inhabiting different environments.

As I mentioned at the outset, I am sceptical of the claim that psychology must be individualistic; there may be other areas of psychology which attribute representations which vary with environment. But I am also sceptical of the claim that psychology must be non-individualistic. Though Burge does not advocate this claim explicitly, it is a natural consequence of his view that explanation in psychology is success-oriented – that it presupposes certain successes in our interaction with the world, and is geared to accounting for them by attributing states which represent that world – and that this success-orientation motivates anti-individualism. Marr's project of explaining how we know what is where in the world by seeing presupposes that we are actually successful in doing so, and the theory accounts for this by arguing that we construct certain representations of the world. But this does not entail that Marr should make an assumption of environmentally specific success in other surroundings, nor does his method suggest that he would do so. Though psychological theories may aim to explain our successes in dealing with our environment, it does not follow that the nature of our successes can be read off that environment, nor that a necessary individuative link between it and our psychological states is needed to explain them.[12]

Acknowledgments

An earlier version of this paper was presented at Cornell University Philosophy Department and in a seminar I taught at Harvard University Philosophy Department in Spring 1992. I am very grateful to the participants in the two discussions for their helpful questions and comments. I would also like to thank Ned Block and Stephen White for valuable comments on earlier drafts.

Notes

1 As my opening questions suggest, when I speak of individualism in this paper I refer to the claim that an individual's intentional states supervene on his or her physical and functional states. So the individualism in question is the weaker of the two forms distinguished by Burge (1986, 4). (The stronger form is a claim about explication.)

2 As Egan (1991, 188) notes, Marr nowhere suggests that this "additional information" is explicitly represented by the visual system.

3 Marr puts it thus: "the critical act in formulating computational theories for such processes [sc. processes for recovering the physical characteristics of a scene from images of it] is the discovery of valid constraints on the way the world behaves that provide sufficient additional information to allow recovery of the desired characteristic" (1982, 330-31). This does not mean that his goal is not the discovery of the constraints our visual systems do in fact exploit; he answers the question of how we in fact solve a problem by developing ways in which the problem could be solved (see, e.g., n.7 below).

4 This reasoning requires that 'normal' should have the same sense in 'normal cause' and 'normal conditions', and that it be read non-rigidly. If it were read rigidly, the content of representations in counterfactual environments would depend on their normal causes in the *actual* environment, and the claim about causal individuation of content would not imply step 3 of Burge's argument; so it is essential that 'normal' refer to what is normal in the counterfactual situation. The same is true of 'local' in "success in representing specific features of the local environment is assumed".

5 See the distinction between developing tools and developing theories, Marr (1982), 345; the discussion of mimicry and mechanisms, 347, 349; and the remarks on mechanisms, mimicry and simile-based thinking, 336, 346, 348.

6 Compare: "once a computational theory has been established for a particular problem, it never has to be done again, and in this respect a result in AI behaves like a result in mathematics or any of the hard natural sciences" (Marr 1977, 130).

7 Marr remarks that though Horn's equations for deriving the shape of objects from shading may be ill-suited to neural networks, he doubts that Horn's effort was misplaced: "Although it will not yield direct information about human shape-from-shading strategies, it probably provides indispensable background information for discovering the particular poor man's version that we ourselves use" (1982, 339).

8 Another way to put this would be to say that Warrington's results reveal the boundaries of the visual module. Discovering this is a first step towards using psychophysical observations to break down the overall computation into a collection of nearly independent, specialized subprocesses or modules, a procedure which Marr describes as fundamental to his approach (see the discussions of modularity at Marr 1982, 99-103, 325, 344-45). Julesz's observations, mentioned in the next paragraph of the text, are an example of the kind of psychophysical evidence which allow the visual process to be separated into modules (Marr 1982, 102). The relationships between Marr's principle of modularity and his three levels of explanation, and between Marr's conception of modularity and that of Fodor (1983), are of considerable interest, and I plan to discuss them elsewhere.

9 Some examples include: perception of the quantized image of Lincoln (Marr 1982, 74), which provides information about the primal sketch; the perception of flow in Glass dot patterns, pp. 83-85, which provide evidence

for virtual lines in the representation of spatial organization; the recovery of shape from silhouettes, p. 217, which indicates the importance of contours as sources of shape information. In discussing Marr's choice of representational primitives for the primal sketch, the only facts Burge mentions as being relevant to that choice are facts about the physical environment (Burge 1986, 33); but Marr appeals to our responses to images shown on pp. 48-51, 74, 77-78, 83-85, 92 and 94-95 to motivate his choice of primitives. The diagram (Marr 1982, 332) illustrating the relationship between representations and processes in Marr's approach also illustrates the role played by psychophysical investigations in suggesting and testing representations and processes. "Everyday experience and coarse psychophysical demonstrations" are depicted as motivating the formulation of representational and computational problems at level 1, while detailed psychophysical investigations are used to test and modify proposed level 2 solutions.

10 Burge responds in this way to Robert Matthews's criticisms of another version of the thought-experiment: "Matthews concentrates on the example instead of the argument" (Burge 1988, 95).

11 McGinn (1989, 66, n.80) confronts Burge with a similar dilemma. Matthews (1988, 82-83) and Segal (1989, 208; 1991, 488) also point out that the importance of behaviour in attributing perceptual contents makes it difficult for the anti-individualist to generate a convincing example.

12 The anti-individualist should resist the temptation to revert at this point to a version of the argument scouted earlier (see p. 7), and to reason thus: the successes psychological theories aim to explain are specified using terms that refer to parts of the physical environment, so those successes are determined by that environment and hence are non-individualistically individuated. Therefore they are to be explained by non-individualistically individuated psychological states. The observation that successes are *identified* in terms of a certain environment does not by itself show that they are *individuated* thus – that interaction with that environment is essential to them.

References

Burge, T. (1986). Individualism and psychology. *Philosophical Review* 95: 3-45

———. (1988). Cartesian error and the objectivity of perception. In R.H. Grimm and D.D. Merrill (eds.), *Contents of Thought*. Tucson: University of Arizona Press

Davies, M. (1991). Individualism and perceptual content. *Mind* 100: 461-84

Egan, F. (1991). Must psychology be individualistic? *Philosophical Review* 100: 179-202

Fodor, J.A. (1983). *The Modularity of Mind*. Cambridge, MA: Bradford/MIT Press

Marr, D. (1981). Artificial intelligence: a personal view. In J. Haugeland (ed.), *MindDesign*. Cambridge, MA: Bradford/MIT Press. First printed in *Artificial Intelligence* 9: 37-48 (1977).

———. (1982). *Vision*. New York: W.H. Freeman

Matthews, R. (1988). Comments on Burge [1988]. In R.H. Grimm and D.D. Merrill (eds.), *Contents of Thought*. Tucson: University of Arizona Press

McGinn, C. (1989). *Mental Content*. Cambridge, MA: Basil Blackwell

Segal, G. (1989). Seeing what is not there. *Philosophical Review* 98: 189-214

——. (1991). In defence of a reasonable individualism. *Mind* 100: 485-94

Sterelny, K. (1990). *The Representational Theory of Mind*. Cambridge, MA: Basil Blackwell

12

Objective Perception

John Haugeland

1

I want to distinguish and characterize what I take to be a special case among broadly sensory or perceptual phenomena. Some might maintain that this case is the only genuine case of perception properly so called; but I will sidestep that largely terminological issue, and simply specify the kind of case I mean as *objective perception* – not worrying about what to call other kinds of case. It is part of my view, though not part of what I will argue for, that objective perception, in this sense, is exclusive to people. This is not to deny that, in some other or wider sense or senses, animals perceive too; nor is it to deny that people also perceive in some or all of these other senses; nor, finally, is it to deny that some other senses of perception may also be distinctive of people (e.g., aesthetic perception). It is only to claim that at least some human perception is "objective" in a special sense, and no animal perception is.[1] Though I will not be defending this claim, I will have it always in mind, and will occasionally take it for granted in choosing illustrations.

The qualifier 'objective' is intended to suggest perception *of objects as objects*. Thus, it is very much part of the undertaking to spell out what is meant by the *object* of a perceiving. It should be clear at the outset, therefore, that 'object' is used in a formal sense, to identify a role or position vis-à-vis (for instance) perception; in particular, it does not carry any implications about the nature of the objects perceived – such as that they be substantial, corporeal or otherwise thing-like. Objectivity in perception is a kind of structure that involves the perceiving, that which is perceived, and the relation between them. The aim is to delineate this distinctive structure and its presuppositions.

Several familiar problem areas in the philosophy of perception will be seen to converge in this topic, among them: (i) picking out what is perceived from among the various causal antecedents of the perceiving; (ii) the normativity of objective perception (that is, the possibility of *mis*perception); (iii) the respect in which objective perception depends on an understanding of what is perceived; (iv) the relevance of language to the possibility of objective perception; and (v) the pre-requisite character of the perceiving self or subject. On the other hand, a number of other important issues connected with perception will not enter directly into the present discussion, including in particular: (i) the peculiar "of-this-ness" or indexicality of perceptual content; (ii) the richness of (apparently) ineffable yet determinate detail in perceptual content; and (iii) the special connection (if any) between perception and imagery or imagination.

2

It is convenient to begin with the identification of what is perceived – the "object" in a broad sense – from among the many causal anteced-ents of the perceiver's perceiving. We can take for granted that, at least in ordinary sensory perception, the perceived object is *one* (or some) of those antecedents. The question is: *which* one? Or, rather, the question is: on what principled basis can we identify one among them as *the* object? For instance, if I look at and see a bicycle, part of the cause of that perceiving in me is the presence and properties of the bike – particularly those properties that determine in detail how it reflects light. But other important causal factors include the ambient light around me (as reflected in part by the bike), the source of the illumi-nation of the bike in the first place, the source of the bike itself, the functioning of my visual system, and so on. We want to say that what I perceive, the object of my perception, is the bicycle, and none of these other factors. The question is: why?

Dretske (1981, chap. 6, especially 155-68) suggests that the object of a perceptual state is whatever that state carries information about in a primary way. "'Carrying information'" is the operative notion. Roughly: given conditions of kind K, a's being F carries the information that b is G just in case a could not have been F in such conditions had b not been G. To put it anthropomorphically, a's being F carries the infor-mation that b is G if you can "tell" from a's being F (and the conditions being K) that b is G. It carries this information in a *primary* way if it does not carry it "via" any other fact, such as c's being H. Intuitively, to say that a's being F carries the information that b is G via c's being H means that it carries that information *only because* it carries the information that c is H, and c's being H carries in turn the information that b is G.[2]

Dretske illustrates the point by explaining why, when someone rings the doorbell, we hear the bell ringing but we don't hear the button being pushed. Under normal conditions, our perceptual response – what Dretske calls the "perceptual experience" – carries both the information that the button is pushed and the information that the bell is ringing. This is because we wouldn't have that experience if the button weren't pushed, nor would we have it if the bell weren't ringing. But the *only reason* we wouldn't have it if the button weren't pushed is that we wouldn't have it if the bell weren't ringing, *and* (under normal conditions) the bell wouldn't ring if the button weren't pushed. Hence, the information about the button is carried via the information about the bell.

To see how this works, consider the (abnormal) conditions in which the bell wires occasionally short, thereby ringing the bell without the button being pushed. Under those conditions, the same experience would still carry the information that the bell was ringing, but it would no longer carry the information that the button was pushed – precisely because the bell's ringing would itself no longer carry that information. So, even in normal conditions, when the perceptual experience does carry the information that the button is pushed, it does so only via the bell's ringing. Hence, the experience does not carry the information about the button in a primary, but only a secondary way. And this is why, according to Dretske, the button is not the object of the perception. Even though we can *tell* that the button is pushed, we do not *perceive* that it is (unless we happen also to be outside watching). What we *hear* is not the button but the bell.

The more interesting and difficult question is why the experience carries even the information about the *bell* in a primary way. It might be argued, for instance, that the experience also carries the information that the air or our eardrum is vibrating in a certain manner, and that, moreover, it carries the information that the bell is ringing only via this information about the air or eardrum.[3] In that case, only the latter information would be carried in a primary way; and then, by the above logic, it would have to be conceded that what we *really* hear, even under normal conditions, is the air or our eardrum, not the bell.

Dretske's reply to this challenge is ingenious, but ultimately, I think, unsuccessful. It has two stages. In the first stage, he points out that one thing's being the case can carry the information that another is, without carrying any information about the intervening causal processes, if (in the relevant conditions) any of several different causal processes might have occurred, and each would have had the same result. Thus, suppose that the mantle bowl only has lemon drops in it when one of the children buys some, and that the children only buy lemon drops when Grandpa provides the funds. Then, if there are lemon drops in the bowl today, that fact carries the information that Grandpa recently paid, but it carries no information as to *which* grandchild fetched – because they're all equally eager and able. *A fortiori*, it can't carry the former information via carrying the latter.

The second stage, then, is to argue that the different ways the air or eardrum might vibrate when we hear the bell ring are like the different grandchildren that might fetch the candy for Grandpa. That is, the perceptual experience must have been caused by some vibration or other that could only have been caused (in the relevant conditions) by the bell ringing; but there are any number of such vibrations that would have sufficed with no difference in effect. Under those conditions, the experience would carry the information that the bell is ringing without carrying any information as to *which* of the sufficient vibrations mediated causally. Thus, the distal information (about the bell) is not carried via any more proximal information (about how the air or eardrum is vibrating), for the simple reason that the proximal information is not carried (by that experience) at all. And this is why it is the bell which we hear after all.

How is this argument made out? Dretske appeals to perceptual constancy effects, which, as he rightly points out, are ubiquitous. We do not perceive the table as changing shape when we walk around it, changing size when we approach, or changing colour as daylight gives way to dusk and then to candles, even though the proximal stimuli – the patterns of light entering our eyes or the patterns of neuron firings in our retinas – vary dramatically. Thus, we see the table as equally square, whether our vantage is such that its retinal projection is itself square, rhomboid or trapezoid. So (under normal conditions), the perception carries the information that the table is square, without carrying any information as to *which* retinal projection happened, on this occasion, to mediate the perceiving causally. Accordingly, it carries the information about the table in a primary way – not via carrying information about any proximal stimulus – and hence it is the *table* which we see.

The essential difficulty here lies in the characterization of the proximal stimulus. Note that the argument depends on the claim that the *same* perceptual experience of the *same* object can be mediated by *different* stimuli; for, if only one stimulus could mediate, then the experience would carry information about it, and hence the information about the object would not be carried in a primary way. For purposes of discussion, we can accept the suggestion, based on perceptual constancy, that in some sense the experience and the object remain the same; the question concerns the sense in which the respective proximal stimuli are different. Of course, it's *qualitative* difference – difference in kind – that's at issue; and whether two instances differ in kind depends on which kinds are being considered.

Which kinds need Dretske consider? Since the argument depends on a non-existence claim, it must, in effect, consider all kinds. For if there were any single kind of stimulus that mediated all and only the constant perceivings (same kind of perception of the same kind of object), then the perception would carry the information that the stimulus was of that kind, and hence would carry the information about the distal object only via the information about the stimulus. Dretske points out that there are respects in which the stimuli differ: some are rhomboid projections, some trapezoid, etc. But that isn't enough; he must argue that there is *no* respect in which these stimuli (and only these) are all alike.

Of course, such a kind would not be as simple as the shape of an instantaneous optical projection on the retina. And Dretske even mentions (1981, 164), as plausible explanations of constancy phenomena, the existence of "'higher order' variables in the stimulus array" and "global characteristics of the entire stimulus pattern" to which our sensory systems are sensitive.[4] Unaccountably, however, he never considers the possibility that such "higher order" and more "global" stimulus *kinds* might undermine his account of why the stimulus itself is not perceived. That is, he never considers the possibility that the perceptual response carries the information that the (proximal) stimulus is of such a (higher order, global) kind, and thus carries information about the (distal) object only via that information about the stimulus.[5]

What's worse, it seems that there *must* be such kinds, if sensory perception is to be possible at all. For if one *can* reliably recognize the squareness of the table from varying perspectives, then there must be *something* – something of a higher order, global, relative to context, or whatever – normally common to all and only the stimuli from such objects, on pain of rendering perception magical. To be sure, perception is not 100 percent reliable, in part because stimuli of the relevant kinds can be produced artificially (or accidentally) even when the corresponding objects are not present. But this is no help to Dretske. Quite the contrary: it not only suggests that there are the stimulus kinds that his account can't allow, but also that perceptual responses track these kinds primarily, and the object kinds only via them.

3

So far, the question has been: why, despite being via (proximal) stimuli, is perception *of* (distal) objects? The answer, as we have seen, cannot depend on the absence of suitable kinds for the stimuli to instantiate. Thus, presumably it must depend instead on something positive about the objects themselves, and about perceiving them. It is crucial, however, not to suppose at the outset that *objects* are an unproblematic, fixed point, and the only issue is how perception gets to be *of them*. In particular, we must not tacitly presuppose that being an object is tantamount to being a temporally and spatially cohesive corporeal lump. Rather, the "objecthood" of perceptual objects and the "of-ness" of perception go hand in hand, and are intelligible only in terms of one another, something like the interdependence of target and aim, or puzzle and solution. So, the deeper question is: *how and why* is such a structure – what we might call the *structure of objectivity* imposed on the physics and physiology of sensation?

In order to avoid the prejudicial presupposition that we know in advance what "objects" are, I shall turn temporarily to a different sort of example, one in which the temptation to equate 'object' with 'body' is perhaps less compelling. In this context, it will be possible to ask what it is about the objects that lets them be objective, without the distraction of supposed "obviousness." That is, the question can really be confronted and maybe even answered. On that basis, then, we will be able to return to the case of ordinary corporeal "things" with clearer horizons.

The special case I want to consider is chess, when the game is played in a visible medium – that is, such that one can *see* positions, threats, moves and the like. I can, for instance, see you castling, early in the midgame; a little later, I can see your knight simultaneously threatening my queen and rook, in a so-called knight fork; and, before long, I can even see the untenability of my entire king-side defence, and infer that I might as well resign. We should not try to imagine that these perceptual abilities are all built up out of a handful of "primitive" or "atomic" abilities, such as identifying the individual pieces and squares. I can recognize a knight fork just as "immediately" as I can recognize a knight or a square; and it may not even be possible to define 'untenable king side' in terms of pieces and locations – suggesting that they can *only* be perceived as gestalts.

What's involved in seeing these things? An instructive first indication is the fact that dogs and cats can't see them at all. Without broaching, for the moment, the question of what exactly they do see, we can be quite sure that no dog or cat could see even a rook as such on the K2 square, never mind the power, daring or foolishness of that position. And the reason is not far to find: dogs and cats don't have a clue about chess. The very possibility of such a game, and all that it entails, is utterly alien to them. We might gather, then, that some grasp or understanding of the game of chess, and maybe also of games more generally, is prerequisite to any ability to perceive the phenomena manifested in chess play. But it will be worth the trouble to proceed more slowly, and explore what such a grasp amounts to, and why it is required.

Surely no creature or system can see a given configuration as a knight fork without having some sense of what a knight fork is. To put it in a familiar but perhaps misleading terminology, nothing can *apply* a concept unless it *has* that concept.[6] Of course, having a sense (or "concept") of what something is cannot be merely an ability to detect it reliably, or discriminate it from other things; locks, for instance, reliably detect the keys that fit them, and it's not out of the question that pigeons could be trained to discriminate (for a given chess set) positions containing knight forks.

In the case of chess, however, even the discrimination problem is harder than that; for chess sets can be implemented in all sorts of styles and media, from labelled slips of paper or computer-screen icons to costumed palace servants or elaborately painted helicopters. Knight forks are equally knight forks in any of these sets; but, to see them, a perceiver would have to "abstract from" the gross and conspicuous differences of implementation, and attend only to the chess-relevant features of the configurations.

Indeed, the matter is still more complicated, because other games, quite different from chess, can be played with the board and pieces that we ordinarily call chess sets. And it could well happen that, in the course of such a game, an arrangement occurs that would be a knight fork were chess being played. But, in fact, it's nothing like a knight fork, because, in this game, the pieces move (or are used) completely differently – the token that would be a knight in chess isn't even a knight in this domain. So, in order to see that a certain configuration is a knight fork, a perceiver must first be able to see, or otherwise appreciate, that it has occurred in the midst of a *chess* game.

These complementary considerations, that chess can be played in widely different media, and that widely different games can be played in the same media, together with the fact that knight forks can occur – and be perceived – in all of the former but none of the latter, show that the ability to perceive knight forks presupposes some grasp or understanding of the game of chess – at least enough to tell when it's being played, regardless of medium. The same point is even more obvious for seeing that a king-side defence is untenable; and a little reflection shows that it is equally true for seeing that some figure is a knight (a *chess* knight), or anything else that occurs only in chess games. Chess games are a kind of *pattern* and chess phenomena can only occur within this pattern, as *subpatterns* of it. The point about different media and different games is that these subpatterns would not be what they are, and hence could not be recognized, except as subpatterns of a superordinate pattern with the specific structure of chess – not a pattern of shape or colour, therefore, but a pattern at what we might call "the chess level." To put it more metaphysically, the game of chess is *constitutive* for chess phenomena, and *therefore* some grasp of it is prerequisite to their perceivability as such.

The pivotal phrase, "some grasp or understanding," has so far been left dangerously vague. It is all too easy to gloss this grasp as: knowing the rules (including the starting and goal configurations) that define the game – what one might get by reading Hoyle or the instructions on the box. But there are several reasons to resist this temptation. In the first place, it's not obvious that reading (and understanding) the rules is the same as, or even sufficient for, understanding the game. Second, and more to the point, it's not obvious that *knowing* the rules is required for understanding the game, at least not if knowing is taken in a sense that implies discursive cognizance of the rules in some explicit formulation (such as one gets by reading). But third, and most important, chess is serving here just as an example: the hope, without which the example would not repay the effort, is to generalize its lessons to less specialized cases – in particular, to cases for which, though there are constitutive prerequisites, these prerequisites have never been (and perhaps cannot ever be) articulated in any "rules according to Hoyle."

4

Too often, I believe, philosophers take it on faith that what essentially distinguishes people is language – "essentially" in the sense that all our other interesting differentia (society, morality, objectivity, self-understanding, history, science, normativity, sense of humour, etc.) flow from, or at least necessarily involve, this one. It seems to me, on the contrary, that some of these – objectivity, in particular – are fundamentally independent of language, and that we misunderstand them if we overlook this independence. Accordingly, I want now to indulge in a brief thought-experiment, by imagining some creatures that are, in certain respects, intermediate between known animals and people.

These creatures – "super-monkeys," we could call them – are sub-human in that they have no linguistic facility whatever: they neither produce nor understand speech (nor any other articulate gestures or signs to the same effect). This is not to say they never cry out in pain, make warning signals or give mating displays; but they never, for instance, tell stories, describe things or formulate rules. On the other hand, they stand out from all other animals in that they learn and play games, including sophisticated games like chess.

Since super-monkeys are animals, and in fact a lot like us, there is no problem about ascribing to them not only various beliefs and desires (at least in the minimal sense of Dennett's 1987 "intentional systems theory") but also a considerable range of affects and moods, emotions and motives. It's perfectly obvious, for instance, that they *like* strawberries (as well as the janitor who brings them), that they *enjoy* frolicking in the pool (but would sometimes rather sleep), that they get *angry* when picked on, because it *hurts*, and that's *why* they strike back. These qualities sharply differentiate supermonkeys from any current or imminent generation of "game-playing" computer.

What should we look for in super-monkeys, if we are to understand them as playing games, even though they don't talk about it? Well, of course, they must *at least* reliably go through the motions: that is, they must actually move the pieces, not merely in accord with the rules, but in a manner more or less suited to winning. And, in the spirit of the above remarks about emotions and motives, we can expect them to be pleased and self-satisfied when they do win (or gain ground), and dejected or frustrated at the opposite. This shows that, in one sense, they are not *just* going through the motions, for the outcomes evidently matter to them. But it does not yet show that the motions are specifically *chess* moves, for it has not been shown that they are made as and only as subpatterns of a superordinate pattern at the chess level. Such further specificity is not hard to add, however: we merely require that our super-monkeys also be able to play chess in various media, and other games in the same media. This is not at all a trivial or inconsequential requirement; but it does not seem to presuppose linguistic facility, so it remains within the parameters of the thought-experiment.

Super-monkeys, as described so far, are clearly guided in their moves by sensory input from the chess board; and so, in at least that limited sense, they are certainly perceiving. When we ask, however, with Dretske, what the perception is *of*, the situation is more complicated. On the one hand, since the *responses* involved are not limited to (and may not even include) inner experiences, but are rather themselves also movings of the chess pieces, we have, so to speak, a new "angle" on the *objects*: they are both perceived *and* acted on. Of course, just as we can ask about perception, why it is of a distal rather than a proximal cause, so we can ask about action why it is of a distal rather than a proximal effect – why it is an action of moving a knight, for instance, rather than of moving an arm and some fingers. But the fact that the piece on the chess board is the one place where these two causal trajectories intersect, and especially if there is continuous feedback, as in visually guided movement, strongly suggests that it is the proper object of both the perception and the action. It is this feedback linkage, I believe, that inclines us to identify, to the extent that we do, the "objects" of ordinary animal perception and action.

On the other hand, we should notice the restricted scope of this feedback argument. It applies to a chess piece only insofar as it is a sensible, manipulable token, and has nothing whatever to do with its role or character in chess. In other words, the question of whether *chess* phenomena can be the objects of perception (or action), even for super-monkeys, has not yet been touched. And, in fact, the earlier argument brought against Dretske's information-based proposal, applies here as well. For, if chess phenomena are the phenomena they are by virtue of the way they are subpatterns within a superordinate pattern at the chess level, then, *inevitably* (under normal conditions), the proximal stimulus patterns are instances of corresponding kinds, according as they are subpatterns of higher order and more global patterns in the proximal stimuli overall. These latter patterns will have to be comparable in "level" to the chess level, in that they abstract from features that are characteristic of the various different media, and depend instead on the global relationships that define chess games as chess. But there is no reason to deny the existence of such patterns, and hence of such stimulus *kinds*.

5

There is, however, one more requirement that super-monkeys will have to meet if they are to be recognized as genuine chess-players; and this last requirement will prove crucial also for objectivity. It can be introduced by asking what happens in the face of an *illegal* move. We have already required, of course, that, as candidate chess-players at all, super-monkeys must *reliably* make legal moves; and in undertaking to play they must, in effect, be counting on this reliability in one another. This cannot mean, however, that they have to be perfect, or that they can take perfection for granted, in the sense of being unprepared to deal with illegality.[7] No system that would blithely ignore the illegality of an opponent's move could properly be deemed a chess-player.

Hence, any genuine chess-player – in fact, any game-player – must, as such, occupy a peculiar position. A player must, on the one hand, be ever *vigilant against* illegal moves, yet, on the other hand, always *count on* consistent legality.[8] These two are more intimately related than they might seem. Let's examine them in turn.

As vigilant, a player needs two quite distinct abilities: (i) to tell in general what move is made (including any relevant context),[9] whenever a player makes a move; and (ii) to tell, for any identifiable move, whether that move would be legal.[10] These abilities together (but neither of them alone) enable players reliably to detect illegal moves – an obvious prerequisite to vigilance. The first ability, in effect, induces a field of recognizable moves (i.e., identifiable phenomena that are either legal or illegal); and the second induces a partition on that field (into the legal and the illegal). Clearly, the field of identifiable moves had better include candidates on both sides of that partition, lest the vigilance be vacuous. That is: it must be possible to identify moves that would be illegal – moves, in other words, that are *ruled out* by those very rules that are constitutive for chess phenomena and their identification at all. To say that these abilities are distinct is to say that they have within them this essential possibility of *discord*.

Counting on consistent legality means more than just expecting it, but something like *insisting* on it – on pain of giving up the game. This insistence is a kind of *commitment* or *resolve* not to tolerate illegality: in case an illegal move is detected, ordinary play is breached, extraordinary measures are called for – and the game itself (i.e., continued play) is at stake in the outcome. The vigilant player's insistence, therefore, is a commitment not to stand for the kind of discord (between the above two abilities), the possibility of which is prerequisite to vigilance in the first place. So the extraordinary measures, when called for, will be an attempt to eliminate this discord, by rectifying either the identification of the move or the determination of its legality. As we shall see, it is this commitment to the definitive standards constitutive for the domain as such (e.g., to the rules of chess) that transmits normative force (including the potential for correction) to the move identification ability, and hence underlies the possibility of its objectivity. Hence, the capacity for such commitment is a prerequisite character of any self or subject that is to be capable also of objective perception (or thought or action).

Suppose, for example, that Bobby Baboon is in the midst of a chess game when his "illegal-move alarm" goes off. As a genuine chessplayer, Bobby is antecedently disposed to take extraordinary measures in the face of such an event, and to adjust accordingly. And among those measures will be to "double-check" his identification of what move was actually made. The details of this double-checking are not important. But we can imagine Bobby looking over the board again, perhaps from different angles, checking for overhanging branches or bad lighting obscuring part of the board, making sure that what he took for a bishop isn't really a knight seen from the back, and so on. We can even imagine that Bobby is still getting used to an unfamiliar chess set, and sometimes has to remind himself (or be reminded) which pieces are which. (Basically similar things could be said about Bobby "double-checking" or "reconsidering" his assessment that the move was illegal – perhaps, e.g., he forgot about capturing *en passant*).

It is crucial that this double-checking be an effort, and that "success" not be automatic. If Bobby turned up a "misperception" every time he looked for one, then the *checking* would be a sham. Rather, we must suppose that the double-checking is an extension, elaboration or more careful mode of the primary recognition ability, together with an ability to tell whether the result is coming up different, and to adjust if so. (Still more impressive would be a capacity to diagnose what went wrong in cases where a misperception is uncovered; but I don't see that this is required.) The enabling assumption is that, almost always, this more careful mode is unnecessary, because it wouldn't make any difference. But, occasionally, it would make a difference; and, in those cases (often flagged by the alarm), the result of the more careful mode is almost always *better.*

What does "better" mean? It means: more conducive to continued chess play, in the long run. Playing a game governed by constitutive standards is a non-trivial *achievement;* dogs and ordinary monkeys, for instance, are utterly incapable of it.[11] The mark of such an achievement is not an ability to articulate those standards as explicit rules, nor is it a disposition to go through any particular motions of play. Rather, it is the ability to play in fact, while at the same time putting the game itself at stake in insisting on the standards; that is, it is the ability to *let the standards govern* the play. Thus, the aforementioned possibility of discord – a possibility which, on the one hand, is reliably avoided, but, on the other hand, is resolutely not tolerated – is fundamental. Realizing a set of dispositions that works with this structure is the achievement; and the fine-tuning effected in the double-checking is best to the extent that it fosters this achievement.

6

Notice that, almost incidentally, we have now assembled the resources needed to answer Dretske's question. What the perception is *of* is that which the constitutive standards govern: the moves, pieces, positions, and so on, in the chess game. Why? Because, when the possibility of a *mis*perception arises, what the issue turns on is telling how things stand with regard to those standards. That's what *accurate* perception is counted on to tell; it's what is checked for in the double-checking; it's the way in which perceptual ability contributes to the game-playing achievement. In other words, the *norms* governing the perceptions as such, and in virtue of which they can be objective, are inseparable from the *standards* governing, and indeed constituting, the chess phenomena as such; or, to make the Kantian paraphrase even more obvious: the conditions of the *possibility of objective perception* as such are likewise the conditions of the *possibility of the objects of that perception.*[12]

To be concrete, suppose that, on a certain occasion, the actual chess position is of one kind, but (due to some quirk in the circumstances) the ambient optic array around Bobby, and hence also his perceptual response, is of the sort usually caused by chess positions of some other kind. Is his response a misperception of the chess position, or an accurate perception of the ambient array? Clearly the former – *because* what's at issue in the perceiving at all, the whole point of *looking* in the first place, is telling what the position is. And this is manifest in the fact that, if Bobby's alarm goes off and he discovers the discrepancy, he will change his response; that is, to the best of his ability, he will bring his response into line with the actual position, rather than the optic array (the entire aim and purpose of double-checking). Therefore, even when there is no discrepancy, it is the position and not the array that is perceived.

This shows, I believe, that our imaginary super-monkeys are capable of objective perception – like people, and unlike any (actual) animals. The fact that these supermonkeys are completely non-linguistic shows further that language is not prerequisite to objective perception, and hence that it is not language that fundamentally separates us from the animals with regard to the possibility of objectivity. On the other hand, the fact that putative perceptions are normatively beholden to their objects, subject to correction in light of double-checking those objects, is integral to the account. What's more, these norms are completely dependent in force and content on the constitutive standards to which the perceived objects are held, and which must therefore be counted primary. And it is, finally, the super-monkeys themselves that "hold" those objects to those standards. Such holding to standards, by simultaneously counting on it and insisting on it, is, when it succeeds, understanding. Thus, the objects of objective perception are ipso facto understood. *Understanding*, not language, is what separates supermonkeys (and us) from "thoughtless brutes."

7

That there might actually be "super-monkeys" that learn and play games like chess without benefit of language is, to be sure, incredible. Hence, the intended point and force of the example calls for explanation. It will help first to rehearse a few notable objections. Thus, it is extremely unlikely that the cognitive and social capacities prerequisite for chess would evolve prior to and independently of those required for language. For, clearly, there is a great deal of overlap in these capacities; and they would have far more survival value if used for language than if used only for formal games. It could even be that our own ability to play chess relies essentially on species-specific "modules" that are integral to our linguistic faculty – such as our ability to parse complex structures, or to see individual tokens as tokens of digital types, or to remember a large "vocabulary" of possible constituents.

Likewise, it is almost impossible to imagine *teaching* chess, even to a creature with all the native capacities of homo sapiens, without verbal instruction and admonition. How could one hope to convey the relevant alternatives and restrictions in various situations without explicit conditionals and modal adverbs? Indeed, if genuine chess presupposes not just that the moves in fact be legal, but that the players insist on this, then they had better have a way of expressing their insistence. Expressions of insistence, moreover, cannot be the same as mere expressions of displeasure, dismay or disapproval; for those could have any number of possible grounds, whereas insistence (as used here) can be grounded only in issues of constitutive legality. But that means that expressions of insistence must be somehow marked as such, marked as concerned with issues of legality, so as to communicate specifically that concern. And wouldn't such specifically marked, communicative expression be tantamount to language?[13]

Objections based on actual or plausible evolutionary history, however, are beside the point. Thus, it might also be that chess-like games could not have emerged until after prehensile hands; but, even if so, that would not say much of interest about the games as such. The arguments that matter, therefore, are those to the effect that chess itself presupposes language, either for learning it or for playing it. But to those, I think, a simple reply is decisive. It is certainly no harder to learn and play chess than it is to learn and speak a natural language. Quite the contrary: games are clearly much less demanding than languages on all counts. In particular, languages are just as constituted by standards, hence just as dependent on speakers' *insistence*, as any game. Yet, it must be possible to learn and speak a language without benefit of (any other or prior) language, on pain of regress. So, in principle, it's possible for games as well.[14]

There remains the idea that chess itself might *be* a language. It goes without saying that languages and games are similar in many ways – to the extent that it has become a philosophical cliché to refer to languages as "games." Nevertheless, there are also many differences, including the following, which is both easy to see and crucial. Chess, like all formal games, is *self-contained* in the sense that what moves would be proper (legal) on any given occasion depends only on factors that are *internal* to the game – previous moves, the locations of other pieces, etc. By contrast, for any genuine language, what it is proper to say on a given occasion – what is true, authorized, materially valid, etc. – depends in general on more than the specifically *linguistic* context. Therefore, no formal game is (in and of itself) a language.

Why belabour the point? I certainly do not deny that language is characteristic of people, and centrally important to what we are. But I

want to resist what strikes me as an all too prevalent tendency to make
of language a magic fulcrum on which every human quality turns – as
if language were the whole essence of what distinguishes us from
machines on the one hand, and beasts on the other. That, I believe, is
a grave distortion for many reasons, most of which go beyond the
present discussion. Even in the context of a theory of perception, however, it is important not to overestimate the role of language (if only
because *correct* perception is prerequisite to dialogue itself).

Playing chess, like speaking, involves interacting with items and
structures in ways that depend – not just causally but normatively –
on their types (roles), their reidentification as individuals (histories),
and their relations to other items and structures ("contexts"). The ability to engage in such interaction is at least the greater part of what is
meant by a *conceptual* grasp. Granted, a person who can talk and the-
orize might have more and richer concepts of chess phenomena than
could a non-linguistic super-monkey. Yet the basic concept of, e.g., a
rook is determined by its role in the game; and any creature that can
play must have mastered that. Concepts are in general articulated by
their relations to one another, as expressed in the detailed contingencies of acceptable practice. Often these contingencies are primarily linguistic, and, in particular, inferential. But, as the chess example shows,
they need not be: proper chess play itself, without verbal accompani-
ment, is sufficiently structured to institute a conceptual articulation of
the corresponding phenomena.

8

It must be acknowledged that chess is not a typical example of a perceptual domain. The question therefore arises whether the account of
objectivity, in terms of constitutive standards, insistence and achievement, might be limited to games and their ilk. We ask, that is, whether
the account depends essentially on any features peculiar to such
domains, or whether it depends only on features characteristic of
objective perception more generally. The following stand out as distinctive of chess and the like – in contrast, for instance, to scientific
observation and everyday perception of sticks and stones.

(i)   Chess is defined by constitutive standards (rules) that are ar-
       bitrary human inventions; they do not have the character of
       empirical discoveries, liable to refutation. (Even so, the rules
       of a playable game must be consistent, complete, and follow-
       able – an achievement that is not at all automatic.)

(ii)   When chess players insist upon legal moves, this is understood primarily in terms of rule-compliance by other players – agents who can be held to account for their behaviour. (Less often an issue, though just as important, is insistence that the board and pieces function properly – by not melting, wandering around, etc.)

(iii) It is almost always easy to tell what move has been made in a chess game, and whether that move is legal – because the game is digital, explicitly defined and relatively simple. (On the other hand, further perceptual skills, such as recognizing strategic weaknesses and opportunities, are not easy and may well not be reducible to these basic discriminations.)

Science, by contrast, seems anything but arbitrary invention: its discoveries are a paragon of the empirical and refutable. Moreover, scientists never hold observable phenomena to account for their behaviour: if some observed phenomenon fails to accord with scientific expectations, it is the observation or those expectations that are at fault, not the phenomenon itself. Finally, scientific investigation is difficult: it takes years of training plus painstaking effort, both to perform reliable experiments and to tell with confidence what results are acceptable.

This, however, is not to deny that the objects of scientific study are held to standards. Donald Davidson (1970, 211 and 219-22), for instance, more or less defines the *physical* as that which can be picked out in terms drawn exclusively from a closed, comprehensive theory with strong constitutive elements and precise, explicit, exception-free laws.[15] This is as much as to say that being subsumable under such a theory – *strict subsumability*, we might call it – is a constitutive standard for the physical: to *be* physical is to be strictly subsumable.

Speaking in a similar vein, but of the history of chemistry, Thomas Kuhn writes: "Changes in the standards governing permissible problems, concepts, and explanations can transform a science. In the next section I shall even suggest a sense in which they transform the world" (1962, 106). And, in the next section, he continues:

> For Dalton, any reaction in which the ingredients did not enter in fixed proportion was *ipso facto* not a purely chemical process. A law that experiment could not have established before Dalton's work, became, once that work was accepted, a constitutive principle that no single set of chemical measurements could have upset.... As a result, chemists came to live in a world where reactions behaved quite differently from the way they had before. (1962, 133f.)

In other words, the principle of fixed proportions became a constitutive standard for what it is to *be* a chemical reaction – and thereby also for being an element or a compound. Kuhn, however, unlike Davidson, is concerned not merely with the notion of standards for *entities*, but with the implications of this view for the conduct of science.

> Finally, at a still higher level, there is another set of commitments without which no man is a scientist. The scientist must, for example, be concerned to understand the world and to extend the precision and scope with which it has been ordered. That commitment must, in turn, lead him to scrutinize, either for himself or through colleagues, some aspect of nature in great empirical detail. And if that scrutiny displays pockets of apparent disorder, then these must challenge him to a new refinement of his observational techniques or to a further articulation of his theories. (1962, 42)

That is to say that scientists are *scientists* by virtue of their *commitments* – in particular, commitments that require what we have earlier called *vigilance*. "Pockets of apparent disorder" are nothing other than apparent breaches of the relevant constitutive standards, the exact analog of apparent illegal moves; and scientists must simultaneously be on the look-out for them, and resolved not to tolerate them. Scientists *insist* that the scientifically observed world be orderly (e.g., strictly subsumable). Moreover, their alternatives in the face of an apparent breach are essentially the same as those available to a chess-player: refinement of observational technique, further articulation of the theory,[16] or giving up the game (scientific breakdown and/or revolution).

The constitutive standards for the objects of scientific research – whether local to particular disciplines, like combining in fixed proportions, or global throughout science as such, like displaying an order with precision and scope – are not arbitrary inventions. On the other hand, they are not exactly empirical discoveries either; for, as Kuhn is at pains to show, accurate observations and discoveries presuppose them, and they are not readily dislodged. They are somehow *both* empirical *and* invented – "synthetic a priori," Davidson says (1970, 221). Standards for the constitution of objects are worked out by fits and starts over many years, such that, in accord with them, ever more objects can be scrutinized in great empirical detail and ordered with precision and scope. "It is hard," Kuhn notes (1962, 135), "to make nature fit a paradigm"; and a fundamental component in that difficulty is coming up with paradigms that nature can be made to fit. Scientists may invent the recipe; but experiment is the proof of the pudding. Like chess – only far more so – science is an *achievement*.

It is an old problem in the philosophy of science to say just what is measured by a scientific instrument. In particular, in what sense can it be said that so-called "theoretical" entities and properties are measured, as opposed to the "phenomenal" or "observational" properties and states of the instrument itself? Notice that this question has essentially the same structure as Dretske's question about how we can say that we hear the bell, and not the vibrations in the air or our eardrums. And the solution, it seems to me, is essentially the same too. What the measurement is *of* is that which the constitutive standards govern: the entities, properties, and relations in terms of which the theory is expressed. Why? Because, when the possibility of a *mis*measurement or experimental *error* arises, what the issue turns on is telling how things stand with regard to those standards. That's what *accurate* instrumentation is counted on to measure; it's what is checked for in double checking; it's the way in which experimental ability contributes to the scientific achievement. Successfully holding those entities to those standards, in the face of ever more precise and detailed experimental testing, is scientific *understanding* – understanding what the entities *are*.

Philosophers of science speak more often of explanation than of understanding, but these come to the same: to *explain* is to render intelligible – to show that and how something can be understood. Thus it is that explanations are of two sorts. An entire domain of phenomena can be constituted and explained when standards to which they can be held are grasped and successfully insisted upon. (Such a success is a *paradigm*.) And, within a domain, particular phenomena, or particular classes of phenomena, are explained by showing how they in particular can be held to the constitutive standards. In case the pertinent standards include strict subsumability, those internal explanations will be, in part, deductive nomological. In case the domain constituting standards are otherwise – for instance: the Davidson/Dennett notion of rationality, the integrated operation of functional systems and organisms, the historical/institutional dynamics of cultures and subcultures – then the explanations and intelligibility will be of different sorts. What they have in common is the structure of *insistence:* practitioners have the ability to recognize phenomena that are ruled out by the standards that are constitutive of that recognizability, and will refuse to accept them.

9

Can the same account be extended also to the objectivity of everyday perception, say of sticks and stones? It would be here, presumably, if anywhere, that dogs and cats would have perceptual abilities comparable to our own. No doubt, we share with higher animals various innate "object-constancy" and "object-tracking" mechanisms that automatically "lock onto" medium-sized lumps – especially ones that are moving and/or staring at us. The question is whether, for us in contrast to animals, there is any more to the objectivity of perceivable "things" than that they trigger such mechanisms – in particular, whether there are constitutive standards to which we, as perceivers, hold them.[17] It seems to me that there are, though they are somewhat vague and difficult to formulate. The essential tenet is something like: *things* are integral bearers of multiple properties. Integrity is the way the properties belong together in space and time, in (at least) two respects: cohesively and compatibly.

A thing is a cohesive spatio-temporal unit. At a time, a thing occupies – that is, its properties are instantiated at – exactly one place, a place which has a definite size and shape, and which is occupied by no other thing. Through time, the place of a thing can vary, as can the properties collected in it there. But mostly these variations can be only gradual – that is, relatively slow and continuous. For otherwise, it would cease to be well-defined which properties belong together as properties of which things; their staying identifiably together in one continuing thing is what fixes their belonging together at all.

The properties of a single thing must always be mutually compatible, and they can be interdependent; that is, some combinations of properties and/or lacks are not permissible in one thing. But no properties or lacks in distinct things are incompatible; that is, any individually possible things are compossible with any others, or none at all (Leibniz not withstanding). This is to say that things are what they are independently of one another, that their properties are intrinsic to them. Properties *as such* are "proper to" the things that have them.[18]

Can we make sense of the suggestion that human perceivers (but not animals) *hold* things to some such standard – *insist* upon it? Consider first (before turning to things) how the members of a family are perceivable (on a corporeal level): each has his or her own characteristic visual appearance, sound of voice, odour, way of moving and so on; and, of course, their various parts stay attached in the same way. But suppose, one day, all these aspects started permuting: what looks like Sister sounds like Father, moves like Grandma, and smells like Kid Brother. Even the parts could mix up: Mother's head (but Father's hair) on Uncle's torso with Baby's limbs – or just two heads with no limbs or torso at all (sounding like a truck and smelling like a watermelon). And moments later, they switch again, with new divisions and new participants. What would you say?

Surely something like: "Egad! Am I going crazy? Am I being tricked or drugged? I can't really be seeing this – it's *impossible*." That is, you would *reject* what you seemed to perceive, you would not accept them as *objects*. Now suppose that, instead of you, it were the family dog who came home to this. We can't ask what it would *say*, because dogs can't talk; and, of course, any estimate of its reaction at all is bound to be largely conjecture and prejudice. But, by way of counterpoint to sharpen the main point, I'll express my own prejudice: I think the dog would *bark*. I expect it would be disoriented and distressed, maybe even frightened. But I can't imagine any part of a dog's reaction amounting to a rejection of the scene, a discounting of its reality, on the grounds that it's impossible. Though Fido can tell Sister from Brother, and humans from cats, I don't think he can distinguish in any sense between possible and impossible. And this, I believe, is the same as to say that he holds no objects to constitutive standards, and therefore understands nothing.

The integrity of family members – people – is certainly a different matter from that of things. Yet analogous permutations of the sensible properties of rocks and blossoms, comets and waterfalls would be equally fantastic. We might occasionally accept, even relish, such disintegrated phantasmagoria in dreams or hallucinations; but no one who understood what it meant could accept them as objective things. That is, the experiences, whatever else they might be, could not be objective perception. To perceive things as objects is to insist upon their coherent integrity the constitutive standard for thinghood – just like insisting upon legality in chess, rationality in interpretation and ordering with precision and scope in empirical science.

Acknowledgments

An earlier version of this paper was read at Indiana University, Bloomington. I am also grateful for comments from Jim Conant, Dan Dennett, Fred Dretske, Christopher Peacocke and Tim van Gelder.

Notes

1 This is not intended as a conceptual or definitional point, but as a factual claim. It could turn out, I suppose, that dolphins or extraterrestrials are capable of objective perception; but (at least in the case of the former) I am highly dubious.

2 Abbreviate "*a*'s being F carries the information that b is G" with "$Fa{\rightarrow}Gb$." Clearly, for a fixed specification of the conditions, this relation is transitive: If $Fa{\rightarrow}Hc$ and $Hc{\rightarrow}Gb$ in the same conditions, then (in those conditions) $Fa{\rightarrow}Gb$. More, however, is required for $Fa{\rightarrow}Gb$ to be *via* Hc than that $Fa{\rightarrow}Hc$ and $Hc{\rightarrow}Gb$ in the same conditions – because, intuitively, it might be that $Fa{\rightarrow}Gb$ independently of Hc. Suppose, however, that there are some

conditions in which $Fa \rightarrow Hc$ but not $Hc \rightarrow Gb$, and some in which $Hc \rightarrow Gb$ but not $Fa \rightarrow Hc$, but the only conditions in which $Fa \rightarrow Gb$ are those in which both $Fa \rightarrow Hc$ and $Hc \rightarrow Gb$. Then, plausibly (and according to Dretske), it is only *via* Hc that $Fa \rightarrow Gb$.

3   It would not be difficult to contrive "abnormal" conditions in which the air or eardrum were vibrated in such a manner as to cause the perceptual experience, even without the bell ringing e.g., using an audio recorder.

4   The terminology is reminiscent of Gibson, whom Dretske in fact cites, in a slightly different context, on the following page.

5   In terms of the earlier illustration, this amounts to suggesting that, although the presence of the lemon drops does not carry any information about *which* child fetched, it does carry the information that *some* child fetched (so, 'child' = the higher-order kind); and, moreover, it carries the information that Grandpa paid only via the information that some child fetched. (Note, by the way, that 'some child' is not in general equivalent to any disjunction: 'child *a*, or child *b*, or...'.)

6   This way of putting it may be misleading because, as I will argue in sections 4 and 5, it is possible in principle for non-linguistic creatures to play chess; the reader, therefore, should not suppose that I intend this mention of conceptual ability to entail linguistic ability. (I will suggest in section 7 that conceptual understanding is possible without language.)

7   An existence proof for illegal moves is not required: Murphy's Law is the best confirmed generalization in all of empirical metaphysics.

8   This counting-on and vigilance are to be understood as implicit in persistent behavioural dispositions, and not (at least, not necessarily) as conscious conviction, or deliberate being-on-the-lookout-for.

9   For non-linguistic players (like our super-monkeys), *telling* what moves are made will be exhibited, in the first instance, in their own legal move-making (in the light of that move, so to speak). But it could also take the form of producing the equivalent moves (and positions) in various alternative media – in effect, "translating" them.

10 In chess, of course, both these abilities are already required in normal play, and are exhibited in a player's ability to make legal moves of its own. Note that these two abilities "to tell" amount to abilities to *recognize*, respectively, the subordinate and superordinate patterns mentioned in section III.

11 If I'm wrong about ordinary monkeys (or even dogs), then so much the better for them; what's important is that there's a line to be drawn, not where.

12 "... the conditions of the *possibility of experience* in general are likewise conditions of the *possibility of the objects of experience* ..."(CPR, A158/B197).

13 This paragraph is based closely on a conversation with Jim Conant.

14 It could be argued that a first language is learnable only by boot-strapping. That is, only a minimal initial "core" is learnable without benefit of language; the remainder of the language is not so learnable, because learning

(and/or speaking) it relies on the core. Then, if it were further maintained that chess is essentially more difficult than this core, the argument in the text would fail. What I find highly dubious in this line of thought, however, is the suggestion that anything *essentially* less sophisticated than chess (and similar formal games) could be in any proper sense a language. Yet, without that, the challenge collapses.

15 I say "more or less" because Davidson, in fact, nowhere offers an explicit definition of the physical, nor do the various remarks on which my attribution is based quite add up to one.

16 For a scientist, of course, "further articulation" can include more than just a better ability to tell what is and isn't permissible; it can include modest modifications ("friendly amendments") to the theory itself.

17 By 'things' here I mean mere things, *realia* – like sticks and stones. "Things" in the sense of paraphernalia or equipment, "things" constituted by their roles and appropriate uses, are also held to constitutive standards, but different ones. Accordingly, the most proper perception of them as objects, and what is insisted upon in such perception, is also different.

18 A fuller discussion would: disengage locatedness at a particular place from the togetherness (collocation) of cohesion; add a requirement for concreteness (complete determinacy) to that for compatibility; connect locatedness and concreteness with actuality (as opposed to mere possibility), and therefore with each other (and with particularity); and so on. But exactly how is another question.

References

Davidson, Donald (1970). Mental events. In Lawrence Foster and J.W. Swanson (eds.), *Experience and Theory*. Amherst: University of Massachusetts Press. Reprinted in Donald Davidson, *Essays on Actions and Events*. Oxford: Oxford University Press (1980). Page references are to the latter edition.

Dennett, Daniel C. (1987). *The Intentional Stance*. Cambridge, MA: Bradford/MIT Press

Dretske, Fred I. (1981). *Knowledge and the Flow of Information*. Cambridge, MA: Bradford/MIT Press

Kant, Immanuel (1929). *Critique of Pure Reason*. Trans. Norman Kemp Smith. London: Macmillan

Kuhn, Thomas S. (1962; 2nd ed. 1970). *The Structure of Scientific Revolutions*. Chicago: University of Chicago Press. Page references are to the second edition.

13

Visual Attention and the Attention-Action Interface

John M. Henderson

1. Introduction

There has been a tendency in experimental psychology to study perception, and especially vision, as though the percept or perceptual experience were the final goal of the perceptual process. However, this approach fails to recognize that visual processes are, to a large extent, one link in a chain from information acquisition to information use. That is, cognitive interaction with the world involves not just perception and thought, but also action and interaction. In fact, visual processes are used to provide information and feedback to motoric interactions with the world virtually all of the time that visual processes are active. This is because the eyes are constantly in motion, either through saccadic eye-movements, which bring new areas of the visual world to the foveae, or through smooth-pursuit eye movements, which allow tracking of moving objects. (Other types of eye movements, such as the vestibulo-ocular reflex, will be ignored for the purposes of this chapter.) This visually guided motoric control exists in addition to the visual guidance of locomotion and visually guided object manipulation, both of which occupy a great deal of the visual day.

In this chapter I will use the arena of eye movement control to explore the perception/action interface. I will suggest that in order to program a motor action directed at a specific object in the visual world (e.g., to direct the eyes to fixate the object, the hands to grasp the object, or the body to move toward the object), the visual system must first explicitly select the location of that object for action. I will further suggest that this selection function (or selective visual attention) operates as the "glue" that ties together not only various representations within the visual system, as argued by Treisman and colleagues (Treisman 1985; Treisman and Gelade 1980), but also visual processing and motor programming.

2. Visual Attention

As William James noted, "we may attend to an object on the periphery of the visual field and yet not accommodate the eye for it" (1890/1950, 437). In his discussion of visual attention, James quoted observations that Helmholtz had published in *Physiological Optik*. In his experiments, Helmholtz designed a box for viewing stereoscopic pictures. The interior of the box was dark except for a pin-hole in the centre that served as a fixation point, and an occasional spark that served briefly to illuminate the picture. Helmholtz observed that:

> although we keep fixating the pin-hole and never allow their combined image to break into two, we can, nevertheless, before the spark comes, keep our attention voluntarily turned to any particular portion we please of the dark field, so as then, when the spark comes, to receive an impression only from such parts of the picture as lie in this region. In this respect, then, our attention is quite independent of the position and accommodation of the eyes, and of any known alteration in these organs; and free to direct itself by a conscious and voluntary effort upon any selected portion of a dark and undifferenced field of view. This is one of the most important observations for a future theory of attention. (Helmoltz, as quoted by James 1890/1950, 438)

These words of Helmholtz turned out to be prophetic. Much of the research and theorizing on attention in the past 15 years have been concerned with an observer's ability to select a portion of the visual field for further analysis. However, the study of visual attention now entails using modern experimental methods, including chronometric techniques designed to examine the time-course of attention processes, as well as the underlying cognitive and neural mechanisms (Allport 1989; Posner and Petersen 1990).

The prototypical experimental paradigm designed to study visual attention was introduced by Posner and colleagues (e.g., Posner 1980; Posner, Snyder and Davidson 1980). In this paradigm, the subject is seated before a visual display consisting of a central fixation point and two empty squares, one to either side of fixation. The subject's task is to press a button if and when a small flash of light appears within one of the squares, and the latency of the subject's response is taken as an indication of processing efficiency. If no flash appears, the subject refrains from responding. In order to examine the effect of visual attention on performance in this task, the subject is induced to direct attention to one or the other of the two squares on a given trial. The subject can be signalled to attend to one square via a central cue, such as an arrow at the fixation point, or a peripheral cue, such as a brightening of the square that should be attended. As an inducement for the subject to attend to the cued square, the target flash appears more often in the cued than in the uncued square (e.g., 80 percent vs. 20 percent). On valid trials, the target flash appears in the cued square, while on invalid trials, the target flash appears in the uncued square. Also, neutral trials are sometimes presented: on these trials, both squares are cued, so that the subject has no reason to attend to one or the other. The main finding from this paradigm is that when the subject is attending to the square in which the flash ultimately appears, response latency is faster than when he is attending to neither location, which in turn is faster than when he is attending to the inappropriate square. Thus, there is facilitation in detecting the flash when attention is directed to the location of the flash and inhibition in detecting the flash when attention is directed to another location.

Posner and colleagues theorized that visual attention can be likened to a spotlight of processing focus. While other metaphors have also been proposed (e.g., Eriksen and Yeh 1985; Henderson 1991; LaBerge and Brown 1989), the spotlight metaphor captures many of the basic characteristics of visual attention: attention can be directed to a particular region of the visual field, "illuminating" visual information at that region and leaving information at other locations "in the dark." Further, the spotlight of attention can be directed both through conscious effort (Posner 1980; Posner et al. 1980) and through an automatic orienting response (Henderson 1991; Jonides 1981), and affects early perceptual processes that are involved in the acquisition (Posner 1980) and representation of visual information (Treisman 1985).

3. Attention and Eye Movements

The research on visual attention indicates that the human observer can attend to various regions of the visual field even while maintaining fixation on a single point. At the same time, we know that during the course of any complex visual task (e.g., visual exploration of the word, picture-viewing or reading), our eyes move from one location to another in a series of rapid eye movements (or saccades) at an average rate of three to four times per second (e.g., Rayner 1978; Tinker 1939; Yarbus 1967). Given these two basic facts, the question arises: how are the overt movements of the eyes and covert movements of attention around the visual field related to each other?

As a rough first pass, there are at least three ways in which covert changes in the locus of visual attention and overt movements of the eyes might be related. First, it could be that when the eyes are free to move, visual attention is always directed toward the stimulus at the point of fixation. On this view, while it might be the case that attention can be allocated away from the point of fixation under appropriate experimental conditions, as described above, this finding would be dismissed as of no functional significance in natural visual tasks. At the other extreme, it might be that covert shifts of visual attention and overt shifts of the eyes are completely decoupled in complex visual tasks, so that there is little relationship between the point of fixation and the focus of visual attention. Finally, in contrast to either of these two positions, it could be that during complex visual tasks there is a functional relationship between the allocation of visual attention and overt movements of the eyes. I will present a review of the behavioural evidence suggesting that this latter hypothesis is correct.

4. Relationship between Eye Movements and Attention

In this section I will review the evidence supporting the view that covert shifts of attention and overt movements of the eyes are functionally related. Most of the studies that I will discuss have employed eye-movement recording to determine the precise location of the fixation position within the visual field. Further, most of these studies used the *eye-contingent display change technique* (McConkie and Rayner 1975), in which the visual stimulus presented to the viewer is changed as a function of eye position. In this experimental paradigm, the subject views a computer monitor on which some type of visual stimulus, such as a digitized scene or text, is presented. The subject's eye movements are recorded while she views the display. Because the display monitor and the eye-tracker are both interfaced with the same computer, the display shown to the subject can be changed contingent on characteristics of the subject's eye movements. An illustration of the set-up is shown in Figure 13.1.

The first experiments using the eye-contingent display change technique involved the use of the *moving window paradigm* in reading. In this paradigm, the observer reads a line of text in which a window or region of normal text is surrounded by regions of uninformative visual information. As the reader moves her eyes through the text, the window moves along with the eyes, so that the window is always defined in terms of the moment-to-moment fixation position. Figure 13.2 presents an example of the moving window technique in which each letter in the text beyond the window is replaced by the letter *x*. The logic of the paradigm is that if text normally used during the course of a fixation is beyond the window region, then the reading process should be disrupted in some way. On the other hand, if some region of text is beyond the window, but reading is not disrupted, then that text is presumably not normally used.

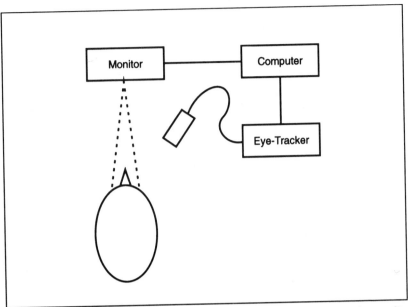

Figure 13.1: Schematic illustration of the experimental set-up for the eye-contingent display change technique. A viewer's eye movements are monitored while she views an image displayed on a computer monitor. Both the eye-tracker and the display system are interfaced with the computer, so the display can be changed in real time, contingent on specific parameters of the subject's eye movements.

```
Base Sentence:   This is an example sentence showing the window.

Fixation n:      xxxx xx xx example sexxxxxx xxxxxxx xxx xxxxxx.
Fixation n+1:    xxxx xx xx xxxxxle sentence xxxxxxx xxx xxxxxx.
Fixation n+2:    xxxx xx xx xxxxxxxx xxxxxxxe showing txx xxxxxx.

Fixation n:      xxxx xx xx example xxxxxxxx xxxxxxx xxx xxxxxx.
Fixation n+1:    xxxx xx xx xxxxxxxx sentence xxxxxxx xxx xxxxxx.
Fixation n+2:    xxxx xx xx xxxxxxxx xxxxxxxe showing xxx xxxxxx.

Fixation n:      xxxx xx xx example sentence xxxxxxx xxx xxxxxx.
Fixation n+1:    xxxx xx xx xxxxxxxe sentence showing txx xxxxxx.
Fixation n+2:    xxxx xx xx xxxxxxxx xxxxxxxe showing the window.
```

Figure 13.2: An example of the moving window technique in reading. In the top example, the reader is shown five character spaces to either side of fixation. In the middle example, the reader is shown only the currently fixated word. In the bottom example, the reader is shown four character spaces to the left of, and 15 character spaces to the right of the currently fixated character.

One of the most robust effects to emerge from studies using the moving window paradigm in reading is that the *perceptual span*, or region from which useful information is acquired during an eye fixation, is asymmetric around the current point of fixation. This is shown by the finding that reading rate (and comprehension) is identical whether the subject is given an asymmetric window with four character spaces to the left and 15 character spaces to the right of the current fixation point or whether the entire line is visible (McConkie and Rayner 1975, 1976; Rayner, Well and Pollatsek 1980; Underwood and McConkie 1985). Thus, the perceptual span generally encompasses the entire word under fixation, and one to two words to the right of the fixated word (Rayner and Pollatsek 1987).

The finding that the perceptual span is asymmetric around the point of fixation is strong evidence that the perceptual span in reading is not determined by visual acuity alone, because simple acuity functions are relatively symmetrical around fixation. One explanation for the asymmetry is that attentional factors contribute to the perceptual span, limiting information use from the left side of the current fixation position and facilitating information use from the right. However, before accepting this explanation, several other possibilities must be ruled out.

One potential alternative explanation for the asymmetry of the perceptual span in reading is that it is due to lateralization of function in the cerebral hemispheres. Because language is left-hemisphere dominant in about 80 percent of the population, and because there is a more direct pathway from retinal cells receiving input from the right visual field to the left hemisphere of the visual cortex, it is possible that the rightward asymmetry of the perceptual span is due to a cortical processing advantage for text in the right visual field. If this explanation were correct, then we would expect that it should hold for any language, regardless of the direction in which that language is read. A study conducted by Pollatsek, Bolozky, Well and Rayner (1981), however, shows that the asymmetry of the perceptual span is not fixed. In this study, bilinguals who could read both English and Hebrew were tested in the moving window paradigm. It was found that when these bilinguals were reading English, their perceptual spans were asymmetric to the right. However, when these same subjects read Hebrew, which is read from right to left, then their perceptual spans reversed such that they were asymmetric to the left. This is exactly the result one would expect if the perceptual span is attentionally constrained rather than constrained by hemispheric specialization.

A second explanation for the asymmetry of the perceptual span, regardless of whether it is rightward or leftward (or downward in the case of Japanese, cf. Osaka and Oda 1991) is that it is intrinsic to the reading process rather than due to a dynamic allocation of visual attention. On this view, one aspect of learning to become a fluent reader involves developing a perceptual module for reading in which the disposition to use information from a particular region of text is either hard-wired or at least automatized. This explanation would suggest that the bilingual readers in the Pollatsek et al. study had developed two reading modules and were switching between them when they switched languages. However, a study conducted by Inhoff, Pollatsek, Posner and Rayner (1989) argues against the notion that the asymmetry is fixed within the reading system. In this study, native readers of English were asked to read from right-to-left text that was presented in several backward formats (e.g., words facing forward but ordered right-to-left; letters within words and words ordered right-to-left). These subjects had no more experience reading from right to left than the average university undergraduate (which is virtually none), and therefore had not had a chance to develop any automatized systems devoted to reading in this manner. Yet, when these readers read the backward text in the moving window paradigm, their perceptual spans were found to be asymmetric to the left, in the direction that the text was being read. Such a result is inconsistent with the hypothesis that the perceptual span is determined by automatized or hard-wired processes developed during reading acquisition (and against the hemispheric specialization hypothhesis), but is what would be expected if the perceptual span is dynamically constrained by selective visual attention.

In sum, the studies that have used the moving window paradigm to explore the acquisition and use of visual information from text during reading show that the perceptual span is asymmetric in the direction the eyes are generally moving. This effect is not due to having learned to read in a particular direction, but instead appears to be dynamically adapted to the reading situation encountered. These findings are consistent with the view that the perceptual span is determined by the allocation of visual attention during each eye fixation. More particularly, it appears that visual attention is allocated to location or object in the visual field toward which the eyes are about to move. The finding that the perceptual span is not determined by acuity factors alone suggests that the term *perceptual span* is somewhat of a misnomer. Instead, the term *attentional span* would seem more appropriate.

5. The Sequential Attention Model

The studies reviewed in the previous section examining the perceptual span in reading indicate that visual attention is generally allocated to that region of text toward which the eyes are moving. One interpretation of this finding is that there is a functional relationship between the covert allocation of visual attention and overt movements of the eyes. In this section I want to outline a particular model of this relationship. The model is based on both empirical evidence and on a consideration of recent theorizing in the cognitive control of eye movements during reading (McConkie 1979; Morrison 1984). Following presentation of the model, I will review further experimental work that bears on various aspects of the model.

5.1 Basic Assumptions

The sequential attention model contains five basic assumptions (Henderson 1988; Henderson 1992; Henderson and Ferreira 1990; Henderson, Pollatsek and Rayner 1989). First, at the beginning of a fixation on a new stimulus, attention is allocated to that stimulus. In reading, the stimulus would generally be the currently fixated word, though the reader would presumably have some control over whether attention were directed at the word, letter or even page level (McConkie and Zola 1987). In scene perception, the stimulus would be at the object level, though again the viewer would have some voluntary control in choosing the level of organization at which attention is directed, e.g., at properties of individual objects, at the level of the entire scene. Second, attention is redirected to a new stimulus when processing on the fixated stimulus is completed. Given that factors at the lexical (Henderson and Ferreira 1990; Just and Carpenter 1980; Rayner and Duffy 1986), syntactic (Ferreira and Henderson 1990; Frazier and Rayner 1982), and semantic (Ehrlich and Rayner 1983) levels can all exert an influence on an individual fixation on a word, and that structural (De Graef et al. 1990) and semantic (Henderson et al. 1989) levels can exert an influence on the durations of individual fixations on an object, "processing completion" probably entails at least partial analysis of the fixated stimulus at all of these levels. Third, the redirection of attention coincides with the signal to generate an eye movement to a new stimulus, and the location of the stimulus toward which attention is redirected is the location toward which the eyes are programmed to move. As I will argue below, this relationship is structurally necessary, given the design of the visual/motor interface. Fourth, the allocation of attention to the new stimulus gates higher-level analysis of that stimulus. By higher-level analysis, I mean acquisition of information beyond that which can be obtained preattentively, such as simple features (e.g., Treisman 1985). Fifth, a saccade brings the eyes to the attended stimulus following the eye movement programming latency. This latency would include the time to compute the eye movement parameters plus the neural transmission time to the ocular muscles, probably on the order of 80 to 100 msec.

5.2 Secondary Assumptions

The sequential attention model suggests a "rubber-band" view of the relationship between visual attention and eye movement control. At a particular point in time, attention is directed away from the center of fixation and toward a new location. After a lag caused by the oculomotor programming latency, the eyes "snap" to the newly attended location. This rubber-band aspect of the model would seem to offer a simple account of where the eyes go from one fixation to the next during natural perception: they go to the location that is currently being attended. However, this answer begs the question of what region will be attended next. I assume that the location to which visual attention is directed is determined on the basis of relatively low-level stimulus features, in the following manner. First, a preattentive representation of likely stimulus locations (i.e., the locations of uninterpreted visual "blobs") is computed. This location map is computed independently of identity information (Ungerleider and Mishkin 1982). Second, stimulus locations are weighted so that attention is allocated to the stimulus location with the largest weight. In reading, the largest weight can generally be assigned to the stimulus location ("blob") immediately to the right of the currently fixated stimulus. This strategy will work except when higher-level language processes require a regressive or backward saccade to a previously read region of text. In this latter case, memory for the location of a particular word will allow for the assignment of weights. (Readers are often quite accurate at sending the eyes directly to a difficult area of text, e.g., Ferreira and Henderson 1990; 1993). In scene perception, the situation is less constrained, but a fairly simple process could assign weights on the basis of a salience measure automatically derived from a low-level (preattentive) analysis of the scene (Mahoney and Ullman 1988). Koch and Ullman (1985) discuss a neurophysiologically plausible model of the allocation of attention based on a location weighting scheme similar to the one proposed here.

An additional secondary assumption of the sequential attention model is that several motor programs may exist in parallel. This assumption derives from the *parallel programming* model of eye-movement control in reading originally proposed by Morrison (1984). In accordance with this model, I assume that it is possible to have several eye-movement programs simultaneously active. Parallel programming is assumed to occur whenever a decision is made to abort a partially programmed movement and instead to make a different movement (Becker and Jurgens 1979). The eye-movement behaviour observed following parallel programming of two saccades will depend on when programming of the second movement begins. For example, if the signal to begin a new program arrives when the first program is not too far along, then the first program can simply be cancelled, with a possible cost in saccade latency (Hogaboam 1983; Pollatsek, Rayner and Balota 1986). In this case, the target of the original saccade would be skipped (but would have been parafoveally processed, Fisher and Shebilske 1985). If the new signal arrives later, then the two programs may overlap, and the landing site of the saccade will be determined by a combination of the two programs. In this case, the eyes may land between the target positions of the two conflicting programs (Becker and Jurgens 1979). Finally, if computation of the first program is well along when the signal arrives to construct a different program, then the first program may be executed. In this case, the eyes will land at the first target location, but the fixation will be brief because the program to move the eyes to the second location is already partially (or completely) computed.

When would parallel eye-movement programs be active according to the sequential attention model? Recall that attention begins at the currently fixated visual stimulus (at location n), but is redirected to a new stimulus (at location $n+1$) when processing of the stimulus at location n is completed. Programming of an eye movement begins when attention is directed away from the stimulus at location n. Now suppose that the stimulus at location $n+1$ is easily processed (e.g., it is easily identified and very predictable). In this case, attention would be redirected again to another stimulus at a new location (location $n+2$) before the eye movement to location $n+1$ had been given time to execute. Because a redirection of attention always initiates eye-movement programming, and because the new locus of attention following redirection is always taken as the target location for the new program, the redirection of attention to location $n+2$ will cause a second program to be readied (to location $n+2$) prior to execution of the first (to location $n+1$). Therefore, two programs will be created that partially overlap in time. Which type of program amalgamation then occurred would depend on how soon the second redirection of attention occurred after the first.

5.3 Evidence Supporting the Sequential Attention Model

5.3.1 Does the model generalize beyond reading? The proposed relationship between visual attention and the programming of saccadic eye-movements is assumed to be a fundamental aspect of visual cognition. However, the studies reviewed above primarily dealt with the

relationship between visual attention and eye movements in reading. The first question to be addressed in this section is whether the sequential attention model generalizes beyond reading.

In order to explore how visual attention and eye movements are related in a complex visual task other than reading, Henderson et al. (1989) had viewers engage in an object-identification task. The viewers examined displays composed of four line drawings of objects positioned at the corners of an imaginary square. The viewer's task was to examine each of the four objects in a prescribed sequence in order to prepare for an immediate probe memory test (e.g., "Was there a tree in the display?"). In order to determine which object or objects were being attended on each fixation, a two-dimensional variation of the moving window paradigm was employed. In the *full display* condition, all four objects were continuously displayed throughout the trial. At the other extreme, in the *one object* condition, only the currently fixated object was displayed, while the other three objects were replaced with a pattern mask composed of meaningless line segments. In the *one+next* condition, the currently fixated object and the object about to be fixated in the prescribed sequence were displayed (with the other two objects replaced by the mask), while in the *one+last* condition, only the currently fixated object and the last object fixated were displayed. Finally, in the *zoom* condition, all four objects were initially displayed, but once the subject moved his eyes to the first object, the trial proceeded as in the one object condition.

The logic of this experiment was similar to that of the moving window studies in reading. If information that is normally used during object identification is outside of the window, then viewing behaviour should be disrupted in comparison to the full display condition. On the other hand, if information that is not normally used is beyond the window, then no disruption should be observed. The prediction of the sequential attention model is that eye-movement behaviour in the one+next condition should be similar to the full display condition, because in both cases the information normally attended is available (the object at fixation and the object about to be fixated), and because information normally acquired preattentively (e.g., information about where potential objects are) is still available due to the pattern masks. On the other hand, eye movement behaviour should be disrupted in the one object, one+last and zoom conditions because the object about to be fixated is not available for processing.

These predictions of the sequential attention model were supported. First, viewing behaviour in the full and one+next conditions were equivalent. Second, viewing behaviour in the one, one+last and zoom conditions were disrupted in comparison to the full display condition, and the former three did not differ among themselves. The finding that in this object-identification task information is acquired only from the object currently fixated and the object about to be fixated shows that the asymmetric attentional span is not unique to reading. Further, because this effect was found regardless of the direction of the impending saccade (horizontal or vertical), it is clear that the asymmetry of the attentional span is not unique to horizontal eye movements. This finding also provides further evidence against the hemispheric lateralization and reading automization explanations for the asymmetry in reading. Finally, even though eye movements were changing direction after each object was fixated, the object about to be fixated was the only object in addition to the object currently fixated that was processed during a given eye fixation. This result indicates that attention is allocated dynamically during each fixation to the location to be fixated next. Together, these results strongly suggest that the sequential relationship between the direction of visual attention and eye-movement programming is a general aspect of visual-cognitive functioning.

5.3.2 Must attention precede a saccade to the target location? A basic assumption of the sequential attention model is that attention *must* precede an eye movement to the target location of that movement. That is, if the eyes are going to move to a particular location, then attention must be directed to that location first. In order to test this notion, Shepard, Findlay and Hockey (1986) conducted a simple but elegant experiment. Subjects were asked to press a button whenever they detected a simple light flash. At the same time, they were to execute an eye movement to a predetermined target location. In one condition, the light flash was most likely to appear at the same location as the target for the saccade. In another condition, the light flash was most likely to appear at a location that was different from the location toward which they were to execute the eye movement. As discussed above, subjects are generally faster to detect such a light flash when they have directed visual attention to the location of the flash. The question here was, when the most likely light flash location and the saccade target location were different, would subjects be able to direct attention (and hence be faster at detecting the flash) at the higher-probability location, or would they have to direct attention (and hence be faster at detecting the light flash) at the lower probability location toward which they were about to direct a saccade? Shepard et al. found that subjects could strategically direct attention to the more likely location *unless* the eye movement was imminent. When an eye movement was imminent, however, subjects could only direct attention to the location that was the target of the saccade. Thus, these results indicate that prior to an eye movement, attention must be allocated to the location about to be fixated.

5.3.3. Is attention directed to a specific location? The sequential attention model clearly predicts that the focus of attention prior to an eye movement will be the *specific* location toward which the eyes will move. However, while the studies discussed above are consistent with this view, they are also consistent with the hypothesis that attention "spreads out" from the fixated location in the general direction of the next eye movement rather than to that specific location. For example, in the reading studies, the asymmetric perceptual span could be due to the reader simultaneously attending the fixated word and all words in the attended hemifield. This position receives some support from the suggestion that visual attention can only be directed to a visual hemifield or at best a visual quadrant (Hughes and Zimba 1985, 1987), though several recent studies show that visual attention can be directed to a specific location in the visual field (Henderson 1991; Henderson and Mcquistan 1993; Klein and McCormick 1989).

I have recently conducted a study designed to test directly whether attention is allocated to the specific location about to be fixated (Henderson 1993). Figure 13.3 illustrates the basic paradigm. The subject began each trial fixating a central cross presented on a computer monitor. Two preview letter strings were then presented to the right of the subject's point of fixation. In the *move* condition, the subject was asked to execute an eye movement to the location of the letter string furthest to the right as soon as the letter strings appeared. The contingent display change technique was employed so that during the saccade the two letter strings could be replaced by a single target word positioned at the location of the letter string toward which the eyes were moving. Because the change was accomplished during the saccade, the subjects never saw the change itself. The task was to name aloud the target word as quickly as possible once the eyes had landed. Naming latency (elapsed time from the onset of the saccade to the initiation of the vocal response) was taken as a measure of word identification time. In order to examine the location from which information was acquired prior to the eye movement, three *preview conditions* were employed. In the *near preview* condition, the letter string closest to the initial point of fixation provided a preview of the target (i.e., was the same as the target word), and the letter string further from the point of fixation but at the location toward which the eyes were about to move did not provide a preview of the target (i.e., was an unpronounceable nonsense letter string). In the *far preview* condition, the letter string positions were reversed so that the preview of the target word occupied the location toward which the eyes would be moving and the nonsense string occupied the closer location. In the *control* condition, the same nonsense letter string occupied both locations. In the second eye-behaviour condition, termed the *no-move* condition, the subject was to maintain fixation on the central location throughout the trial, and his eye movements were monitored to ensure that he did so. The same three preview conditions were again used, but the target word appeared at the fixation location after a 200 msec presentation of the preview. The value of 200 msec. was used because it was the average saccade latency in the eye-movement condition, thus ensuring an equivalent amount of time for the preview in both the move and no-move conditions. Again, the subject was to name the target word as quickly as possible after it appeared foveally.

The sequential attention model generates two predictions about the results of this experiment. Both predictions involve the *preview benefit*, or amount of benefit derived from having a preview of the target word available extrafoveally prior to fixation on that word. The preview benefit is calculated as the difference in naming latency between the

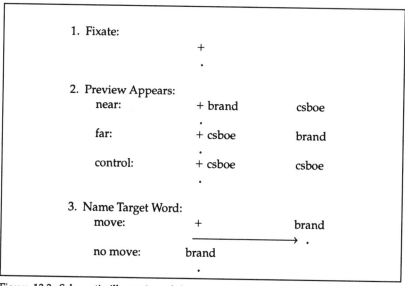

Figure 13.3: Schematic illustration of the experimental paradigm used by Henderson (1993) to examine the spatial specificity of visual attention prior to a saccadic eye-movements. The subject began each trial fixating a central cross. Two letter strings then appeared to the right of fixation, with a preview of the target word appearing close to the fixation point (near), far from the fixation point (far), or not at all (control). The subject then either executed an eye movement to the far letter string (move) and named the word that appeared there, or maintained fixation (no move) and named the word that appeared at that location.

control condition and a particular preview condition (i.e., control condition minus preview condition). The first prediction is that in the move condition, attention should shift to the location about to be fixated (the far location) and information at that specific location should be used to begin identifying the stimulus located there. Therefore, a greater preview benefit should be observed for the far location (control minus far preview) in the move condition compared to the no-move condition, because in the no-move condition there is no reason for the subject to attend the far location over the near location (a preview was equally likely to occur at either location). The second prediction is that the preview benefit should not be greater for the near location (control minus near preview) in the move condition compared to the no-move condition, because attention is allocated specifically to the location toward which the eyes are about to move. If, on the other hand, attention is allocated generally in the direction that the eyes will move (i.e., "oozes" out from the fixated location to the about-to-be-fixated location), then both the near and far preview conditions should show a greater preview benefit in the move condition compared to the no-move condition.

The results of this experiment were clear. Considering first the far preview condition, the results indicated that when the subject was maintaining fixation on the central cross (no-move condition), preview of the target word at the far location provided no preview benefit. In contrast, when the subject was about to execute an eye movement (move condition), a preview of the target word at that far location led to significant preview benefit. These data indicate that attention precedes an eye movement to the location toward which the eyes are about to move. Consider now the near preview condition. The amount of preview benefit derived from the near location when the eyes were moving to the far location was *less* than the amount derived when the eyes remained stationary. The finding that the preview benefit at the near location was reduced in the move compared to the no-move condition is opposite to the results at the far location, and clearly inconsistent with the view that attention is allocated in the general direction that the eyes are about to move. Instead, these data suggest that attention moves away from the fixation point prior to the saccade. Because the near word is closer to the fixation point, when attention is directed away in the move condition, the preview benefit derived from the near location is reduced.

In summary, the results of this experiment indicate that visual attention is directed to the specific location toward which the eyes are about to move rather than in the general direction that the eyes are about to move.

5.3.4. Is visual attention shared between the currently fixated and to-be-fixated stimulus? The studies discussed above suggest that prior to an eye movement, attention is directed to the specific location of the stimulus about to be fixated. However, it could be the case that attention is directed in parallel to both the location of the fixated stimulus and the stimulus about to be fixated, rather than to one and then the other in a sequential manner. In other words, attention might be discretely split between the fixated stimulus and the stimulus about to be fixated. Such a parallel attention hypothesis could account for the finding that spatially intermediate stimuli were not attended in the Henderson (1993) study discussed above because splitting attention between two noncontiguous locations need not involve attending to locations intermediate between the two.

The parallel attention hypothesis predicts that the processing difficulty of the stimulus to be fixated next should affect information acquisition from the currently fixated stimulus. This prediction follows because on the parallel hypothesis, attention is shared between the two stimuli. On the other hand, the sequential attention hypothesis predicts independence between difficulty of one stimulus and information acquisition from the other, because attention is directed to each stimulus consecutively (and therefore there is no temporal overlap in processing).

The finding that the processing difficulty of the currently fixated stimulus affects the preview benefit derived from the stimulus to be fixated next seems to support the parallel attention hypothesis. However, as outlined above, the parallel allocation hypothesis also predicts that an increase in the difficulty of the stimulus about to be fixated should decrease information acquisition from the currently fixated stimulus. This prediction follows because attention is assumed to be shared between the two stimuli. However, an examination of previous experiments provides no support for this prediction. I will present here a few illustrative examples.

First, Henderson (1988) employed the object identification version of the moving window paradigm, in which four objects were viewed successively in two preview conditions. Subjects began each trial fixated in the centre of the array of objects. They then executed a saccade to the first object, and subsequently to each object in turn. When the first object was fixated, either that object and a good preview of the object to be fixated next (preview condition), or that object and a visual mask composed of meaningless line segments (control condition), became visible on the screen in the location of the object to be fixated next. As usual, once the subjects directed their eyes to the location of the second object, it always became visible. The results of this experiment showed a large preview benefit (control minus preview conditions), indicating that subjects did acquire information from the to-be-fixated object when it was visible. If it were the case that attention is shared between the currently fixated stimulus and the stimulus to be fixated next, then processing time (and therefore fixation durations) on the currently fixated object should be increased when two objects were visible. Contrary to this prediction, however, fixation times on the first object were identical in the preview and control conditions. Thus, there was no difference in processing time on the currently fixated object as a function of the availability of information from the next object.

Similar examples derive from reading studies. For example, Henderson and Ferreira (1990) conducted a reading study in which the difficulty of the fixated word and the availability of preview information for the next word were independently manipulated. Subjects read simple sentences while their eye movements were recorded. As far as the subjects were concerned, they were simply reading these sentences in a natural manner in order to prepare for comprehension questions. However, the experiments employed the *boundary technique* (Rayner 1975), a variant of the eye-contingent display change technique in which only a single letter string changes as a function of eye position. For example, consider the sentence *Mary bought a chest despite the high price.* In this example, the boundary was placed between the penultimate and final letters of the word *chest*, designated word *n*. Either a *same preview* (despite) or a *different preview* (zqdloyv) of word *n*+1 (despite) was displayed as long as the subject was fixating somewhere to the left of the boundary. When the subject shifted fixation past the boundary, the preview was then replaced by the target word (despite). Because the boundary was crossed during a saccade from word *n* to word *n*+1, subjects were not consciously aware that display changes were taking place.[1] If more attention were being expended on the preview when it was a word (as should be the case, given that the word provided useful information and was clearly used by the reader prior to fixation), then processing time on word *n* should have been increased when word *n*+1 was a word. This did not happen. Similarly, Blanchard, Pollatsek and Rayner (1989) alternated the size of the window from fixation to fixation in a moving window study. On some fixations the foveal word and the next word were displayed, and on some fixations only the foveal word was displayed. They found that the availability of a preview of the upcoming word had no effect on the duration of the fixation on the current word. Again, if attention were shared between the currently and to-be-fixated words in reading, then the availability of the upcoming word should have increased processing time for the current word.

Finally, in a recent study, we examined whether processing time on a given word in a sentence would vary as a function of lexical factors about the word to be fixated next (Henderson and Ferreira 1993). In that study, the sentences up to and including a critical word (word n) were identical, but the next word (word n+1) was either a short, high-frequency, function word, or a longer, lower frequency, content word. Previous research indicates that function words are far easier to identify and therefore are skipped more often and, when they are fixated, receive shorter fixations in reading (Just and Carpenter 1987). The question here, however, was whether the difficulty of word n+1 would influence fixation times on word n. The results of the study were clear-cut. While there was a marked effect of word n+1 on processing of that word (function words were skipped more often, and were fixated for less time), no effects of word n+1 were observed during fixations on word n. Therefore, effects due to the difficulty of the upcoming word do not become manifest until processing on the current word is completed, as predicted by the sequential attention hypothesis.

In sum, the difficulty of the upcoming stimulus has no effect on the acquisition of information from the currently fixated stimulus. This effect provides strong evidence against the parallel allocation hypothesis, and is consistent with the sequential attention hypothesis.

5.3.5. What is the neurophysiological evidence for an interdependence between visual attention and saccadic programming? In addition to the behavioural evidence discussed above, there is also neurophysiological evidence suggesting that prior to a saccadic eye-movement, visual attention is directed to the location toward which the saccade is aimed.

In these experiments, microelectrodes are inserted into the brain of the monkey in order to allow the recording of activity from a single cell. The monkey is also trained to participate in the behavioural part of the experiment, which might include maintaining fixation and responding manually to a visual stimulus, or executing an eye movement to a particular region of the visual field. By recording from a cell while the monkey maintains fixation, the receptive field of the cell can be mapped. The receptive field of a cell is the area within which a presented stimulus evokes a response from that cell. Mapping of the receptive field entails presenting a visual stimulus at various locations in the field and monitoring for cell activity.

Several studies using single-cell recording from awake and behaving monkeys suggests that the receptive fields of visually responsive neurons respond to changes in the focus of attention that are tied to saccadic eye-movements (Wurtz, Goldberg and Robinson 1988). In these experiments, the monkey is induced (via reward) to execute a saccade to a location within the receptive field of the recorded cell. The finding is that while the cell responds to a stimulus in its receptive field (by definition), the intensity of the response increases when the monkey is about to execute a saccade to that location. For example, the rate of activity of neurons in the superior colliculus is selectively enhanced prior to an eye movement when the receptive fields cover the location toward which a saccade is directed (Goldberg and Wurtz 1972). Importantly, the same cells do not respond when saccades are executed in darkness, suggesting that they are not reacting to the saccade itself. Further, given a visual stimulus in the receptive field of the cell, responses are not enhanced when a saccade is directed to another location in the visual field nor when the monkey responds to the visual stimulus manually rather than with an eye movement. Thus, cells in the superior colliculus seem to be at least partially tuned to the combination of a visual stimulus at a particular location and the preparation of a saccade to that location. Very similar results have been found when recording from cells in the frontal eye fields (Goldberg and Bushnell 1982).

It has been argued that because the single-cell studies show that the enhanced responses of cells in superior colliculus and the frontal eye fields are specific to saccadic eye-movements rather than to other types of responses (e.g., manual responses) cells in these areas cannot be reflecting attentional processes (Goldberg and Bruce 1985; Peterson and Robinson 1986; Wurtz 1986). The argument is that because visual attention can be dissociated from eye movements but enhanced responses of cells in these areas cannot, these areas must not be reflecting attentional processes. I would like to suggest, however, that these areas may be reflecting the operation of a visual-attentional process specifically tied to the onset of a saccadic eye-movement. That is, the enhanced activity of a cell to a visual stimulus prior to a saccade to that stimulus seems to be an exact neurophysiological correlate of the behavioural evidence that I have reviewed above. Thus, while these neural systems may not be involved in a more general attentional system, they do seem to reflect a part of the attentional system that is particular to the visual system.

In addition to cells that show enhanced responsiveness to stimulation prior to a saccade, there are also cortical cells that seem to be enhanced due to more general motor programming. For example, cells in posterior parietal cortex (area 7) and parts of the pulvinar (Pdm) show enhanced activity prior to a saccade to the location of the visual stimulus (and not other locations), but also show enhancement when the monkey releases a lever in response to the stimulus, or reaches for the stimulus (Bushnell, Goldberg and Robinson 1981; Petersen and Robinson 1983; see Robinson and Petersen 1986, for a review). Cells in these areas, then, seem to reflect the link between a visual stimulus and the response to that stimulus, regardless of the type of response that is made. Some researchers have argued that these cells represent the type of selective enhancement that would be expected of a general attentional system (Goldberg and Bruce 1985; Robinson and Petersen 1986; Wurtz 1986). However, while these cells probably do reflect such a system, it is important to note that attentional selectivity can be based upon many stimulus dimensions within vision (e.g., location, colour, movement, size, particular features), and that selection can also take place in the other modalities. Therefore, while it is important to discover the neural correlates of a general attentional system, it would be unwise to assume that there is only such a general system and no other, more specific, systems. The cells in the areas discussed (superior colliculus, frontal eye fields, posterior parietal cortex and pulvinar) clearly reflect a selectivity for visual information at a particular location prior to a saccadic eye-movement (and sometimes to other types of motor responses controlled by that stimulus), and therefore appear to reflect attentional processes. Finally, it is important to note that not all cortical cells show these effects; for example, neurons in striate (area 17) and prestriate (area 18) cortex do not show spatially selective enhancement, but instead seem to be enhanced by the general arousal level of the system (Wurtz and Mohler 1976; Robinson, Baizer and Dow 1980).

6. Attention and Action

The evidence discussed above provides a good deal of support for the view that visual attention precedes a saccadic eye-movement to a particular location in the visual field in a time-locked fashion. In this section, I want to offer some speculations concerning the potential computational significance of this time-locked attentional link between visual processing and motoric response.

Perhaps the most influential theory concerning the role of visual attention in visual processing is the Feature Integration Theory (FIT) proposed by Ann Treisman (Treisman and Gelade 1980; Treisman 1985).[2] I will use this theory to illustrate the role of attention in the perception/action interface. According to the feature integration theory, visual stimuli are initially represented as collections of independent features that are coded by separate representational (and neural) systems. For example, different representational "maps" would code features such as colour, orientation and curvature. Because each of these maps is independent, the specific values that "go together" across maps to form conjunctions that define a particular object (e.g., red + horizontal) must be conjoined in some way. This issue of how to make sure that independently represented primitives combine appropriately is sometimes called the "binding problem." According to the feature integration theory, the process that ensures the correct conjunction of features across representational maps is visual attention. Attention is theorized to operate over a master map of stimulus locations. Because each feature is implicitly coded according to location, making location explicit allows correct feature binding. This general idea is illustrated in Figure 13.4.

In keeping with the spirit of feature integration theory, I propose that visual attention allows the perceptuo-motor system to bind the location of a particular stimulus with a motor action. In other words, in addition to the role of combining features across visual maps, visual attention may also work to combine visual and motoric representations of the world. On this view, when the spatial co-ordinates of a visual stimulus are made explicit through the operation of visual attention, those co-ordinates become available for motor systems that are involved in programming movements associated with that stimulus and, in particular, movements that are directed toward that stimulus. In a sense, directing attention to a stimulus allows the binding of visual and motor representations. This general idea is shown in Figure 13.5.

Another way to conceptualize the binding of visual and motoric representations is to think of a motor attention system analogous to

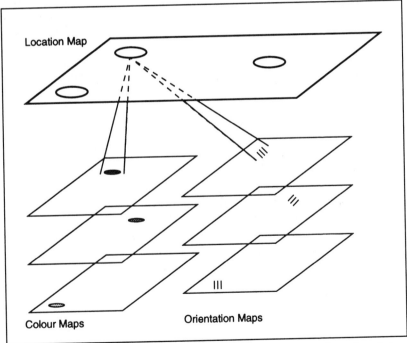

Figure 13.4: The feature integration theory (after Treisman 1985). Independent feature maps are integrated via a master map of stimulus locations.

the visual attention system that selects one motor program for action from among the many motor programs possible. Michael Goldberg and colleagues have recently provided evidence that at the neural level many conflicting motor signals are available at any given time (Goldberg and Bruce 1985; Goldberg and Segraves 1987). They have also speculated that selection from among these signals entails a process similar to visual attention (Goldberg and Segraves 1987). The evidence for simultaneously contradictory motor signals derives from two sources. First, there is evidence that some neurons have both sensory and motor components to their discharge. For example, some neurons in the intermediate layer of the superior colliculus of the monkey discharge both when a visual stimulus is present in their receptive fields in the absence of saccade and also prior to a saccade in the absence of visual stimulation (Wurtz and Goldberg 1972). Presumably, how the signal is interpreted depends on the area doing the interpretation; motor areas would interpret the signal as a motor signal, and visual areas would interpret the signal as visual stimulation. The implication is that, given several visual stimuli, several motor signals would be simultaneously generated, and some selection process would be needed to filter them.

A second source of evidence for competing motor signals derives from studies showing that cells in the intermediate layers of superior colliculus in monkeys discharge both prior to all saccades, and also discharge with the same intensity in the absence of a saccade (Mohler

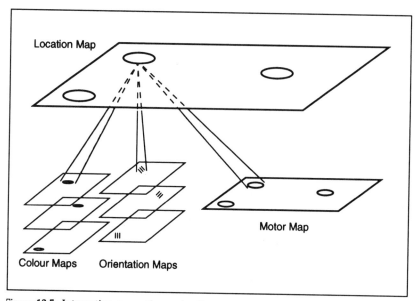

Figure 13.5: Integrating perception and action.

and Wurtz 1976). So, the execution of a saccade requires a discharge, but a discharge does not force a saccade. The hypothesis is that some selection process must select for action among the available saccade signals (Wurtz and Segraves 1987).

Given that many possible motor actions are available within the perceptuo-motor system at any given time, each one potentially linked to a visual stimulus, the issue of motoric selection becomes obvious. To anthropomorphize, the question for the motor system is, "How can I select a motor action until the target stimulus for that action has been selected?" The answer is: "Wait until a visual stimulus has been selected for further visual analysis, and choose a motor action suitable for directing action toward that stimulus." Thus, for the eye movement system, a saccadic program would be readied based on visual selection of a particular stimulus. Presumably, for other action systems, such as reaching, a similar selection of a target would be necessary. Of course, selecting whether to fixate, reach for or swat at a given stimulus would require another level of selection – perhaps equivalent to selecting to attend to the visual, auditory or somatosensory modalities in perception. The point, though, is that in order to direct a motor action toward a visual stimulus, that stimulus must first be selected. The proposal I am offering here is that selection for motor action is both functionally and structurally linked with the system that selects a visual stimulus for further perceptual analysis.

Notes

1 The inability to detect such changes is a regular observation in eye movement research that employs eye-contingent display changes. In initially testing the computer program for this experiment, I ran myself through the several trials and was convinced that the program was not working because I had no phenomenal experience of the changes. This was despite the fact that I knew exactly where the changes should be! It was only when I stood behind my collaborator, Fernanda Ferreira, and watched the computer screen as she ran through the same trials, that I could see that the program was working properly.
2 Modifications to FIT have been proposed by several investigators (e.g., Wolfe et al. 1989), but these modifications do not affect the more general points I wish to make here.

References

Allport, A. (1989). Visual attention. In M.I. Posner (ed.), *Foundations of Cognitive Science*. Cambridge, MA: MIT Press

Becker, W., and R. Jurgens (1979). An analysis of the saccadic system by means of double-step stimuli. *Vision Research* 19: 967-83

Blanchard, H.E., A. Pollatsek and K. Rayner (1989). Parafoveal processing during eye fixations in reading. *Perception and Psychophysics* 46: 85-94

Bushnell, M.C., M.E. Goldberg and D.L. Robinson (1981). Behavioral enhancement of visual responses in monkey cerebral cortex: I. Modulation in posterior parietal cortex related to selective visual attention. *Journal of Neurophysiology* 46: 755-72

De Graef, P., D. Christiaens and G. d'Ydewalle (1990). Perceptual effects of scene context on object identification. *Psychological Research* 52: 317-29

Ehrlich, K., and K. Rayner (1983). Pronoun assignment and semantic integration during reading: Eye movements and immediacy of processing. *Journal of Verbal Learning and Verbal Behaviour* 22: 75-87

Eriksen, C.W., and Y. Yeh (1985). Allocation of attention in the visual field. *Journal of Experimental Psychology: Human Perception and Performance* 11: 583-97

Ferreira, F., and J.M. Henderson (1990). The use of verb information in syntactic parsing: Evidence from eye movements and word-by-word self-paced reading. *Journal of Experimental Psychology: Learning, Memory, and Cognition* 16: 555-69

Ferreira, F., and J.M. Henderson (forthcoming). Reading processes during syntactic analysis and reanalysis. *Canadian Journal of Psychology*

Fisher, D.F., and W.L. Shebilske (1985). There is more that meets the eye than the eyemind assumption. In R. Groner, G.W. McConkie and C. Menz (eds.), *Eye Movements and Human Information Processing*. North Holland: Elsevier Science

Frazier, L., and K. Rayner (1982).Making and correcting errors during sentence comprehension: Eye movements in the analysis of structurally ambiguous sentences. *Cognitive Psychology* 14: 178-210

Goldberg, M.E., and C. J. Bruce (1985). Cerebral cortical activity associated with the orientation of visual attention in the rhesus monkey. *Vision Research* 25: 471-81

Goldberg, M.E., and M.C. Bushnell (1982). Behavioral enhancement of visual responses in monkey cerebral cortex: II. Modulation in frontal eye fields specifically related to saccades. *Journal of Neurophysiology* 46: 773-87

Goldberg, M.E., and M.A. Segraves (1987). Visuospatial and motor attention in the monkey. *Neuropsychologia* 25: 107-18

Goldberg, M.E., and R.H. Wurtz (1972). Activity of superior colliculus in behaving monkey: II. The effect of attention on neuronal responses. *Journal of Neurophysiology* 35: 560-74

Henderson, J.M. (1988). Visual Attention and the Acquisition of Etrafoveal Information during Eye Fixations. Unpublished doctoral dissertation, Amherst, MA: University of Massachusetts

———. (1991). Stimulus discrimination following covert attentional orienting to an exogenous cue. *Journal of Experimental Psychology: Human Perception and Performance* 17: 91-106

———. (1992). Visual attention and eye movement control during reading and scene perception. In K. Rayner (ed.), *Eye Movements and Visual Cognition: Scene Perception and Reading*. New York: Springer-Verlag

———. (1993). Visual attention and saccadic eye-movements. In G. d'Ydewalle and J. Van Rensbergen (eds.), *Perception and Cognition: Advances in Eye Movement Research*. Amsterdam: North-Holland

Henderson, J.M., and F. Ferreira (1990). Effects of foveal processing difficulty on the perceptual span in reading: Implications for attention and eye movement control. *Journal of Experimental Psychology: Learning, Memory, and Cognition* 16: 417-29

Henderson, J.M., and F. Ferreira (1993). Eye movement control in reading: Fixation measures reflect foveal but not parafoveal processing difficulty. *Canadian Journal of Experimental Psychology* 47:201-21

Henderson, J.M., and A.D. Macquistan (1993). Covert orienting to an exogenous cue: Support for a gradient model of visual attention. *Perception and Psychophysics*, 53: 221-30

Henderson, J.M., A. Pollatsek and K. Rayner (1989). Covert visual attention and extrafoveal information use during object identification. *Perception and Psychophysics* 45: 196-208

Hogaboam, T.W. (1983). Reading patterns in eye movement data. In K. Rayner (ed.), *Eye Movements in Reading: Perceptual and Language Processes*. New York: Academic Press

Hughes, H.C., and L.D. Zimba (1985). Spatial maps of directed visual attention. *Journal of Experimental Psychology: Human Perception and Performance* 11: 409-30

Hughes, H.C., and L.D. Zimba (1987). Natural boundaries for the spread of directed visual attention. *Neuropsychologia* 2: 5-18

Inhoff, A.W., A. Pollatsek, M.I. Posner, and K. Rayner (1989). Covert attention and eye movements in reading. *Quarterly Journal of Experimental Psychology* 41A: 63-89

James, W. (1890/1950). *The Principles of Psychology*. Vol. 1. New York: Dover

Jonides, J. (1981). Voluntary versus automatic control over the mind's eye's movement. In J. Long and A. Baddeley (eds.), *Attention and Performance IX* (pp. 187-203). Hillsdale, NJ: Erlbaum

Just, M.A., and P.A. Carpenter (1980). A theory of reading: From eye fixations to comprehension. *Psychological Review* 87: 329-54

Just, M.A., and P.A. Carpenter (1987). *The Psychology of Reading and Language Comprehension*. Newton, MA: Allyn and Bacon

Klein, R., and P. McCormick (1989). Covert visual orienting: Hemifield activation can be mimicked by zoom lens and midlocation placement strategies. *Acta Psychologica* 770: 235-50

Koch, C., and S. Ullman (1985). Shifts in selective visual attention: towards the underlying neural circuitry. *Human Neurobiology* 4: 219-27

LaBerge, D., and V. Brown (1989). Theory of attentional operations in shape identification. *Psychological Review* 96: 101-24

Mahoney, J.V., and S. Ullman (1988). Image chunking defining spatial building blocks for scene analysis. In Z. Pylyshyn (ed.), *Computational Processes in Human Vision: An Interdisciplinary Perspective.* Norwood, NJ: Ablex

McConkie, G.W. (1979). On the role and control of eye movements in reading. In P.A. Kolers, M.E. Wrolstad and H. Bouma (eds.), *Processing of Visible Language* Vol. 1, 37-48. New York: Plenum Press

McConkie, G.W., and K. Rayner (1975). The span of the effective stimulus during a fixation in reading. *Perception and Psychophysics* 17: 578-86

McConkie, G.W., and K. Rayner (1976). Asymmetry of the perceptual span in reading. *Bulletin of the Psychonomic Society* 8: 365-68

McConkie, G.W., and D. Zola (1987). Visual attention during eye fixations in reading. *Attention and Performance Xll* 327-62. London: Erlbaum

Mohler, C.W., and R.H. Wurtz (1976). Organization of monkey superior colliculus: Intermediate layer cells discharging before eye movements. *Journal of Neurophysiology* 39: 722-44

Morrison, R.E. (1984). Manipulation of stimulus onset delay in reading: Evidence for parallel programming of saccades. *Journal of Experimental Psychology: Human Perception and Performance* 10: 667-82

Osaka, N., and K. Oda (1991). Effective visual field size necessary for vertical reading during Japanese text processing. *Bulletin of the Psychonomic Society* 29: 345-47

Petersen, S.E., and D.L. Robinson (1983). Two types of behavioral enhancement of visual responses in the pulvinar of alert rhesus monkeys. *Investigative Ophthalmology and Visual Science* 24: 106

Pollatsek, A., S. Bolozky, A.D. Well, and K. Rayner (1981). Asymmetries in the perceptual span for Israeli readers. *Brain and Language* 14: 174-80

Pollatsek, A., K. Rayner and D.A. Balota (1986). Inferences about eye movement control from the perceptual span in reading. *Perception and Psychophysics* 40: 123- 30

Posner, M.I., and S.E. Petersen (1990). The attention system of the human brain. *Annual Review of Psychology* 13: 25-42

Posner, M.I. (1980). Orienting of attention. *Quarterly Journal of Experimental Psychology* 32: 3-25

Posner, M.I., C.R.R. Snyder and B.J. Davidson (1980). Attention and the detection of signals. *Journal of Experimental Psychology: General* 109: 160-74

Rayner, K. (1975). The perceptual span and peripheral cues in reading. *Cognitive Psychology* 7: 65-81

Rayner K. (1978). Eye movements in reading and information processing. *Psychological Bulletin* 85: 618-60

Rayner, K., and S.A. Duffy (1986). Lexical complexity and fixation times in reading: Effects of word frequency, verb complexity, and lexical ambiguity. *Memory and Cognition* 14: 191-201

Rayner, K., and A. Pollatsek (1987). Eye movements in reading: A tutorial review. *Attention and Performance Xll* 327-62. London: Erlbaum

Rayner K., A.D. Well and A. Pollatsek (1980). Asymmetry of the effective visual field in reading. *Perception and Psychophysics* 27: 537-44

Robinson, D.L., and S.E. Petersen (1986). The neurobiology of attention. In J.E. LeDoux and W. Hirst (eds.), *Mind and Brain: Dialogues in Cognitive Neuroscience.* New York: Cambridge University Press

Robinson, D.L., J.S. Baizer and B.M. Dow (1980). Behavioral enhancement of visual responses of prestriate neurons of the rhesus monkey. *Investigative Ophthalmology and Visual Science* 19: 1120-23

Shepherd, M., J.M. Findlay and R..J. Hockey (1986). The relationship between eye movements and spatial attention. *Quarterly Journal of Experimental Psychology* 38A: 475-91

Tinker, M.A. (1939). Reliability and validity of eye-movement measures of reading. *Journal of Experimental Psychology* 19: 732-46

Treisman, A. (1985). Preattentive processing in vision. *Computer Vision, Graphics, and Image Processing* 31: 156-77

Treisman, A., and G. Gelade (1980).A feature integration theory of attention. *Cognitive Psychology* 12: 97-136

Underwood, N.R., and G.W. McConkie (1985). Perceptual span for letter distinctions during reading. *Reading Research Quarterly* 20: 153-62

Ungerleider, L.G., and M. Mishkin (1982). Two cortical systems. In D.J. Ingle, M.A. Goodale and R.J.W. Mansfield (eds.), *Analysis of Visual Behavior.* Cambridge, MA: MIT Press

Wolfe, J.M., K.R. Cave and S.L. Franzel (1989). A modified feature integration model for visual search. *Journal of Experimental Psychology: Human Perception and Performance* 15: 419-33

Wurtz, R.H. (1986). Stimulus selection and conditional response mechanisms in the basal ganglia of the monkey. In M.I. Posner and O.S.M. Marin (eds.), *Attention and Performance XI* 441-55. Hilldale, NJ: Erlbaum

Wurtz, R.H., and M.E. Goldberg (1972). Activity of superior colliculus in behaving monkey: III. Cells discharging before eye movements. *Journal of Neurophysiology* 35: 575-86

Wurtz, R.H., M.E. Goldberg and D.L. Robinson (1982). Brain mechanisms of visual attention. *Scientific American,* 124-35

Wurtz, R.H., and C.W. Mohler (1976). Organization of monkey superior colliculus: Enhanced visual response of superficial layer cells. *Journal of Neurophysiology* 39: 745-65

Yarbus, A.L. (1967). *Eye Movements and Vision.* New York: Plenum Press

14

The Perception of Time

C. Randy Gallistel

The belief that there is nothing in the mind that was not first in the senses lies deeply embedded in our philosophy and psychology. This belief makes the experience of time perplexing, because it is not clear what the sensory basis of the experience is. Insights gained from experiments on the timing of animal behaviour offer a way out of this perplexity, but only by recognizing that there are in fact things in the mind that did not come through the senses. Time is in the mind because clocks are built into the brain. Because the mind gets time values from built-in clocks, and because it may calculate the durations of intervals from these time values during the process of recollecting experiences, there is no sensory basis for the experience of time.

Insofar as 'perception' refers to experiences rooted in sensory input, to sensible properties of the world, my title is a misnomer. There is no perception of time. Kant was on the right track when he argued that time is not so much an experience in and of itself as it is an obligatory aspect of all experience. Our experiences stand in time. I will suggest an hypothesis about how memory works that makes clear, I hope, how and why they do so.

1. The Internal Clock

Philosophers and psychologists are not the only ones who are or have been deeply committed to the view that behaviourally significant activity in the brain or mind must be engendered by the action of stimuli falling on sensory receptors. This conviction held sway over physiologists until the last few decades. All action was taken to be reflex action, and reflex action depended by definition on exogenously generated neural activity. Thirty years ago, the endogenous basis of most rhythmic biological activities was still intensely controversial, although there had been strong evidence for it since the dawn of scientific attempts to find a material basis for vital phenomena. Harvey (1628) observed that isolated pieces of heart muscle contracted rhythmically. In the centuries that followed, it was widely known that the isolated heart of a turtle would beat for hours in a Petri dish filled with Ringer's solution. Nonetheless, there were persistent attempts to explain the rhythmic contraction of the heart muscle as driven by the rhythmic stimulus of the entering blood. Toward the end of the nineteenth century, the rhythmic electrical activity of the sinoatrial node was shown to drive the rhythmic contractions of the heart, and the endogenous nature of cardiac activity became generally accepted, but the behavioural physiologists who suggested that other rhythmic activities were also endogenous (Brown 1914; Bünning 1936; Holst 1939; Stein-Beling 1935; Szymanski 1920) went unheeded.

In the 1970s, resistance to the notion that rhythmic activities arose within the nervous system itself abruptly gave way in the face of overwhelming evidence from behavioural, neurophysiological and cellular investigations. One line of evidence came from the study of the circadian rhythm, the daily cycle in the activity of animals. This activity is measured by recording the output of an activity-sensing device on a slowly moving chart recorder. When the animal moves around, the resulting squiggles merge into a blur of ink; when it is quiescent, the pen traces a straight line on the chart. Figure 14.1B shows the circadian activity of a roach, while Figure 14.1A shows how displays like this are created by cutting up the chart paper into 24-hour segments and mounting them one beneath another, so that changes in the timing of the daily onset of activity can be traced by scanning down the display.

For the first 20 days charted in Figure 14.1B, a bout of sustained activity begins abruptly soon after lights-out (objective dusk). One might suppose that this activity was triggered by the extinction of the lights (although notice that the roach became intermittently active about two hours prior to lights-out). However, the endogenous nature of this 24-hour rhythm in the roach's activity is revealed when, at day 20, it is blinded by painting its eyes with fingernail polish. Thereafter, there continues to be an abrupt onset of sustained activity once in each 24-hour segment, but the onset occurs 30 minutes earlier each day. In other words, the period of the animal's activity cycle is 23 hours and 30 minutes, so that when the record is cut into 24-hour segments corresponding to the 24-hour solar cycle, the onsets drift steadily leftward (by 30 minutes/day) as one scans down the display. This is called phase drift.

Phase drift in the activity cycle is seen whenever one deprives an animal of the dark-light transitions at approximately 24-hour intervals that keep the animal's internal clock synchronized with the solar cycle. When the internal clock is synchronized with an external day-night cycle, it is said to be entrained. When it is not synchronized with an external day-night cycle, it is said to run free. The rate of drift (the

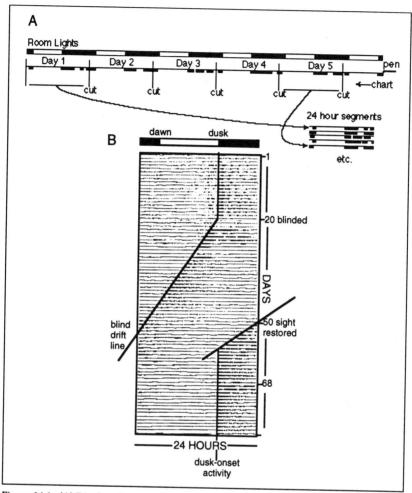

Figure 14.1: (A) Displays that reveal consistent patterns in the period and phase of an animal's circadian activity are created by cutting the continuous chart of activity into 24-hour segments and mounting the segments one below the other. (B) The circadian activity of a roach. The black-white bar at the top shows the dark-light cycle of the artificial light in the roach's cage. During the first 20 days, the onset of sustained activity (subjective dusk) is synchronized with the turning off of the lights (objective dusk). On day 20, the roach was reversibly blinded. Its internal clock was no longer entrained by the external dark-light cycle and it ran free with its own natural period, which in this case was 23 hours and 30 minutes. The onset of activity at subjective dusk occurred 30 minutes earlier each day producing the leftward drift (blind drift line). At day 50, when the subjective dusk coincided with objective dawn, sight was restored. The entraining effect of the dark-light cycle accelerated the daily phase shift in subjective dusk until it again coincided with objective dusk. Thereafter, the entraining effect of the external cycle again kept the circadian oscillation synchronized with the dark-light cycle. Modified from Roberts (1965), with permission.

number of minutes gained or lost per solar day) in the free-running activity cycle varies from animal to animal, because animal clocks are like human clocks: every one has a rhythm of its own, with a period at least slightly different from every other. When it was first discovered that animals kept in seemingly constant conditions nonetheless showed a daily activity rhythm, there were attempts to explain this rhythm in terms of some subtle external rhythmic stimulus, undetected by the experimenter, such as cosmic rays. These exogenous causation hypotheses were not tenable in the face of evidence that, in a colony of free-running animals, their cycles drifted out of phase (out of synchrony) with each other. One was forced to posit as many undetected external cyclical stimuli as there were animals in the colony and, further, to postulate that each animal was sensitive to a different external stimulus cycle. It became much more plausible to assume that each animal had its own internal clock.

In recent years, dramatic progress has been made in localizing this clock within the nervous system. Several different tissues in the heart are capable of rhythmic activity with a period (cycle duration) of approximately one second, including the heart muscle itself, but under normal circumstances the beating of the heart is driven by cyclical changes in the electrical polarization of specialized pacemaker cells in the sinoatrial node. Similarly, many different neural and non-neural tissues are capable of generating cyclical activity with a period of about a day, but under normal circumstances the circadian rhythm seen in most mammalian bodily functions is driven by the neurons in a small nucleus called the suprachiasmatic nucleus, which is in the hypothalamus, at the base of the brain, just above the roof of the mouth. There is a pronounced circadian rhythm in the activity of the cells in this nucleus (Schwartz and Gainer 1977), whether they are in situ or are removed and kept in cell culture or as a living tissue slice (Green and Gillette 1982; Newman, Hospod, Patlak and Moore 1992) and, finally, destroying this nucleus causes the permanent disappearance of the daily rhythm of activity in the intact rodent (Rusak and Zucker 1979)

The hypothesis that the suprachiasmatic nucleus is the master clock has recently received definitive confirmation through transplant experiments. Some years ago, a mutant hamster was discovered in the laboratory of Martin Ralph and Michael Menaker, leading researchers in the neurobiology of circadian rhythms. Normal "wild-type" hamsters have a clock with a period within an hour of 24 hours; under free-running conditions their activity cycle gains or loses less than 60 minutes a day. The mutant hamster's clock had a period of about 19 hours (Ralph and Menaker 1988); its free-running activity gained five hours a day. A strain of such hamsters has now been bred. Recently Ralph and his collaborators (Ralph, Foster, Davis and Menaker 1990) extirpated the suprachiasmatic nuclei in two groups of wild-type hamsters and two groups of short-cycle hamsters. After monitoring the activity of all four groups of hamsters for several weeks under free-running conditions to verify that the removal of this nucleus had led to the disappearance of the circadian activity rhythm, the experimenters transplanted fetal suprachiasmatic nucleus tissue into the brains of the lesioned hosts at a site close to the site of the destroyed nucleus. The transplants came from either wild-type or short-cycle donors. In the animals in which a circadian activity rhythm became evident following the transplant, the period of the rhythm was invariably that of the donor animal. Wild-type hamsters were converted to short-cycle hamsters and short-cycle hamsters to wild-type hamsters by means of these transplants (Figure 14.2).

In the just described transplant experiments, time was taken out of the mind of the hamsters when the lesions destroyed the master clock, and it was put back into their mind by the transplant of a clock from another hamster, a clock that kept different time. There is a rather close analogy between this dramatic and philosophically interesting experiment and the destruction of the calendar-clock chip on the mother board of contemporary microcomputers – which deprives the computer of regular access to the signal that indicates the current date and time – followed by the replacement of that chip – which restores the computer's ability to assign dates and times to the file records.

A clock in the brain would be of little use if it were not synchronized with the daily solar cycle. The process by which external dark-light transitions synchronize the internal circadian clock is called entrainment. There is a specialized visual input to the suprachiasmatic nucleus, which provides the clock with the morning solar time signal that it uses to reset itself each day so as to remain in synchrony with the solar cycle. (The short-cycle hamsters cannot remain in synchrony because the daily gain in their clocks is too great for the resetting process to overcome.) There appear to be a number of adaptive specializations in this visual pathway that suit it to its very specialized function (Foster et al. 1991; Takahashi, De Coursey, Bauman and Menaker 1984).

2. The Chronobiology of Memory

The modern microcomputer needs a calendar/clock chip because recording the time and date at which a file has last been accessed is a basic aspect of the way in which its operating system stores and accesses files. I want to suggest that recording the time of an event to

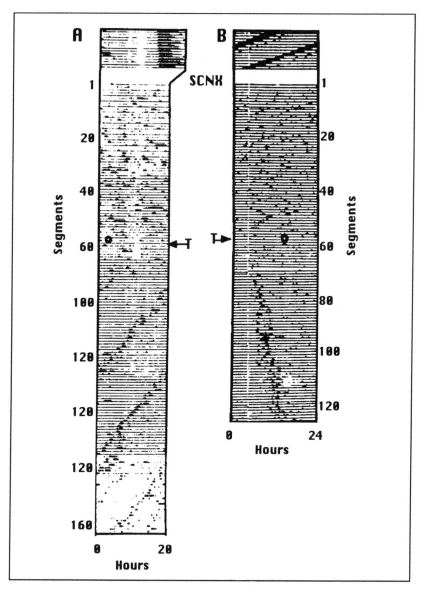

Figure 14.2: (A) Free-running circadian activity record from a wild-type hamster into which suprachiasmatic fetal tissue from a homozygous mutant short-cycle donor was transplanted. The endogenous rhythm of the host before its suprachiasmatic nucleus was removed was very slightly longer than 24 hours, so that the onset of its activity occurred about 3 minutes later each day (14 segments at top of record, before lesion of suprachiasmatic nucleus, *SCNX*). Its suprachiasmatic nucleus was extirpated at *SCNX*. At this point the length of each record segment is reduced to 20 hours (from 24 hours) in order to show better the appearance of short-cycle activity following the eventual transplant. In segments 1 to 50, there is no regular cycle in the animal's activity. At *T*, it

be remembered is an even more basic aspect of the operation of animal brains; indeed, that these recordings of time (and place) are the key to our ability to recall events. To lend even a modicum of plausibility to this radical suggestion, I must first review the evidence that animals routinely learn the time at which something happens and that this "time stamp" plays an important role in their subsequent use of the information gained from that experience.

The availability of food is often a function of the time of day, and animals routinely learn the time at which food is available. For example, different species of flowers produce nectar at different times of day, and bees learn the time of day at which a flower of a given colour and odour at a given location produces nectar. This was first demonstrated by students of von Frisch in the 1930s (Beling 1929; Wahl 1932; Wahl 1933). Bees are particularly well suited for experiments of this kind, because the foraging bee is looking for food primarily for the hive not for itself. A foraging worker bee spends the day transporting food from its sources to the hive. Unlike most foraging animals, it does not cease to visit a source when it has eaten its fill.

In one of his experiments, Wahl (1932) set up two feeding stations at different directions and distances from a hive, and trained the foraging bees from the hive to visit both of them. The feeding stations were tables with a beaker containing sugar water. The beaker on one table (table A) contained sugar water only between 9:00 and 10:30 in the morning, while the beaker on the other table (B) contained sugar water only between 4:00 and 5:30 in the afternoon. On the test day, neither beaker was ever filled.

On the test day, Wahl tallied the number and kind of visits to the empty beakers per half-hour (Figure 14.3). Between 7:00 and 9:00, that 's, in the two hours prior to the time at which the beaker on table A had been filled on previous days, the number of visits to table A per half-hour built to a peak, and a majority of the these visits were landing visits, in which the bee landed on and entered the beaker. (The beakers were so constructed that bees could not determine whether

---

received fetal suprachiasmatic (SCN) tissue from a donor in the strain that has an endogenous cycle of about 19 hours. By segment 80, there is a clear cycle in the host's activity and the period of this cycle is 19.5 hours, so that activity onset occurs 30 minutes earlier in each successive 20-hour segment (leftward drift seen in segments 80 to 165). (B) Free-running activity record from a heterozygous short-cycle host into which SCN tissue from a wild-type donor was transplanted. In the records above SCNX one sees the rapid leftward drift characteristic of the heterozygotic host whose endogenous clock gained about 2.3 hours per day. Its suprachiasmatic nucleus was extirpated at SCNX, leading to an aperiodic activity record in segments 1 to 60. After receiving fetal SCN tissue from a wild-type donor at T, cyclic activity becomes apparent by segment 70 and the period of this cycle is 24.2 hours (slight rightward drift seen in segments 70 to 125). Reproduced with minor modifications from Ralph et al. (1990), with permission.

they contained nectar or not except by landing and entering.) During this same period, there was also a crescendo in the visits to the other table (where the bees had not been fed in the morning during training), but a majority of these visits were "fly-by" visits, in which the bee did not land and enter the beaker. A failure to land during a visit indicates only a weak expectation of finding nectar (see the Kolterman experiment below). Because bees use the presence of other bees as a landing cue, it is likely that these fly-by visits were to check whether

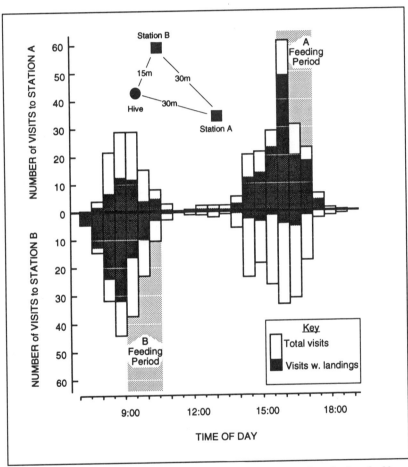

Figure 14.3: Numbers and types of visits to two feeding stations whose beakers had been stocked at different times of day during the training period. The bars indicate total visits; the filled portion of each bar gives the proportion of land-and-enter visits. Note changes in these proportions as a function of the time of day. Data from Wahl (1932, 544, 546, 547). Reproduced from Gallistel (1990), with permission.

other bees were foraging at that site. By noon, visits to both stations had all but ceased, but between 2:00 and 4:00 in the afternoon, there was a second crescendo of visits to both tables, only now the relative proportions of land-and-enter visits to fly-by-only visits at the two tables were reversed. Most of the visits to the afternoon feeding station were land-and-enter visits, while most of the visits to the morning feeding station were now only fly-bys.

In another experiment, Wahl varied the concentration of the sugar in the water, making it higher during one or two periods of the day, and lower the rest of the time. On the test day, when the beaker was empty all day, there were marked increases in the bees' return visits to the beaker just prior to, and during, the hours of the day when the "nectar" had been sweetest.

In similar experiments, Koltermann (1971) let foraging bees experience the odour of geranium while visiting a feeding beaker at around 9:00 in the morning and then the odour of thyme while visiting the same station at 3:00 in the afternoon. The next day. at 9:00 and again at 3:00, he tested their preference between two (empty) beakers, one smelling of geranium and the other of thyme. They preferred the geranium beaker in the morning and the thyme beaker in the afternoon (Figure 14.4). If they foraged from a blue-green beaker in the morning and a violet beaker in the afternoon, when they subsequently had to choose between a blue-green and a violet beaker (both empty), they preferred the blue-green in the morning and the violet in the afternoon (Figure 14.5).

In sum, it would appear that in the foraging bee, each feature of its remembered experience – the location, the surrounding colour, the ambient odour, and the sweetness of previously experienced nectar – is stamped with the time of day. The time-stamp in memory, together with the current reading on the bee's internal clock, determines how the bee behaves toward that stimulus on subsequent occasions. The bee's estimates of time of day – both for its time stamps and for the current time, are readings of the bee's internal clock. They are not derived from external variables that change with the time of day (such as the elevation of the sun), because bees seek food at a station 24 hours after they lasted obtained it there, even when the experiment is run indoors in the absence of any 24-hour cycle in the world external to the bee (Wahl 1932).

The fundamental role played by the time of day at which an event is experienced is in no way peculiar to the bee. When rats are given a shock for stepping through the doorway between the white and black compartments of an apparatus created to test for what is called "one

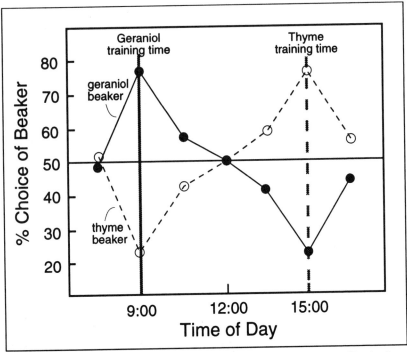

Figure 14.4: Percentage choice of (barren) geraniol-smelling and thyme-smelling beakers, as a function of time of day, in bees that had experienced geraniol odour at 9:00 and thyme odour at 15:00 on the preceding training day. Redrawn from Koltermann (1971), with permission.

trial passive avoidance" and then tested at various times of day thereafter, they are maximally reluctant to venture through the doorway again when the test is at the same time of day as the training experience (Holloway and Wansley 1973). If the rats have contradictory experiences on stepping through the door into the dark chamber – sugared milk on one occasion, a shock on the next – the extent to which the positive experience counteracts their hesitancy following the negative experience is a function of whether the two experiences occurred at the same times of day or not. If they did (even when they occurred on separate days), then the positive experience helps overcome their hesitancy following the negative experience. If, however, the positive experience was at a different time of day, then it has little effect on the hesitancy of rats tested at the time of day when they experienced the shock (Hunsicker and Mellgren 1977).

Rats like bees learn the time(s) of day at which food is available, and like bees, they show this by an increase in activity that occurs in antic-

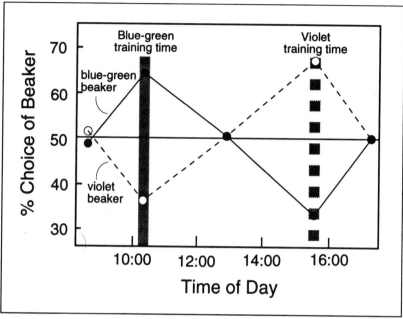

Figure 14.5: Percentage choice of (barren) beakers on blue-green or violet paper, as a function of the time of day, in bees that had experienced blue-green at 10:00 and violet at 15:00 on the preceding training day. Redrawn from Koltermann (1971) p. 64, with permission of author and publisher.

ipation of this time (Bolles and Moot 1973). That this anticipatory behaviour depends on the time indicated by the internal clock has been shown in an elegant series of experiments by Rosenwasser, Pelchat and Adler (1984). They trained rats to anticipate feeding at various times of day while the rats were entrained to an artificial day-night cycle. Then they restored the rats to unrestricted feeding (food always available) and they changed the setting of the internal clock (its position in its own cycle at a given point in the solar day), either by changing the times of day at which the light in the home cage came on and went off (shifting the artificial "solar" cycle that entrains the rats' clock), or by putting the rats in constant illumination, allowing their internal clocks to run free. When the setting of the internal clock had been shifted relative to the solar day in one of these two ways, they took away the rats' food for several days. There was no daily feeding during these tests, but the rats showed anticipatory activity, and this anticipatory activity occurred at the phase of their internal clock at which the anticipatory activity had occurred during the training period (Figure 14.6).

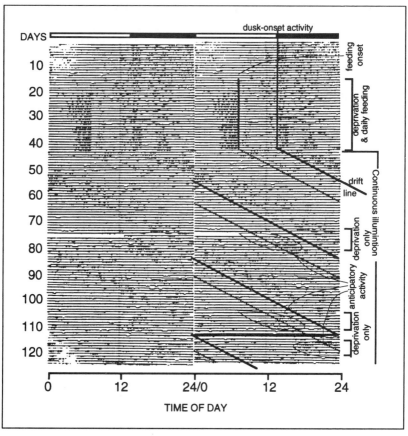

Figure 14.6: Double-day record of activity, demonstrating that a rat has learned to anticipate feeding at a given reading on its internal clock. In a double-day plot, each 24-hour segment of the activity record is shown twice, first on the right (the second half of the plot), then on the left on the line below (the first half of the plot). This permits easier visualization of phase drifts. The entraining light-dark cycle was present until the end of restricted feeding (day 40). During restricted feeding, the rat had access to food only from 10:00 to 12:00 each day, during the period when it is normally inactive. Note the anticipatory activity that terminates abruptly at 10:00 when food becomes available. (The heavy vertical line on the right half of the plot from day 15 to day 40 marks the onset of food availability). Thereafter, the rat was in constant illumination (free-running conditions). The activity onset at subjective dusk occurred 48 minutes later each day. The rightward drift in subjective dusk indicated by solid drift line on the right half of the plot, the (subjective) phase at which food onset has been experienced by the heavy dotted line. The absence of all food on days 74 through 80, and again from days 105 through 109, and yet again from days 115 through 119, caused the reappearance of anticipatory activity at the same phase of the subject's endogenous activity cycle as the phase of food availability during the restricted feeding regime months earlier (activity straddling the heavy dotted drift line for the food onset phase). Modified from Rosenwasser et al. (1984), with permission.

3. The Role of Time (and Space) in Recollection

The assumption that animals record the time of an experience, in the form of readings from an internal calendar-clock, is central to my principal thesis, which is that all experience is recorded in conjunction with an obligatory specification of time and place. I suggest that the specifications of time and place associated with the records of experiences play a unique and fundamental role in our ability to recollect experience in useful ways. The records of time and place mediate the unification of the many different aspects into which the modules in our sensory-perceptual apparatus divide our experience of the world.

Our sensory-perceptual faculties confront a formidable challenge. Our perceptions are based on properties of the proximal stimuli, the stimuli that actually excite our sensory receptors, such as the images formed on our retinas. What we need to know, however, are properties of distal stimuli, the objects that reflected the light that forms images on our retina. The problem is that simple properties of distal stimuli – for example, the size and distance of an object and the reflectance characteristics of the material of which it is composed – are not specified in a simple way by first-order properties of the proximal stimulus. To derive properties of the distal stimulus from the proximal stimulus, our sensory perceptual system must invert the very complex function that maps from simple aspects of the distal stimulus to complex properties of the proximal stimulus. The very long times required by ray-tracing 3-D rendering programs give an indication of just how complex this function is; inverting it is a formidable computational task.

While there is much that we do not understand about how our sensory-perceptual mechanisms derive a representation of the distal stimulus from the proximal stimulus, one thing is clear: they divide in order to conquer. Our sensory-perceptual system is composed of a large number of specialized components or modules, each of which extracts from incoming sensory signals a different partial description of the stimulus. This principle is evident already in the externally observable specializations that create the sensory modalities – vision, hearing, olfaction, and so on, but the principle goes much deeper. In the process of transducing the proximal stimulus into neural signals and at every stage of neural processing thereafter, the sensory input is processed by specialized circuits or modules working in parallel. By the time the signals generated by visual input get to the later stages of the visual cortex – to the regions where it may plausibly be assumed that neural activity determines percepts – there are dozens of these modules. Each module is located in a different region of the cortex, and each appears to specify different aspects of the distal stimulus.

Neural activity in one part of the cortex seems to specify aspects of shape; activity in another region specifies aspects of motion; activity in yet another region specifies the reflectance characteristics of surfaces (colour); and so on (see Gallistel 1990 for review).

Phenomenologically, the world does not present itself to us as a collection of unrelated aspects. Also, diverse aspects of the distal stimulus must be taken into account in the genesis of behaviour. For example, the behaviour of a foraging bee returning to and landing on a flower demonstrably takes into account the bee's previous experience of the sweetness, the location, the colour, the odour and the time of nectar production. If these diverse aspects of the same experience have been extracted by different parts of the nervous system, how are they united? We know from the psychophysical work of Treisman and others that there is a process of some kind that knits together the diverse aspects of one experience, such as the shape and colour of a perceived object, and that this process can err, producing what are called illusory conjunctions, incorrectly perceived (or remembered) conjunctions of, for example, colour and shape (Treisman and Schmidt 1982). Phenomenologically, these erroneous conjunctions are just as real as correct conjunctions; when queried immediately after the presentation of a display, subjects recall seeing a green circle and a red square, although the display in fact comprised a green square and a red circle.

A fundamental question about the relation between perception and memory is whether the conjoining of different aspects of experience, such as the colour and shape of a perceived object, occurs prior to the storage of experience in memory – as I think is commonly implicitly assumed – or after the storage of experience in memory, at the time of recollection. My thesis is that phenomenological experience is primarily recollective – it is read out from storage buffers rather than from the neural activity induced by the stimuli – and that the obligatory specifications of time and place that accompany recorded aspects of experience mediate the bringing together in recollection of diverse aspects of an experience.

The specifications of time and place that I imagine to mediate the unity of remembered experience may be thought of as psychological world-lines. For a physicist, a particle of matter, such as an electron, traces a path in the space-time manifold. This path is called the world-line of the particle. A world-line is a locus (a collection of adjacent points) in the "space" defined by the three spatial and one temporal dimension within which all physical phenomena occur. "Space" is enclosed in single quotes in the preceding sentence to indicate that it is being used in its mathematical sense. A space in the mathematical sense may have any number of dimensions, whereas space in its physical sense (its everyday sense) has three dimensions. For the mathematician, the space in which physical events, such as the motion of a particle, are defined is a four-dimensional space, which is often called the space-time manifold because the "space-time space" is a distinctly odd locution. Three of the dimensions of the space-time manifold are the dimensions of space as ordinarily conceived, and one is the time dimension.

I assume that our sensory perceptual mechanisms locate the distal sources of sensory input in a three-dimensional space that corresponds to the conventional Euclidean space in which (non-relativistic) physical events are located and that the brain itself adds to this three-dimensional spatial localization a fourth dimension, the temporal dimension. The spatial location of a stimulus source is computed from sensory input, but the temporal location is not. The temporal location (the values of time corresponding to the values that specify the position of something in ordinary space) are signalled by the brain's calendar-clock. The resulting locus of points in a psychological space of four dimensions is a psychological world-line.

The abstract spaces of mathematicians, which may have any number of dimensions, are also useful in conceptualizing the contemporary understanding of how the neural activity in a cortical module specifies an aspect of the stimulus. It appears that each cortical module is devoted to assigning a stimulus to a locus in a descriptive space of modest dimensionality. The three-dimensional colour space, which contains the psychological representation of the reflectance characteristics of a point on a surface, is an example.

From a mathematical standpoint, the physical specification of the reflectance characteristics of a point on a surface is a point in a space of infinite dimensionality, because there are infinitely many wavelengths of light within the range of wavelengths to which our visual system is sensitive, and the reflectance characteristics of a point are given by specifying for each wavelength the percent of incident light that is reflected. The visual system, however, reduces the description of reflectance spectra to a space of only three dimensions, called the colour space. The reduction of spectral information to a space of three dimensions occurs at the transduction stage, where the spectral composition of a light reflected from a point on a distal surface to a point on the retina, is coded by means of the signals coming from three light transducers with different spectral absorption curves (the three cones).

The signals from the three kinds of cones at a given point in the retinal image do not, however, determine the ultimate psychological representation of the reflectance spectrum of the corresponding point on the distal surface, that is, they do not determine the perceived colour of the distal point. There is no simple relation between the reflectance spectrum of the point on a surface and the spectrum of the light in the corresponding point of the retinal image. Here, as usual in perception, a simple attribute of the distal point does not correspond to any simple attribute of any one point in the proximal stimulus. To compute the representation of the reflectance spectrum of the distal point, the visual system must take into account the relation between the spectrum of the light at the corresponding point in the retinal image and the spectrum of the light from all other points.

In the course of computing the ultimate representation of the reflectance spectrum of a distal point, the visual system does a number of co-ordinate transformations. The net result of these transformations is the phenomenological colour space, which has three bipolar dimensions – red-green, yellow-blue, and white-black (Jameson 1972). A point on a surface is experienced as having some amount of red or green, but not both, because these terms designate the opposite ends of one dimension of our phenomenological experience of colour. A point is also perceived as having some amount of yellow or blue, but not both, because this is another orthogonal dimension of our phenomenological experience. A point is also experienced as having and some amount of whiteness or blackness.

To the mathematician, these "amounts" are just values along descriptive dimensions – the red-green dimension, the yellow-blue dimension and the white-black dimension. These amounts are the co-ordinates of the point (its location) in colour space. A strong violet lies well out toward the red end of the red-green dimension and well out toward the blue end of the yellow-blue dimension but near the neutral point on the white-black dimension; whereas army green lies some way out toward the green end of the red-green dimension, some way out toward the yellow end of the yellow-blue dimension, and some way out toward the black end of the white-black dimension. It appears that there are modules in the visual cortex devoted to specifying the locus of distal points in this colour space. Through some as yet not fully understood aspect of its activity, such a module signals location in colour space.

The colour space is just one of a large number of descriptive spaces created by neural mechanisms in the brain for the purpose of encoding properties of the experienced world. The number of dimensions in these other descriptive spaces and how those dimensions should be labelled is generally unclear, but there is some consensus that each module (each cortical field) specifies via its activity the position of a stimulus in its descriptive space, the descriptive space unique to that module. The question is, how are these diverse descriptions of the same experience unified in our phenomenological experience and in the genesis of behaviour?

Recent research in perception suggests that the perceptual system creates primitive object markers or "object files," to which it then ascribes various properties (Albright 1992, Kahneman, Treisman and Gibbs 1992; Kanwisher and Driver 1992). An object marker or object file has no intrinsic sensory properties; these must be assigned to it by the perceptual process. Illusory conjunctions arise when properties are misassigned (or also, on my hypothesis, when the property assigned to one world-line is erroneously retrieved by a probe specifying a different world-line); the colour that should have been associated with one world-line is associated with another (or the colour assigned on one world-line is retrieved by a probe specifying a nearby world-line). The only property intrinsic to an object marker is a location in ordinary space, which may be perceived as changing with time, that is, the propertyless object may be perceived as moving or having moved. Because they are defined simply as paths in space-time, without other intrinsic properties, the object markers or object files posited by some contemporary students of perception may be thought of as psychological world-lines, trajectories in the psychological space-time manifold, with which sensible properties such as shape and colour may be associated

My hypothesis is that the diverse aspects of experience extracted by diverse sensory-perceptual modules are not united prior to the recording of experience in memory. Rather, I suggest that the records of experience in memory are as fragmented as the sensory-perceptual process itself. I suggest that each sensory-perceptual module keeps its own records (Figure 14.7). These records contain only two types of information. In data-base terminology, they have only two fields. Both fields specify loci (sets of adjacent points) in what are spaces in the mathematical sense. One space is the descriptive space unique to a given sensory-perceptual module. The other space is the psychological space-time manifold.

Thus, every separate record in the memory file for a given sensory-perceptual module has a distinct world-line in one field (position in space as a function of time) and in the other field it has position in the descriptive space as a function of time. Or better, if still more abstractly, we can think of every record as a trajectory in a space of between 7 and perhaps 15 or 20 dimensions. The first four dimensions, which give the position of the source as a function of time, are part of the records made by every module. I will call these the world-line dimensions. The remaining dimensions, which describe sensible properties of a stimulus, are specific to a given perceptual module.

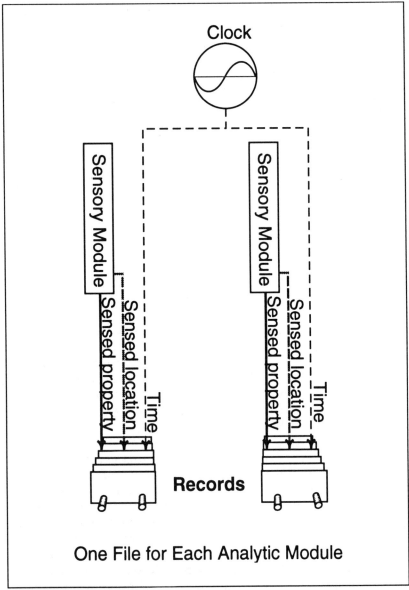

Figure 14.7: Schematic representation of the hypothesized structure of memory. Each analytic (perceptual) module keeps its own records. These records contain specifications of the temporal and spatial locus of the stimulus source together with the locus of those of its sensible properties that are specified by that particular module. The values of the co-ordinates that specify the spatial location of the stimulus source and a subset of its sensible properties derive from sensory input, but the values on the temporal dimension derive from the brain's built-in clock.

The world-line dimensions in a record – the data about the place and time – mediate the unification of experience during recollection. Recollection begins with the retrieval of a record based on a sensible property pertinent to the momentary behavioural or computational goals of the animal. For example, a bee about to set out on a foraging expedition might retrieve a record from its nectar characteristics file on the basis of its sweetness. (The nectar characteristics file contains all the records generated by a hypothetical taste module that analyzes ingesta on the basis of those dimensions that define its value as nectar.)

The decision process that determines where the bee directs its foraging flight begins by retrieving the sweetest record on file. It then uses the spatial information in this record – the values that specify where in the world that sweetness was experienced – to probe its nectar characteristics file again. This probe retrieves all the records of nectar characteristics at that locus or region in the world. By looking at the manner in which the sweetness at that site varies from record to record as a function of the times indicated in each record, the bee can determine whether its recorded experiences indicate a consistent occurrence of high sweetness at the present time of day at that location. If it does, that location becomes the goal of the bee's foraging flight. The spatial co-ordinates specifying the site are used to determine the orientation and distance of the flight the bee makes. This flight brings it to the vicinity of the source, and there it begins the search pattern designed to locate the flower or flower patch that was the source itself. In what follows, it must be understood that different species of flowers often grow close together and that different species produce nectar at different times of day.

In executing the search for the flowers from which the previously experienced high-quality nectar came, the bee uses remembered information extracted by other sensory/perceptual modules that provide descriptions of other characteristics of nectar sources – modules that provide descriptions of shapes (Gould 1985), modules that provide descriptions of odours, modules that provide descriptions of colour, and so on. It also uses information about the configuration of landmarks surrounding the source (Cartwright and Collett 1983; Cartwright and Collett 1987; Cheng, Collett, Pickhard and Wehner 1987). On the current hypothesis, each different kind of information about the flowers that were the source of the high quality nectar resides in separate records in different files. The bee brings together this information by using the world-line data from its nectar-characteristics data to retrieve from the other files the records that have the same or nearby world-lines, the records in the other files that were made at that place at those times. These records give it the other aspects of remembered experience that it needs to find the flowers from which it got the high-quality nectar at that time of day.

Notice that what the bee is in effect doing is recalling previous episodes of its experience in their multifaceted richness. But the multiple facets of these episodes are not united in memory itself; they are only united by the recollective process. Which facets of an episode are recalled together depends not on the original experience itself but rather on the purpose for which information is being retrieved. The use of time and place information to retrieve records need not be confined to finding records in different files that all have the same time and place values. Information is generally recalled for some purpose. The purpose may require the recollection of data from sources at some temporal or spatial remove from the initial or pivotal record. For example, the bee may need data on landmarks encountered en route to a site or data on experiences such as rainstorms the preceding day that predict nectar production in that kind of flower. Relevant records from loci removed in space and time can be retrieved by using the space and time data in the starting record to calculate the space and time values for the records to be retrieved next, then using these calculated worldlines to retrieve the needed records from the pertinent files.

The records of event times also provide a basis for the recollection of duration. The interval between two events or the duration of a single event may be determined from the time-of-occurrence information in the records that preserve information about the sensible aspects of the events. On this view, duration is not itself a sensible aspect of events. It exists only in recollection. This resolves the paradox surrounding the phenomenological question: exactly when we may be said to experience a duration? Do we experience the duration of an interval only at the end of the interval? Is there an ongoing experience of duration, etc. On the current hypothesis, duration is not a sensible property of an event. It is not like colour or shape, etc. Duration is an aspect of phenomenological experience that is created in the process of recollection.

This is, to put it charitably, a speculative hypothesis. Is there any evidence for it? On the spatial side, there are some experiments by Nissen (Isenberg and Nissen 1990; Nissen 1985) that show that spatial position plays a privileged role in enabling us to recollect one property of an object, such as its shape, given another property, such as its colour.

On the temporal side, there is only one well-established fact that seems to me to favour this hypothesis. It is the fact of retrograde amnesia. Retrograde amnesia is among the most common of neuropsychological phenomena because it is observed in most cases of concussive injury to the head. As a consequence of the concussion, there is a period during recovery from the injury when the experiences falling within some interval of time prior to the injury are unrecallable. The interval of past experience from which memories cannot be retrieved, which may be as short as a few minutes or as long as many years, is called the amnestic interval. Memories falling within the amnestic interval cannot be retrieved no matter what their subject matter nor how important they are to the patient emotionally or practically.

We know that it is the retrieval process that is at fault, not the destruction of the records themselves, because as recovery from the injury progresses, the amnestic interval shrinks radically. Most patients eventually can recollect what happened during all but perhaps the last few minutes or hours of what may have once been an amnestic interval measured in weeks, months or years (see Gallistel, 1990, chap. 15, for review and citations).

The phenomenon of retrograde amnesia shows that the time at which memories were laid down plays a fundamental role in their subsequent recollection. Most contemporary theories of memory offer no ready explanation of this well-established neuropsychological fact, because time does not play a privileged role in retrieving memories. On the present hypothesis, however, the ability to specify a certain time in probing the many different files in which information about our past experiences is kept is indispensable. If the system were to lose the ability to specify a certain range of past times, then it would lose the ability to make any effective use of all the records that were laid down during the no-longer specifiable range of past times. When the system recovered the ability to specify times within that range, it would recover the ability to retrieve records that were related to each other in behaviourally useful ways.

In summary, there is no question that there are clocks built into the brains of animals. There is also no question that the readings on these clocks and the intervals between readings play a fundamental role in the determination of behaviour. Thus, time is in the mind not because it is a sensible property of the world, but rather because clocks are in the brain and the time signals from these clocks are incorporated into the records through which past experience may help to inform future behaviour. If we pursue this line of thought to its logical conclusion, we are led to an hypothesis about how memory is structured and how recollection works that makes it clear what it is Kant may have been groping to express when he argued that time was an obligatory aspect of all experience.

References

Albright, T.D. (1992). Form-cue invariant motion processing in primate visual cortex. *Science* 255: 1141-43

Beling, I. (1929). Über das Zeitgedächtnis der Bienen. *Zeitschrift für vergleichende Physiologie* 9: 259-338

Bolles, R.C., and S.A. Moot (1973). The rat's anticipation of two meals a day. *Journal of Comparative and Physiological Psychology* 83: 510-14

Brown, T.G. (1914). On the nature of the fundamental activity of the nervous centres; together with an analysis of the conditioning of rhythmic activity in progression, and a theory of evolution of function in the nervous system. *Journal of Physiology* 48: 18-46

Bünning, E. (1936). Die endonome Tagesperiodik als Grundlage der photoperiodischen Reaktion. *Bericthe deutsches botanisches Gesellschaft* 54: 590-607

Cartwright, B.A., and T.S. Collett (1983). Landmark learning in bees: experiments and models. *Journal of Comparative Physiology* 151: 521-43

Cartwright, B.A., and T.S. Collett (1987). Landmark maps for honey bees. *Biological Cybernetics* 57: 85-93

Cheng, K., T.S. Collett, A. Pickhard and R. Wehner (1987). The use of visual landmarks by honey bees: Bees weight landmarks according to their distance from the goal. *Journal of Comparative Physiology* 161: 469-75

Foster, R.G., I. Provencio, D. Hudson, S. Fiske, W. De Grip and M. Menaker (1991). Circadian photoreception in the retinally degenerate mouse *(rd/rd)*. *Journal of Comparative Physiology, Series A* 169: 39-50

Gallistel, C.R. (1990). *The Organization of Learning*. Cambridge, MA: MIT Press

Gould, J.L. (1985). How bees remember flower shapes. *Science* 227: 1492-94

Green, D.J., and M.U. Gillette (1982). Circadian rhythm of firing rate recorded from single cells in rat suprachiasmatic brain slice. *Brain Research* 245: 198-200

Harvey, W. (1628/1910). *Exercitatio anatomica de motis cordis et sanguinis in animalibus*. Translated by Robert Willis. Harvard Classics, vol. 39. New York: Colliers

Holloway, F.A., and R.A. Wansley (1973). Multiple retention deficits at periodic intervals after active and passive avoidance learning. *Behavioral Biology* 9: 1-14

Holst, E.von (1939). Die relative Koordination als Phänomen und als Methode zentralnervöser Funktionsanalyze. *Ergebnisse der Physiologie* 42: 228-306

Hunsicker, J.P., and R.L. Mellgren (1977). Multiple deficits in the retention of an appetitively motivated behavior across a 24-h. period in rats. *Animal Learning and Behavior* 5: 14-26

Isenberg, L., M.J. Nissen and L. Case (1990). Attentional processing and the independence of color and orientation. *Journal of Experimental Psychology: Human Perception and Performance* 16 (4): 869-78

Jameson, D. (1972). Theoretical issues of color vision. In D. Jameson and L.M. Hurvich (eds.), *Handbook of Sensory Physiology, Vol. VII/4.1, Visual Psychophysics* Berlin: Springer Verlag

Kahneman, D., A. Treisman and B.J. Gibbs (1992). The reviewing of object files: Object-specific integration of information. *Cognitive Psychology, 24*, 175-219

Kanwisher, F., and J. Driver (1992). Objects, attributes, and visual attention: Which, what, and where. *Current Directions in Psychological Science* 1: 26-31

Koltermann, R. (1971). 24-Std-Periodik in der Langzeiterrinerung an Duft- und Farbsignale bei der Honigbiene. *Zeitschrift für vergleichende Physiologie* 75: 49-68

Newman, G.C., F.E. Hospod, C.S. Patlak and R.Y. Moore (1992). Analysis of *in vitro* glucose utilization in a circadian pacemaker model. *Journal of Neurocience* 12 (6): 2015-21

Nissen, M.J. (1985). Accessing features and objects: Is location special? In M.I. Posner and O.S. Marin (eds.), *Attention and Performance XI*, pp. 205-219. Hillsdale, NJ: Erlbaum

Ralph, M.R., R.G. Foster, F.C. Davis and D.M. Menaker (1990). Transplanted suprachiasmatic nucleus determines circadian period. *Science* 247: 975-77

Ralph, M.R., and M. Menaker (1988). A mutation of the circadian system in golden hamsters. *Science* 241 (4870): 1225-27

Roberts, S.K. (1965). Photoreception and entrainment of cockroach activity rhythms. *Science* 148: 958-60

Rosenwasser, A.M., R.J. Pelchat and N.T. Adler (1984). Memory for feeding time: possible dependence on coupled circadian oscillators. *Physiology and Behavior* 32: 25-30

Rusak, B., and I. Zucker (1979). Neural regulation of circadian rhythms. *Physiological Reviews* 59: 449-526

Schwartz, W.J., and H. Gainer (1977). Suprachiasmatic nucleus: Use of ^{14}C-labeled deoxyglucose uptake as a functional marker. *Science* 197: 1089-91

Stein-Beling, I.von (1935). Über das Zeitgedächtnis bei Tieren. *Biological Reviews* 10: 18-41

Szymanski, J.S. (1920). Activität und Ruhe bei Tieren und Menschen. *Zeitschrift der allgemeinen Physiologie* 18: 105-62

Takahashi, J.S., P.J. De Coursey, L. Bauman and M. Menaker (1984). Spectral sensitivity of a novel photoreceptive system mediating entrainment of mammalian circadian rhythms. *Nature* 308: 186-88

Triesman, A., and H. Gibbs (1982). Illusory conjunctions in the perception of objects. *Cognitive Psychology* 14: 107-41

Wahl, O. (1932). Neue Untersuchungen über das Zeitgedächtnis der Bienen. *Zeitschrift für vergleichende Physiologie* 16: 529-89

———. (1933). Beitrag zur Frage der biologischen Bedeutung des Zeitgedächtnisses der Bienen. *Zeitschrift für vergleichende Physiologie* 18: 709-17